Programming
ASP.NET Core

Dino Esposito

Programming ASP.NET Core

Published with the authorization of Microsoft Corporation by:
Pearson Education, Inc.

Copyright © 2018 by Pearson Education, Inc.

ISBN-13: 978-1-50-930441-7
ISBN-10: 1-50-930441-X

Library of Congress Control Number: 2018938486

1   18

Trademarks

Microsoft and the trademarks listed at http://www.microsoft.com on the "Trademarks" webpage are trademarks of the Microsoft group of companies. All other marks are property of their respective owners.

Warning and Disclaimer

Every effort has been made to make this book as complete and as accurate as possible, but no warranty or fitness is implied. The information provided is on an "as is" basis. The author, the publisher, and Microsoft Corporation shall have neither liability nor responsibility to any person or entity with respect to any loss or damages arising from the information contained in this book or from the use of the CD or programs accompanying it.

Special Sales

For information about buying this title in bulk quantities, or for special sales opportunities (which may include electronic versions; custom cover designs; and content particular to your business, training goals, marketing focus, or branding interests), please contact our corporate sales department at corpsales@pearsoned.com or (800) 382-3419.

For government sales inquiries, please contact governmentsales@pearsoned.com.

For questions about sales outside the U.S., please contact intlcs@pearson.com.

Editor-in-Chief
Greg Wiegand

Acquisitions Editor
Trina Fletcher MacDonald

Development Editor
Mark Renfrow

Managing Editor
Sandra Schroeder

Senior Project Editor
Tracey Croom

Copy Editor
Rick Kughen

Indexer
Ken Johnson

Proofreader
Abigail Manheim

Technical Editor
Christophe Navarre

Editorial Assistant
Courtney Martin

Cover Designer
Twist Creative, Seattle

Compositor
codemantra

Contents at a Glance

Contents

About the Author

Dino Esposito is a digital strategist at BaxEnergy who has authored more than 20 books and 1,000 articles to date. His programming career has so far spanned 25 years. It is commonly recognized that his books and articles helped the professional growth of thousands of .NET developers and architects worldwide. Dino started back in 1992 as a C developer and witnessed the debut of .NET, the rise and fall of Silverlight and the ups and downs of various architectural patterns. He now looks ahead to Artificial Intelligence 2.0 and Blockchain and is the author of "The Sabbatical Break", a theatrical-style work to travel the uncontaminated spaces of imagination hyperlinking software, literature, science, sport, technology, art. Get in touch at http://youbiquitous.net.

http://twitter.com/despos

http://instagram.com/desposofficial

http://facebook.com/desposofficial

Introduction

"We need men who can dream of things that never were, and ask why not."

—President John F. Kennedy, Speech to the Irish Parliament, June 1963

Some aspects of the ASP.NET Core story remind me of the beginning of the ASP.NET adventure more than 15 years ago. A very young Scott Guthrie—now a Microsoft VP—presented a new thing called ASP+ to a small audience of web developers in London in the fall of 1999. Those were the days of Active Server Pages, and ASP+ was trying to introduce a new syntax for moving the VBScript code back to the server and express it through a compiled language. ASP+ was a real breakthrough.

At the time of the presentation, there was no public awareness of the .NET thing yet, which would not be publicly disclosed until the following summer. The demos Scott showed, including a jaw-dropping Web Service example, were coming out of a stand-alone runtime environment based on a custom worker process—a console application—capable of listening on the port 80. The first demos used plain Visual Basic and C++ code against the Win32 API. In a short time, the whole ASP+ thing was quickly consumed by the new .NET Framework and eventually became ASP.NET.

ASP.NET Core, too, was first presented as a new standalone framework rewritten from scratch to take the Microsoft web stack to another level of scalability and performance. However, in doing so, the team glimpsed the enticing opportunity to make the ASP.NET Core framework available on multiple platforms. To achieve that goal, a subset of the .NET Framework had to be made available on target platforms, and this meant a new .NET Framework had to be created. And, in the end, this is just what happened.

For too long, ASP.NET Core was a moving target and the mechanics moving the target were not clear to anyone, and they weren't always communicated timely and effectively. Twenty years ago, we (thankfully?) lacked the instant sharing attitude that social media imposes today. Also, ASP+ probably was a moving target, but nobody outside Microsoft—and the people directly involved—ever knew about that.

While the pillars of the ASP.NET and ASP.NET Core stories might be seen as being the same, runtime conditions are fairly different. The web before ASP.NET was a web in its infancy, with limited availability of scalable server-side technologies and without scalability itself being the serious issue it is today. At the same time, a great many applications were potentially ready to be rewritten for the web, and they were just awaiting a reliable platform from a reliable vendor.

Today, many frameworks exist today that could be used instead of ASP.NET Core. However, ASP.NET Core is not just frontend; ASP.NET Core is also backend, Web API, and small and compact web (containerized) monoliths to be deployed standalone or within a service fabric. ASP.NET Core also can be used on multiple hardware/software platforms.

It's really hard to say whether ASP.NET Core is a must in the near future—or even at present—of every company and team. For sure, ASP.NET Core is the natural follow up for ASP.NET developers and the incarnation of another full-stack solution for web development on a variety of platforms.

Who should read this book

This book is not for absolute beginners, at least not in the sense of newbies without at least a superficial understanding of web development. It is tailor-made for existing ASP.NET developers especially those with an MVC background. At the same time, this book is a good fit for expert web developers, especially those with an MVC background but who are new to ASP.NET. Even though ASP.NET Core is brand-new, it does have a lot of common points with ASP.NET MVC (and to a much less extent, Web Forms).

If you're on the Microsoft stack, or if you are considering moving there, ASP.NET Core offers an excellent choice for the entire stack, including a tight connection with the Azure cloud.

Assumptions

This book expects that you have at least a minimal understanding of web development—preferably matured—but not necessarily, on the Microsoft stack.

This might not be for you if...

If you're an absolute newbie to web programming who has never heard about ASP.NET and you're subsequently looking for a step-by-step guide to ASP.NET Core, this book might not be ideal.

Organization of this book

This book is divided into five sections.

- Part I, "The New ASP.NET at a Glance," provides a quick overview of the foundation of ASP.NET Core and introduces the hello-world application.

- Part II, "The ASP.NET MVC Application Model," focuses on the MVC application model and outlines its core parts, such as controllers and views.

- Part III, "Cross-cutting Concerns," touches on common aspects of development such as authentication, configuration, and data access.

- Part IV, "Frontend," is dedicated to technologies and additional frameworks for building a usable and effective presentation layer.

- Part V, "The ASP.NET Core Ecosystem," is about the runtime pipeline, deployment, and migration strategies.

System requirements

You will need the following hardware and software to complete the practice exercises in this book:

- Window 7 or higher or MacOS 10.12 or higher.

- Alternatively, you can use one of many Linux distros, as described at https://docs.microsoft.com/en-us/dotnet/core/linux-prerequisites.

- Visual Studio 2015, any edition, or superior; Visual Studio Code.

- Internet connection to download software or chapter examples.

Downloads: Code samples

All the code illustrated in the book, including possible errata and extensions, can be found at https://aka.ms/ASPNetCore/downloads.

Errata, updates, & book support

We've made every effort to ensure the accuracy of this book and its companion content. You can access updates to this book—in the form of a list of submitted errata and their related corrections—at:

https://aka.ms/ASPNetCore/errata

If you discover an error that is not already listed, please submit it to us at the same page.

If you need additional support, email Microsoft Press Book Support at mspinput@microsoft.com.

Please note that product support for Microsoft software and hardware is not offered through the previous addresses. For help with Microsoft software or hardware, go to http://support.microsoft.com.

Stay in touch

Let's keep the conversation going! We're on Twitter: *http://twitter.com/MicrosoftPress*.

The New ASP.NET at a Glance

Welcome to ASP.NET Core.

It's been over fifteen years since Microsoft introduced ASP.NET and the .NET Framework. Of course, web development has changed dramatically in that time. Developers have learned much, and clients want radically different solutions delivered in new ways to new devices. ASP.NET Core reflects all of this, and it anticipates much of what's likely to happen next. Part I places ASP.NET Core in context, and it helps you quickly get started with it.

Chapter 1, *Why Another ASP.NET?*, explains why ASP.NET Core exists, where it might be familiar (especially to ASP.NET MVC developers), and the many ways it's radically different. You'll explore ASP.NET Core in the context of the compact, modular, open source, and cross-platform .NET Core Framework, and you'll see how it promotes better support for both minimal web services and full sites. You'll also get a quick first look at its Command-line Interface (CLI) developer tools.

Then, in Chapter 2, *The First ASP.NET Core Project*, you'll quickly create your first application. A few things seem never to change, so I've kept the familiar "Hello World" convention for the first apps. But even here, you'll get a taste of ASP.NET Core's striking minimalism[md]and what it makes possible.

CHAPTER 1

Why Another ASP.NET?

If we want things to stay as they are, things will have to change.
—Giuseppe Tomasi di Lampedusa, "The Leopard"

I think it was probably the summer of 1999. Writing software for the Windows operating system at that time required C/C++ skills and big libraries like Microsoft Foundation Classes (MFC) and ActiveX Template Library (ATL) existed to make development easier. The Component Object Model (COM) was becoming the bare bones of any application running on Windows. Everything, including data access, was going to be redesigned to be COM-compliant and COM-aware. However, the choice of the programming language and the development tool was a still a relevant discriminant, especially if data access or sophisticated user interface was necessary in a Windows application. If you opted for Visual Basic, then you could have trivially easy database access and a quick and nice user interface, but you couldn't play with the function pointer and couldn't access—not easily and reliably at least—all the functions in Windows SDK. On the other hand, if you opted for C or C++, there were no high-level facilities for data access, and building a menu or a toolbar was a sore way to walk in comparison to what it was in Visual Basic.

As a software professional, it was not an easy world to live in, but we all managed to find our own most comfortable nests, and we managed to run and grow our businesses quite nicely. Suddenly, however, .NET arrived, and everything changed. And thankfully it changed for the best.

The Current .NET Platform

The .NET platform was announced in the summer of 2000 and reached the second beta stage a year later. Version 1.0 was released in early 2002, though in software terms, it might as well have been three geological eras ago.

Highlights of the .NET Platform

The .NET platform is made of a framework of classes and a virtual machine called the Common Language Runtime (CLR). The CLR is essentially an execution environment for code conceptually written in an intermediate language (IL) like the Java's bytecode. The CLR provides running code with a variety of services such as memory management and garbage collection, exception handling, security, versioning, debugging, and profiling. More than anything, though, the CLR can provide those services in a cross-language way.

On top of the CLR, there are language compilers and the concept of a "managed language." A managed language is a plain programming language for which a compiler exists; the compiler can generate IL code for the CLR to consume. Any .NET compiler produces IL code, but IL code is not directly runnable under the host Windows operating system. So, another tool was put on the table—the just-in-time compiler. This compiler turned IL code into binary code that could execute on the specific hardware/software platform.

The .NET Framework

At the time, the aspect of .NET that most struck me was the ability to mix different programming languages in the same project. You could easily create a library in, say Visual Basic, and call it from code written in any other managed language. Also, a new, extremely powerful language was offered—the now ubiquitous C# language, which was born as the legendary phoenix from the ashes of the Java language.

Overall, the biggest change for developers was the availability of classes to access most of the underlying Windows SDK. That is the Base Class Library (BCL), which is a common substrate of code that any .NET application could target. The BCL is a collection of reusable types that are closely integrated with CLR, such as primitive types, LINQ, and classes and types helpful in common operations such as I/O, dates, collections, and diagnostics.

The BCL is complemented by a set of additional and highly specialized libraries, such as ADO.NET for database access, Windows Forms for desktop Windows applications, ASP.NET for web applications, XML, and a few others. Over the years, the set of additional libraries has grown to incorporate giant frameworks such as Windows Presentation Foundation (WPF), Windows Communication Foundation (WCF), and Entity Framework (EF).

Altogether, BCL and additional frameworks form the .NET Framework.

The ASP.NET Framework

In the fall of 1999, Microsoft started unveiling a new web framework slated to replace Active Server Pages (ASP). In the first public demos, the framework was called ASP+, and it was based on its own C/C++ engine, which then flowed into the .NET platform becoming today's ASP.NET.

The ASP.NET framework consists of an extension to Internet Information Services (IIS) capable of capturing incoming HTTP requests and running them through the ASP.NET runtime environment. Within the runtime environment, the request is resolved by finding a special component that can handle that request and preparing an HTTP response packet for the browser. The runtime environment is structured like a pipeline: The request comes in and goes through various stages until it is fully processed, and the response is written back to the output stream.

Unlike its competitors, ASP.NET provided a stateful and event-based programming model that allowed implicit context to flow from one request to the other. This model was well known by desktop application developers, and it opened the world of web programming to many developers with limited or no skills at all in HTML and JavaScript. Because of the thick abstraction layer over HTTP and HTML initially featured in ASP.NET, it attracted swarms of Visual Basic, Delphi, C/C++, and even Java programmers.

The Web Forms Model

Originally, the ASP.NET runtime environment was devised with two main goals:

- The first goal was providing a programming model that could shield developers as much as possible from HTML and JavaScript. Deeply inspired to the classic client/server request model, the Web Forms model worked beautifully and created an ecosystem of free and commercial server components offering more and more advanced capabilities such as smart data grids, input forms, wizards, date pickers, and so forth.

- The second goal was to aim as much as possible at blending ASP.NET and IIS together. ASP.NET was envisioned to be the operational wing of IIS, and not just a plugin, and its runtime environment destined to become a structural part of IIS. This milestone was fully reached with the release of IIS 7 back in 2008. The Integrated Pipeline mode of IIS 7 and superior is a working mode in which IIS and ASP.NET share the same pipeline. The path a request goes through when it knocks at the IIS gate is just the path it would go through within ASP.NET. ASP.NET code is simply responsible for processing the request and for intercepting and preprocessing any specific requests it wants.

About 2009, the Web Forms programming model was paired with the ASP.NET MVC framework, which was inspired by a completely different principle that represents a complete turnaround from the original goal of ASP.NET. In the Web Forms model, ASP.NET pages produce their HTML via server controls, which are the main reason for the success and rapid adoption of ASP.NET. These server controls are black-box components (declaratively or programmatically configured) that generate HTML and JavaScript for the browser. However, the developer has limited control over the HTML being generated and people requirements change over time.

The ASP.NET MVC Model

ASP.NET MVC is designed from the ground up to work close to the HTTP metal; it doesn't attempt to hide any of the features of HTTP, and it requires developers to be very aware of the mechanics of HTTP requests and responses. Ideally, developers using ASP.NET MVC should possess JavaScript and CSS skills. ASP.NET MVC is the result of a profound rework of the programming model driven by new cross-cutting requirements, such as separation of concerns, modularization, and testability.

It was probably a tough decision, but ASP.NET MVC didn't get its own runtime environment and ended up being coded as a plugin for the existing ASP.NET runtime. This is good and bad news at the same time. It is good news because you can handle incoming requests either through the Web Forms model or the ASP.NET MVC model, which makes it easy to start with an existing Web Forms application and slowly evolve it to ASP.NET MVC piecemeal. It is bad news, however, because very few of the structural shortcomings of ASP.NET (in light of modern requirements) could be addressed. For example, the ASP.NET MVC team managed to make the entire HTTP context mockable but couldn't build in the framework a full and canonical dependency-injection infrastructure.

Yet, the ASP.NET MVC programming model is the most flexible and understandable way to handle web requests that have to return HTML content. Except that at some point, with the explosion of the mobile space, HTML stopped being the sole possible output of an HTTP request.

The Web API Framework

Particularly with the advent of devices, a web endpoint could be requested to serve any type of content (for example, JSON, XML, images, and PDF) to any type of client. Any piece of code that could place an HTTP request is a potential client of a web endpoint. And, the scalability level of certain solutions became critical.

In the ASP.NET space, there was not much else to do to expand the infrastructure to play well in new scenarios: extreme scalability, cloud, and platform independence. The Web API framework has been an attempt to offer a temporary solution to the high demand of thin servers capable of exposing a RESTful interface and capable of dialoging with any HTTP client without any assumptions and restrictions. The Web API framework is an alternate set of classes to create HTTP endpoints designed to be only aware of the full HTTP syntax and semantics. The Web API framework offers a programming interface nearly identical to ASP.NET MVC; it includes controllers, routing, and model binding but runs them within a brand-new runtime environment.

With the ASP.NET Web API, the point of creating a web framework decoupled from the web server started taking root, and this led to the definition of the Open Web Interface for .NET standard (OWIN). OWIN is a specification that sets the rules for a web server and a web application to interoperate. With OWIN, the second original goal of ASP.NET—strong and tight coupling between web host and web application—was dismissed as obsolete.

Web API has the potential to be hosted in any application that complies with the OWIN standard. However, to be usable, Web API must be hosted under IIS, which requires an ASP.NET application. The use of Web API within an ASP.NET application, whether Web Forms or MVC, just increases the memory footprint of the application because two runtime environments are used.

The Need for Super-Simple Web Services

Another significant change in the software industry landscape that happened in recent years is the need for minimal, super-simple web services—just a thin web server layer around a piece of business logic.

A minimal web server is an HTTP endpoint that can be called by a client to get extremely basic, mostly text-based content. Such a web server does not need to run a sophisticated and customizable pipeline. All it needs is to receive the HTTP request, process it as appropriate, and return an HTTP response. All this should happen without any overhead or just with the overhead required by the context. The use of client-side programming models (such as Angular) just fuels the need for such web services.

ASP.NET and all its runtime environments are just not designed for similar scenarios. While the ASP.NET runtime (which supports both Web Forms and MVC applications) is to some extent customizable (disable session, output caching, and even authentication) it doesn't reach the level of granularity and control that some business scenarios require these days. As an example, it is nearly impossible to turn ASP.NET into an effective static file server.

.NET Fifteen Years Later

Fifteen years is quite a long time for any software, and the .NET Framework is no exception. ASP.NET was devised in the late 1990s, and the web evolved very quickly. In about 2014, the ASP.NET team started making plans for a new ASP.NET and designed a brand-new runtime environment following the OWIN specification quite closely.

Removing any dependencies upon the old ASP.NET runtime—symbolized by the *system.web* assembly—has been the primary goal of the team. However, another crucial objective of the team was to give developers full control over the pipeline so that building both a minimal web service and a full website could be possible. In doing so, the team faced another nontrivial problem: to ensure throughput and make any solution cloud-effective in terms of costs: the footprint of the application had to be drastically reduced. Also, the .NET Framework then had to undergo a special treatment to lose weight.

The guidelines for the new ASP.NET can be summarized as below:

- Making ASP.NET able to access both the full existing .NET Framework and a shrink-wrapped version of it devoid of all little-used—and little useful—dependencies to web developers.

- Decoupling the new ASP.NET environment from the host web server.

However, once this plan was implemented, a bunch of other issues and opportunities came along. And they were too appealing to let them pass.

A More Compact .NET Framework

The new ASP.NET was designed side by side with a new .NET Framework that in the end was named .NET Core Framework. The new framework can be seen as a subset of original .NET Framework specifically designed to be more granular, compact and, more importantly, cross-platform. This design goal was achieved in two ways: dropping some functionalities and rewriting other functionalities to improve effectiveness in some cases and to make up for existing dependencies on dropped functionalities.

The .NET Core Framework was primarily designed to work with ASP.NET applications. This was the ultimate vector that guided the choice of which libraries to include in the library and which to drop. The .NET Core Framework comes with a new runtime for application execution called CoreCLR. The CoreCLR follows the same layout and architecture of the current .NET CLR and does things like loading the IL code, compiling to machine-level code, and collecting garbage. The CoreCLR doesn't support some features of the current CLR, such as application domains and code access security, that proved unnecessary or too specific for the Windows platform and then hard to port out to the other platform. Furthermore, the set of class libraries in the .NET Core Framework is articulated in packages, and packages have a very fine granularity and are much smaller than the current .NET Framework.

The entire .NET Core platform is fully open source. Links to repositories are shown Table 1-1.

TABLE 1-1 Github links to .NET Core source code

Platform	Description	Link
CoreCLR	CLR and related tools	http://github.com/dotnet/coreclr
CoreFX	.NET Core Framework	http://github.com/dotnet/corefx

In a nutshell, the differences between the full .NET Framework and the .NET Core Framework can be summarized in the following points:

- The .NET Core Framework is more compact and modular.

- The .NET Core Framework (and related tools) is open source.

- The .NET Core Framework cannot be used to write anything other than ASP.NET and console applications.

- The .NET Core Framework can be deployed side by side with the application, whereas the full .NET Framework can only be installed on the target machine and shared by all applications. As you can see, this poses a nontrivial issue of versioning.

Once devoid of platform dependencies, a new and more compact .NET framework is also code that could be adapted to work on a variety of alternative operating systems. This makes for another huge difference between the .NET Core Framework and the existing .NET Framework. The .NET Core Framework can be used to write cross-platform applications that also run on Linux and Mac operating systems.

> **Note** With the release of .NET Core 2.0, the functional gap between the full .NET Framework and the .NET Core Framework is reducing because more classes and namespaces have been ported to the Core Framework (*System.Drawing* and data-table classes, for example). However, considering the .NET Core Framework to be a copy of the full .NET Framework is a mistake. It's another framework redesigned from scratch that looks very similar and works in a cross-platform way.

Decoupling ASP.NET from the Host

To address the requirement of a web application model that could be used to write both minimal web services and full websites, decoupling ASP.NET from IIS proved to be a necessary step. The entire OWIN philosophy (see *http://owin.org*) is about

- Separating the functions of the web server from the functions of the web application.

- Encouraging the development of simpler modules for .NET web development that when composed together can reach the full horsepower of a real-world web site.

Figure 1-1 shows the overall architecture found in OWIN.

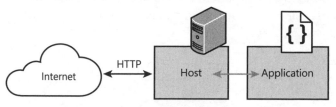

FIGURE 1-1 The open web interface architecture

With an OWIN-based architecture in place, the host web server is no longer forced to be IIS. Also, the host interface can be implemented by a console application or a Windows service. However, beyond these limited scenarios, the true power of a web application model inspired by the OWIN open interface is that the same application can be hosted on any compliant web server, regardless of the system platform.

HTTP is a platform agnostic protocol, and the moment a new version of the .NET Framework is built without tight dependencies on a specific platform like Windows, then building a web application model that works in a cross-platform manner becomes, suddenly, a realistic and quite appealing project.

> **Important** Back in 2008 when IIS started supporting the Integrated Pipeline mode, Microsoft's vision of the web was totally different from today's vision. And to some extent, the world was different. Per the Integrated Pipeline vision, IIS and ASP.NET had to work together and look like a unified engine. The model built for the new ASP.NET overturns the Integrated Pipeline vision, which says that ASP.NET is a standalone environment and could be hosted behind any web server. This model says this standalone environment could even work—in some situations—when directly exposed to the public.

The New ASP.NET Core

ASP.NET Core is a new framework for building a variety of Internet-based applications, most notably (though not limited to) web applications. In fact, special flavors of web applications can be considered IoT-embedded servers and web-exposed services, such as the back end of a mobile application.

ASP.NET Core applications can be written to target the .NET Core Framework or the existing full .NET Framework. ASP.NET was designed to be cross-platform so that developers can create applications that run on Windows, Mac, and Linux. ASP.NET Core consists of an embedded web server and a runtime environment that runs the application code. The application code is written using a slightly reworked ASP.NET MVC framework and relies on a collection of system modules designed to be extremely small, which provides more opportunity to build applications that require minimal overhead to run. Figure 1-2 presents the overall architecture of ASP.NET Core.

Note A web server, such as IIS or Apache, is not strictly required because the embedded web server (Kestrel) can be exposed directly. Your need for a separate web server mostly depends on whether Kestrel serves your needs.

FIGURE 1-2 The overall architecture of ASP.NET Core

The new ASP.NET relies on the tools of the .NET Core SDK to build and run applications. We'll learn more about the .NET SDK and the command-line tools in the next section. I'll cover the ASP.NET Core runtime in depth in Chapter 14, "The ASP.NET Core Runtime Environment."

.NET Core Command-line Tools

In .NET Core, the entire set of fundamental development tools—those used to build, test, run, and publish applications—is also available as command-line applications. Together, such applications are referred to as the .NET Core Command-line Interface (CLI).

Installing CLI Tools

CLI tools are available for all development and deployment platforms that .NET Core applications can target. They usually come with the install package tailor-made for the platform, such as RPM or DEB packages on Linux and MSI packages on Windows. Once you've run the installer, CLI tools are safely stored in a globally accessible location on the disk. Figure 1-3 shows the folder of CLI tools on a Windows computer.

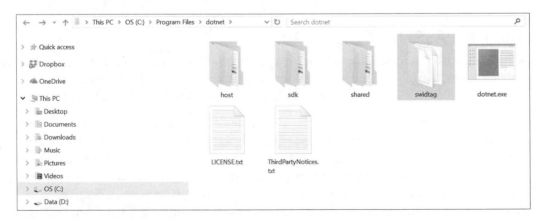

FIGURE 1-3 Installed CLI tools

Notice that you can have multiple versions of CLI tools running side by side. When multiple versions are installed, then by default the most recent runs.

The *dotnet* Driver Tool

The CLI is generally referred to as a collection of tools, but instead, it is a collection of commands run by a host tool known as the driver. This tool is *dotnet.exe* (see Figure 1-3). Any command-line instruction takes the following form:

```
dotnet [host-options] [command] [arguments] [common-options]
```

The *[command]* placeholder refers to the command to execute within the driver tool whereas *[arguments]* refers to the arguments being passed to the command. Host and common options are detailed below.

When multiple versions of the CLI are installed, and you don't want to run the latest, then you create a *global.json* file in the same folder of the application and ensure it contains at least the following:

```json
{
  "sdk": {
    "version": "2.0.0"
  }
}
```

The value of the *version* property determines the version of the CLI tooling to use.

> **Note** This version of the CLI tooling is not the same as the version of the .NET Core runtime the application will use. The runtime version is specified in the project file, and you can comfortably edit it from within the user interface of the IDE of your choice. If you want, instead, to edit the project file manually, then it is as easy as editing the *.csproj* XML file and changing the value of the *TargetFramework* element. The value refers to the moniker that identifies the version (such as *netcoreapp2.0*).

Host Options

On the command line of the *dotnet* tool, host options are passed before the command moniker and refer to the configuration of the *dotnet* tool. There are three supported values to get general information about the tooling and the runtime environment, to get the version number of the CLI, and to enable diagnostics. (See Table 1-2.)

TABLE 1-2 Host options of CLI

Platform	Description
-d or --diagnostics	Enables diagnostic output
--info	Displays information about the runtime environment and the .NET CLI
--version	Displays the .NET CLI version number

Common Options

The common CLI options in Table 1-3 refer to options common to all commands, such getting help or enabling verbose output.

TABLE 1-3 Common options of CLI

Platform	Description
-v or --verbose	Enables verbose output
-h or --help	Shows general help about how to use a *dotnet* tool

Predefined *dotnet* Commands

By default, installing the CLI tools makes available the commands listed in Table 1-4. Note that the order commands appear in the table attempts to resemble a realistic order of use.

TABLE 1-4 Usual CLI commands

Command	Description
new	Creates a new .NET Core application starting from one of the available templates. Default templates include console applications as well as ASP.NET MVC applications, test projects, and class libraries. Additional options let you indicate the target language and the name of the project.
restore	Restores all the dependencies of the project. Dependencies are read from the project file and restored as NuGet packages consumed from a configured feed.
build	Builds the project and all its dependencies. Parameters for the compilers (such as whether to build a library or an application) should be specified in the project file.
run	Compiles the source code if required, generates an executable and runs it. It relies on the command *build* for the first step.
test	Runs unit tests in the project using the configured test runner. Unit tests are class libraries with a dependency on a particular unit test framework and its runner application.
publish	Compiles the application if required, reads the list of dependencies from the project file and then publishes the resulting set of files to an output directory.
pack	Creates a NuGet package out of the project binaries.
migrate	Migrates an old *project.json*-based project to a *msbuild*-based project.
clean	Cleans the output folder of the project.

To learn more about the detailed way to invoke any of the above commands, you can type the following from the command line:

```
dotnet <command> --help
```

More commands can be added by referencing portable console applications within the project or globally by copying the executable in a directory associated to the *PATH* environment variable.

Summary

The .NET platform has been around for more than fifteen years, and in all this time, it has attracted a lot of investment and has become very popular. The world, however, is in continuous change and the famous quote from the novel, "The Leopard," by Giuseppe Tomasi di Lampedusa at the beginning of this chapter—"If we want things to stay as they are, things will have to change"—says it all. So, the original .NET platform, centered around a single, comprehensive class library and a few application models (ASP.NET, Windows Forms, and WPF), is now undergoing a significant redesign. I said "undergoing" here because the redesign, which started in 2014, reached a first firm milestone with version 2.0, but it will definitely continue in the future.

Business-wise, you might or might not feel the rush to embrace the new platform yet, but I believe the new platform will become the way to go (and migrate to) in no more than a couple of years. The highlights of the new platform are its extreme modularity and cross-platform nature. Any code you write targeting .NET Core will also run on Linux, Mac, or Windows, albeit with different runtimes. Because of the strong orientation to cross-platform development, all the core tools to operate the platform (building, running, testing, and publishing) are exposed as command-line tools on which IDEs can build. The command-line interface of .NET Core goes under the name of CLI tools.

In the next chapter, we start focusing on the core topic of this book—ASP.NET and web development.

CHAPTER 2

The First ASP.NET Core Project

All animals are equal but some animals are more equal than others.

—George Orwell, "Animal Farm"

ASP.NET Core is the web-oriented application model that works on top of the .NET Core platform. Although the name of the application model contains the old familiar ASP.NET moniker, nothing in ASP.NET Core is really the same as in the preceding version of ASP.NET. First and foremost, ASP.NET Core has a brand-new runtime environment that supports a single application model—ASP.NET MVC. This means that the new web framework has nothing like Web Forms and even nothing exactly like Web API. Everything is brand new, and a bit of code and skills reuse is only possible in the realm of the ASP.NET MVC programming model—controllers, views, and routes.

> **Important** In this chapter and in the rest of the book, we'll make references to features and implementation aspects of non-.NET Core ASP.NET (including Web Forms, ASP.NET MVC, and Web API), and compare them to features of ASP.NET Core. To avoid misunderstandings, we'll use the term *classic ASP.NET* to refer to any application model of ASP.NET available before ASP.NET Core.

Anatomy of an ASP.NET Core Project

There are a few options to create a new ASP.NET Core project. First, you can use one of the canonical project templates available in your version of Visual Studio. Alternatively, you can use the New command in the CLI tool. If you opt for another IDE, such as JetBrains's Rider, then you have a bunch of other ASP.NET project templates from which to choose. Finally, if you just want files generated to arrange in a project under your total control, then the best option is probably the ASP.NET generator in Yeoman.

Yeoman is a language-agnostic project generator that, when properly configured, can generate all the files that make up the skeleton of a web application, including ASP.NET Core applications. (For more information, see *http://yeoman.io/learning*.)

Note The project files you get using Visual Studio, Rider, CLI tools, and Yeoman are slightly different. Visual Studio offers two options—a barebone project and a full project with membership and Bootstrap. The New command in the CLI tool also generates a rich ASP.NET project. The default ASP.NET Core application from Rider is something in between an empty project and a fully configured project devoid of application logic. Yeoman is probably the most flexible generator as it offers a few options from which you can choose.

Structure of the Project

As you can see in Figure 2-1, Visual Studio comes with predefined templates to create classic non-.NET Core Web applications that target the full .NET Framework as well as ASP.NET Core applications. The option highlighted in the figure—ASP.NET Core Web Application (.NET Core)—instead creates an ASP.NET Core application targeting the .NET Core framework.

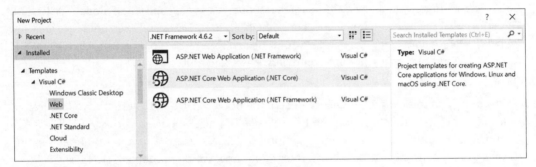

FIGURE 2-1 Creating a new ASP.NET Core project in Visual Studio

The next step in the wizard requires you to specify the amount of code you want to be generated for the first run of the application. Overall, I believe that at least for learning purposes the best approach is starting with a barebone but functioning project. In this regard, the Empty option of Visual Studio is the ideal option, as shown in Figure 2-2.

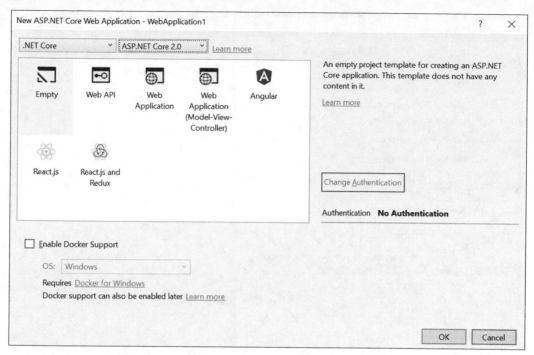

FIGURE 2-2 Selecting an empty project

Once you confirm the selection, Visual Studio creates a few files and configures a new project. At this point, you're ready to inspect the files and try to build them into an executable.

A First Look at the Empty Project

The content of the solution might trigger different reactions depending on your developer background. As a former ASP.NET developer, for example, you'll typically notice an unusual *wwwroot* project folder and the lack of one of the fundamental files of the past ASP.NET: *global.asax*. The other crucial file of the past ASP.NET configuration—the *web.config* file—is still there, but its content differs significantly from expectations. (See Figure 2-3.)

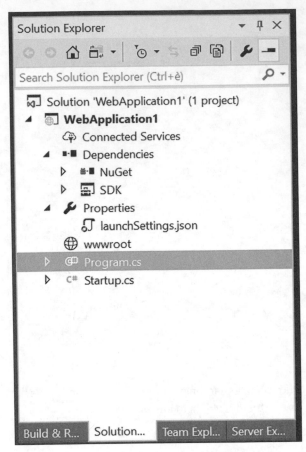

FIGURE 2-3 The content of solution explorer for an empty project

As Figure 2-3 shows, the solution includes two new files: *startup.cs* and *program.cs*. Having startup.cs available might not be a complete surprise if you've practiced a bit with OWIN-based frameworks such as Web API or ASP.NET SignalR. However, having *program.cs* in a web application might also be a shock. A console program file in a web application? How is that possible?

Well, it's all about the new runtime infrastructure that hosts and runs ASP.NET Core applications. Let's find out more about the new entries of a barebone ASP.NET Core project.

Purpose of the *wwwroot* Folder

As far as static files are concerned, the ASP.NET Core runtime distinguishes between the content root folder and the web root folder.

The *content root* is generally the current directory of the project, and in production, it is the root folder of deployment. It represents the base path for any file search and access that might be required by the code. Instead, the *web root* is the base path for any static files that the application might serve to web clients. Generally, the web root folder is a child folder of the content root and is named *wwwroot*.

The interesting thing is that the web root folder must be created on the production machine, but it is completely transparent to client browsers requesting static files. In other words, if you have an images subfolder below *wwwroot* with a file named *banner.jpg,* then the valid URL to grab the banner is the following:

```
/images/banner.jpg
```

However, the physical image file must go under *wwwroot* on the server; otherwise, it won't be retrieved. The location of both root folders may be changed programmatically in the *program.cs* file. (More on this in a moment.)

> **Note** A clear, system-level distinction between content root and web root doesn't exist in classic ASP.NET. In classic ASP.NET, the content root is automatically defined to be the root folder where the application is installed. Having a clearly identified web root folder, however, is a good practice that most teams have implemented, and it has been turned into a system feature in ASP.NET Core. Personally, I tend to call my web root folder *Content*, but I see that many others like to call it *Assets*. At any rate, in classic ASP.NET, the definition of the web root folder is virtual, and the folder must be included in any URL that points to a static file stored inside.

Purpose of the Program File

As weird as it may sound, an ASP.NET Core application is nothing more than a console application launched by the *dotnet* driver tool we already met in Chapter 1. The source code of the (required) console application is in the *program.cs* file. The role of the console application is well illustrated in Figure 2-4.

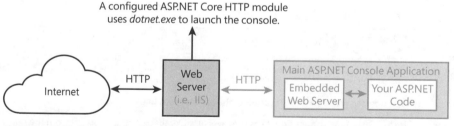

FIGURE 2-4 Bird's eye view of how an ASP.NET Core application works

The web server (IIS, for example) communicates with a fully decoupled executable over a configured port and forwards the incoming request to the console application. The console application is spawned from the IIS process space, care of a required HTTP module that enables IIS to support ASP.NET Core. Analogous extension modules are required to host ASP.NET Core applications on other Web servers such as Apache or NGINX.

Important It is interesting to note that the ASP.NET Core architecture depicted in Figure 2-4 has some analogy to the original architecture linking ASP.NET 1.x and IIS back in 2003. At that time, ASP.NET had its own worker process communicating with IIS through named pipes. Later, the tasks of the ASP.NET worker process have been absorbed by the built-in IIS worker process (*w3wp.exe*), creating the concept of application pools. In ASP.NET Core two independent, unrelated and fully decoupled executables communicate, but the ASP.NET executable is not a multi-tenant worker process. It is simply an instance of the application that hosts a basic async web server to process incoming requests.

Internally, the console application is built around the following few lines of code taken from the *program.cs* file.

```
public static void Main(string[] args)
{
    var host = new WebHostBuilder()
        .UseKestrel()
        .UseContentRoot(Directory.GetCurrentDirectory())
        .UseIISIntegration()
        .UseStartup<Startup>()
        .Build();
    host.Run();
}
```

An ASP.NET Core application requires a host in which to execute. The host is responsible for the application startup and lifetime management. *WebHostBuilder* is the class responsible for building a fully configured instance of a valid ASP.NET Core host. Table 2-1 briefly explains the tasks performed by the methods invoked in the code snippet above.

TABLE 2-1 Extension methods for the ASP.NET Core host

Method	Effect
UseKestrel	Instructs the host about the embedded web server to use. The embedded web server is responsible for accepting and processing HTTP requests in the context of the host. Kestrel is the name of the default cross-platform ASP.NET embedded web server.
UseContentRoot	Instructs the host about the location of the content root folder.
UseIISIntegration	Instructs the host about using IIS as the reverse proxy that will grab requests from the public Internet and pass them on to the embedded server.
	Note that for an ASP.NET Core application having a reverse proxy might be recommended for security and traffic reasons but it is not necessary at all from a purely functional point of view.
UseStartup<T>	Instructs the host about the type that contains initialization settings for the application.
Build	Builds an instance of the ASP.NET Core host type.

The *WebHostBuilder* class has quite a few extension methods that would let you further customize the behavior.

Also, ASP.NET Core 2.0 offers a simpler way to build the web host instance. By using a "default" builder, a single call can return a freshly created instance of the web host. Here's how the *program.cs* file can be rewritten.

```
public class Program
{
    public static void Main(string[] args)
    {
        BuildWebHostInstance(args).Run();
    }

    public static IWebHost BuildWebHostInstance(string[] args) =>
        WebHost.CreateDefaultBuilder(args)
            .UseStartup<Startup>()
            .Build();
}
```

The static method *CreateDefaultBuilder* does all the work for you and adds Kestrel, IIS configuration, and the content root as well as other options, such as logging providers and configuration data that up until ASP.NET Core 1.1 could only be added in the startup class. The best way to make sense of the things that the *CreateDefaultBuilder* method does for you is taking a look at its source code: *http://github.com/ aspnet/MetaPackages/blob/dev/src/Microsoft.AspNetCore/WebHost.cs#L150*.

Purpose of the Startup File

The *startup.cs* file contains the class designated to configure the request pipeline that handles all requests made to the application. The class contains at least a couple of methods that the host will call back during the initialization of the application. The first method is called *ConfigureServices* and is used to add in the dependency injection mechanism services that the application expects to use. The *ConfigureServices* is optional to have in a startup class, but having one is necessary in most realistic scenarios.

The second method is called *Configure* and, as its name suggests, serves the purpose of configuring previously requested services. For example, if you declared your intention to use the ASP.NET MVC service in the method *ConfigureServices*, then in *Configure* you can specify the list of valid routes you intend to handle by calling the *UseMvc* method on the provided *IApplicationBuilder* parameter. The *Configure* method is required. Note that the startup class is not expected to implement any interface or inherit from any base class. Both *Configure* and *ConfigureServices*, in fact, are discovered and invoked via reflection.

> **Note** As weird as it may sound, ASP.NET Core allows you to write web applications but not necessarily ASP.NET MVC applications with controllers, views, and routes. Hence, if you intend to write a canonical ASP.NET MVC, you must first request MVC-specific services.

In a way, the operations you perform in the folds of the startup class recall closely the operations that, in classic ASP.NET, you would have coded in the *Application_Start* method of *global.asax* and in some sections of the *web.config* file.

Note that the name of the startup class is not set in stone. The name *Startup* is a reasonable choice, but you can change it to your liking. Needless to say, if you rename the startup class, then you must pass in the right type in the call to *UseStartup<T>*. Also, notice that the *UseStartup* extension method offers a few additional overloads for you to indicate the startup class. For example, you can pass its name as a class-assembly string or as a *Type* object as follows.

```
// Using a non-conventional and nostalgic name
// for the startup class (GlobalAsax)
// ...
var host = new WebHostBuilder()
        .UseKestrel()
        .UseContentRoot(Directory.GetCurrentDirectory())
        .UseIISIntegration()
        .UseStartup<GlobalAsax>()
        .Build();
```

Important As previously mentioned, we're only scratching the surface of the ASP.NET runtime and hosting environment in this chapter. The purpose is to go straight to the substance of how to build applications and how to make them behave as expected. However, an insightful look at the ASP.NET Core runtime environment is necessary to comprehend the potential of the platform and the best ways to use it, even on different operating systems. Hence, a tour of the ASP.NET system is in order and will take place in Chapter 14, "The ASP.NET Core Runtime Environment."

Interacting with the Runtime Environment

All ASP.NET Core applications are hosted in a runtime environment, and they consume a few available services. The great news is that the number and quality of these services is entirely up to the development team. You don't get any services that you don't want. Also, you must declare explicitly all the services you need to have up and running for the application to work.

Note A mistake that I made quite often in my early days with the ASP.NET Core platform was forgetting to require the static-files service with the subsequent refusal of the system to serve any images or JavaScript files, even when they were regularly deployed under the web root folder.

Next, you'll learn more about the interaction that takes place between the application and the hosting environment.

Resolving the Startup Type

One of the first tasks the host takes on is resolving the startup type. You explicitly indicate a startup type of any name either through the *UseStartup<T>* generic extension method or by passing it as a parameter to the nongeneric version . It is also possible to pass the name of a referenced assembly that contains a *Startup* type.

The conventional name of the startup class is *Startup,* and you can definitely change it to your liking. However, if you maintain the conventional name, you get a few extra benefits. In particular, you can have multiple startup classes configured in the application, one per development environment. You can have a startup class to use in development and others to use in the staging or production environments. Furthermore, you can also define custom development environments if you like.

Let's say that you have a couple of classes in your project named *StartupDevelopment* and *StartupProduction,* and you use the following code to create the host:

```
var host = new WebHostBuilder()
    .UseKestrel()
    .UseContentRoot(Directory.GetCurrentDirectory())
    .UseIISIntegration()
    .UseStartup(Assembly.GetEntryAssembly().GetName().Name)
    .Build();
```

You're now telling the host to resolve the startup class from the current assembly. In this case, the host attempts to find a loadable class that matches the following pattern: *StartupXXX* where *XXX* is the name of the current hosting environment. By default, the hosting environment is set to *Production* but can be changed to any string you like. For example, it could be *Staging* or *Development* or whatever else that makes sense for you. If the hosting environment is not set, then the system will simply try to locate a plain *Startup* class and throws an error if it fails.

In a nutshell, you can defnitely rename the startup class but, more realistically, you might want the host to resolve the class based on the current hosting environment. Great, but how do you set the current hosting environment?

The Hosting Environment

The *Development* environment results from the value of an environment variable named ASPNETCORE_ENVIRONMENT. In a Visual Studio project, the variable is set to *Development* by default, and the variable can be set to any string you wish, such as *Production* or *Staging.*

The ASPNETCORE_ENVIRONMENT variable can be set in any way you can set an environment variable on a given operating system. For example, on Windows, you can use the Control Panel, PowerShell, or the *set* tool from the command prompt. Of course, you can also set the variable programmatically or from within Visual Studio in the Properties dialog of the project, as shown in Figure 2-5. Bear in mind that if, for whatever reason, the ASPNETCORE_ENVIRONMENT variable is not set, then the hosting environment is assumed to be *Production.*

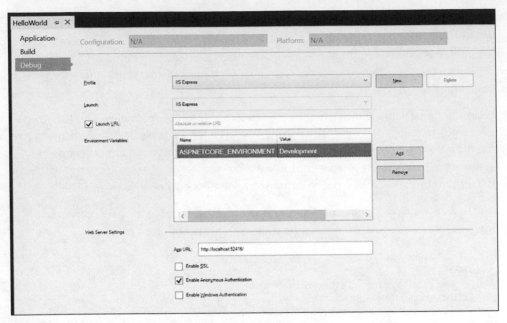

FIGURE 2-5 Setting an environment variable in Visual Studio

The configuration of the hosting environment is exposed programmatically through the members of the *IHostingEnvironment* interface (see Table 2-2).

TABLE 2-2 The IHostingEnvironment interface

Member	Description
ApplicationName	Gets or sets the name of the application. The host sets the value of the property to the assembly that contains the application entry point.
EnvironmentName	Gets or sets the name of the environment overriding the value of the ASPNETCORE_ ENVIRONMENT variable. You can use the setter of this property to set the environment programmatically.
ContentRootPath	Gets or sets the absolute path to the directory that contains the application files. This property is usually set to the root installation path.
ContentRootFileProvider	Gets or sets the component that must be used to retrieve content files. The component can be any class that implements the *IFileProvider* interface. The default file provider uses the file system to retrieve files.
WebRootPath	Gets or sets the absolute path to the directory that contains the static files that clients can request via URL.
WebRootFileProvider	Gets or sets the component that must be used to retrieve web files. The component can be any class that implements the *IFileProvider* interface. The default file provider uses the file system to retrieve files.

The *IFileProvider* interface represents a read-only file provider, and it works by taking a string that describes a file or directory name and returning an abstraction of the content. An interesting alternate implementation of the *IFileProvider* interface is one that retrieves the file and directory contents from a database.

An object that implements the *IHostingEnvironment* interface is created by the host and made publicly available to the startup class and all other classes in the application via dependency injection. (More on this in the next section, "Enabling System and Application Services.")

 Note The constructor of the startup class can optionally receive the reference to a couple of system services: *IHostingEnvironment* and *ILoggerFactory*. In particular, the latter is the ASP.NET Core abstraction for creating instances of a logger component.

Enabling System and Application Services

If defined, the *ConfigureServices* method is invoked before *Configure* to give developers a chance to wire up system and application services to the request pipeline. Configuration of wired services might take place directly in *ConfigureServices,* or it can be postponed until *Configure* is called. It depends ultimately on the programming interface of the service. Here's the prototype of the *ConfigureServices* method.

```
public void ConfigureServices(IServiceCollection services)
```

As you can see, the method receives a collection of services and just adds its own services. In general, services that have a substantial setup phase provide an *AddXXX* extension method on *IServiceCollection* and accept a few parameters. In the code snippet below, you see how to add the Entity Framework *DbContext* to the list of available services. The *AddDbContext* method accepts a few options, such as the database provider to use and the actual connection string.

```
public void ConfigureServices(IServiceCollection services)
{
    var connString = "...";
    services.AddDbContext<YourDbContext>(options => options.UseSqlServer(connString));
}
```

Adding a service to the *IServicesCollection* container makes the service further available to the rest of the application via the ASP.NET Core built-in dependency injection system.

Configuring System and Application Services

The *Configure* method is used to configure the HTTP request pipeline and to specify the modules that will have a chance to process incoming HTTP requests. Modules and loose code that can be added to the HTTP request pipeline are collectively referred to as *middleware*.

The *Configure* method receives an instance of a system object that implements the *IApplication-Builder* interface and will add middleware through extension methods of the interface. Also, the *Configure* method may receive an instance of *IHostingEnvironment* and *ILoggerFactory* components. Here's a possible way to declare the method.

```
public void Configure(IApplicationBuilder app, IHostingEnvironment env)
{
    ...
}
```

A very common action you would take in the *Configure* method is enabling the ability to serve static files and a centralized error handler.

```
public void Configure(IApplicationBuilder app, IHostingEnvironment env)
{
    app.UseExceptionHandler("/error/view");
    app.UseStaticFiles();
}
```

The extension method *UseExceptionHandler* acts as a centralized error handler and redirects to the specified URL in case of unhandled exceptions. Its overall behavior is analogous to the *Application_Error* method in *global.asax* in classic ASP.NET. To receive the developer's friendly messages in case of exceptions, you might want to use the *UseDeveloperExceptionPage* instead. At the same time, you might want to see developer's friendly messages only in development mode. This scenario represents an excellent use-case for the methods of some of the extension methods of the *IHostingEnvironment* interface.

```
public void Configure(IApplicationBuilder app, IHostingEnvironment env)
{
    if (env.IsDevelopment())
    {
        app.UseDeveloperExceptionPage();
    }
    else
    {
        app.UseExceptionHandler("/Error/View");
    }

    app.UseStaticFiles();
}
```

Extension methods like *IsDevelopment*, *IsProduction,* and *IsStaging* are predefined to check the current development mode. If you define a custom environment, you can check it through the *IsEnvironment* method. Note that environment names are not case-sensitive in Windows and Mac, but they are case-sensitive in Linux.

Because any code you write in *Configure* ends up configuring the runtime pipeline, the order in which services are configured is important. For this reason, the first thing you want to do in *Configure* is set up error handling right after the static files.

Environment-Specific Configuration Methods

In a startup class, the names of *Configure* and *ConfigureServices* methods can also be made environment-specific. The pattern is *ConfigureXxx* and *ConfigureXxxServices; Xxx* refers to an environment name.

Creating a single startup class using the default name of *Startup* and registering it with the host via *UseStartup<T>* is probably the ideal way to configure the startup of an ASP.NET Core application. Then, in the body of the class, you create environment-specific methods, such as *ConfigureDevelopment* and *ConfigureProduction*.

The host will take care of resolving the method based on the environment currently set. Note that if you rename the startup class to anything other than *Startup,* then the built-in logic for automatic resolution of types will fail.

The ASP.NET Pipeline

The *IApplicationBuilder* interface provides the means to define the structure of the ASP.NET pipeline. The pipeline is a chain of optional modules that preprocess and postprocess an incoming HTTP request, as shown in Figure 2-6.

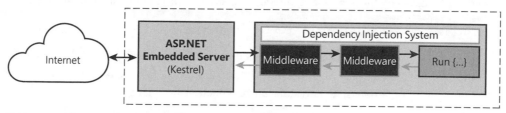

FIGURE 2-6 The ASP.NET Core pipeline

The pipeline is made of middleware components registered in *Configure* and invoked in the registered order for each request. Every middleware component is built around the following pattern:

```
app.Use(async (httpContext, next) =>
{
    // Pre-process the request
    ...

    // Yield to the next middleware module in the chain
    await next();

    // Post-process the request
    ...
});
```

All middleware components are given a chance to process the request before it is actually run by the ASP.NET code. By calling the next module, each middleware component pushes the request down to the next request in the queue. When the last registered module has preprocessed the request, the request executes. After that, the chain of middleware components is traversed backward, and all registered modules have a chance to postprocess the request usually by looking at the updated context and its response. On the way back to the client, middleware modules are invoked in the reverse order.

You can register your own middleware with a code snippet, as shown above, and indicate the code through a lambda expression. Alternatively, you can wrap up the logic in a class and create an ad hoc *UseXxx* method to register it in the pipeline within the *Configure* method. I'll return to the ASP.NET pipeline and its customization in Chapter 14.

The chain of middleware components ends with the request runner, namely the code that will actually perform the action intended for the request. This code is also referred to as *terminating middleware*. In classic ASP.NET MVC, the request runner is the action invoker that selects the appropriate controller class, determines the correct method, and invokes it. As mentioned, though, in ASP.NET Core, the MVC programming model is just one option. This means that the request runner takes a more abstract form:

```
app.Run(async context =>
{
    await context.Response.WriteAsync("Courtesy of 'Programming ASP.NET Core'");
});
```

The code processed by the terminating middleware has the form of the following delegate:

```
public delegate Task RequestDelegate(HttpContext context);
```

The terminating middleware takes an instance of the *HttpContext* object and returns a task. The HTTP context object is a container of HTTP-based information, including the response stream, authentication claims, input parameters, session state, and connection information.

If the terminating middleware is defined explicitly through a *Run* method, then any request is served directly from there with no need to have controllers and views around. With a *Run* middleware method implemented, any request can be served with nearly no overhead in the fastest possible way and with the bare minimum of memory footprint. I'll demonstrate this feature in the next section of the chapter.

The Dependency Injection Subsystem

The overview of the ASP.NET runtime environment couldn't be completed without a look at the built-in dependency injection (DI) subsystem.

Dependency Injection at a Glance

DI is a design principle that promotes loose coupling between classes. For example, let's say you have the following class:

```
public class FlagService
{
    private FlagRepository _repository;

    public FlagService()
    {
        _repository = new FlagRepository();
    }

    public Flag GetFlagForCountry(string country)
    {
        return _repository.GetFlag(country);
    }
}
```

The class *FlagService* depends on the class *FlagRepository* and given the tasks that both classes accomplish, a tight relationship is unavoidable. The DI principle helps keep a loose relationship between the *FlagService* and its dependencies. The core idea of DI is to make *FlagService* dependent only on an abstraction of the functions provided by *FlagRepository*. With DI in mind, the class can be rewritten as follows:

```
public class FlagService
{
    private IFlagRepository _repository;

    public FlagService(IFlagRepository repository)
    {
        _repository = repository;
    }

    public Flag GetFlagForCountry(string country)
    {
        return _repository.GetFlag(country);
    }
}
```

Now, any class that implements *IFlagRepository* can safely work with an instance of *FlagService*. By using DI, we turned a tight dependency between *FlagService* and *FlagRepository* into a looser relationship between *FlagService* and an abstraction of the services it needs to import from the outside. The responsibility of creating an instance of the repository abstraction has been moved away from the service class. This means that some other code is now responsible for taking a reference to an interface (an abstraction) and returning a usable instance of a concrete type (a class). This code can be written manually every time it is needed.

```
var repository = new FlagRepository();
var service = new FlagService(repository);
```

Or, this code can be run by an ad hoc layer of code that inspects the constructor of the service and resolves all its dependencies.

```
var service = DependencyInjectionSubsystem.Resolve(FlagService);
```

Refactoring your types by following this injection pattern will also help you write unit tests more easily because mocked implementation can be passed at any time to the constructors.

ASP.NET Core comes with its own DI subsystem so that any class, including controllers, can just declare in the constructor (or members) all necessary dependencies; the system will ensure that valid instances are created and passed.

Dependency Injection in ASP.NET Core

To use the DI system, you need to register the types the system must be able to instantiate for you. The ASP.NET Core DI system is already aware of some types, such as *IHostingEnvironment* and *ILoggerFactory,* but it needs to know about application-specific types. Let's see what it takes to add new types to the DI system.

Registering Types with the DI System

The *IServicesCollection* parameter that your code receives in the method *ConfigureServices* is the handle to access all types currently registered with the DI system. To register a new type, you add code to the *ConfigureServices* method.

```
public void ConfigureServices(IServiceCollection services)
{
    // Register a custom type with the DI system
    services.AddTransient<IFlagRepository, FlagRepository>();
}
```

The method *AddTransient* instructs the DI system to serve a fresh new instance of the type *FlagRepository* every time an abstraction like the *IFlagRepository* interface is requested. With this line in place, any class whose instantiation is managed by ASP.NET Core can simply declare a parameter of type *IFlagRepository* to have a fresh instance served by the system. Here's a common use of the DI system:

```
public class FlagController
{
    private IFlagRepository _flagRepository;
    public FlagController(IFlagRepository flagRepository)
    {
        _flagRepository = flagRepository;
    }

    ...
}
```

Controller and view classes are very common examples of ASP.NET Core classes that take advantage of the DI system.

Resolving Types Based on Runtime Conditions

Sometimes you want to register an abstract type with the DI system, but you need to decide about the concrete type only after verifying some runtime conditions (appended cookies, HTTP headers, or query string parameters, for example). Here's how to do it:

```
public void ConfigureServices(IServiceCollection services)
{
    services.AddTransient<IFlagRepository>(provider =>
    {
        // Create the instance of the actual type to return
        // based on the identity of the currently logged user.
        var context = provider.GetRequiredService<IHttpContextAccessor>();
        return new FlagRepositoryForUser(context.HttpContext.User);
    });
}
```

Notice that you can have the HTTP context injected in a programming context where it is not natively available by asking the DI container to inject an instance of *IHttpContextAccessor*.

Resolving Types on Demand

In some cases, you need to create instances of types that have their own dependencies. A very good example is *FlagService*, the class we introduced earlier to play with the concept of dependency injection. (See the section, "Dependency Injection at a Glance," earlier in this chapter.)

```
public class FlagService
{
    public FlagService(IFlagRepository repository)
    {
        _repository = repository;
    }
    ...
}
```

How would you create an instance of the class without first manually resolving all its dependencies? Note that dependencies can be nested to many levels, so it could be that to instantiate a type that implements *IFlagRepository,* one first must instantiate many other types. Any DI system can help with this problem, and the ASP.NET Core system is no exception.

Usually, a DI system is centered around a root object known as the container that traverses the tree of dependencies and resolves abstract types. In the ASP.NET Core system, the container is represented by the *IServiceProvider* interface. To resolve an instance of the *FlagService*, you have two options: using the classic *new* operator and providing a valid instance of the *IFlagRepository* implementation dependency or leveraging *IServiceProvider*, as below:

```
var flagService = provider.GetService<FlagService>();
```

To get an instance of the *IServiceProvider* container, you just define *IServiceProvider* as a parameter of the constructor wherever needed, and the DI will kindly inject the expected instance. Here's an example of a controller:

```
public class FlagController
{
    private FlagService _service;
    public FlagController(IServiceProvider provider)
    {
        _service = provider.GetService<FlagService>();
    }

    ...
}
```

Injecting *IServiceProvider* or injecting the actual dependency has the same effect on your code. There's no way to get a static, global reference to the service provider. However, in the context of ASP.NET Core, you don't need it. Your code, in fact, will always run within an ASP.NET Core class that supports dependency injection. As far as custom classes are concerned, all you have to do is design them to accept dependencies through the constructor.

Controlling the Lifetime of Objects

There are three different ways to register a type with the DI system, and the lifetime of the returned instance differs for each. Let's have a look at Table 2-3.

TABLE 2-3 Lifetime options for DI-created objects

Method	Behavior
AddTransient	Every caller receives a freshly created instance of the specified type.
AddSingleton	All requests receive the same instance of the specified type created the first time after application startup. If for some reason no cached instance is available, it is re-created. The method also features an overload that allows you to pass yourself the instance to cache and return on demand.
AddScoped	Each call to the DI system within the context of a given request receives the same instance created at the beginning of the request processing. This option is like a singleton except that it is scoped to the request lifetime.

The code below shows how to register a user-created instance to be served as a singleton.

```
public void ConfigureServices(IServiceCollection services)
{
    services.AddSingleton<ICountryRepository>(new CountryRepository());
}
```

Every abstract type can be mapped to multiple concrete types. When this happens, the system uses the last registered concrete type to resolve the dependency. If no concrete type can be found, then null is returned. If a concrete type is found, but it cannot be instantiated, then an exception is thrown.

Integrating with External DI Libraries

Over the years, classic ASP.NET MVC progressively increased the level of customization of the out-of-the-box features. In the latest version, for example, the *IDependencyResolver* interface defines the methods to locate available services and to resolve dependencies. It has more of a service locator than a dependency injection framework, but it provides the requested functionality. The biggest difference between Service Locator and Dependency Injection is that the former offers a global object—the service locator—that must be explicitly asked to resolve a dependency. With the Dependency Injection pattern, instead, type resolution is implicit, and all a class must do is declare—through supported injection points—the dependencies. The Service Locator pattern is much easier to add to an existing framework. The Dependency Injection pattern is ideal for a framework built from the ground up.

The DI framework in ASP.NET Core is not a fully-fledged DI framework and hardly competes with any of the top-industry frameworks out there. It does basic tasks, does them well, and serves the needs of the ASP.NET Core platform. The biggest difference with other popular DI frameworks is injection points.

Injection Points

Generally speaking, a dependency can be injected in a class in three different ways: as an additional parameter in the constructor, in a public method, or through a public property. The DI implementation in ASP.NET Core, however, has been kept deliberately simple and it doesn't fully support advanced use-cases like other popular DI frameworks, including Microsoft's Unity, AutoFac, Ninject, Structure-Map, and so forth.

So in ASP.NET Core, dependency injection can only occur via the constructor, and this is by design.

However, when using DI in a fully enabled MVC context, then you can use the *FromServices* attribute to mark a public property of a class or a method parameter as an injection point. The drawback is that the *FromServices* attribute belongs to the ASP.NET model binding layer and it is not technically a part of the DI system. For this reason, you can use *FromServices* only when the ASP.NET MVC engine is enabled and only within the realm of a controller class. We'll demonstrate this feature in Chapter 3, "Bootstrapping ASP.NET MVC," after introducing MVC controllers.

> **Note** Another feature of most industry-leading DI frameworks that the ASP.NET Core implementation doesn't support is the ability to map the same abstract type to multiple concrete types—each with a different and unique key. By passing the key (usually, an arbitrary string) to the service provider, you can have the abstract type resolved in a particular way. This feature can be simulated in ASP.NET Core either using a factory class for the abstract type or, if possible, through a callback-based type resolution.

Using External DI Frameworks

If you find the ASP.NET Core DI infrastructure too simple for your needs, or if you have a large code-base written against a different DI framework, then you can configure the ASP.NET Core system to switch to using the external DI framework of choice. For this to happen, though, it is required that the external framework supports ASP.NET Core and provides a bridge to connect to the ASP.NET Core infrastructure.

Supporting ASP.NET Core means providing a class library compatible with the .NET Core framework and a custom implementation of the *IServiceProvider* interface. As part of this support effort, the external DI framework must also be able to import the collection of services natively or programmatically registered with the ASP.NET Core DI system.

```
public IServiceProvider ConfigureServices(IServiceCollection services)
{
    // Add some services using the ASP.NET Core interface
    services.AddTransient<IFlagRepository, FlagRepository>();

    // Create the container of the external DI library
    // Using StructureMap here.
    var structureMapContainer = new Container();

    // Add your own services using the native API of the DI library
    // ...

    // Add services already registered with the ASP.NET Core DI system
    structureMapContainer.Populate(services);
```

```
// Return the implementation of IServiceProvider using internally
// the external library to resolve dependencies
return structureMapContainer.GetInstance<IServiceProvider>();
}
```

It is important to note that you can register an external DI framework in *ConfigureServices*. In doing so, though, you must change the return type of the method in the startup class from *void* to *IServiceProvider*. Finally, keep in mind that only a few of the DI frameworks out there have been ported to .NET Core. Among the few, there are Autofac and StructureMap. You can get Autofac for .NET Core through the *Autofac.Extensions.DependencyInjection* NuGet package. If you're interested in Structure-Map, instead, you can grab it from Github at the following address: *http://github.com/structuremap/ StructureMap.Microsoft.DependencyInjection*.

Building a Mini Website

As mentioned, ASP.NET Core is a framework to build web applications, and it doesn't support some of the application models of classic ASP.NET, most notably the Web Forms application model. It does support the ASP.NET MVC application model with a good level of compatibility instead. In fact, most of the existing controllers and Razor views can be ported as-is under the realm of an ASP.NET Core application that uses the MVC services.

In fact, you don't strictly need the MVC and Razor engines to build fully functioning websites. This aspect of the ASP.NET Core platform enables you to create mini website or website with a short pipeline and a tiny memory footprint.

> **Note** Creating a mini website that can run without a large footprint isn't easy to do with classic ASP.NET. In classic ASP.NET you could disable some unwanted HTTP modules, thus reducing the length of the request pipeline, but a lot happens before your code gets to run. To my best knowledge, the fastest way to have your custom code run in classic ASP.NET is to use an HTTP handler. You cannot get close to that with either ASPX files or MVC controllers. As far as Web API is concerned, things don't change much if the Web API server is hosted within the boundaries of an ASP.NET site.

Creating a Single Endpoint Website

As we'll see in much more detail later in the book, any middleware components added to the pipe-line can inspect and modify every aspect of the request, and any middleware components can add response cookies and headers and even write to the output stream, thus producing some actual output for the client.

The Hello World Application

Let's start seeing what it takes to create a true hello-world web application with ASP.NET Core. While it was not possible with classic ASP.NET, ASP.NET Core allows you to create a minimalistic application that just prints out a simple message. Here's the code:

```
public void Configure (IApplicationBuilder app, IHostingEnvironment env)
{
    app.Run(async (context) =>
    {
        await context.Response
            .WriteAsync("Courtesy of <b>Programming ASP.NET Core</b>!" +
            "<hr>" +
            "ENVIRONMENT=" + env.EnvironmentName);
    });
}
```

The code above belongs to the startup class. In addition to this code, all you need is a *program.cs* file and a project file. Figure 2-7 shows the output in the browser.

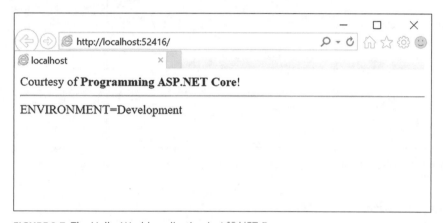

FIGURE 2-7 The Hello-World application in ASP.NET Core

The code necessary to generate the output in the figure is not long, but you can actually make it even shorter. Here's a simple echo website that writes out the segment of the URL that follows the server name.

```
using Microsoft.AspNetCore.Hosting;
using Microsoft.AspNetCore.Builder;
using Microsoft.AspNetCore.Http;

namespace Echo
{
    public class Program
    {
        public static void Main(string[] args)
        {
            var host = new WebHostBuilder()
                .UseKestrel()
                .UseIISIntegration()
```

```
                .Configure(app => {
                    app.Run(async (context) => {
                        var path = context.Request.Path;
                        await context.Response.WriteAsync(path); });
                })
                .Build();
            host.Run();
        }
    }
}
```

You don't even need a startup class and a startup file. The terminating middleware, in fact, is attached directly to the host instance. And you still have access to the HTTP request internals to figure out the origin URL and query string parameters (see Figure 2-8). There's still room in the terminating middleware for some minimally complex business logic.

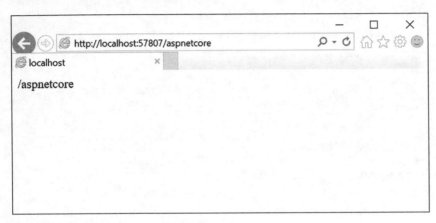

FIGURE 2-8 The Echo sample application

Launching the Website

Within Visual Studio, you can test the website through IIS (including IIS Express) or by launching the console application directly (see Figure 2-9).

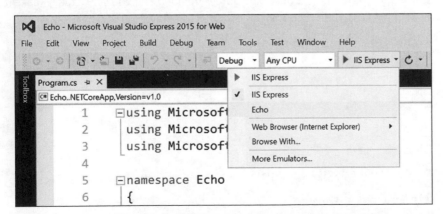

FIGURE 2-9 Launch options for an ASP.NET Core application in Visual Studio

When you launch the console application directly, the effect is that the application starts and begins listening on the configured port (port 5000, by default). At the same time, a browser window is opened for you to make requests (see Figure 2-10).

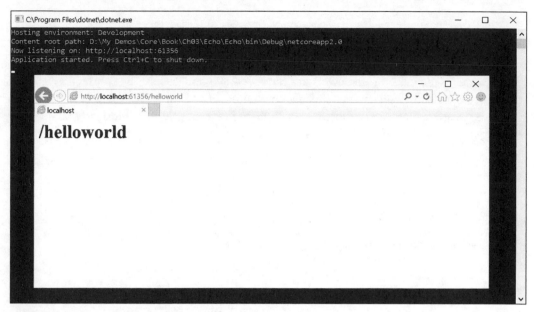

FIGURE 2-10 The application listening on configured port

The Country Server

Let's take this approach one step further and try to build a very thin but functional mini website. In the example, the website will hold a JSON file with a list of the world's countries and return a filtered list based on the hints provided by the query string.

The business logic required to set up the Country mini website is limited to the code that loads the content of the JSON file into memory and runs a few LINQ queries on it. The JSON file is added to the content root folder as a project file and remains invisible from the web channel. A repository class manages the interaction between the mini website and the list of countries. The repository is abstracted to the *ICountryRepository* interface:

```
namespace CoreBook.MiniWeb.Persistence.Abstractions
{
    public interface ICountryRepository
    {
        IQueryable<Country> All();
        Country Find(string code);
        IQueryable<Country> AllBy(string filter);
    }
}
```

To be honest, in the perspective of saving as much code as possible, having an interface here to abstract the country repository is probably overkill. However, the approach taken in the demo illustrates a practice that is highly recommended in real-world code—at least for testability reasons. The repository is registered with the DI system and is made available as a singleton through the application.

```
public void ConfigureServices(IServiceCollection services)
{
    services.AddSingleton<ICountryRepository>(new CountryRepository());
}
```

Here's the full code of the repository. As you can see, the code is nearly identical to the code you would write for the full .NET Framework in a classic ASP.NET application. The only (minor) noticeable difference is the actual API necessary to read the content of a text file. In the .NET Core framework, you still have stream readers but no more overloads that can accept a file name. Instead, you now have a *File* singleton object for more direct access to file content.

```
public class CountryRepository : ICountryRepository
{
    private static IList<Country> _countries;

    public IQueryable<Country> All()
    {
        EnsureCountriesAreLoaded();
        return _countries.AsQueryable();
    }

    public Country Find(string code)
    {
        return (from c in All()
                where c.CountryCode.Equals(code, StringComparison.CurrentCultureIgnoreCase)
                select c).FirstOrDefault();
    }

    public IQueryable<Country> AllBy(string filter)
    {
        var normalized = filter.ToLower();
        return String.IsNullOrEmpty(filter)
            ? All()
            : (All().Where(c => c.CountryName.ToLower().StartsWith(normalized)));
    }

    #region PRIVATE
    private static void EnsureCountriesAreLoaded()
    {
        if (_countries == null)
            _countries = LoadCountriesFromStream();
    }

    private static IList<Country> LoadCountriesFromStream()
    {
        var json = File.ReadAllText("countries.json");
        var countries = JsonConvert.DeserializeObject<Country[]>(json);
        return countries.OrderBy(c => c.CountryName).ToList();
    }
    #endregion
}
```

The full solution is shown in Figure 2-11.

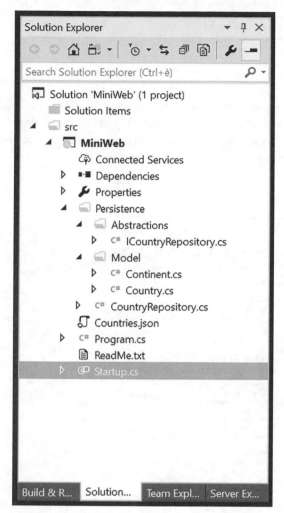

FIGURE 2-11 The Mini Web solution

Aside from the business logic that retrieves country information, the entire application is built around the terminating middleware in the startup class:

```
public void Configure(IApplicationBuilder app,
        IHostingEnvironment env,
        ICountryRepository country)
{
    // NOTE
    // You can inject ICountryRepository through the method's signature or
    // request the DI container (IServiceProvider) through the signature and
    // ask it to resolve ICountryRepository.
    //
    // var country = provider.GetService<ICountryRepository>();
```

```
    app.Run(async (context) =>
    {
        var query = context.Request.Query["q"];
        var listOfCountries = country.AllBy(query).ToList();
        var json = JsonConvert.SerializeObject(listOfCountries);
        await context.Response.WriteAsync(json);
    });
}
```

The country hint passed through the query string is retrieved directly from the HTTP *Request* object, and they are used to filter the countries. Next, the list of matching *Country* objects is serialized to JSON. Also, note that the API of the HTTP *Request* object to read the query string is slightly different from that in classic ASP.NET. The mini site in action is shown in Figure 2-12.

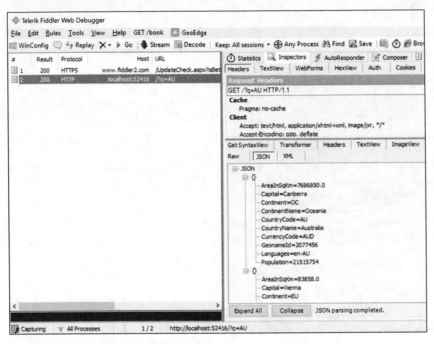

FIGURE 2-12 The country server in action

Blinking at Microservices

A mini website is conceptually similar to a dedicated, company-wide content delivery network. Imagine a scenario in which you have a lot of client-side code, spread across multiple web and mobile applications, and that it's continually retrieving the same information, such as weather forecasts, user pictures, zip codes, or country information.

Incorporating the same data retrieval logic in all web applications is an option but isolating that logic into a distinct web API promotes reusability and modularity. Isolating that logic is the core principle of *microservices*. How would you code such a website? In classic ASP.NET, there will be a lot that happens outside your control before the actual request is processed. In ASP.NET code, building a mini website or web microservices is a reality.

Accessing Files on the Web Server

In ASP.NET Core, no feature is available until you enable it explicitly. Enabling a feature means adding the appropriate NuGet package to the project, registering the service with the DI system, and configuring the service in the startup class. The rule doesn't have exceptions even for the MVC engine that must be registered. Likewise, you must register a service that guarantees access to static files located under the web root folder.

Enabling the Static Files Service

To enable retrieval of static files such as HTML pages, images, JavaScript files, or CSS files you need to add the following line to the *Configure* method of the startup class:

```
app.UseStaticFiles();
```

The above line requires the installation of the *Microsoft.AspNetCore.StaticFiles* NuGet package. Any files below the configured web root are now available for request. This includes any files that must be served as-is to the client without passing for any form of dynamic code, such as a controller method.

Enabling the static files service doesn't let your users browse the content of the specified directory. To also enable directory browsing you need the following:

```
public void ConfigureServices(IServiceCollection services)
{
    services.AddDirectoryBrowsing();
}
public void Configure(IApplicationBuilder app)
{
    app.UseStaticFiles();
    app.UseDirectoryBrowser();
}
```

With the above code in place, directory browsing is enabled for all directories under the web root. You can also restrict browsing to just a few directories.

```
public void Configure(IApplicationBuilder app)
{
    app.UseDirectoryBrowser(new DirectoryBrowserOptions()
    {
        FileProvider = new PhysicalFileProvider(
            Path.Combine(Directory.GetCurrentDirectory(), @"wwwroot", "pics"))
    });
}
```

The middleware adds a directory configuration that enables browsing for the wwwroot/pics folder only. If you want to enable browsing for other directories as well, just duplicate the *UseDirectory-Browser* call changing the path to the desired directory.

Note that static files and directory browsing are independent settings. You can have both enabled, none, or only one of the two. Realistically, though, you want to have at least static files enabled in any web application.

> **Important** Enabling directory browsing is not a feature that's recommended to have because it can lead users to sneak into your files and possibly learn secrets of your website.

Enabling Multiple Web Roots

Sometimes, you want to be able to serve static files from *wwwroot* as well as from other directories. This is definitely possible in ASP.NET Core, and all that is required is multiple calls to *UseStaticFiles*, as illustrated below.

```
public void Configure(IApplicationBuilder app)
{
    // Enable serving files from the configured web root folder (i.e., WWWROOT)
    app.UseStaticFiles();

    // Enable serving files from \Assets located under the root folder of the site
    app.UseStaticFiles(new StaticFileOptions()
    {
        FileProvider = new PhysicalFileProvider(
            Path.Combine(Directory.GetCurrentDirectory(), @"Assets")),
        RequestPath = new PathString("/Public/Assets")
    });
}
```

The code contains two calls to *UseStaticFiles*. The former enables the application to serve files only from the configured web root folder—*wwwroot* by default. The latter enables the application also to serve files located under the *Assets* folder located under the root directory of the site. However, in this case, what would be the URL used to retrieve files from the *Assets* physical folder? That's precisely the role of the *RequestPath* property of the *StaticFileOptions* class. To access *test.jpg* from *Assets,* a browser should call the following URL: */public/assets/test.jpg*.

```
<!DOCTYPE html>
<html>
<head>
    <meta charset="utf-8" />
    <title>Programming ASP.NET Core -- Ch03</title>
    <link rel="stylesheet" href="/css/site.css" />
</head>
<body>
    <h1>FILE SERVER demo</h1>
    <hr />
    <img alt="test" src="/public/assets/test.jpg" />
</body>
</html>
```

Even HTML pages are subject to the action of the static files service, as long as they are static files and not dynamic markup served by some controller (see Figure 2-13).

FIGURE 2-13 Serving files in ASP.NET Core

Note that as far as static files are concerned, no authorization layer exists that lets you control which users get which files. All files under the jurisdiction of the static file service are considered publicly accessible. This is how most websites work and is certainly not a specific feature of ASP.NET Core applications.

If you need to apply some level of authorization to some static files, then you have just one option: storing the physical files outside of *wwwroot* and any other directory configured with the static files service and serving them via a controller action. I'll discuss this in more detail in Chapter 3.

> **TIP** File names are case-insensitive under Windows but not under Mac and Linux. If you develop ASP.NET Core applications that can be hosted outside IIS and the Windows platform, you should keep this aspect in mind.

Note IIS has its own HTTP module to handle static files, named *StaticFileModule*. When an ASP.NET Core application is hosted under IIS, the default static file handler is bypassed by the ASP.NET Core Module. However, if the ASP.NET Core Module in IIS is misconfigured or missing, then the *StaticFileModule* will not be bypassed, and files will be served outside your control. To avoid that, as an additional measure, it is recommended to disable the *StaticFileModule* of IIS for an ASP.NET Core application.

Supporting Default Files

A default web file is an HTML page automatically served when the user navigates to a folder within the site. The default page is usually named *index.** or *default.** with allowed extensions of *.html* and *.htm*. Those files should be placed in *wwwroot* but ignored unless you add the following middleware:

```
public void Configure(IApplicationBuilder app)
{
    app.UseDefaultFiles();
    app.UseStaticFiles();
}
```

Note that default files middleware must be enabled before the static files middleware. In particular, the default files middleware will check for the following files in the following order: *default.htm*, *default.html*, *index.htm*, and *index.html*. The search stops at first match found.

You are welcome to completely redefine the list of default file names. Here's how:

```
var options = new DefaultFilesOptions();
options.DefaultFileNames.Clear();
options.DefaultFileNames.Add("home.html");
options.DefaultFileNames.Add("home.htm");
app.UseDefaultFiles(options);
```

If it bothers you to deal with different types of file-related middleware, then you can consider using the *UseFileServer* middleware that combines the functions of static files and default files. Note that *UseFileServer* doesn't enable directory browsing by default, but it supports options to change that behavior and also to add the same level of configuration we have seen for *UseStaticFiles* and *UseDefaultFiles* middleware.

Adding Your Own MIME Types

The static files middleware can recognize and serve over 400 different file types. However, if your website misses a MIME type, you can still add it. Here's how.

```
public void Configure(IApplicationBuilder app)
{
    // Set up custom content types -associating file extension to MIME type
    var provider = new FileExtensionContentTypeProvider();
```

```
    // Add a new mapping or replace if it exists already
    provider.Mappings[".script"] = "text/javascript";

    // Remove JS files
    provider.Mappings.Remove(".js");

    app.UseStaticFiles(new StaticFileOptions()
    {
        ContentTypeProvider = provider
    });
}
```

For classic ASP.NET web applications, adding a missing MIME type is a configuration task you perform within IIS. However, in the context of an ASP.NET Core application, IIS (as well as web servers on other platforms) plays the bare role of a reverse proxy and simply forwards incoming requests to the ASP.NET Core embedded web server (Kestrel) and from there up through the request pipeline. The pipeline, though, must be configured programmatically.

Summary

In this chapter, we have taken a look at a few sample ASP.NET Core projects. An ASP.NET Core application is a plain console application usually triggered within the boundaries of a fully-fledged web server such as IIS, Apache Server, or NGINX. However, you don't strictly need a full web server to run an ASP.NET Core application. All ASP.NET Core applications are equipped with their own basic web server (Kestrel) that can still receive HTTP requests over a configured port.

The console application builds a host environment where requests will be processed through a pipeline. In this chapter, we've scratched the surface of the HTTP pipeline and web server architecture and discussed how to arrange mini websites and sites that can serve static files. In the next chapter, we'll attack dynamic processing of requests, and we'll introduce routes, controllers, and views.

The ASP.NET MVC Application Model

You've already had your first taste of ASP.NET Core development and what it can do. Now, it's time to explore its powerful ASP.NET Model-View-Controller (MVC) application model.

If you've coded with ASP.NET MVC, you'll find much that's familiar here. In fact, the MVC concepts implemented by ASP.NET Core won't surprise users of platforms such as Rails and Django, or front-end frameworks like Angular. Of course, the details matter, so Part II drills down on these, helping you make the most of ASP.NET Core's modern application model whatever your background.

Chapter 3, *Bootstrapping ASP.NET MVC*, helps you get your MVC infrastructure up and running. You'll enable the MVC application model, register the MVC service, enable and configure routing, and see how routing fits into the workflow of an ASP.NET MVC request.

Next, Chapter 4, *ASP.NET MVC Controllers* introduces the fundamental pillar of the ASP.NET MVC application model, showing how controllers govern request processing[md]from capturing input to organizing a valid response.

Chapter 5, *ASP.NET MVC Views*, introduces the framework's view engine for generating HTML markup that browsers can process. Finally, Chapter 6, *The Razor Syntax*, introduces Microsoft's improved Razor markup language for building modern HTML pages more simply and efficiently.

CHAPTER 3

Bootstrapping ASP.NET MVC

It is not down in any map; true places never are.

—Herman Melville, "Moby Dick"

ASP.NET Core fully supports the specific ASP.NET Model-View-Controller (MVC) application model in which the URL of an incoming request is resolved to a pair of controller/action items. The *controller* item identifies a class name; the *action* item identifies a method on the controller class. The processing of the request, therefore, is a matter of executing the given *action* method of the given *controller* class.

The ASP.NET MVC application model in ASP.NET Core is nearly identical to the MVC application model available in classic ASP.NET, and it doesn't even differ too much from implementations of the same MVC pattern you find in other web platforms such as CakePHP for PHP, Rails for Ruby, and Django for Python. The MVC pattern is also pretty popular among front-end frameworks, most notably Angular and KnockoutJS.

In this chapter, we'll go through the preliminary steps that ultimately set up the ASP.NET MVC Core pipeline and pick up the handler responsible for the actual processing of any incoming requests.

Enabling the MVC Application Model

If you're coming to ASP.NET Core from an ASP.NET background, having to explicitly enable the MVC application model might seem strange. First and foremost, ASP.NET Core is a fairly generic web framework that allows requests to be handled through a centralized endpoint—the terminating middleware.

Also, ASP.NET supports a more sophisticated endpoint based on controller actions. However, if this is the application model you want, then you have to enable it so that the terminating middleware—the *Run* method we discussed in Chapter 2—is bypassed.

Registering the MVC Service

The beating heart of the MVC application model is the *MvcRouteHandler* service. Although publicly documented, the service is not one that you want to use directly in your application code. However, its role is crucial for the whole ASP.NET MVC machinery. The MVC route handler is the engine responsible for resolving the URL to an MVC route, invoking the selected controller method, and processing the results of the action.

 Note *MvcRouteHandler* is also the name of a class used in the implementation of classic ASP.NET MVC. In classic ASP.NET MVC, however, the class played a more limited role than it does in ASP.NET Core. For capturing the big picture of what the class does in ASP.NET Core, rather than just relying on the ability of a search engine, it is preferable to look directly at its implementation, which can be found at *http://bit.ly/2kOrKcJ*.

Adding the MVC Service

To add the MVC route handler service to the ASP.NET host, you proceed in the same way as for any other application service such as static files, authentication, or Entity Framework Core. You just add a line of code to the *ConfigureServices* method of the startup class.

```
public void ConfigureServices(IServiceCollection services)
{
    // Package required: Microsoft.AspNetCore.Mvc or Microsoft.AspNetCore.All (only in 2.0)
    services.AddMvc();
}
```

Note that the code requires a reference to an additional package that the IDE (Visual Studio, for instance) typically offers to restore for you. The *AddMvc* method has two overloads. The parameter-less method accepts all default settings for the MVC service. The second overload, as below, allows you to select ad hoc options.

```
// Receives an instance of the MvcOptions class
services.AddMvc(options =>
{
    options.ModelBinderProviders.Add(new SmartDateBinderProvider());
    options.SslPort = 345;
});
```

Options are specified through an instance of the *MvcOptions* class. The class is a container of configuration parameters you can change in the MVC framework. For example, the code snippet above adds a new model binder that parses specific strings into valid dates and specifies the SSL port to be used when the controller class is decorated with the *RequireHttpsAttribute*. The full list of configurable options can be found here: *http://docs.microsoft.com/en-us/aspnet/core/api/microsoft.aspnetcore.mvc.mvcoptions*.

Additional Services Enabled

The *AddMvc* method is only an umbrella method under which many other services are initialized and added to the pipeline. Table 3-1 provides the full list.

TABLE 3-1 List of MVC services enabled by the *AddMvc* method

Service	Description
MVC Core	Set of core services of the MVC application model including routing and controllers
API Explorer	Service responsible for gathering and exposing information about controllers and actions for dynamic discovery of capabilities and help pages
Authorization	Service behind authentication and authorization
Default Framework Parts	Service that adds input tag helpers and URL resolution helpers to the list of application parts
Formatter Mappings	Service that sets up default media type mappings
Views	Service to process action results as HTML views
Razor Engine	Registers the Razor view and page engine into the MVC system
Tag Helpers	Service to reference the part of the framework about tag helpers
Data Annotations	Service to reference the part of the framework about data annotations
JSON Formatters	Service to process action results as JSON streams
CORS	Service to reference the part of the framework about cross-origin resource sharing (CORS)

For more details, see the method's source code at *http://bit.ly/2l3H8QK*.

If you have memory constraints—for example, you're hosting the application in the cloud—you might want the application to reference nothing but the bare metal of the framework. The list of services in Table 3-1 can be made shorter; how much shorter mostly depends on the actual features you need to have in the application. The following code is enough to serve plain HTML views without more advanced features, such as data annotations for form validation and tag helpers.

```
public void ConfigureServices(IServiceCollection services)
{
    var builder = services.AddMvcCore();
    builder.AddViews();
    builder.AddRazorViewEngine();
}
```

The code above, though, is not enough to return formatted JSON data. To add that capability as well, you just add:

```
builder.AddJsonFormatters();
```

Note that some of the services in Table 3-1 are useful only if you are exposing a web API. These services are API Explorer, Formatter Mappings, and CORS. Tag helpers and default application parts can also be blissfully dropped if you're happy to content yourself with a programming experience like that of classic ASP.NET MVC.

Activating the MVC Service

In the *Configure* method of the startup class, you call the *UseMvc* method to configure the ASP.NET Core pipeline to support the MVC application model. At this point, everything around the MVC application model is completely set up except conventional routing. As we'll see in a moment, conventional routing consists of a bunch of pattern rules that identify all valid URLs the application intends to process.

In the MVC application model, that's not the only way to bind actions to URLs. For example, if you decide to associate actions to URLs through attributes (as we'll see in Chapter 4), then you're done. Otherwise, for the MVC service to be effective, you also must list the URL routes that the application intends to handle.

A route is a URL template that your application can recognize and process. A route is ultimately mapped to a pair of controller and action names. As we'll see in a moment, you can add as many routes as you wish, and those routes can take nearly any shape you like them to be. An internal MVC service is responsible for request routing; it is automatically registered when you enable MVC Core services.

Enabling Conventional Routing

To be usable, your application should provide rules to select the URLs it wants to handle. However, not all feasible URLs must be listed explicitly; one or more URL templates with placeholders will do the job. A default routing rule exists, which is sometimes referred to as conventional routing. Usually, the default route is enough for the entire application.

Adding the Default Route

If you don't have any special concerns about routes, the simplest and easiest method is to use the default route only.

```
public void Configure(IApplicationBuilder app)
{
    app.UseMvcWithDefaultRoute();
}
```

The actual code behind the *UseMvcWithDefaultRoute* method is shown below.

```
public void Configure(IApplicationBuilder app)
{
    app.UseMvc(routes =>
    {
        routes.MapRoute(
            name: "default",
            template: "{controller=Home}/{action=Index}/{id?}");
    });
}
```

As per the previous code, any requested URL will be parsed in segments:

- The first segment right after the server name will be matched to a route parameter named *controller*.

- The second segment will be matched to a route parameter named *action*.

- The third segment (if any) will be matched to an optional route parameter named *id*.

In light of this, the URL *Product/List* will be matched to a controller name of *Product* and an action method of *List*. If the URL contains fewer than two segments, default values apply. For example, the root URL of the website will match a controller name of *Home* and an action method of *Index*. The default route also supports an optional third segment whose content is matched to a named value of *Id*. Note that the *?* symbol indicates that the argument is optional.

Route parameters—and in particular, route parameters named *controller* and *action*—play a key role in the overall processing of an incoming request because they point in some way to the code that will actually produce the response. Any request successfully mapped to a route will be processed by executing a method on a controller class. The route parameter named *controller* identifies the controller class, and the route parameter named *action* identifies the method to invoke. We'll cover controllers in detail in the next chapter.

When No Routes Are Configured

The *UseMvc* method can also be invoked without parameters. When this happens, the ASP.NET MVC application is fully functional but has no configured routes it can handle.

```
public void Configure(IApplicationBuilder app)
{
    app.UseMvc();
}
```

Note that the code above is fully equivalent to the snippet below:

```
app.UseMvc(routes => { });
```

It would be interesting to see what happens when no routes are configured. For doing so, let me briefly anticipate how a simple controller class might look. Say you add a new class to the project, named *HomeController.cs*, and then invoke the *home/index* URL from the address bar.

```
public class HomeController : Controller
{
    public IActionResult Index()
    {
        // Writes out the Home.Index text
        return new ContentResult { Content = "Home.Index" };
    }
}
```

Conventional routing would map the URL *home/index* to the *Index* method of the *Home* controller. As a result, you should see a blank page with the text **Home.Index** printed. If you use conventional routing with the above configuration, all you get is an HTTP 404 page-not-found error.

Let's add now some terminating middleware to the pipeline and try it again. Figure 3-1 shows the new output you get.

```
app.Run(async (context) =>
{
    await context.Response.WriteAsync(
        "I'd rather say there are no configured routes here.");
});
```

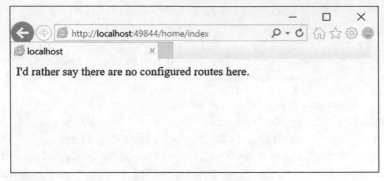

FIGURE 3-1 No routes are configured in the application

Now, let's go back the default route and try again. Figure 3-2 shows the result.

```
public void Configure(IApplicationBuilder app)
{
    app.UseMvcWithDefaultRoute();
    app.Run(async (context) =>
    {
        await context.Response.WriteAsync(
            "I'd rather say there are no configured routes here.");
    })
}
```

FIGURE 3-2 The default route is configured in the application

The conclusion is twofold. On the one hand, we can say that *UseMvc* changes the structure of the pipeline bypassing any terminating middleware you may have defined. On the other hand, if a matching route can't be found, or doesn't work (as a result of a missing controller or method), then the terminating middleware regains a place in the pipeline and runs as expected.

Let's learn a bit more about the internal behavior of the *UseMvc* method.

The Routing Service and the Pipeline

Internally, the *UseMvc* method defines a route builder service and configures it to use the provided routes and a default handler. The default handler is an instance of the *MvcRouteHandler* class. This class is responsible for finding a matching route and for extracting controller and action method names from the template.

Also, the *MvcRouteHandler* class will also try to execute the action method. If successful, it marks the context of the request as handled so that no further middleware will ever touch the generated response. Otherwise, it lets the request proceed through the pipeline until fully processed. Figure 3-3 summarizes the workflow with a diagram.

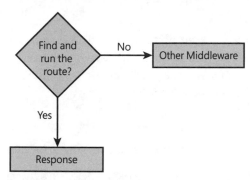

FIGURE 3-3 Routes and pipeline

 Note In classic ASP.NET MVC, failing to find a matching route for a URL would result in an HTTP 404 status code. In ASP.NET Core, instead, any terminating middleware is given a chance to process the request.

Configuring the Routing Table

Historically, the primary way to define routes in ASP.NET MVC is to add URL templates to an in-memory table. It is worth noting that ASP.NET Core also supports routes defined as attributes of controller methods, as you'll learn in Chapter 3.

Whether defined through a table entry or through an attribute, conceptually, a route is always the same and always contains the same amount of information.

Anatomy of a Route

A route is essentially given by a unique name and a URL pattern. The URL pattern can be made of static text or can include dynamic parameters whose values are excerpted from the URL and possibly the whole HTTP context. The full syntax for defining a route is shown below.

```
app.UseMvc(routes =>
{
    routes.MapRoute(
        name: "your_route",
        template: "...",
        defaults: new { controller = "...", action = "..." },
        constraints: { ... },
        dataTokens: { ... });
})
```

The *template* argument refers to the URL pattern of your choice. As mentioned, for the default conventional route, it is equal to:

```
{controller}/{action}/{id?}
```

Defining additional routes can take any form you like and can include both static text and custom route parameters. The *defaults* argument specifies default values for the route parameters. The *template* argument can be fused to the *defaults* argument. When this happens, the *defaults* argument is omitted, and the *template* argument takes the following form.

```
template: "{controller=Home}/{action=Index}/{id?}"
```

As mentioned, if the *?* symbol is appended to the parameter name, then the parameter is optional.

The *constraints* argument refers to constraints set on a particular route parameter such as acceptable values or required type. The *dataTokens* argument refers to additional custom values associated with the route but not used to determine whether the route matches a URL pattern. We'll return on these advanced aspects of a route in a moment.

Defining Custom Routes

Conventional routing figures out controller and method name automatically from the segments of the URL. Custom routes just use alternative algorithms to figure out the same information. More often, custom routes are made of static text explicitly mapped to a controller/method pair.

While conventional routing is fairly common in ASP.NET MVC applications, there's no reason for not having additional routes defined. Typically, you don't disable conventional routing; you simply add some ad hoc routes to have some controlled URLs to invoke a certain behavior of the application.

```
public void Configure(IApplicationBuilder app)
{
    // Custom routes
    app.UseMvc(routes =>
    {
        routes.MapRoute(name: "route-today",
            template: "today",
            defaults: new { controller="date", action="day", offset = 0 });
        routes.MapRoute(name: "route-yesterday",
            template: "yesterday",
            defaults: new { controller = "date", action = "day", offset = -1 });
```

```
        routes.MapRoute(name: "route-tomorrow",
            template: "tomorrow",
            defaults: new { controller = "date", action = "day", offset = 1 });
    });

    // Conventional routing
    app.UseMvcWithDefaultRoute();

    // Terminating middleware
    app.Run(async (context) =>
    {
        await context.Response.WriteAsync(
            "I'd rather say there are no configured routes here.");
    });
}
```

Figure 3-4 Shows the output of the newly defined routes.

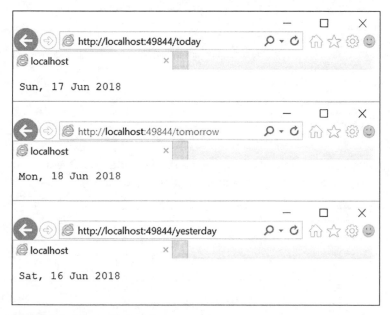

FIGURE 3-4 New routes in action

All the new routes are based on a static text mapped to the method *Day* on the controller *Date*. The only difference is the value of an additional route parameter—the *offset* parameter. For the sample code to work as shown in the Figure 3-4, a *DateController* class is required in the project. Here's a possible implementation:

```
public class DateController : Controller
{
    public IActionResult Day(int offset)
    {
        ...
    }
}
```

It's interesting to notice what happens when you invoke a URL like the following /date/day?offset=1. Not surprisingly, the output is the same as invoking /tomorrow. This is the effect of having custom routes and conventional routing working side by side. Instead, the URL /date/day/1 won't be recognized properly, but you won't get an HTTP 404 error or a message from the terminating middleware. The URL is resolved as if you had called /today or /date/day.

As expected, the URL /date/day/1 doesn't match any of the custom routes. However, it is perfectly matched by the default route. The controller parameter is set to Date, and the action parameter is set to Day. However, the default route features a third optional parameter—the id parameter—whose value is excerpted from the third segment of the URL. The value 1 of the sample URL is then assigned to a variable named id, not to a variable named offset. The parameter offset that is passed to the Day method in the controller implementation only gets the default value of its type—0 for an integer.

To give a URL like /date/day/1 the meaning of one day after today, you must slightly rework the list of custom routes and add a new one at the end of the table.

```
routes.MapRoute(name: "route-day",
            template: "date/day/{offset}",
            defaults: new { controller = "date", action = "day", offset = 0 });
```

Also, you could even edit the route-today route as below:

```
routes.MapRoute(name: "route-today",
            template: "today/{offset}",
            defaults: new { controller = "date", action = "day", offset = 0 });
```

Now any text following /date/day/ and /today/ will be assigned to the route parameter named offset and made available within the controller class action methods (see Figure 3-5).

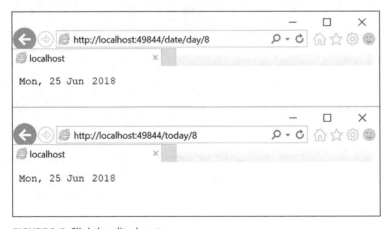

FIGURE 3-5 Slightly edited routes

At this point, a good question would be: Is there a way to force the text being assigned to the offset route parameter to be a number? That's just what route constraints are for. However, we have a couple of other topics to cover before approaching route constraints.

Important The *MapRoute* method maps the URL to a pair of controller/method regardless of the HTTP verb used for the request. You are also welcome to map to a specific URL verb using other mapping methods such as *MapGet, MapPost,* and *MapVerb*.

Order of Routes

When you work with multiple routes, the order in which they appear in the table is important. The routing service, in fact, scans the route table from top to bottom and evaluates routes as they appear. The scan stops at the first match. In other words, very specific routes should be given a higher position in the table so that they are evaluated before more generic routes.

The default route is a fairly generic one because it determines controller and action directly from the URL. The default route is so generic that it can even be the only route you use in an application. Most of the ASP.NET MVC applications I have in production only use conventional routing.

If you have custom routes, however, make sure you list them before enabling conventional routing; otherwise, you risk that the greedier default route will capture the URL. Note, however, that in ASP.NET MVC Core, capturing the URL is not limited to extracting the name of the controller and method. A route is selected only if both the controller class and the related method exist in the application. For example, let's consider a scenario in which conventional routing is enabled as the first route and is followed by all custom routes we saw in Figure 3-5. What happens when the user requests */today*? The default route would resolve it to the *Today* controller and *Index* method. However, if the application lacks a *TodayController* class, or an *Index* action method, then the default route is discarded, and the search proceeds with the next route.

It might be a good idea to have a catch-all route at the very bottom of the table, after the default route. A catch-all route is a fairly generic route that is matched in any case and works as a recovery step. Here's an example of it:

```
app.UseMvc(routes =>
{
    // Custom routes
});

// Conventional routing
app.UseMvcWithDefaultRoute();

// Catch-all route
app.UseMvc(routes =>
{
    routes.MapRoute(name: "catch-all",
        template: "{*url}",
        defaults: new { controller = "error", action = "message" });
});
```

The catch-all route map to the Message method of the ErrorController class that accepts a route parameter named *url*. The asterisk symbol indicates that this parameter grabs the rest of the URL.

Accessing Route Data Programmatically

The information available about the route that matches the requested URL is saved to a data container of type *RouteData*. Figure 3-6 provides a glimpse of the internals of *RouteData* during the execution of a request for *home/index*.

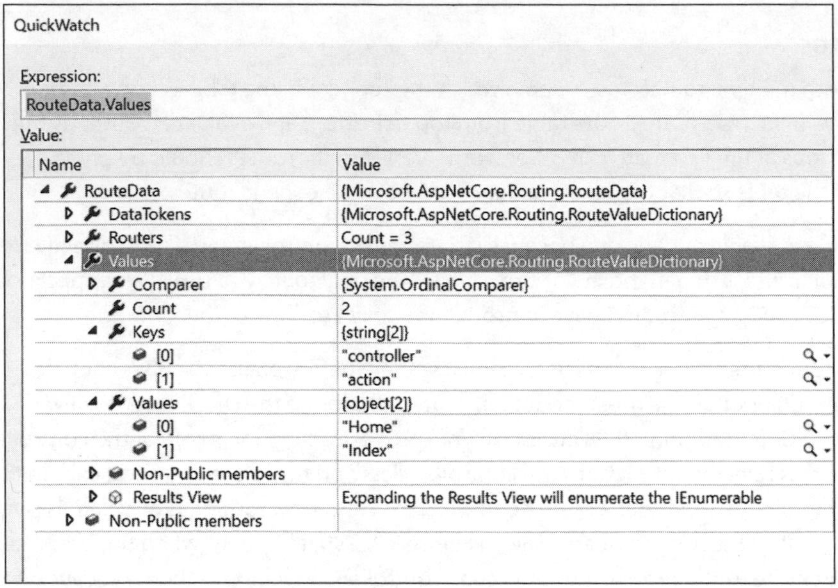

FIGURE 3-6 RouteData internals

The incoming URL has been matched to the default route and, because of the URL pattern, the first segment is mapped to the *controller* route parameter while the second segment is mapped to the *action* route parameter. Route parameters are defined within the URL template through the *{parameter}* notation. The *{parameter=value}* notation, instead, defines a default value for the parameter to be used in case the given segment is missing. Route parameters can be accessed programmatically using the following expression:

```
var controller = RouteData.Values["controller"];
var action = RouteData.Values["action"];
```

The code works nicely if you are in the context of a controller class that inherits from the base *Controller* class.

As we'll see in Chapter 4, though, ASP.NET Core also supports plain-old CLR object (POCO) controllers, namely controller classes that do not inherit from *Controller*. In this case, getting the route data is a bit more complicated.

```
public class PocoController
{
    private IActionContextAccessor _accessor;
    public PocoController(IActionContextAccessor accessor)
    {
        _accessor = accessor;
    }
    public IActionResult Index()
    {
        var controller = _accessor.ActionContext.RouteData.Values["controller"];
        var action = _accessor.ActionContext.RouteData.Values["action"];
        var text = string.Format("{0}.{1}", controller, action);
        return new ContentResult { Content = text };
    }
}
```

You need to have an action context accessor injected into the controller. ASP.NET Core provides a default action context accessor but binding it to the services collection is a responsibility of the developer.

```
public void ConfigureServices(IServiceCollection services)
{
    // More code may go here
    ...

    // Register the action context accessor
    services.AddSingleton<IActionContextAccessor, ActionContextAccessor>();
}
```

To access route data parameters from within controllers, you don't strictly need to use any of the techniques illustrated here. As we'll see in Chapter 4, the model binding infrastructure will automatically bind HTTP context values to declared parameters by name.

> **Important** We don't recommend injecting the *IActionContextAccessor* service because it performs poorly and, more importantly, is rarely really needed. Model binding is a much clearer and faster way to grab input HTTP data even in POCO controllers.

Advanced Aspects of Routing

A route can be further characterized by constraints and data tokens. A constraint is a sort of a validation rule that is associated with a route parameter. If a constraint is not validated the route is not matched. Data tokens, instead, are simple bits of information associated with a route made available to the controller but not used to determine if a URL matches the route.

Route Constraints

Technically speaking, a constraint is a class that implements the *IRouteConstraint* interface and essentially validates the value passed to a given route parameter. For example, you can use a constraint to ensure that a route is matched only if a given parameter receives a value of the expected type. Here's how you define a route constraint:

```
app.UseMvc(routes =>
{
    routes.MapRoute(name: "route-today",
                    template: "today/{offset}",
                    defaults: new { controller="date", action="day", offset=0 }
                    constraints: new { offset = new IntRouteConstraint() });
});
```

In the example, the *offset* parameter of the route is subject to the action of the *IntRouteConstraint* class, one of the predefined constraint classes in the ASP.NET MVC Core framework. The following code shows the skeleton of a constraint class.

```
// Code adapted from the actual implementation of IntRouteConstraint class.
public class IntRouteConstraint : IRouteConstraint
{
    public bool Match(
            HttpContext httpContext,
            IRouter route,
            string routeKey,
            RouteValueDictionary values,
            RouteDirection routeDirection)
    {
        object value;
        if (values.TryGetValue(routeKey, out value) && value != null)
        {
            if (value is int) return true;
            int result;
            var valueString = Convert.ToString(value, CultureInfo.InvariantCulture);
            return int.TryParse(valueString,
                            NumberStyles.Integer,
                            CultureInfo.InvariantCulture,
                            out result);
        }
        return false;
    }
}
```

constraint class extracts the value of the *routeKey* parameter from the dictionary of route values makes reasonable checks on it. The *IntRouteConstraint* class simply checks that the value can be ccessfully parsed to an integer.

Note that a constraint can be associated with a unique name string that explains how the constraint is used. The constraint name can be used to specify the constraint more compactly.

```
routes.MapRoute(name: "route-day",
                template: "date/day/{offset:int}",
                defaults: new { controller = "date", action = "day", offset = 0 });
```

The name of the *IntRouteConstraint* class is *int* meaning that *{offset:int}* associates the action of the class to the *offset* parameter. IntRouteConstraint is one of the predefined route constraint classes in ASP.NET MVC Core, and their names are set at startup and fully documented. If you create a custom constraint class, you should set the name of the constraint when you register it with the system.

```
public void ConfigureServices(IServiceCollection services)
{
    ...
    services.Configure<RouteOptions>(options =>
            options.ConstraintMap.Add("your-route", typeof(YourRouteConstraint)));
}
```

Based on that you can now use the *{parametername:contraintprefix}* notation to bind the constraint to a given route parameter.

Predefined Route Constraints

Table 3-2 presents the list of predefined route constraints and their mapped names.

TABLE 3-2 Predefined route constraints

Mapping Name	Class	Description
Int	IntRouteConstraint	Ensures the route parameter is set to an integer
Bool	BoolRouteConstraint	Ensures the route parameter is set to a Boolean value
datetime	DateTimeRouteConstraint	Ensures the route parameter is set to a valid date
decimal	DecimalRouteConstraint	Ensures the route parameter is set to a decimal
double	DoubleRouteConstraint	Ensures the route parameter is set to a double
Float	FloatRouteConstraint	Ensures the route parameter is set to a float
Guid	GuidRouteConstraint	Ensures the route parameter is set to a GUID
Long	LongRouteConstraint	Ensures the route parameter is set to a long integer
minlength(N)	MinLengthRouteConstraint	Ensures the route parameter is set to a string no shorter than the specified length
maxlength(N)	MaxLengthRouteConstraint	Ensures the route parameter is set to a string no longer than the specified length
length(N)	LengthRouteConstraint	Ensures the route parameter is set to a string of the specified length
min(N)	MinRouteConstraint	Ensures the route parameter is set to an integer greater than the specified value
max(N)	MaxRouteConstraint	Ensures the route parameter is set to an integer smaller than the specified value
range(M, N)	RangeRouteConstraint	Ensures the route parameter is set to an integer that falls within the specified range of values
alpha	AlphaRouteConstraint	Ensures the route parameter is set to a string made of alphabetic characters
regex(RE)	RegexInlineRouteConstraint	Ensures the route parameter is set to a string compliant with the specified regular expression
required	RequiredRouteConstraint	Ensures the route parameter has an assigned value in the URL

As you might have noticed, the list of predefined route constraints doesn't include a fairly common one: Ensuring that the route parameter takes a value from a known set of possible values. To constrain a parameter in this way, you can use a regular expression, as shown below.

```
{format:regex(json|xml|text)}
```

A URL would match the route with such a *format* parameter only if the parameter takes any of the listed substrings.

Data Tokens

In ASP.NET MVC, a route is not limited to the information within the URL. The URL segments are used to determine whether a route matches a request, but additional information can be associated with a route and retrieved programmatically later. To attach extra information to a route you use data tokens.

A data token is defined with the route and is nothing more than a name/value pair. Any route can have any number of data tokens. Data tokens are free bits of information not used to match a URL to the route.

```
app.UseMvc(routes =>
{
    routes.MapRoute(name: "catch-all",
        template: "{*url}",
        defaults: new { controller = "home", action = "index" },
        constraints: new { },
        dataTokens: new { reason = "catch-all" });
});
```

Data tokens are not a critical, must-have feature of the ASP.NET MVC routing system, but they are sometimes useful. For example, let's say you have a catch-all route mapped to a controller/action pair that is also used for other purposes and imagine that the *Index* method of the *Home* controller is used for a URL that doesn't match any of the routes. The idea is to show the home page if a more specific URL can't be determined.

How can you distinguish between a direct request for the home page and the home page displayed because of a catch-all routing? Data tokens are an option. Here's how you can retrieve data tokens programmatically.

```
var catchall = RouteData.DataTokens["reason"] ?? "";
```

Data tokens are defined with routes but are only used programmatically.

Map of ASP.NET MVC Machinery

Routing is the first step of the longer process that takes an HTTP request to produce a response. The ultimate result of the routing process is the paired controller/action that will process requests not mapped to a physical static file. In Chapter 4, we'll take a closer look at controller classes—the central console of any ASP.NET MVC applications. Until then, though, an overall look at the entire ASP.NET MVC machinery is in order.

In the rest of the book, in fact, we'll focus on parts and how to configure and implement them, but it would be nice to see the big picture and analyze how those parts relate to each other (see Figure 3-7).

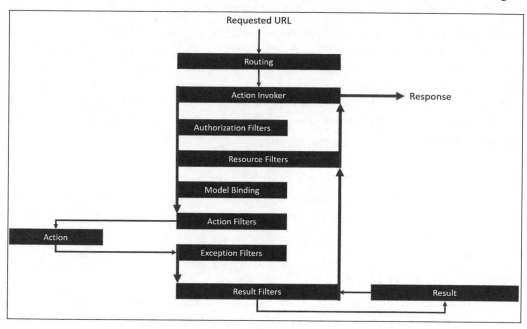

FIGURE 3-7 The full route of an ASP.NET MVC request

The machinery is triggered by an HTTP request that doesn't map to a static file. First, the URL goes through the routing system and is mapped to a controller name and an action name.

> **Important** In this chapter, we used the terms "action" and "method" interchangeably. That was just right for the current level of abstraction. However, in the overall architecture of ASP.NET MVC, the concept of an "action" and the concept of a "method" are related but are not the same. The term "method" refers to a plain public method defined on a controller class not marked with the *NonAction* attribute. Such a method is commonly referred to as an "action method." Instead, the term, "action," refers to a plain string for the name of the action method to invoke on a controller class. By convention, the value of the *action* route parameter usually matches the name of an action method on the controller class. However, as we'll see in the next chapter, a level of indirection is possible, and a method with a custom name can be mapped to a particular action name.

The Action Invoker

The action invoker is the beating heart of the entire ASP.NET MVC infrastructure and the component that orchestrates all the steps necessary to process a request. The action invoker receives the controller factory and the controller context, a container object populated with route data and HTTP request information. As shown in Figure 3-7, the invoker runs its own pipeline of action filters and provides hooks for some ad hoc application code to run before and after the actual execution of the request.

The invoker uses reflection to create an instance of the selected controller class and to invoke the selected method. In doing so, it also resolves the method's and constructor's parameters, reading from the HTTP context, route data, and the system's DI container.

As we'll see in the next chapter, any controller method is expected to return an object wrapped in a *IActionResult* container. As the name suggests, the controller method returns just data to be used for the production of the actual response that will be sent back to clients. In no way is the controller method responsible for writing directly to the response output stream. The controller method does have programmatic access to the response output stream, but the recommended pattern is that the method packages data into an action result object and gives instruction to the invoker on how to further process it.

> **Note** For more information about the actual behavior of the ASP.NET MVC action invoker, refer to the implementation of the class *ControllerActionInvoker* at *http://bit.ly/2kQfNAA*.

Processing Action Results

The controller method's action result is a class that implements the *IActionResult* interface. The ASP.NET MVC framework defines several such classes for the various types of output a controller method might want to return: HTML, JSON, plain text, binary content, and specific HTTP responses.

The interface has one single method—*ExecuteResultAsync*—that the action invoker calls to have the data embedded in the specific action result object processed. The ultimate effect of executing an action result is writing to the HTTP response output filter.

Next, the action invoker runs its internal pipeline and calls out the request. The client—most typically the browser—will then receive any generated output.

Action Filters

An action filter is a piece of code that runs around the execution of a controller method. The most common types of action filters are filters that run before or after the controller method executes. For example, you can have an action filter that only adds an HTTP header to a request or an action filter that refuses to run the controller method if the request is not coming via Ajax or from an unknown IP address or referrer URL.

Action filters can be implemented in either of two ways: as method overrides within the controller class or, preferably, as distinct attribute classes. We'll find out more about action filters in Chapter 4.

Summary

Architecturally speaking, the most relevant fact about ASP.NET Core is that it is a true web framework that just enables developers to build HTTP frontends. It doesn't force you to a particular application model. In the past, classic ASP.NET was offered as a web framework with a specific application model simply bolted on, whether Web Forms or MVC.

ASP.NET Core has open middleware for you to plug in and receive and process incoming requests to your liking. In ASP.NET Core you can effectively have code that sits there over the communication port, captures any requests and returns responses. It could just be you, HTTP, and your code with no intermediaries. At the same time, though, you can enable a more sophisticated application model like MVC. When you do so, some side tasks become necessary such as defining the URL templates that your application will recognize and the components responsible for handling those requests. In this chapter, we focused on URL templates and request routing. In Chapter 4, we move on to controllers for actual request processing.

ASP.NET MVC Controllers

"Well, everybody does it that way, Huck."

"Tom, I am not everybody."

—*Mark Twain, "The Adventures of Tom Sawyer"*

Despite the explicit reference to the Model-View-Controller pattern in the name, the ASP.NET MVC application model is essentially centered on one pillar—the controller. The controller governs the entire processing of a request. It captures input data, orchestrates the activity of business and data layers, and finally wraps up raw data computed for the request into a valid response for the caller.

Any request that passes the URL routing filter is mapped to a controller class and served by executing a given method on the class. Therefore, the controller class is the place where developers write the actual code required to serve a request. Let's briefly explore some characteristics of controller classes, including implementation details.

Controller Classes

The writing of a controller class can be summarized in two steps: implementing a class that is discoverable as a controller and adding a bunch of public methods that are discoverable as actions at runtime. However, a couple of important details remain to be clarified: How the system gets to know the controller class to instantiate and how it figures out the method to invoke.

Discovering the Controller Name

All that the MVC application receives is a URL to process, and the URL must be mapped in some way to one controller class and one public method. Regardless of the routing strategy, you might have chosen (convention-based routing, attribute routing, or both) to fill the route table. In the end, a URL is mapped to a controller based on the routes registered in the system's route table.

Discovery via Convention-based Routing

If a match is found between the incoming URL and one of the predefined conventional routes, then the name of the controller results from the parsing of the route. As seen in the previous chapter, the default route is defined as follows:

```
app.UseMvc(routes =>
{
    routes.MapRoute(
        name: "default",
        template: "{controller=Home}/{action=Index}/{id?}");
});
```

The controller name is inferred from the URL template parameter as the first segment of the URL that follows the server name. Conventional routing sets the value of the controller parameter via explicit or implicit route parameters. An explicit route parameter is a parameter defined as part of the URL template, as shown above. An implicit route parameter is a parameter that doesn't appear in the URL template and is treated as a constant. In the example below, the URL template is *today,* and the value of the controller parameter is statically set through the *defaults* property of the route.

```
app.UseMvc(routes =>
{
    routes.MapRoute(
        name: "route-today",
        template: "today",
        defaults: new { controller="date", action="day", offset=0 });
}
```

Note that the controller value that is inferred from the route may not be the exact name of the controller class to be used. More often, though not always, is a sort of a nickname. Hence, some extra work may be required to turn the controller value into an actual class name.

Discovery via Attribute Routing

Attribute routing allows you to decorate controller classes or methods with special attributes that indicate the URL template that will end up invoking methods. The major benefit of attribute routing is that route definitions are placed close to their corresponding actions. In this way, whoever reads the code has a clear idea of when and how that method is will be invoked. Furthermore, choosing attribute routing keeps the URL template independent from the controller and the action used to serve the request. Later, if you change the URLs for evolutionary or marketing reasons, you don't have to refactor the code.

```
[Route("Day")]
public class DateController : Controller
{
    [Route("{offset}")]     // Serves URL like Day/1
    public ActionResult Details(int offset) { ... }
}
```

Routes specified via attributes will still flow into the global route table of the application, the same table explicitly populated programmatically when you use convention-based routing.

Discovery via Mixed Routing Strategy

Convention-based and attribute routing are not mutually exclusive. Both can be used in the context of the same application. Both attribute routing and convention-based routing populate the same route table used to resolve URLs. Conventional routing must be explicitly enabled in the sense that convention-based routes must always be added programmatically. Attribute routing is always on and needs no explicit enablement. Note that this was not the case with attribute routing in Web API and previous versions of ASP.NET MVC.

Because attribute routing is always on it turns out that routes defined via attributes take precedence over convention-based routes.

Inherited Controllers

A controller class is usually a class that inherits—either directly or indirectly—from a given base class, the *Microsoft.AspNetCore.Mvc.Controller* class. Note that in all versions of ASP.NET MVC released before ASP.NET Core, inheriting from the base class *Controller* was a strict requirement. In ASP.NET Core, instead, you can also have controller classes that are plain C# classes with no inherited functionality. I'll say more on this flavor of controller classes in a moment, but for the time being, let's assume that controllers must originally inherit from the system's base class.

Once the system has successfully resolved the route, it holds a controller name. The name is a plain string—sort of a nickname. The nickname (for example, *Home* or *Date*) must be matched to a real class included or referenced in the project.

Class Name with Suffix

The most common scenario for having a valid controller class that the system can easily discover is giving the class name the suffix, "Controller," and inheriting it from the aforementioned *Controller* base class. This means that the corresponding class of a controller name, Home, will be the *HomeController* class. If such a class exists, the system is happy and can successfully resolve the request. This is the way that things worked in past versions of ASP.NET MVC before ASP.NET Core.

The namespace of the controller class is unimportant in ASP.NET Core, though tooling and many examples available in the community tend to place controller classes under a folder named Controllers. The reality is that you can place your controller classes in any folder and any namespace you wish. As long as the class has the "Controller" suffix and inherits from *Controller,* it will always be discovered.

Class Name without Suffix

In ASP.NET Core, the controller class also will be successfully discovered if it lacks the "Controller" suffix. There are a couple of caveats, though. The first caveat is that the discovery process works only if the class inherits from base class *Controller.* The second caveat is that the name of the class must match the controller name in the route analysis.

If the controller name extracted from the route is, say, *Home*, then it is acceptable to have a class named *Home* that inherits from base class *Controller*. Any other name won't work. In other words, you can't just use a custom suffix, and the root part of the name must always match the name in the route.

> **Note** In general, a controller class inherits directly from the class Controller, and it gets environment properties and capabilities from the Controller class. Most notably, the controller inherits the HTTP context from its base class. You can have intermediate custom classes that inherit from Controller from which the actual controller classes bound to URLs inherit. Having such intermediate classes depends on how much abstraction you need given the specific requirements of the application you're writing. It's mostly a design decision.

POCO Controllers

The action invoker injects the HTTP context into the controller's instance and the code running within the controller class can access it through the handy *HttpContext* property. Inheriting your controller class from a system-provided base class gives you all the necessary plumbing for free. In ASP.NET Core, however, inheriting any controller from a common base class is no longer necessary. In ASP.NET Core, a controller class can be a plain old C# object (POCO), simply defined as shown below:

```
public class PocoController
{
    // Write your action methods here
}
```

For the system to successfully discover a POCO controller, either the class name has the "Controller" suffix, or the class is decorated with the *Controller* attribute.

```
[Controller]
public class Poco
{
    // Write your action methods here
}
```

Having a POCO controller is a form of optimization and optimization usually comes from dropping some features to reduce overhead and/or memory footprint. Consequently, not inheriting from a known base class might preclude some common operations or make them a bit more verbose to implement. Let's review a few scenarios.

Returning Plain Data

A POCO controller is a fully testable plain C# class that has no dependencies on the surrounding ASP.NET Core environment. It should be noted that a POCO controller only works well if you don't need any dependencies on the surrounding environment. If your task is creating a super-simple web service that barely represents a fixed endpoint for returning data, then a POCO controller might be a good choice. (See the following code.)

```
public class PocoController
{
    public IActionResult Today()
    {
        return new ContentResult() { Content = DateTime.Now.ToString("ddd, d MMM") };
    }
}
```

This code also works well if you must return the contents of a file—whether the file exists or it is to be created on the fly.

Returning HTML Content

You can send plain HTML content back to the browser via the services of *ContentResult*. All you do differently from the example above is set the *ContentType* property to an appropriate MIME type and build the HTML string to your liking.

```
public class Poco
{
    public IActionResult Html()
    {
        return new ContentResult()
        {
            Content = "<h1>Hello</h1>",
            ContentType = "text/html",
            StatusCode = 200
        };
    }
}
```

Any HTML content you can build in this way is created algorithmically. If you want to connect to the view engine (see Chapter 6) and output the HTML resulting from a Razor template, then more work is required and, more importantly, more intimate knowledge of the framework is required.

Returning HTML Views

Accessing the ASP.NET infrastructure that deals with HTML views is not immediate. From within a controller method, you must return an appropriate *IActionResult* object (more on this soon), but all the available helper methods for doing that quickly and effectively belong to the base class and are not available in a POCO controller. Here's a workaround to return HTML based on a view. As a disclaimer, most of the artifacts shown in the code snippet will be fully explained later in this chapter or in Chapter 5. The primary point of the following code snippet is to show that a POCO controller has a smaller memory footprint but lacks some built-in facilities.

```
public IActionResult Index([FromServices] IModelMetadataProvider provider)
{
    // Initialize a ViewData dictionary to make data available within the view
    var viewdata = new ViewDataDictionary<MyViewModel>(provider, new ModelStateDictionary());

    // Fill the data model for the view
    viewdata.Model = new MyViewModel() { Title = "Hi!" };
```

```
        // Invoke the view passing data
        return new ViewResult() { ViewData = viewdata, ViewName = "index" };
}
```

The additional parameter in the method signature deserves more explanation. It is a form of dependency injection that is widely used (and recommended) around ASP.NET Core. To create an HTML view, you need at least a reference to *IModelMetadataProvider* that comes from the outside. Frankly, without externally injected dependencies you won't be able to do much. Have a look at the following code snippet that attempts to simplify the code above.

```
public IActionResult Simple()
{
    return new ViewResult() { ViewName = "simple" };
}
```

You can have a Razor template named "simple" and whatever HTML is being returned comes from the template. However, you are unable to pass your own data to the view to make the rendering logic smart enough. Also, you are unable to access any data posted your way whether through a form or the query string.

> **Note** Roles and features of the ViewResult class and the Razor language for creating HTML views will be discussed in Chapter 5.

Accessing the HTTP Context

The most problematic aspect of a POCO controller is the lack of the HTTP context. In particular, this means that you can't inspect the raw data being posted, including query string and route parameters. This context information, however, is available and can be attached to the controllers only where you need it. There are two ways to do that.

The first approach consists of injecting the current context for the action. The context is an instance of the *ActionContext* class and wraps the HTTP context and route information. Here's what's required on your end.

```
public class PocoController
{
    [ActionContext]0
    public ActionContext Context { get; set; }
    ...
}
```

Based on this example, you can now access the *Request* object or the *RouteData* object as if you were in a regular, non-POCO controller. The following code allows you to read the controller name from the *RouteData* collection.

```
var controller = Context.RouteData.Values["controller"];
```

Another approach uses a feature called model binding, which I explain later in this chapter. Model binding can be seen as injecting specific properties available in the HTTP context into the controller method.

```
public IActionResult Http([FromQuery] int p1 = 0)
{
    ...
    return new ContentResult() { Content = p1.ToString() };
}
```

By decorating a method parameter with the *FromQuery* attribute, you instruct the system to try to find a match between the name of the parameter (say, *p1*) and one of the parameters on the query string of the URL. If a match is found and types are convertible, then the method parameter automatically receives the value passed. Analogously, by using the *FromRoute* or *FromForm* attributes, you can access data in the *RouteData* collection or that has been posted through an HTML form.

> **Note** In ASP.NET Core, the notion of global data is quite blurred. Nothing can really be global in the sense of being globally accessible from anywhere in the application. Any data intended to be globally accessible must be passed around explicitly. More exactly, it must be imported in any context where it might be used. To make this happen, ASP.NET Core comes with a built-in Dependency Injection (DI) framework through which developers register abstract types (like interfaces) and their concrete types, leaving on the framework the burden of returning an instance of the concrete type whenever a reference to the abstract type is requested. We have seen already a few examples of this (common) programming technique. So far, however, all the examples were special in the sense types involved were all types registered implicitly. In Chapter 8, we'll see in a lot more detail how to code for the DI system.

Controller Actions

The final output of the route analysis of the URL of an incoming request is a pair made of the name of the controller class to instantiate and the name of the action to perform on it. Executing an action on a controller invokes a public method on the controller class. Let's see how action names are mapped to class methods.

Mapping Actions to Methods

The general rule is that any public method on a controller class is a public action with the same name. As an example, consider the case of a URL like */home/index*. Based on the routing facts we have discussed earlier, the controller name is "home," and it requires an actual class named *HomeController* available in the project. The action name extracted from the URL is "index." Subsequently, the *HomeController* class is expected to expose a public method named *Index*.

There are some additional parameters that might come into play, but this is the core rule of mapping actions to methods.

Mapping by Name

To see all aspects of action-to-method mapping in the MVC application model, let's consider the following example.

```
public class HomeController : Controller
{
    // Implicit action name: Index
    public ActionResult Index()
    {
        ...
    }

    [NonAction]
    public ActionResult About()
    {
        ...
    }

    [ActionName("About")]
    public ActionResult LoveGermanShepherds()
    {
        ...
    }
}
```

Because the method *Index* is public and not decorated with any attributes, it is implicitly bound to an action with the same name. This is the most common scenario: Just add a public method, and its name becomes an action on the controller you can invoke from the outside using any HTTP verb.

Interestingly, the method *About* in the example above is also a public method, but it is decorated with the *NonAction* attribute. The attribute doesn't alter the visibility of the method at compile time but makes the method invisible to the routing system of ASP.NET Core at runtime. You can call it from within the server-side code of the application, but it is not bound to any action that can be called from browsers and JavaScript code.

Finally, the third public method in the sample class has the fancy name of *LoveGermanShepherds* but is decorated with the *ActionName* attribute. The attribute binds the method explicitly to the action *About*. Hence, every time the user requests the action About, the method *LoveGermanShepherds* runs. The name *LoveGermanShepherds* can only be used in calls within the realm of the controller class or in any scenario (quite unlikely indeed) where an instance of the *HomeController* class is programmatically created and used via developer's code.

So far, we haven't considered the role of HTTP verbs, such as GET or POST. Another level of method-to-action mapping is based on the HTTP verb used for the request.

Mapping by HTTP Verbs

The MVC application model is flexible enough to let you bind a method to an action only for a specific HTTP verb. To associate a controller method with an HTTP verb, you either use the parametric *AcceptVerbs* attribute or direct attributes such as *HttpGet*, *HttpPost*, and *HttpPut*. The *AcceptVerbs* attribute allows you to specify which HTTP verb is required to execute a given method. Let's consider the following example:

```
[AcceptVerbs("post")]
public IActionResult CallMe()
{
    ...
}
```

Given that code, it turns out that the *CallMe* method can't be invoked using a GET request. The *AcceptVerbs* attribute takes strings to refer to HTTP verbs. Valid values are strings that correspond to known HTTP verbs such as *get*, *post*, *put*, *options*, *patch*, *delete*, and *head*. You can pass multiple strings to the *AcceptVerbs* attribute, or you can repeat the attribute multiple times on the same method.

```
[AcceptVerbs("get", "post")]
public IActionResult CallMe()
{
    ...
}
```

Using *AcceptVerbs* or multiple individual attributes, such as *HttpGet*, *HttpPost*, *HttpPut* is entirely a matter of preference. The following code is equivalent to the code above using *AcceptVerbs*.

```
[HttpPost]
[HttpGet]
public IActionResult CallMe()
{
    ...
}
```

Over the web, you perform an HTTP GET command when you follow a link or type the URL into the address bar. You perform an HTTP POST when you submit the content of an HTML form. Any other HTTP command can be performed from the Web only via AJAX, and from any client code that sends requests to the ASP.NET Core application.

When Distinct Verbs Are Helpful

Here's a common scenario you'll face every time you have MVC views hosting an HTML form. You need a method to render the view that displays the form, and you also need a method to process the values the form will post. The request to render typically comes with GET; the request to process typically comes through a POST. How do you handle that within the controller?

An option might be to have just one method that can handle requests regardless of the HTTP verb used.

```
public IActionResult Edit(Customer customer)
{
    var method = HttpContext.Request.Method;
    switch(method)
    {
        case "GET":
          return View();
        ...
    }

    ...
}
```

In the body of the method, you must determine whether the user intended to display the form or process the posted values. The best source of information you have is the *Method* property of the *Request* object in the HTTP context. By using verb attributes, you can break up the code into distinct methods.

```
[HttpGet]
public ActionResult Edit(Customer customer)
{
    ...
}

[HttpPost]
public ActionResult Edit(Customer customer)
{
    ...
}
```

There are two methods now bound to distinct actions. This is acceptable for ASP.NET Core, which will invoke the appropriate method based on the verb. It is not acceptable for a Microsoft C# compiler, though, which won't let you have two methods with the same name and signature in the same class. Here's a rewrite:

```
[HttpGet]
[ActionName("edit")]
public ActionResult DisplayEditForm(Customer customer)
{
    ...
}

[HttpPost]
[ActionName("edit")]
public ActionResult SaveEditForm(Customer customer)
{
    ...
}
```

Methods now have distinct names, but both are bound to the same action, albeit for different verbs.

Attribute-based Routing

Attribute-based routing is an alternate way of binding controller methods to URLs. The idea is that instead of defining an explicit route table at the startup of the application, you decorate controller methods with ad hoc route attributes. Internally, the route attributes will populate the system's route table.

The *Route* Attribute

The *Route* attribute defines the URL template that is valid for invoking the given method. The attribute can be placed both at the controller class level and at the method level. If placed in both places, then the URLs will be concatenated. Here's an example.

```
[Route("goto")]
public class TourController : Controller
{
    public IActionResult NewYork()
    {
        var action = RouteData.Values["action"].ToString();
        return Ok(action);
    }

    [Route("nyc")]
    public IActionResult NewYorkCity()
    {
        var action = RouteData.Values["action"].ToString();
        return Ok(action);
    }

    [Route("/ny")]
    public IActionResult BigApple()
    {
        var action = RouteData.Values["action"].ToString();
        return Ok(action);
    }
}
```

The *Route* attribute at the class level is quite intrusive. With the attribute in place, you can't invoke any method on a class named *TourController* that includes the controller name of the tour. The only way to call a method on the controller class is through the template specified by the *Route* attribute. How would you invoke the *NewYork* method, then?

The method doesn't have its own *Route* attribute and inherits the parent template. To invoke the method, therefore, the URL to use is */goto*. Note that */goto/newyork* will return a 404 error (URL not found). Try adding another method following the same routing pattern of *NewYork*.

```
// No [Route] specified explicitly
public IActionResult Chicago()
{
    var action = RouteData.Values["action"].ToString();
    return Ok(action);
}
```

Now the controller class contains two methods devoid of their own *Route* attribute. Subsequently, invoking */goto* results in ambiguity. (See Figure 4-1.)

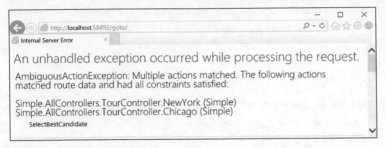

FIGURE 4-1 Ambiguous action exception when methods lack the route attribute

When a controller method has its own *Route* attribute, things are clearer. The specified URL template is the only way to invoke the method, and if the same *Route* attribute is also specified at the class level, the two templates will be concatenated. For example, to invoke the *NewYorkCity* method, you must invoke */goto/nyc*.

In the example above, the method *BigApple* addresses yet another scenario. As you can see, in this case, the value of the *Route* attribute begins with a backslash. In this case, the URL is intended to be an absolute path and won't be concatenated with the parent template. As a result, to invoke the *BigApple* method, you must use the URL */ny*. Note that an absolute path is identified by URL templates beginning with / or ~/.

Using Route Parameters in Routes

Routes also support parameters. Parameters are custom values collected from the HTTP context. Interestingly, if you also have conventional routing enabled in your application, then you can use the detected controller and action names in the routes. Let's rewrite the *NewYork* method of the previous example as below:

```
[Route("/[controller]/[action]")]
[ActionName("ny")]
public IActionResult NewYork()
{
    var action = RouteData.Values["action"].ToString();
    return Ok(action);
}
```

Even though the method belongs to a *TourController* class with a root *Route* attribute of *goto*, it is now available on the */tour/ny* URL because of the combined effect of the parametric route and the *ActionName* attribute. Because of conventional routing, controller and action parameters are defined in the *RouteData* collection and can be mapped to parameters. The *ActionName* attribute just renames *NewYork* to *ny*. That's why it works!

Here's another nice example:

```
[Route("go/to/[action]")]
public class VipTourController : Controller
{
    public IActionResult NewYork()
    {
        var action = RouteData.Values["action"].ToString();
        return Ok(action);
    }

    public IActionResult Chicago()
    {
        var action = RouteData.Values["action"].ToString();
        return Ok(action);
    }
}
```

All methods in the controller will now be available as URLs in the form */go/to/XXX* where *XXX* is the just the name of the action method (see Figure 4-2).

FIGURE 4-2 Routes with route parameters

Using Custom Parameters in Routes

The route can host custom parameters as well, namely parameters sent to the method via the URL, query string or the body of the request. We'll get to tools and techniques to collect input data in just a moment. For the time being, let's just consider the following controller method in the same *VipTourController* class seen above.

```
[Route("{days:int}/days")]
public IActionResult SanFrancisco(int days)
{
    var action = string.Format("In {0} for {1} days",
        RouteData.Values["action"].ToString(),
        days);
    return Ok(action);
}
```

The method receives a parameter named *days* of type integer. The *Route* attribute defines the location of the parameter *days* (note the different *{ }* notation for custom parameters) and adds a type constraint to it. As a result, the fancy URL *go/to/sanfrancisco/for/4/days* now works beautifully (Figure 4-3).

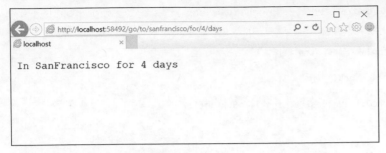

FIGURE 4-3 Routes with CUSTOM parameters

Note that if you try a URL in which the *days* parameters can't be converted to an integer, you get a 404 status code because the URL might not be found. However, if you omit the type constraint and just set the custom parameter *{days}* then the URL will be recognized, the method has a chance to process it, and internally the *days* parameter gets the default value for the type. In case of integers, it is 0. Just for fun, see what happens with the URL *go/to/sanfrancisco/for/some/days*.

Note In ASP.NET Core you can also specify route information in verb-specific attributes like *HttpGet* and *HttpPost*. As a result, instead of specifying the route and then the verb attribute you can pass the route URL template to the verb attribute.

Implementation of Action Methods

The signature of a controller action method is up to you and is not subject to any constraints. If you define parameter-less methods, you then make yourself responsible for programmatically retrieving any input data your code requires from the request. If you add parameters to the method's signature, ASP.NET Core will offer automatic parameter resolution through model binder components.

In this section, we'll first discuss how to retrieve input data from within a controller action method manually. Next, we'll turn to automatic parameter resolution via model binders—the most common choice in ASP.NET Core applications. Finally, we'll look into the codification of action results.

Basic Data Retrieval

Controller action methods can access any input data posted with the HTTP request. Input data can be retrieved from various sources, including form data, a query string, cookies, route values, and posted files. Let's get into some details.

Getting Input Data from the *Request* Object

When writing the body of an action method, you can directly access any input data that comes through the familiar *Request* object and its child collections, such as *Form*, *Cookies*, *Query*, and *Headers*. As you'll see in a moment, ASP.NET Core offers quite compelling facilities (for example, model binders) that you might want to use to keep your code cleaner, more compact, and easier to test. However, nothing prevents you from writing old-style *Request*-based code as shown below.

```
public ActionResult Echo()
{
    // Capture data in a manual way from the query string
    var data = Request.Query["today"];
    return Ok(data);
}
```

The *Request.Query* dictionary contains the list of parameters and respective values extracted from the query string of the URL. Note that the search for a matching entry is case insensitive.

While fully functional, this approach suffers from two major problems. First, you must know where to get the value, whether from the query string, the list of posted values, the URL, and the like. You must use a different API for any different source. Second, any value you get is coded as a string, and any type conversion is on your own.

Getting Input Data from the Route

When you use conventional routing, you can insert parameters in the URL template. These values are captured by the routing module and are made available to the application. Route values, though, are not exposed to applications via the *Request* property inherited from Controller. You must use a slightly different approach to retrieve them programmatically. Suppose you have the following route registered when the application starts up.

```
routes.MapRoute(
    name: "demo",
    template: "go/to/{city}/for/{days}/days",
    defaults: new { controller = "Input", action = "Go" }
);
```

The route has two custom parameters—*city* and *days*. The name of the controller and method are set statically via the *defaults* property. How would retrieve the values of *city* and *days* in code?

```
public ActionResult Go()
{
    // Capture data in a manual way from the URL template
    var city = RouteData.Values["city"];
    var days = RouteData.Values["days"];
    return Ok(string.Format("In {0} for {1} days", city, days));
}
```

Route data is exposed through the *RouteData* property of the *Controller* class. Also, in this case, the search for a matching entry is conducted in a case-insensitive way. The *RouteData.Values* dictionary is a *String/Object* dictionary. Any necessary type conversion is up to you.

Model Binding

Using native request collections of input data works but from a readability and maintenance standpoint, it is preferable to use an ad hoc model to expose data to controllers. This model is sometimes referred to as the *input model*. ASP.NET MVC provides an automatic binding layer that uses a built-in set of rules for mapping raw request data from a variety of value providers to properties of input model classes. As a developer, you are largely responsible for the design of input model classes.

> **Note** Most of the time, the built-in mapping rules of the model-binding layer are enough for controllers to receive clean and usable data. However, the logic of the binding layer can be customized to a large extent, thus adding unprecedented levels of flexibility as far as the processing of input data is concerned.

The Default Model Binder

Any incoming request passes through the gears of a built-in binder object that corresponds to an instance of the *DefaultModelBinder* class. Model binding is orchestrated by the action invoker and consists in investigating the signature of the selected controller method and looking at formal parameter names and types trying to find a match with the names of any data uploaded with the request, whether through the query string, form, route or perhaps cookies. The model binder uses convention-based logic to match the names of posted values to parameter names in the controller's method. The *DefaultModelBinder* class knows how to deal with primitive and complex types, as well as collections and dictionaries. In light of this, the default binder works just fine most of the time.

Binding Primitive Types

Admittedly, model binding may sound a bit magical at first, but there's no actual wizardry behind it. The key fact about is that it lets you focus exclusively on the data you want the controller method to receive. You completely ignore the details of how you retrieve that data, whether it comes from the query string, the body, or the route.

> **Important** The model binder matches parameters to incoming data in a precise order. First it checks if a match can be found on route parameters, next on form posted data, and finally, it checks query string data.

Let's suppose you need a controller method to repeat a given string a given number of times. The input data you need is a string and a number. Here's what you do:

```
public class BindingController : Controller
{
    public IActionResult Repeat(string text, int number)
    {
        ...
    }
}
```

Designed in this way, there's no need for you to access the HTTP context to grab data. The default model binder reads the actual values for *text* and *number* from the full collection of values available in the context of the request. The binder looks for a feasible value trying to match formal parameter names (*text* and *number* in the example) to named values found within the request context. In other words, if the request carries a form field, a query string field, or a route parameter named *text*, the carried value is automatically bound to the *text* parameter. The mapping occurs successfully if the parameter type and the actual value are compatible. If a conversion cannot be performed, an argument exception is thrown. The next URL, for example, works just fine:

```
/binding/repeat?text=Dino&number=2
```

Conversely, the following URL may generate invalid results.

```
/binding/repeat?text=Dino&number=true
```

The query string field text contains *Dino*, and the mapping to the *string* parameter *text* on the method *Repeat* takes place successfully. The query string field *number*, on the other hand, contains *true*, which can't be successfully mapped to an *int* parameter. The model binder returns a parameter dictionary, where the entry for *number* contains the default value of the type, therefore 0. What happens exactly depends on the code used to process the input. It can return some empty content or even throw an exception.

The default binder can map all primitive types, such as *string*, *int*, *double*, *decimal*, *bool*, *DateTime*, and related collections. To express a Boolean type in a URL, you resort to the *true* and *false* strings. These strings are parsed using .NET Framework native Boolean parsing functions, which recognize *true* and *false* strings in a case-insensitive manner. If you use strings such as *yes/no* to mean a Boolean, the default binder won't understand your intentions and will place a *false* value in the parameter dictionary, which might affect the actual output.

Forcing Binding from a Given Source

In ASP.NET Core, you can alter the fixed order of model binding data sources by forcing the source for a particular parameter. You can do this through any of the following new attributes: *FromQuery*, *FromRoute*, and *FromForm*. As the names indicate, those attributes force the model binding layer to map values from query strings, route data, and post data, respectively. Let's consider the following controller code.

```
[Route("goto/{city}")]
public IActionResult Visit([FromQuery] string city)
{
    ...
}
```

The *FromQuery* attribute forces the binding of parameter code to whatever comes from the query string with a matching name. Suppose the URL */goto/rome?city=london* is requested. Where are you going, Rome or London? The value Rome is passed through a higher-priority dictionary, but the actual method parameter is bound to any value coming over the query string. Hence, the value of the *city* parameter is London. The interesting thing is that if the forced source doesn't contain a matching value, then the parameter takes the default value for the declared type rather than any other matching value being available. Put another way, the net effect of any of the *FromQuery*, *FromRoute,* and *FromForm* attributes is constraining the model binding to exactly the specified data source.

Binding from Headers

In ASP.NET Core, a new attribute makes its debut to simplify getting information stored in HTTP headers in the context of controller methods. The new attribute is *FromHeader*. You might wonder why HTTP headers aren't automatically subjected to model binding. There are two aspects to consider. In my opinion, the first aspect is more philosophical than technical. HTTP headers may not be considered plain user input and model binding is just devised to map user input to controller methods. HTTP headers carry information that in some circumstances can be helpful to check inside the controller. The most illustrious example of this is authentication tokens, but then again, the authentication token is not exactly "user input." The second aspect of not having HTTP headers automatically resolved by the model binder is purely technical and has to do with naming conventions of HTTP headers.

Mapping a header name like *Accept-Language*, for example, would require a parameter named accordingly, except that dashes are not acceptable in a C# variable name. The *FromHeader* attribute just solves this problem.

```
public IActionResult Culture([FromHeader(Name ="Accept-Language")] string language)
{
    ...
}
```

The attribute gets the header name as an argument and binds the associated value to the method parameter. As a result of the previous code, the *language* parameter of the method will receive the current value of the *Accept-Language* header.

Binding from Body

Sometimes it is worthwhile passing request data not via the URL or headers but as part of the request body. To enable the controller method to receive body content you must explicitly tell the model binding layer to parse the body content to a particular parameter. This is the job of the new *FromBody* attribute. All that is required on your end is decorating a parameter method with the attribute, as below.

```
public IActionResult Print([FromBody] string content)
{
    ...
}
```

The entire content of the request (GET or POST) will be processed as a single unit and mapped wherever possible to the parameter standing possible type constraints.

Binding Complex Types

There's no limitation on the number of parameters you can list on a method's signature. However, a container class is often better than a long list of individual parameters. For the default model binder, the result is nearly the same whether you list a sequence of parameters or just one parameter of a complex type. Both scenarios are fully supported. Here's an example:

```
public class ComplexController : Controller
{
    public ActionResult Repeat(RepeatText input)
    {
        ...
    }
}
```

The controller method receives an object of type *RepeatText*. The class is a plain data-transfer object defined as follows:

```
public class RepeatText
{
    public string Text { get; set; }
    public int Number { get; set; }
}
```

As you can see, the class just contains members for the same values you passed as individual parameters in the previous example. The model binder works with this complex type as well as it did with single values.

For each public property in the declared type—*RepeatText* in this case—the model binder looks for posted values whose key names match the property name. The match is case-insensitive.

Binding Arrays of Primitive Types

What if the argument that a controller method expects is an array? For example, can you bind the content of a posted form to an *IList<T>* parameter? The *DefaultModelBinder* class makes it possible but doing so requires a bit of contrivance of your own. Have a look at the figure 4-4.

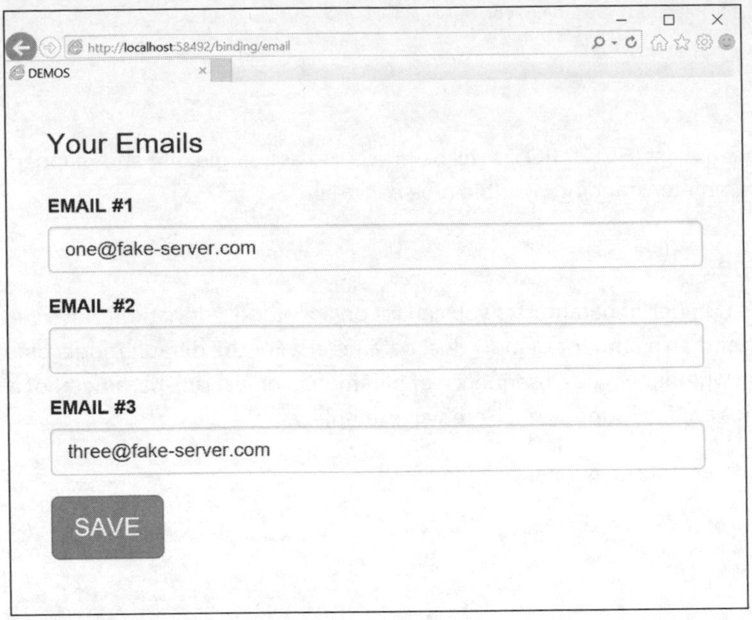

FIGURE 4-4 Sample view posting an array of email strings

When the user clicks the button, the form sends out the content of the various text boxes. If each textbox has a unique name, then you can only collect those values individually by name. However, if you name the textboxes appropriately, you can leverage the binder's ability to build arrays. Here's some ad hoc HTML you might want to use to create forms to post multiple related pieces of information.

```
<input name="emails" id="email1" type="text">
<input name="emails" id="email2" type="text">
<input name="emails" id="email3" type="text">
```

As you can see, each input field has a unique ID, but the value of the *name* attribute is the same. The information that browsers send is the following:

```
emails=one@fake-server.com&emails=&emails=three@fake-server.com
```

There are three items with the same name, and the model binder automatically groups them in an enumerable collection (see Figure 4-5).

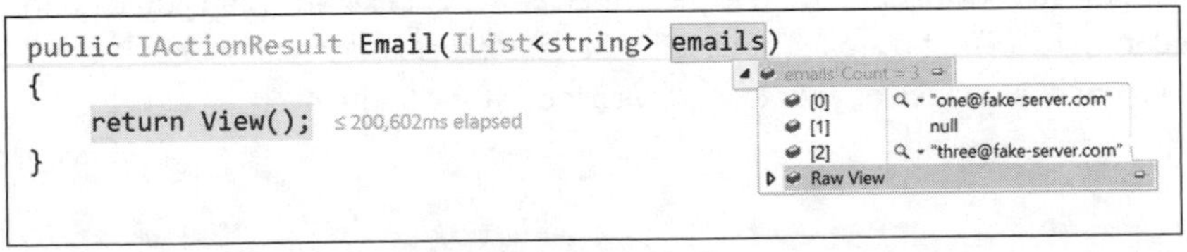

FIGURE 4-5 An array of strings has been posted

In the end, to ensure that a collection of values is passed to a controller method, you need to ensure that elements with the same name are uploaded. Next, the name must match the controller method's signature according to the normal rules of the binder.

Taking Control of Binding Names

An interesting point to consider is just the name of the input field you would use. In the code snippet above, all input fields were named *emails*. A plural name like that works beautifully on the controller's side where you would expect to receive an array of strings. However, on the HTML side, you would be naming a single email field with a plural name. It's not a matter of whether it works or not; it's a matter of calling things with the name they have in the real world. ASP.NET Core offers the *Bind* attribute to fix things.

```
<input name="email" id="email1" type="text">
<input name="email" id="email2" type="text">
<input name="email" id="email3" type="text">
```

In the HTML source code, you would use the singular, and in the controller code, you force the binder to map an incoming name to the specified parameter.

```
public IActionResult Email([Bind(Prefix="email")] IList<string> emails)
```

Note that HTML is strict about the characters allowed in an ID name. For example, the value assigned to an ID attribute can't contain square brackets. However, these constraints are released for the *name* attribute. This characteristic comes in handy to bind arrays of complex types.

Binding Arrays of Complex Types

Suppose your HTML form collects multiple aggregates of information such as addresses. Realistically, you might define an address as below:

```
public class Address
{
    public string Street { get; set; }
    public string City { get; set; }
    public string Country { get; set; }
}
```

Moreover, an address might be part of a larger data structure such as *Company*:

```
public class Company
{
    public int CompanyId { get; set; }
    public IList<Address> Addresses { get; set; }
    ...
}
```

Let's assume the input form matches the structure of the *Company* class. When the form is posted, the server receives a collection of addresses. How does it work with model binding? Again, it's a matter of how you define the HTML markup. In case of complex types, the array must be explicitly created also in the markup.

```
<input type="text" id="..." name="company.Addresses[0].Street" ... />
<input type="text" id="..." name="company.Addresses[0].City" ... />
<input type="text" id="..." name="company.Addresses[1].Street" ... />
<input type="text" id="..." name="company.Addresses[1].City" ... />
```

The above HTML structure will be matched nicely by the following controller method signature:

```
public IActionResult Save(Company company)
```

The bound object is an instance of the *Company* class where the *Addresses* collection property contains two elements. This approach is quite elegant and functional but not perfect.

In particular, it works nicely if you know exactly how many items populate the collection but might fail otherwise. Also, if the sequence of indexes in the posted values has holes, then binding fails. Indexes usually start from 0, but regardless of the starting index the bound collection is truncated at the first missing index. For example, if you have *addresses[0]* and then *addresses[2]* and *addresses[3]* then only the first one will be automatically passed to the controller method.

> **Important** Be aware that the notion of missing information here refers exclusively to the data being recognized and processed by the model binder. Browsers correctly post all the data entered into the HTML form. However, without model binding, you must arrange a fairly sophisticated parsing algorithm yourself to retrieve all posted data and relate the pieces to each other.

Action Results

An action method can produce various results. For example, an action method can just act as a web service and return a plain string or a JSON string in response to a request. Likewise, an action method can determine that there's no content to return or that a redirect to another URL is required. An action method typically returns an instance of a type implementing *IActionResult*.

The type *IActionResult* refers to a common programming interface to execute some further operations on behalf of the action method. All these further operations relate to producing some response for the requesting browser.

Predefined Action Result Types

ASP.NET Core comes with a variety of concrete types that implement the *IActionResult* interface. A few types are listed in Table 4-1. The table below doesn't include action result types related to security and Web API.

TABLE 4-1 Some of the predefined *IActionResult* types

Type	Description
ContentResult	Sends raw text content (not necessarily HTML) to the browser
EmptyResult	Sends no content to the browser
FileContentResult	Sends the content of a file to the browser. The content of the file is expressed as a byte array
FileStreamResult	Sends the content of a file to the browser. The content of the file is represented through a *Stream* object
LocalRedirectResult	Sends an HTTP 302 response code to the browser to redirect the browser to the specified URL local to the current site. It only accepts a relative URL
JsonResult	Sends a JSON string to the browser. The *ExecuteResult* method of this class sets the content type to JSON and invokes the JavaScript serializer to serialize any provided managed object to JSON
NotFoundResult	Returns a 404 status code
PartialViewResult	Sends HTML content to the browser that represents a fragment of the whole page view
PhysicalFileResult	Sends the content of a file to the browser. The file is identified via its path and content type
RedirectResult	Sends an HTTP 302 response code to the browser to redirect the browser to the specified URL
RedirectToActionResult	Like *RedirectResult*, it sends an HTTP 302 code to the browser and the new URL to navigate to. The URL is built based on action/controller pair
RedirectToRouteResult	Like *RedirectResult*, it sends an HTTP 302 code to the browser and the new URL to navigate to. The URL is built based on a route name
StatusCodeResult	Returns the specified status code
ViewComponentResult	Sends HTML content to the browser taken from a view component
ViewResult	Sends HTML content to the browser that represents a full page view
VirtualFileResult	Sends the content of a file to the browser. The file is identified via its virtual path

You use file-related action result classes if you want to reply to a request with the download of some file content or even some plain binary content expressed as a byte array.

> **Note** *JavascriptResult* and *FilePathResult* action result types available in previous versions of ASP.NET MVC are no longer supported in ASP.NET Core. *FilePathResult* has been split into *PhysicalFileResult* and *VirtualFileResult*. To return Javascript instead, you now use *ContentResult* with the appropriate MIME type. Also, *HttpStatusCodeResult*, *HttpNotFoundResult* and *HttpUnauthorizedResult* are no longer available. However, they have been just renamed to *StatusCodeResult*, *NotFoundResult*, and *UnauthorizedResult* respectively.

Security Action Results

ASP.NET Core provides more action result types specific to security actions, such as authentication and authorization. Table 4-2 summarizes the action result types.

TABLE 4-2 Security-related *IActionResult* types

Type	Description
ChallengeResult	Returns a 401 status code (unauthorized) and redirects to the configured access denied path. Returning an instance of this type or explicitly calling challenge methods of the framework has the same effect
ForbidResult	Returns a 403 status code (forbidden) and redirects to the configured access denied path. Returning an instance of this type or explicitly calling forbid methods of the framework has the same effect
SignInResult	Signs the user in. Returning an instance of this type or explicitly calling sign-in methods of the framework has the same effect
SignOutResult	Signs the user out. Returning an instance of this type or explicitly calling sign-out methods of the framework has the same effect
UnauthorizedResult	Just returns a 401 status code (unauthorized) without taking any further action

As far as the sign-in process is concerned, returning a *SignInResult* object from a controller method has the same effect as explicitly calling the method in the new authentication API (see Chapter 8) to sign users in. If you are within a controller method call (e.g., the post method after a login form) then causing the creation of a principal object via the action result is probably cleaner from a design perspective. However, it's mostly a matter of preference in my opinion.

Web API Action Results

The list of action result types in ASP.NET Core also includes a bunch of types specifically created for the Web API framework and not part of the ASP.NET MVC framework in previous versions. Table 4-3 lists the action result types specific to Web API.

TABLE 4-3 Web API-related *IActionResult* types

Type	Description
AcceptedResult	Returns a 202 status code and returns the URI to monitor the status of the request
AcceptedAtActionResult	Returns a 202 status code and returns the URI to monitor the status of the request as a controller/action pair
AcceptedAtRouteResult	Returns a 202 status code and returns the URI to monitor the status of the request as a route name
BadRequestObjectResult	Returns a 400 status code and optionally sets an error in the model state dictionary
BadRequestResult	Returns a 400 status code
CreatedResult	Returns a 201 status code along with the URI of the resource created

Type	Description
CreatedAtActionResult	Returns a 201 status code along with the URI of the resource expressed as controller/action pair
CreatedAtRouteResult	Returns a 201 status code along with the URI of the resource expressed as a route name
CreatedResult	Returns a 201 status code along with the URI of the object created
NoContentResult	Returns a 204 status code and null content. Similar to *EmptyResult* except that *EmptyResult* returns null content but sets a status code of 200
OkObjectResult	Returns a 200 status code and does content negotiation before serializing provided content
OkResult	Returns a 200 status code
UnsupportedMediaTypeResult	Returns a 415 status code

In previous versions of ASP.NET, the Web API framework was available as a separate framework for accepting and serving requests in a pure REST style. In ASP.NET Core, the Web API framework, including its own set of controller services and action result types, has been integrated into the main framework.

Action Filters

An action filter is a piece of code that runs around the execution of an action method and can be used to modify and extend the behavior coded in the method itself.

Anatomy of Action Filters

An action filter is fully represented by the following interface:

```
public interface IActionFilter
{
    void OnActionExecuting(ActionExecutingContext filterContext);
    void OnActionExecuted(ActionExecutedContext filterContext);
}
```

As you can see, it offers a hook for you to run code before and after the execution of the action. From within the filter, you have access to the request and controller context and can read and modify parameters.

Native Implementation of Action Filters

Each user-defined controller that inherits from the class *Controller* ends up getting a default implementation of the *IActionFilter* interface. The base *Controller* class, in fact, exposes a pair of overridable methods called *OnActionExecuting* and *OnActionExecuted*. This means that each controller class gives you the chance to decide what to do before, after, or both before and after a given method is invoked, simply overriding methods of the base class. This feature won't work for POCO controllers.

Here's some code that adds an ad hoc response header any time the method *Index* is invoked.

```
public class FilterController : Controller
{
    protected DateTime StartTime;
    public override void OnActionExecuting(ActionExecutingContext filterContext)
    {
        var action = filterContext.ActionDescriptor.RouteValues["action"];
        if (string.Equals(action, "index", StringComparison.CurrentCultureIgnoreCase))
        {
            StartTime = DateTime.Now;
        }
        base.OnActionExecuting(filterContext);
    }

    public override void OnActionExecuted(ActionExecutedContext filterContext)
    {
        var action = filterContext.ActionDescriptor.RouteValues["action"];
        if (string.Equals(action, "index", StringComparison.CurrentCultureIgnoreCase))
        {
            var timeSpan = DateTime.Now - StartTime;
            filterContext.HttpContext.Response.Headers.Add(
                "duration", timeSpan.TotalMilliseconds.ToString());
        }
        base.OnActionExecuted(filterContext);
    }

    public IActionResult Index()
    {
        return Ok("Just processed Filter.Index");
    }
}
```

Figure 4-6 demonstrates how the method counts the milliseconds it takes to execute, and the method writes that number to a new response header called *duration*.

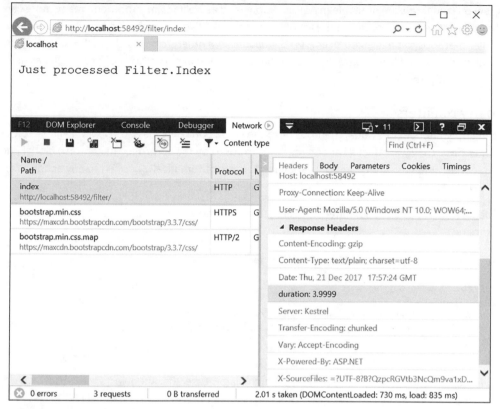

FIGURE 4-6 A custom response header added to the method *Index*

Classification of Filters

Action filters are just one type of filters invoked in the ASP.NET Core pipeline. Filters are classified into different types according to the tasks they actually accomplish. Table 4-4 lists the types of filters that intervene in the ASP.NET Core pipeline.

TABLE 4-4 Types of filters in the ASP.NET Core pipeline

Type	Description
Authorization filters	The first class of filters that runs in the pipeline to determine whether the requesting user is authorized for the current request
Resource filters	Run right after authorization before the rest of pipeline and after all the pipelined component. Useful for caching
Action filters	Run before and after a controller method action
Exception filters	If registered, are triggered in case of unhandled exceptions
Result filters	Run before and after the execution action method results

Filters can have a synchronous or asynchronous implementation. Using either is a matter of preference and opportunity.

A few built-in filters are available in ASP.NET Core, and as we'll see in a moment, many more can be created for specific purposes. In the list of built-in filters, I like to emphasize *RequireHttps* to force controller methods to be invoked over HTTPS, *ValidateAntiForgeryToken* to check the token sent over an HTML post to avoid sneaky attacks, and *Authorize,* which makes methods of a controller available only to authenticated users.

Visibility of Filters

You can apply filters to individual methods or to the entire controller class. If you apply filters to the controller class, they will affect all action methods exposed by the controller. In contrast, global filters are those that, when registered at application startup, are automatically applied to any action of any controller class.

Global filters are plain action filters that are just registered programmatically at startup, as demonstrated here:

```
public void ConfigureServices(IServiceCollection services)
{
    services.AddMvc(options =>
    {
        options.Filters.Add(new OneActionFilterAttribute());
        options.Filters.Add(typeof(AnotherActionFilterAttribute));
    });
}
```

Filters can be added by instance or by type. In the latter case, the actual instance is obtained through the ASP.NET Core DI framework. Global filters are the first to be invoked. Next are filters defined at the controller level, and last are filters defined on action methods. Note that if the controller class overrides *OnActionExecuting* its code runs before any method-level filter applied. If the controller overrides *OnActionExecuted* then this code runs after any method-level filter applied.

Little Gallery of Action Filters

Overall, action filters form an embedded aspect-oriented framework within ASP.NET Core. When it comes to writing an action filter, you typically inherit from *ActionFilterAttribute* and just add your own behavior.

Let's go through a short list of sample action filters.

> **Note** Action filters are custom components that encapsulate a specific behavior. You write an action filter whenever you want to isolate this behavior and replicate it with ease. Reusability of the behavior is one of the factors for deciding whether to write action filters, but it's not the only one. Action filters also serve the purpose of keeping the controller's code lean and mean. As a general rule, whenever your controller's method code is padded with branches and conditional statements, stop and consider whether some of those branches (or repetitive code) can be moved to an action filter. The readability of the code will be largely improved.

Adding a Custom Header

A common example of an action filter is a filter that adds a custom header to every request for a given action method. Earlier in the chapter, you saw how to achieve this by overriding the *OnActionExecuted* controller method. The following code shows how to move that code out of the controller to a distinct class.

```
public class HeaderAttribute : ActionFilterAttribute
{
    public string Name { get; set; }
    public string Value { get; set; }

    public override void OnActionExecuted(ActionExecutedContext filterContext)
    {
        if (!string.IsNullOrEmpty(Name) && !string.IsNullOrEmpty(Value))
            filterContext.HttpContext.Response.Headers.Add(Name, Value);
        return;
    }
}
```

You now have an easily managed piece of code. You can attach it to any number of controller actions, to all actions of a controller, and even globally to all controllers. All you need to do is to add an attribute, as shown here:

```
[Header(Name="Action", Value="About")]
public ActionResult About()
{
    ...
}
```

Let's see a slightly more sophisticated example that involves the localization of an application's views.

Setting the Request Culture

ASP.NET Core provides a fully functional and tailor-made infrastructure to support multi-lingual applications. A similar specific framework doesn't exist in any previous versions of ASP.NET, though individual tools to build the framework exist. If you have a large codebase of legacy ASP.NET MVC code, the chances are that you have logic to read the user's preferred culture and restore it on every incoming request.

In Chapter 8, we'll look at the ASP.NET Core new middleware for dealing with multiple cultures and switching between them. Here, instead, I'll show how to rewrite the same logic using a global action filter. As you can see, the idea is the same but implemented through the ASP.NET Core middleware triggered by any culture switches earlier in the pipeline.

```
[AttributeUsage(AttributeTargets.Class|AttributeTargets.Method, AllowMultiple = false)]
public class CultureAttribute : ActionFilterAttribute
{
    public string Name { get; set; }
    public static string CookieName
    {
        get { return "_Culture"; }
    }
```

```
public override void OnActionExecuting(ActionExecutingContext filterContext)
{
    var culture = Name;
    if (string.IsNullOrEmpty(culture))
        culture = GetSavedCultureOrDefault(filterContext.HttpContext.Request);

    // Set culture on current thread
    SetCultureOnThread(culture);

    // Proceed as usual
    base.OnActionExecuting(filterContext);
}

private static string GetSavedCultureOrDefault(HttpRequest httpRequest)
{
    var culture = CultureInfo.CurrentCulture.Name;
    var cookie = httpRequest.Cookies[CookieName] ?? culture;
    return culture;
}

private static void SetCultureOnThread(string language)
{
    var cultureInfo = new CultureInfo(language);
    CultureInfo.CurrentCulture = cultureInfo;
    CultureInfo.CurrentUICulture = cultureInfo;
}
}
```

Right before executing the action method, the code checks for a custom cookie named _Culture that might contain the user's choice of the language. If no cookie is found, the filter defaults to the current culture and assigns it to the current thread. To ensure that the *Culture* filter acts on every controller method you register it globally:

```
public void ConfigureServices(IServiceCollection services)
{
    services.AddMvc(options =>
    {
        options.Filters.Add(new CultureAttribute());
    });
}
```

> **Note** A filter registered globally is not different from a filter explicitly assigned to the class or method level. When writing an action filter, you can control the scope of the filter by using the *AttributeUsage* attribute.
>
> ```
> [AttributeUsage(AttributeTargets.Class|AttributeTargets.Method, AllowMultiple = false)]
> ```
>
> In particular, the *AttributeTargets* enumeration lets you indicate where the attribute can be placed and the *AllowMultiple* property lets you determine the number of times it can be used in the same place. Note that the *AttributeUsage* attribute works with any custom attribute you create and not just with action filters.

Restricting a Method to AJAX Calls Only

The action filters considered thus far are components aimed at intercepting a few stages of the execution of action methods. What if you want to add some code to help decide whether a given method is fit to serve a given action? For this type of customization, another category of filters is required: *action selectors*.

Action selectors come in two distinct flavors: *action name* selectors and *action method* selectors. Name selectors decide whether the method they decorate can be used to serve a given action name. Method selectors decide whether a method with a matching name can be used to serve a given action. Method selectors typically give their response based on other runtime conditions. The canonical example of an action name selector is the system's *ActionName* attribute we used earlier. Common examples of action method selectors, instead, are *NonAction* and *AcceptVerbs* attributes. Let's see how to write a custom method selector that accepts a method call only if the request is made via JavaScript.

All you need is a class that inherits from *ActionMethodSelectorAttribute* and overrides the *IsValidForRequest* method:

```
public class AjaxOnlyAttribute : ActionMethodSelectorAttribute
{
    public override bool IsValidForRequest(RouteContext routeContext, ActionDescriptor action)
    {
        return routeContext.HttpContext.Request.IsAjaxRequest();
    }
}
```

The method *IsAjaxRequest* is an extension method of the *HttpRequest* class.

```
public static class HttpRequestExtensions
{
    public static bool IsAjaxRequest(this HttpRequest request)
    {
        if (request == null)
            throw new ArgumentNullException("request");
        if (request.Headers != null)
            return request.Headers["X-Requested-With"] == "XMLHttpRequest";
        return false;
    }
}
```

Any method marked with the *AjaxOnly* attribute is only enabled to serve calls placed via the browser's *XMLHttpRequest* object.

```
[AjaxOnly]
public ActionResult Details(int customerId)
{
    var model = ...;
    return PartialView(model);
}
```

If you try to invoke a URL that, according to routes, should be mapped to an Ajax-only method, well, you'll get a not-found exception.

 Note The same approach can be used to check, for example, the user-agent of the requesting client and recognize calls coming from a mobile device.

Summary

Controllers are the heart of an ASP.NET Core application. Controllers mediate between the user requests and the capabilities of the server system. Controllers are linked to user-interface actions and are in touch with the middle tier. Controllers perform actions aimed at getting results but don't return results directly. In a controller, the processing of the request is neatly separated from any further action that makes the results available, most notably the rendering of an HTML view.

From a design perspective, controllers are part of the presentation layer as they hold tight references to the runtime environment and know about the HTTP context of the request. While ASP.NET Core introduces and supports POCO controllers, I use non-POCO controllers much more often.

Controller action methods can return a long list of action result types such as file content, JSON, plain text, and redirect responses. In Chapter 5, we'll look at the most common action result type of a web application—HTML views.

CHAPTER 5

ASP.NET MVC Views

You do not need to accept everything as true, you only have to accept it as necessary.
—*Franz Kafka, "The Trial"*

The majority of ASP.NET MVC requests require that HTML markup is served back to browsers. Architecturally speaking, there's no difference at all between requests that return HTML markup and requests that return plain text or JSON data. However, because producing HTML markup might sometimes require a lot of work (and always require a lot of flexibility), ASP.NET MVC comes with a dedicated system component—the view engine—responsible for producing plain HTML for the browser to process. In doing so, the view engine mixes application data and a markup template to create HTML markup.

In this chapter, we'll explore structure and behavior of the view engine and the margin for customizing its behavior. Lastly, we'll look into controller-less pages (also known as Razor pages), which essentially are HTML templates invoked directly without the intermediation of a controller action method.

Serving HTML Content

In ASP.NET Core, an application can serve HTML in a variety of ways with a growing level of sophistication and control from the developer's side.

Serving HTML from Terminating Middleware

As discussed in Chapter 2, an ASP.NET Core application can just be a very thin web server built around some terminating middleware. The terminating middleware is a chunk of code that gets to process the request. Basically, it's a function that processes the HTTP request. Your code can do everything, including returning a string that the browser will treat as HTML. Here's a sample *Startup* class for the purpose.

```
public class Startup
{
    public void Configure(IApplicationBuilder app)
    {
        app.Run(async context =>
        {
            var obj = new SomeWork();
            await context.Response.WriteAsync("<h1>" + obj.Now() + "</h1>");
        });
    }
}
```

By simply writing HTML-formatted text in the response's output stream (and possibly setting the appropriate MIME type), you can serve HTML content to the browser. It all happens in a very straight-forward way, with no filters and no intermediation. It works, but we're far from having a maintainable and flexible solution.

Serving HTML from Controllers

More realistically, an ASP.NET Core application leverages the MVC application model and makes use of controller classes. As discussed in Chapter 4, "ASP.NET MVC Controllers," any request is mapped to a method on a controller class. The selected method is given access to the HTTP context, can inspect the incoming data, and determine the action to take. Once the method has gathered all the necessary data, it is ready to prepare the response. HTML content can be arranged algorithmically on the fly, or it can be more comfortably created from a selected HTML template with placeholders for computed data.

Serving HTML as Plain Text from Action Methods

The code below illustrates the pattern of a controller method that retrieves data in some way and then formats it to some valid HTML layout.

```
public IActionResult Info(int id)
{
    var data = _service.GetInfoAsHtml(id);
    return Content(html, "text/html");
}
```

When the controller method regains control of the flow, it holds a text string that it knows is made of HTML markup. The controller then just returns the text decorated with the proper HTML MIME type. This approach is only a bit better than writing HTML directly to the output stream because it allows for input data to be mapped to comfortable .NET types via model binding, and it relies on more structured code. The physical generation of HTML still happens algorithmi-cally; by that, I mean that to change the layout, changes to the code are required, which will need subsequent compiling.

Serving HTML from Razor Templates

The most common approach for serving HTML content is relying on template files for expressing the desired layout and a standalone engine to parse the template and fill it out with live data. In ASP.NET MVC, Razor is the markup language used for expressing HTML-like templates, and the *view engine* is the system component that renders templates out to consumable HTML.

```
public IActionResult Info(int id)
{
    var model = _service.GetInfo(id);
    return View("template", model);
}
```

The view engine is triggered by the call of the *View* function, which returns an object that packages the name of the Razor template file to use—a file with a *.cshtml* extension—and a view model object containing the data to show in the final HTML layout.

The benefit of this approach is in the neat separation between the markup template—the foundation of the final HTML page—and the data that will be shown in it. The view engine is a system tool that orchestrates the activity of other components, such as the Razor parser and page compiler. From a developer's perspective, it suffices to edit the Razor template—an HTML-like file—to change the layout of the HTML that is served back to the browser.

Serving HTML from Razor Pages

In ASP.NET Core 2.0, Razor pages are an additional way to serve HTML content. Basically, it's about having Razor template files that can be used directly without going through a controller and a controller action. As long as the Razor page file is located under the *Pages* folder, and its relative path and name matches the URL, then the view engine will process the content and produce HTML.

The big difference between a Razor page and a regular controller-driven view is that a Razor page can be a single file—much like an ASPX page—that contains code and markup. If you're used to MVC controllers, then I expect you will find Razor pages fundamentally useless and pointless, perhaps only useful in those rare scenarios in which you have a controller method that renders out a view without any business logic. If you're new to the MVC application model, then Razor pages can represent a lower entry point barrier to make progress on the framework.

Note The weird thing about Razor pages is that they fit well as long as your view is just a bit more complex than a static HTML file. Razor pages, though, can be made quite complex. They can perform database access, dependency injection, and they can post and redirect. With these features in place, however, the gap with a regular controller-driven view is very thin.

The View Engine

The view engine is the central component of the MVC application model responsible for creating HTML from your views. Views are usually a mix-up of HTML elements and C# code snippets. First, let's review the trigger of the view engine in the most common case—the *View* method on the *Controller* base class.

Invoking the View Engine

From within a controller method, you invoke the view engine by calling the *View* method, as below:

```
public IActionResult Index()
{
    return View(); // same as View("index");
}
```

The *View* method is a helper method responsible for creating a *ViewResult* object. The *ViewResult* object needs to know about the view template, an optional master view, and the raw data to be incorporated into the final HTML.

The *View* Method

Even though the method *View* is parameter-less in this code snippet, it doesn't mean no data is actually passed on. Here's the complete signature of the method:

```
protected ViewResult View(String viewName, String masterViewName, Object viewModel)
```

Here's a more common pattern for a controller method:

```
public IActionResult Index(...)
{
    var model = GetRawDataForTheView(...);
    return View(model);
}
```

In this case, the name of the view defaults to the name of the action whether implicitly inferred from the method's name or explicitly set through the *ActionName* attribute. The view is a Razor file (with a *.cshtml* extension) located under the *Views* project folder. The master view defaults to a Razor file named *_Layout.cshtml* and is the HTML layout on which the view is based. Finally, the variable *model* indicates the data model to be incorporated into the template to generate the final HTML.

More details about the syntax of the Razor language are in Chapter 6.

Processing the *ViewResult* Object

The *View* method packages up the name of the Razor template, the master view, and the view model to return a single object that implements the *IActionResult* interface. The class is named *ViewResult* and abstracts the result obtained after processing the action method. When the controller method returns, no HTML has been generated yet, and nothing has been written to the output stream yet.

```
public interface IActionResult
{
    Task ExecuteResultAsync(ActionContext context)
}
```

As you can see, at its core, the *IActionResult* interface comprises a single method with the self-explanatory name of *ExecuteResultAsync*. Inside of the *ViewResult* class—and in any other class that serves as an action result class—there's a piece of logic that processes embedded data to shape up the response.

However, the trigger for the *ExecuteResultAsync* method is not the controller. When the controller returns, the action invoker picks up the action result and executes it. When an instance of the *ViewResult* class has its *ExecuteResultAsync* method invoked, the view engine is triggered to produce the actual HTML.

Putting it All Together

The view engine is the component that physically builds the HTML output for the browser. The view engine kicks in for each request that ends up in a controller action that returns HTML. It prepares the output by mixing a template for the view and any data the controller passes in.

The template is expressed in an engine-specific markup language (for example, Razor); the data is passed packaged in dictionaries or in strongly typed objects. Figure 5-1 shows the overall picture of how a view engine and controller work together.

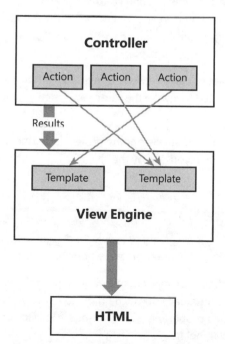

FIGURE 5-1 Controllers and view engines

The Razor View Engine

In ASP.NET Core, a view engine is merely a class that implements a fixed interface—the *IViewEngine* interface. Each application can have one or more view engines and use all of them in different cases. In ASP.NET Core, however, each application is armed by just one default view engine—the *RazorViewEngine* class. The aspect of the view engine that most impacts the development is the syntax it supports for defining the template of the view.

The Razor syntax is quite clean and friendly. A view template is essentially an HTML page with a few code placeholders. Each placeholder contains an executable expression—much like a code snippet. The code in the snippets is evaluated when the view gets rendered, and the resulting markup is integrated into the HTML template. Code snippets can be written in C# or other .NET languages supported by the .NET Core platform.

> **Note** It is possible to implement your own view engine based on your custom syntax in addition to the *RazorViewEngine* class provided by ASP.NET Core.

Generalities of the Razor View Engine

The Razor view engine reads templates from a physical location on disk. Any ASP.NET Core project has a root folder named *Views* where the templates are stored in a specific structure of subdirectories. The *Views* folder usually has some subfolders—each named after an existing controller. Each controller-specific subdirectory contains physical files whose name is expected to match the name of an action. The extension has to be *.cshtml* for the Razor view engine. (If you're writing your ASP.NET Core application in, say, Visual Basic, then the extension must be *.vbhtml*.)

ASP.NET MVC requires that you place each view template under the directory named from the controller that uses it. In case multiple controllers are expected to invoke the same view, then you move the view template file under the *Shared* folder.

It is important to note that the same hierarchy of directories that exists at the project level under the *Views* folder must be replicated on the production server when you deploy the site.

View Location Formats

The Razor view engine defines a few properties through which you can control how view templates are located. For the internal working of the Razor view engine, it is necessary to provide a default location for master, regular, and partial views both in a default project configuration and when areas are used.

Table 5-1 shows the location properties supported by the Razor view engine with the predefined value. The *AreaViewLocationFormats* property is a list of strings, each of which points to a placeholder string defining a virtual path. Also, the *ViewLocationFormats* property is a list of strings, and each of its contained strings refers to a valid virtual path for the view template.

TABLE 5-1 The default location formats of the Razor view engine

Property	Default location format
AreaViewLocationFormats	~/Areas/{2}/Views/{1}/{0}.cshtml
	~/Areas/{2}/Views/Shared/{0}.cshtml
ViewLocationFormats	~/Views/{1}/{0}.cshtml
	~/Views/Shared/{0}.cshtml

As you can see, locations are not fully qualified paths but contain up to three placeholders.

- The placeholder {0} refers to the name of the view, as it is being invoked from the controller method.

- The placeholder {1} refers to the controller name as it is used in the URL.

- Finally, the controller {2}, if specified, refers to the area name.

> **Note** If you're familiar with classic ASP.NET MVC development, you might be surprised to see that in ASP.NET Core, there's nothing like view location formats for partial views and layouts. In general, as we'll see in Chapter 6, views, partial views, and layouts are similar and are treated and discovered in the same way by the system. This is probably the rationale behind such a decision. Therefore, to add a custom view location for partial views or layout views, you simply add it to the *ViewLocationFormats* list.

Areas in ASP.NET MVC

Areas are a feature of the MVC application model used to group related functionalities within the context of a single application. Using areas is comparable to using multiple sub-applications, and it is a way to partition a large application into smaller segments.

The partition that areas offer is analogous to namespaces, and in an MVC project, adding an area (which you can do from the Visual Studio menu) results in adding a project folder where you have a distinct list of controllers, model types, and views. This allows you to have two or more HomeController classes for different areas of the application. Area partitioning is up to you and is not necessarily functional. You can also consider using areas one-to-one with roles.

In the end, areas are nothing technical or functional; instead, they're mostly related to the design and organization of the project and the code. When used, areas have an impact on routing. The name of the area is another parameter to be considered in the conventional routing. For more information refer to http://docs.microsoft.com/en-us/aspnet/core/mvc/controllers/areas.

Customizing Location Formats

If I look back at almost a decade of ASP.NET MVC programming, I realize that in nearly any production application of medium complexity, I have ended up having a custom view engine or, more often, a customized version of the default Razor view engine.

The primary reason for using a configuration different from the default is always the need of organizing views and partial views in specific folders to make it simpler and faster to retrieve files when the number of views and partial views exceeds a couple of dozens. Razor views can be given any name following any sort of naming convention. Although neither a naming convention nor a custom organization of folders is strictly required, in the end, both are useful to manage and maintain your code.

My favorite naming convention is based on the use of a prefix in the name of views. For example, all my partial views begin with *pv_* whereas layout files begin with *layout_*. This guarantees that even when quite a few files are found in the same folder, they are grouped by name and can be spotted easily. Also, I still like to have a few additional subfolders at least for partial views and layouts. The code below shows how you can customize the view locations in ASP.NET Core.

```
public void ConfigureServices(IServiceCollection services)
{
    services
        .AddMvc()
        .AddRazorOptions(options =>
        {
            // Clear the current list of view location formats. At this time,
            // the list contains default view location formats.
            options.ViewLocationFormats.Clear();

            // {0} - Action Name
            // {1} - Controller Name
            // {2} - Area Name
            options.ViewLocationFormats.Add("/Views/{1}/{0}.cshtml");
            options.ViewLocationFormats.Add("/Views/Shared/{0}.cshtml");
            options.ViewLocationFormats.Add("/Views/Shared/Layouts/{0}.cshtml");
            options.ViewLocationFormats.Add("/Views/Shared/PartialViews/{0}.cshtml");
        });
}
```

The call to *Clear* empties the default list of view location strings so that the system will only work according to custom location rules. Figure 5-2 presents the resulting folder structure as it appears in a sample project. Note that now partial views will only be discovered if located under *Views/Shared* or *Views/Shared/PartialViews*, and layout files will only be discovered if located under *Views/Shared* or *Views/Shared/Layouts*.

FIGURE 5-2 Customized view locations

 Note If you are a bit unfamiliar with the concept of partial views and layout files, don't worry. In the next chapter, they will be fully explained with examples.

View Location Expanders

View location formats are a static setting for the view engine. You define view location formats at the application startup, and they remain active for the entire lifetime. Each time a view must be rendered, the view engine goes through the list of registered locations until it finds a location that contains the desired template. If no template is found, an exception is thrown. So far so good.

What if, instead, you need to determine the path to the view dynamically on a per-request basis? If it sounds like a weird use-case, think about multi-tenant applications. Imagine you have an application that is consumed as a service by multiple customers concurrently. It's always the same codebase, and it's always the same set of logical views, but each user can be served a specific version of the view, maybe styled differently or with a different layout.

A common approach for this type of application is defining the collection of default views and then allowing customers to add customized views. For example, let's say customer Contoso navigates to the view *index.cshtml* and expects to see *Views/Contoso/Home/index.cshtml* instead of the default view at *Views/Home/index.cshtml*. How would you code this?

In classic ASP.NET MVC, you had to create a custom view engine and override the logic to find views. It was not a huge amount of work—just a few lines of code—but yet you had to roll your own view engine and learn a lot about its internals. In ASP.NET Core, view location expanders are a new type of component made to resolve views dynamically. A view location expander is a class that implements the *IViewLocationExpander* interface.

```
public class MultiTenantViewLocationExpander : IViewLocationExpander
{
    public void PopulateValues(ViewLocationExpanderContext context)
    {
        var tenant = context.ActionContext.HttpContext.ExtractTenantCode();
        context.Values["tenant"] = tenant;
    }

    public IEnumerable<string> ExpandViewLocations(
            ViewLocationExpanderContext context,
            IEnumerable<string> viewLocations)
    {
        if (!context.Values.ContainsKey("tenant") ||
            string.IsNullOrWhiteSpace(context.Values["tenant"]))
                return viewLocations;

        var tenant = context.Values["tenant"];
        var views = viewLocations
                .Select(f => f.Replace("/Views/", "/Views/" + tenant + "/"))
                .Concat(viewLocations)
                .ToList();
        return views;
    }
}
```

In *PopulateValues*, you access the HTTP context and determine the key value that will determine the view path to use. This could easily be the code of the tenant you extract in some way from the requesting URL. The key value to be used to determine the path is stored in the view location expander context. In *ExpandViewLocations*, you receive the current list of view location formats, edit as appropriate based on the current context, and return it. Editing the list typically means inserting additional and context-specific view location formats.

According to the code above, if you get a request from *http://contoso.yourapp.com/home/index* and the tenant code is "contoso," then the returned list of view location formats can be as shown in Figure 5-3.

```
0 references
public IEnumerable<st      [0]   Q ▾ "/Views/contoso/{1}/{0}.cshtml"          ExpanderContext context, IEn
{                          [1]   Q ▾ "/Views/contoso/Shared/{0}.cshtml"
     var overriddenVie     [2]   Q ▾ "/Views/contoso/Shared/Layouts/{0}.cshtml"
         .Select(f =>      [3]   Q ▾ "/Views/contoso/Shared/PartialViews/{0}.cshtml"
         .Concat(viewL     [4]   Q ▾ "/Views/{1}/{0}.cshtml"                    t.Values["tenant"] + "/"))
         .ToList();        [5]   Q ▾ "/Views/Shared/{0}.cshtml"
     return overridder     [6]   Q ▾ "/Views/Shared/Layouts/{0}.cshtml"
}                          [7]   Q ▾ "/Views/Shared/PartialViews/{0}.cshtml"
                         ▷ ● Raw View
                        ◢ ● overriddenViewNames Count = 8 ⌐
```

FIGURE 5-3 Using a custom location expander for a multi-tenant application

Tenant-specific location formats have been added at the top of the list, meaning that any overridden view will take precedence over any default view.

Your custom expander must be registered in the startup phase. Here's how to do it.

```
public void ConfigureServices(IServiceCollection services)
{
    services
        .AddMvc()
        .AddRazorOptions(options =>
        {
            options.ViewLocationExpanders.Add(new MultiTenantViewLocationExpander());
        });
}
```

Note that by default the no view location expander is registered in the system.

Adding a Custom View Engine

In ASP.NET Core the availability of view location expander components drastically reduces the need of having a custom view engine, at least for the need of customizing the way that views are retrieved and processed. A custom view engine is based on the *IViewEngine* interface, as shown below.

```
public interface IViewEngine
{
    ViewEngineResult FindView(ActionContext context, string viewName, bool isMainPage);
    ViewEngineResult GetView(string executingFilePath, string viewPath, bool isMainPage);
}
```

The method *FindView* is responsible for locating the specified view, and in ASP.NET Core, its behavior is largely customizable through location expanders. Instead, the method *GetView* is responsible for creating the view object, namely the component that will then be rendered to the output stream to capture the final markup. Typically, there's no need to override the behavior of *GetView* unless you need to something unusual, such as changing the template language.

These days, the Razor language and the Razor view are largely sufficient for most needs, and examples of alternate view engines are rare. However, some developers started projects to create and evolve alternate view engines that use the Markdown (MD) language to express HTML content. In my opinion, that is one of the few cases for really having (or using) a custom view engine.

At any rate, if you happen to have a custom view engine, you can add it to the system through the following code in *ConfigureServices*.

```
services.AddMvc()
        .AddViewOptions(options =>
            {
                options.ViewEngines.Add(new SomeOtherViewEngine());
            });
```

Also, note that RazorViewEngine is the sole view engine registered in ASP.NET Core. Hence, the code above just adds a new engine. If you want to replace the default engine with your own engine, you must empty the *ViewEngines* collection before registering the new engine.

Structure of a Razor View

Technically speaking, the primary goal of a view engine is to produce a view object from a template file and provide view data. The view object is then consumed by the action invoker infrastructure and leads to the generation of the actual HTML response. Every view engine, therefore, defines its own view object. Let's find out more about the view object managed by the default Razor view engine.

Generalities of the View Object

As discussed, the view engine is triggered by a controller method that calls into the *View* method of the base controller class to have a particular view rendered. At this point, the action invoker—the system component that governs the execution of any ASP.NET Core requests—goes through the list of registered view engines and gives each a chance to process the view name. This happens through the services of the *FindView* method.

The *FindView* method of the view engine receives the view name and verifies that a template file with given name and due extension exists in the tree of folders it supports. If a match is found, the *GetView* method is triggered to parse the file content and arrange for a new view object. Ultimately, the view object is an object that implements the *IView* interface.

```
public interface IView
{
    string Path { get; }
    Task RenderAsync(ViewContext context);
}
```

The action invoker just calls *RenderAsync* to have HTML generated and written to the output stream.

Parsing the Razor Template

The Razor template file is parsed to separate static text from language code snippets. A Razor template is essentially an HTML template with some interspersed chunks of programmatic code written in C# (or in general in any language the ASP.NET Core platform supports). Any C# code snippet must be prefixed with the @ symbol. A sample Razor template file is shown below.

(This sample template shows only a glimpse of what we'll cover in Chapter 6; there, we'll delve deeper into all syntax aspects of Razor templates.)

```
<!-- test.cshtml located in Views/Home -->

<h1>Hi everybody!</h1>
<p>It's @DateTime.Now.ToString("hh:mm")</p>
<hr>
Let me count till ten.
<ul>
@for(var i=1; i<=10; i++)
{
    <li>@i</li>
}
</ul>
```

The content of the template file is split into a list of text items of two types: Static HTML content and code snippets. The list built by the Razor parser looks like what's shown in Table 5-2.

TABLE 5-2 List of items found out of parsing the sample Razor template

Content	Type of content
<h1>Hi everybody!</h1><p>It's	Static content
DateTime.Now.ToString("hh:mm")	Code snippet
</p><hr>Let me count till ten.<ul>	Static content

for(var i=1; i<=10; i++)
{
   :
}
	Code snippet

<li>	Static content *(recursively processed in the for loop)*
I	Code snippet *(recursively processed in the for loop)*
</li>	Static content *(recursively processed in the for loop)*
</ul>	Static content

The @ symbol is used to tell the parser where a transition occurs between static content and a code snippet. Any text following the @ symbol is then parsed according to the syntax rules of the supported language—in this case, the C# language.

Building the View Object out of the Razor Template

The text items discovered in the Razor template file form the groundwork for dynamically building a C# class that fully represents the template. A C# class is dynamically created and compiled using the compiler services of the .NET platform (Roslyn). Assuming that the sample Razor file is named *test.cshtml* and it is located in *Views/Home*, following is the code that the actual Razor view class silently generates.

```
// The code below is NOT an exact printout of the actual code being generated. However
// it shows the fundamental things. Other lines, not relevant for our purposes, have
// been removed for clarity and brevity. The substance of the behavior, though, is all here.

public class _Views_Home_Test_cshtml : RazorPage<dynamic>
{
    public override async Task ExecuteAsync()
    {
        WriteLiteral("<h1>Hi everybody!</h1>\r\n<p>It\'s ");
        Write(DateTime.Now.ToString("hh:mm"));
        WriteLiteral("</p>\r\n<hr>\r\nLet me count till ten.\r\n<ul>\r\n");
        for(var i=1; i<=10; i++)
        {
            WriteLiteral("<li>");
            Write(i);
            WriteLiteral("</li>");
        }
        WriteLiteral("</ul>\r\n");
    }
}
```

The class inherits from *RazorPage<T>*, which in turn implements the *IView* interface. Because of the predefined members of the *RazorPage<T>* base page (available in the *Microsoft.AspNetCore.Mvc.Razor* namespace), you can use apparently magic objects to access the request and your own data in the body of a Razor template. Noticeable examples are *Html, Url, Model,* and *ViewData*. We'll see these property objects in action in Chapter 6 when we discuss the Razor syntax available to produce HTML views.

More often than not, a Razor view results from the combination of multiple *.cshtml* files, such as the view itself, the layout file, and two optional global files named *_viewstart.cshtml* and *_viewimports.cshtml*. The role of these two files is explained below.

TABLE 5-3 Global files in the Razor system

File name	Purpose
_ViewStart.cshtml	Contains code that is being run before any view is rendered. You can use this file to add any configuration code that is common to all views in the application. You commonly use this file to specify a default layout file for all views This file must be located in the root *Views* folder and is also supported in classic ASP.NET MVC
_ViewImports.cshtml	Contains Razor directives that you want to share across all views. You're allowed to have multiple copies of this file in various view folders. The scope of its content affects all views in the same folder or below it unless another copy of the file exists at an inner level. This file is not supported in classic ASP.NET. In classic ASP.NET, though, the same purpose is achieved using a *web.config* file

When multiple Razor files are involved, the compile process proceeds in steps. The layout template is processed first, followed by *_ViewStart* and the actual view. The output is then merged so that the common code in *_ViewStart* is rendered before the view and the view outputs its content within the layout.

Note Files in Table 5-3 are the only files you might globally need to run ASP.NET Core MVC applications. In Visual Studio 2017, some of the predefined application templates create some other files (such as_ValidationScriptsPartial.cshtml) that you can happily and blissfully ignore unless you find them useful for your purposes.

Razor Directives

The behavior of the Razor parser and code generator is driven by a few optional directives you can use to configure the rendering context further. Table 5-4 presents commonly used Razor directives.

TABLE 5-4 Most popular Razor directives

Directive	Purpose
@using	Adds a namespace to the compilation context. Same as the *using* instruction of C# @using MyApp.Functions
@inherits	Indicates the actual base class to use for the dynamically generated Razor view object. By default, the base class is *RazorPage<T>*, but the @inherits directive lets you use a custom base class that in turn must inherit from *RazorPage<T>* @inherits MyApp.CustomRazorPage
@model	Indicates the type of the class being used to pass data to the view. The type specified through the @model directive becomes the generic parameter *T* of *RazorPage<T>*. If not specified, *T* defaults to *dynamic* @model MyApp.Models.HomeIndexViewModel
@inject	Injects in the view context an instance of the specified type bound to the given property name. The directive relies on the system's DI infrastructure @inject IHostingEnvironment CurrentEnvironment

The @using and @model directives are pretty common in nearly any Razor view. The @inject directive, instead, represents the connecting point between a Razor view and the DI system of ASP.NET Core. Through @inject, you can resolve any registered type and have a fresh instance of it in the view. The injected instance will be available via a property with that name in the dynamically generated code for the Razor view.

Precompiled Views

Razor views are generated and compiled on the fly when the view is invoked. The generated assembly is cached and dropped only when the system detects that the Razor view template has been modified. When this is detected, the view is regenerated and recompiled on first access.

Starting with ASP.NET Core 1.1, you can optionally precompile Razor views and deploy them as an assembly with your application. Precompilation is relatively easy to request and consists of making a change in the .csproj file either manually or through the interface of your IDE (if supported).

All you need to do is reference the package *Microsoft.AspNetCore.Mvc.Razor.ViewCompilation* and ensure the *.csproj* file contains the following:

```
<PropertyGroup>
  <TargetFramework>netcoreapp2.0</TargetFramework>
  <MvcRazorCompileOnPublish>true</MvcRazorCompileOnPublish>
  <PreserveCompilationContext>true</PreserveCompilationContext>
</PropertyGroup>
```

All in all, there are two reasons for considering precompiled views. Determining the relevance of such reasons, however, is up to the development team. If you deploy precompiled views, then the first user who hits a given view will get the page a little faster. Second, while going through the precompilation step, any undetected compile errors show up quickly and can be fixed immediately. To me, the second reason sounds much more compelling than the first.

Passing Data to a View

There are three different, non-exclusive ways to pass data to a Razor view. In ASP.NET Core, you also have a fourth way—dependency injection via the @inject directive. You can use one of the two built-in dictionaries—*ViewData* and/or *ViewBag*—or you use strongly-typed view model classes. No difference exists between these approaches from a purely functional point of view, and even from a performance perspective, the difference is negligible.

However, a huge difference exists regarding design, readability, and subsequently, maintenance. The difference is all in favor of using strongly-typed view model classes.

Built-in Dictionaries

The simplest way for a controller to pass data to a view is stuffing any information into a name/value dictionary. This can be done in either of two ways.

The *ViewData* Dictionary

ViewData is a classic name/value dictionary. The actual type of the property is *ViewDataDictionary* which is not derived from any of the system's dictionary types but still exposes the common dictionary interfaces as defined in the .NET Core framework.

The base *Controller* class exposes a *ViewData* property, and the content of that property is automatically flushed into the dynamically created instance of the *RazorPage<T>* class behind the view. This means that any value stored in controller *ViewData* is available in the view without any further effort on your end.

```
public IActionResult Index()
{
    ViewData["PageTitle"] = "Hello";
    ViewData["Copyright"] = "(c) Dino Esposito";
```

```
        ViewData["CopyrightYear"] = 2017;

    return View();
}
```

The *index.cshtml* view doesn't need to declare a model type and can just read back any passed data. This is where the first crack in the wall appears. The developer responsible for writing the view might have no clue about the data being passed through the dictionary. She must rely on internal documentation and live communication channels, or perhaps she can place a breakpoint and inspect the dictionary in Visual Studio (see Figure 5-4). In any case, it's not going to be a pleasant experience even when the same person writes the controller and the view.

Also, consider that just because *ViewData* entries are identified by name (for example, magic strings) your code is constantly subject to typos and in this case not even precompiled views can protect you against unexpected runtime exceptions or unpredictably wrong content. The use of constants instead of magic strings mitigates the issue but at the cost of forcing internal documentation of those constants and the entire collection of data being passed to the view.

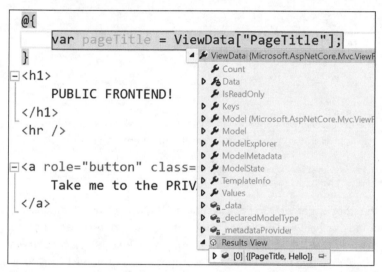

FIGURE 5-4 Inspecting the content of the *ViewData* dictionary in Visual Studio

The *ViewData* dictionary is a *string/object* dictionary, which means any data you store in it is exposed as a generic *object*. This might not be a big deal if you're only displaying the content in the view from a relatively small dictionary. For a large dictionary, you might incur boxing/unboxing performance issues. If you need to use some of the *ViewData* items for comparisons or other type-sensitive operations, then you must perform a type cast before getting a usable value.

The most compelling reason for using a weakly typed dictionary like *ViewData* is simplicity and immediateness of programming. However, this always comes at the cost of making your code brittle, and any effort to make it less brittle inevitably forces you to put in an effort comparable to using strongly typed classes without the inherent clarity that results from using classes.

> **Important** While we wouldn't recommend an extensive use of *ViewData* dictionary in a web application, we recognize that it can be a life-saver in some edge cases, such as when you find it problematic to update a strongly typed model (for example, you don't own the source code) and still need to pass additional data to the view. As mentioned, in fact, dictionaries and view models can be blissfully used together. Another tricky scenario in which dictionaries can sometimes be used side by side with strongly-typed view models is when you're passing data from a view to a child partial view. We'll cover this scenario in Chapter 6 when we discuss partial views.

The *ViewBag* Dynamic Object

ViewBag is another property defined on the base *Controller* class whose content is flushed automatically into the view class. *ViewBag* differs from *ViewData* because it allows direct programming access to properties, thus avoiding the dictionary standard access supported by *ViewData*. Here's an example:

```
public IActionResult Index()
{
    ViewBag.CurrentTime = DateTime.Now;
    ViewBag.CurrentTimeForDisplay = DateTime.Now.ToString("HH:mm");

    return View();
}
```

Note that any access to use an indexer on *ViewBag* will miserably fail, which will result in an exception. In other words, the following two expressions are not equivalent and the only former works.

```
ViewBag.CurrentTimeForDisplay = DateTime.Now.ToString("HH:mm");      // works
ViewBag["CurrentTimeForDisplay"] = DateTime.Now.ToString("HH:mm");   // throws
```

The interesting part of the story is that *ViewBag* doesn't contain anywhere any definitions for properties like *CurrentTime* and *CurrentTimeForDisplay*. You can type any property name next to the *ViewBag* object reference, and the C# compiler will never complain. The reason is that *ViewBag* is defined on the *Controller* base class as a *DynamicViewData* property, and *DynamicViewData* is an ASP.NET Core type defined as follows:

```
namespace Microsoft.AspNetCore.Mvc.ViewFeatures.Internal
{
  public class DynamicViewData : DynamicObject
  {
     :
  }
}
```

The C# language supports dynamic features through the Dynamic Language Runtime (DLR), and the *DynamicObject* class is part of it. Whenever it encounters a reference to a dynamic type variable, the C# compiler skips type checking and emits code that boils down to the DLR to resolve the call at runtime. This means that errors (if any) will only be discovered at runtime even in case of precompiled views.

Another interesting aspect of *ViewBag* is that its content is automatically synced up to the content of the *ViewData* dictionary. This happens because the constructor of the *DynamicViewData* class receives a reference to the *ViewData* dictionary and just reads and writes any received value from and to a corresponding *ViewData* entry. As a result, the following expressions are equivalent.

```
var p1 = ViewData["PageTitle"];
var p2 = ViewBag.PageTitle;
```

So what's the point of using *ViewBag*?

All in all, *ViewBag* is only apparently cool. It just prettifies your code a bit by getting rid of ugly dictionary-based code, and it does so at the cost of resorting to DLR-interpreted code for any reads and writes. In doing so, it lets you define properties that might not actually exist, so it doesn't even save you from null reference exceptions at runtime.

> **Note** Dynamic objects like *ViewBag* make little sense in the context of passing data from an ASP.NET Core controller and the view but having dynamic features in C# is highly rewarding. LINQ and social network APIs, for example, take advantage of such dynamic features in the language.

Strongly Typed View Models

Some developers seem to hate using view model classes because it's just a bunch of more classes to write and doing so requires a bit of forethought. However, as a general rule, strongly typed view models are the preferable approach to passing data to a view because it forces you, as a developer, to focus on the data flow going in and out of the view.

Compared to using dictionaries, a view model class is just a different way to lay out the data to pass to the view. Instead of looking like a collection of sparse object values, with a view model class, the data is laid out nicely in a hierarchical structure where each piece of data retains its own real type.

Guidelines for a View Model Class

A view model class is a class that fully represents the data being rendered into the view. The structure of the class should match, as closely as possible, the structure of the view. While some reuse is always possible (and to some extent advisable), in general terms, you should aim at having one ad hoc view model class per Razor view template.

A common mistake is using an entity class as a view model class. For example, let's say that your data model has an entity of type *Customer*. How should you pass data to the Razor view that allows editing a customer record? You might be tempted to pass the view just the reference to the *Customer* object you want to edit. This might or might not be a good solution. In the end, it all depends on the actual structure and content of the view. For example, if the view allows you to change the country of the customer, then you probably need to pass the view the list of countries from which to choose. Generally, the ideal view model is a class similar to the class below:

```
public class CustomerEditViewModel
{
    public Customer CurrentCustomer { get; set; }
    public IList<Country> AvailableCountries { get; set; }
}
```

The only case in which it could be acceptable to have an entity model passed directly to the view is when you really have a CRUD view. But, frankly, pure CRUD views these days exist only in tutorials and summary articles.

I recommend you always start from common base class to create your view model classes. Here's a simple and effective starting point.

```
public class ViewModelBase
{
    public ViewModelBase(string title = "")
    {
        Title = title;
    }

    public string Title { get; set; }
}
```

Because the class is primarily expected to model an HTML view, then at the very minimum, it has to expose a *Title* property to set the title of the page. More properties can be added as long as you identify other properties common to all pages in the application. Also, it's a good idea to have formatting methods in the view model base class instead of placing the same large amount of C# code inside the Razor view.

Should you derive all of your view model classes from something like the *ViewModelBase* class above? Ideally, you should have one base view model class for each layout class you use. These view model classes will extend *ViewModelBase* with the properties common to the specific layout. Finally, each view based on a particular layout will be fed by an instance of a class derived from the layout base view model class.

Centralizing the Flow of Data into the View

Let's take a look at the following basic, but still relevant, snippet of Razor code. It simply features a DIV element that renders the current time internally and offers a link to navigate back to the previous page.

```
@model IndexViewModel
@using Microsoft.Extensions.Options;
@inject IOptions<GlobalConfig> Settings
```

```
<div>
   <span>
      @DateTime.Now.ToString(Settings.Value.DateFormat)
   </span>
   <a href="@Model.ReturnUrl">Back</a>
</div>
```

There's no single flow of data into the view. Data actually flows in from three distinct sources: the view model (*Model* property), the injected dependency (*Settings* property), and the static reference to the system's *DateTime* object. While not compromising at all, the view functionality the preceding approach might be problematic to handle in large applications with hundreds of views and quite complex.

Direct use of static references and even DI-injected references (the pride and joy of ASP.NET Core) should be avoided in Razor views because they enlarge the bandwidth through which data flows in. If you're looking for guidance on how to build maintainable views, then you should aim at giving each view only one way to get to its data: the view model class. Hence, if your view needs a static reference or a global reference simply add those properties to the view model class. In particular, the current time could be just one more property that can be added to the super *ViewModelBase* class.

Injecting Data through the DI System

In ASP.NET Core, you also have the possibility of injecting into the view an instance of any type registered with the DI system. You do this through the @inject directive. As mentioned, the @inject directive adds one more channel through which data can flow into the view, and this might be a problem to maintain the code easily in the long run.

However, for short-lived applications or just as a shortcut injection of external references to a view is a fully supported feature that you are welcome to use. No matter the possible benefits of a different design, it should be noted that the *ViewData* dictionary and the @inject directive together offer a powerful and extremely quick way to retrieve any data you may need from within a Razor view. This is not a practice I apply or encourage, but it's supported, and it definitely works.

Razor Pages

In classic ASP.NET MVC, there's no way to reference a Razor template via a direct URL. A URL can be used to either link a static HTML page or the HTML output arranged by a controller action method. ASP.NET Core is no exception. However, starting with ASP.NET Core 2.0, a new feature is available—Razor pages—that allow you call a Razor template directly via the URL without any controller intermediation.

Discovering the Rationale behind Razor Pages

Sometimes, though, you have controller methods that simply serve some fairly static markup. Canonical examples are the About Us or Contact Us pages of a standard website. Let's take a look at the following code.

```
public class HomeController
{
    public IActionResult About()
    {
        return View();
    }

    public IActionResult ContactUs()
    {
        return View();
    }
}
```

As you can see, there's no data being passed from the controller to the view and nearly no rendering logic is expected in the actual view. Why should you use the filter and the overhead of a controller for such a simple request? Razor pages serve this purpose.

Another scenario for using Razor pages is that their use in some way lowers the barrier to proficient ASP.NET programming. Let's see how.

Implementation of Razor Pages

The main reason for Razor pages is to save the costs of a controller when all you need is a bit more than static HTML and much less than a full Razor view with all of its infrastructure. Razor pages can support rather advanced programming scenarios such as accessing a database, posting a form, validating data, and the like. However, if this is what you need, then why use a plain page?

The @page Directive

The following code shows the source code of a simple, yet functional, Razor page. The excessive simplicity of the Razor code is not coincidental.

```
@page
@{
    var title = "Hello, World!";
}

<html>
  <head>
    <title>@title</title>
  </head>
  <body>
    <!-- Some relatively static markup -->
  </body>
</html>
```

A Razor page is like a layout-less Razor view except for the root directive—the @page directive. A Razor page fully supports all aspects of the Razor syntax, including the @inject directive and the C# language.

The @page directive is crucial to turn a Razor view into a Razor page because it is this directive that, once processed, instructs the ASP.NET Core infrastructure to treat the request as an action even though it was not bound to any controller. It is key to notice that the @page directive must be the first Razor directive on a page as it affects the behavior of other supported directives.

Supported Folders

Razor pages are regular *.cshtml* files located under the new *Pages* folder. The *Pages* folder is typically located at the root level. Within the *Pages* folder, you can have as many levels of subdirectories as you like, and each directory can contain Razor pages. In other words, the location of Razor pages is much the same as the location of files in a file system directory.

Razor pages can't be located outside the *Pages* folder.

Mapping to URLs

The URL to invoke a Razor page depends on the physical location of the file in the *Pages* folder and the name of the file. A file named *about.cshtml,* located right in the Pages folder, is reachable as */about*. Similarly, a file named *contact.cshtml,* located under *Pages/Misc,* is reachable as */misc/contact*. The general mapping rule is that you take the path of the Razor page file relative to *Pages* and drop the file extension.

What happens if your application also has a *MiscController* class with a *Contact* action method? In this case, when the URL */misc/contact* is invoked, will it be run through the *MiscController* class or the Razor page? The controller will win.

Note also that if the name of the Razor page is *index.cshtml* then also the name index can be dropped in the URL and the page can be reached both via */index* and via */.*

Posting Data from a Razor Page

Another realistic scenario for a Razor page is when all the page can do is post a form. This feature is ideal for basic form-based pages like the contact-us page.

Adding a Form to Razor Page

The following code shows a Razor page with a form and illustrates how to initialize the form and post its content.

```
@inject IContactRepository ContactRepo
@functions {
    [BindProperty]
    public ContactInfo Contact { get; set; }

    public void IActionResult OnGet()
    {
        Contact.Name = "";
        Contact.Email = "";

        return Page();
    }
}
```

```
        public void IActionResult OnPost()
        {
            if (ModelState.IsValid)
            {
                ContactRepo.Add(Contact);
                return RedirectToPage();
            }
            return Page();
        }
}

<html>
<body>
    <p>Let us call you back!</p>
    <div asp-validation-summary="All"></div>
    <form method="POST">
      <div>Name: <input asp-for="ContactInfo.Name" /></div>
      <div>Email: <input asp-for="ContactInfo.Email" /></div>
      <button type="submit">SEND</button>
    </form>
</body>
</html>
```

The page is split into two main parts: The markup zone and the code zone. The markup zone is a regular Razor view with all of the features of a Razor view, including tag helpers and HTML helpers. The code zone contains all the code to initialize the page and process its posted data.

Initializing the Form

The @functions directive acts as the container of all code around the page. It is typically made of two methods—*OnGet* and *OnPost*. The former is invoked to initialize the input elements of the markup. The latter is invoked to process any content posted from the form.

Binding between HTML input elements and code elements is performed using the model binding layer. Decorated with the *BindProperty* attribute, the *Contact* property is initialized in *OnGet* and has its values rendered in HTML. When the form posts back, the same property contains (via model binding) the posted values.

Processing the Input of the Form

The *OnPost* method can use the *ModelState* property to check for errors—the entire validation infrastructure works as it would work in a controller scenario—and if all is good faces the problem of processing the posted data. If errors are detected, the page is rendered back calling the *Page()* function, which results in a GET request for the same URL.

Processing the input of a form realistically means accessing a database. You can access the database directly through the *DbContext* object of the application or via some dedicated repository. In both cases, the reference to the tool must be injected via DI in the page. Likewise, you can use the @inject directive to make available any necessary information in the context of the Razor page.

Important If you check out the documentation of Razor pages, you will find a few more supported options and tools available for more advanced scenarios. Quite frankly, though, the real power of Razor pages lies in the quick coverage they allow for basic scenarios. Going beyond this level makes the complexity of Razor pages and the complexity of controllers nearly the same. And controllers provide for much deeper layering of the code and far more separation of concerns. Beyond the level of complexity discussed here, using Razor pages over controllers is only a matter of personal preference.

Summary

Views are the foundation of web applications, and in ASP.NET Core, views are the result of processing a template file—typically a Razor template file—and mixing it with some data provided by the caller—typically, but not necessarily, a controller method. In this chapter, we first discussed the view engine architecture and then dug into the rendering of a Razor view. Next, we proceeded to compare the various approaches to pass data to a view. We concluded the chapter with a look at Razor pages, which are useful for quickly arranging extremely simple and basic views; they're also a tool for learning web programming in ASP.NET Core from a different perspective.

This chapter contained many snippets of Razor code. Razor is a markup language whose syntax looks like HTML but allows for numerous extensions and specific features. We'll analyze the syntax of Razor in Chapter 6, "The Razor Syntax."

The Razor Syntax

A man should stand up to his bad luck, to his mistakes, to his conscience and all that sort of thing. Why—what else would you have to fight against?

—Joseph Conrad, "The Shadow Line"

An ASP.NET Core application is typically, but not necessarily, made of controllers, and controller methods typically, but not necessarily, return *ViewResult* objects as the result of their action. The action result is then processed by the action invoker system component to produce the actual response. If the action result is a *ViewResult* object, the view engine is kicked off to produce some HTML markup. The view engine is architected to consume templates from a given folder structure and fill it out with some provided data. The way templates are expressed and the way data is injected into them depends on the internal implementation of the view engine component and the internal markup language they understand and parse on the way to generating HTML.

ASP.NET Core ships with one default view engine—the Razor view engine. And Razor is the markup language you use to define the layout of your application's HTML views. We've already seen a few examples of the Razor language in past chapters. In this chapter, we're aimed at providing structured and comprehensive coverage of the language elements.

Elements of the Syntax

A Razor file is a text file that contains two main syntax items—HTML expressions and code expressions. HTML expressions are emitted verbatim; code expressions, instead, are evaluated, and their output is merged with HTML expressions. Code expression refers to the syntax of a predefined programming language.

The programming language is identified from an extension of the Razor file. By default, the extension is *.cshtml,* and the programming language for expressions is C#. Regardless of the selected programming language, the @ character always denotes the start of a Razor code expression.

Processing Code Expressions

In Chapter 5, we have seen how the Razor parser processes the source code and how it comes up with an ordered list of static HTML expressions and dynamic code expression. A code expression can be a direct value to be emitted inline (for example, a variable or a plain expression) or it can be a complex statement made of control flow elements such as loops and conditions.

Interestingly, in Razor, you must always indicate the start of a code snippet, but after that, the internal parser uses the syntax of the selected programming language to figure out where the code expression ends.

Inline Expressions

Let's consider the following example:

```
<div>
    @CultureInfo.CurrentUICulture.DisplayName
</div>
```

In the code snippet, the *CultureInfo.CurrentUICulture.DisplayName* expression is evaluated, and the output is emitted to the output stream. Another example of an inline expression is the following:

```
@{
    var message = "Hello";
}

<div>
    @message
</div>
```

The *@message* expression emits the current value of the *message* variable. In this second snippet, though, we see another syntax element—the *@{ ... }* code block.

Code Blocks

The code block allows for multi-line statements—both declarations and calculations. The content of a *@{ ... }* block is assumed to be code unless the content is wrapped up in a markup tag. The markup tag will mostly be an HTML tag, but in principle, you can even use non-HTML custom tags if that makes sense in your specific scenario. Let's consider the following case:

```
@{
    var culture = CultureInfo.CurrentUICulture.DisplayName;
    Your culture is @culture
}
```

In this case, the code block needs to contain both code and static markup. Let's say the markup you wish to send to the browser is plain text without any surrounding HTML elements (not even elements that have no visual clue, such as *SPAN)*. The net effect of the snippet above is that the parser attempts to treat the text "Your culture is ..." according to the syntax of the current programming language. This would likely result in a compile error. Here's how to rewrite it.

```
@{
    var culture = CultureInfo.CurrentUICulture.DisplayName;
    <text>Your culture is @culture</text>
}
```

The *<text>* tag can be used to mark some static text as verbatim without having some surrounding markup element being rendered to the response.

Statements

Any Razor code snippet can be mixed with plain markup, even when the snippet contains control flow statements such as *if/else* or *for/foreach*. Here's a brief example that shows how to build an HTML table:

```
<body>
    <h2>My favorite cities</h2>
    <hr />
    <table>
        <thead>
            <th>City</th>
            <th>Country</th>
            <th>Ever been there?</th>
        </thead>
    @foreach (var city in Model.Cities) {
        <tr>
            <td>@city.Name</td>
            <td>@city.Country</td>
            <td>@city.Visited ?"Yes" :"No"</td>
        </tr>
    }
    </table>
</body>
```

Note that the closing curly brace, which is placed in the middle of the source (you can see it in the line of *@foreach*), is correctly recognized and interpreted by the parser.

Multiple tokens (for example, markup and code) can be combined in the same expression using round brackets:

```
<p> @("Welcome, " + user) </p>
```

Any variable you create can be retrieved and used later as if the code belonged to a single block.

Output Encoding

Any content being processed by Razor is automatically encoded, which makes your HTML output extremely secure and resistant to XSS script injections without any additional effort on your end. Keep this in mind and avoid explicitly encoding output because it would possibly result in a double encoded text.

However, there might be situations in which your code just needs to emit unencoded HTML markup. In this case, you resort to using the *Html.Raw* helper method. Here's how to do it.

```
Compare this @Html.Raw("<b>Bold text</b>")
to the following: @("<b>Bold text</b>")
```

Where does the *Html* object come from? Technically, it's called an HTML helper, and it is just one of the predefined properties on the base *RazorPage* class from which any Razor view is derived. As we'll see in a moment, there are quite a few interesting HTML helpers available in Razor.

HTML Helpers

An HTML helper is an extension method of the *HtmlHelper* class. Abstractly speaking, an HTML helper is nothing more than an HTML factory. You call the method in your view; some HTML is inserted that results from provided input parameters (if any). Internally, an HTML helper simply accumulates markup into an internal buffer and then outputs it. A view object incorporates an instance of the *HtmlHelper* class under the property name, *Html*.

ASP.NET Core supplies a few HTML helpers out of the box, including *CheckBox*, *ActionLink*, and *TextBox*. The stock set of HTML helpers is presented in Table 6-1.

TABLE 6-1 The stock set of HTML helper methods

Method	Type	Description
BeginForm, BeginRouteForm	*Form*	Returns an internal object that represents an HTML form that the system uses to render the <form> tag
EndForm	*Form*	A void method, closes the pending </form> tag
CheckBox, CheckBoxFor	*Input*	Returns the HTML string for a check box input element
Hidden, HiddenFor	*Input*	Returns the HTML string for a hidden input element
Password, PasswordFor	*Input*	Returns the HTML string for a password input element
RadioButton, RadioButtonFor	*Input*	Returns the HTML string for a radio button input element
TextBox, TextBoxFor	*Input*	Returns the HTML string for a text input element
Label, LabelFor	*Label*	Returns the HTML string for an HTML label element
ActionLink, RouteLink	*Link*	Returns the HTML string for an HTML link
DropDownList, DropDownListFor	*List*	Returns the HTML string for a drop-down list
ListBox, ListBoxFor	*List*	Returns the HTML string for a list box
TextArea, TextAreaFor	*TextArea*	Returns the HTML string for a text area
ValidationMessage, ValidationMessageFor	*Validation*	Returns the HTML string for a validation message
ValidationSummary	*Validation*	Returns the HTML string for a validation summary message

As an example, let's see how to use an HTML helper to create a text box with programmatically determined text.

```
@Html.TextBox("LastName", Model.LastName)
```

Each HTML helper has a bunch of overloads to let you specify attribute values and other relevant information. For example, here's how to style the text box by using the class attribute:

```
@Html.TextBox("LastName",
              Model.LastName,
              new Dictionary<String, Object>{{"class", "myCoolTextBox"}})
```

In Table 6-1, you see a lot of *xxxFor* helpers. In what way are they different from other helpers? An *xxxFor* helper differs from the base version because it accepts only a lambda expression, such as the one shown here:

```
@Html.TextBoxFor(model => model.LastName,
                 new Dictionary<String, Object>{{"class", "myCoolTextBox"}})
```

For a text box, the lambda expression indicates the text to display in the input field. The *xxxFor* variation is especially useful when the data to populate the view is grouped in a model object. In this case, your view results are clearer to read and strongly typed.

There are strong pros and strong cons around the use of HTML helpers. They've been first introduced as HTML subroutines—call it, pass it parameters, get the desired markup. The most sophisticated HTML helpers become the more C# code you have to write to pass parameters—often deep graphs of parameters. To some extent, HTML helpers hide the intricacy of rendering complex markup. At the same time, though, just because the markup structure is hidden as a developer, you lose the perspective of it and use it as a black box. Even styling an internal piece with CSS requires a design effort because the CSS property must be exposed in the API.

While HTML helpers are fully supported in ASP.NET Core, their use is much less appealing than it was a few years ago. ASP.NET Core provides *tag helpers* (see later) as an additional tool to render complex HTML in a way that is both flexible and expressive. Personally, I haven't been using HTML helpers much lately with one exception—the *CheckBox* helper.

The Strange Case of Booleans and Check boxes

Suppose you have a check box in an HTML form. An excellent example is the *Remember me* check box of a canonical login form. If you don't use the *CheckBox* helper, then you end up with plain HTML as below:

```
<input name="rememberme" type="CheckBox" />
```

According to the HTML standard, browsers will post the following if the check box is checked.

```
rememberme=on
```

If the check box is not checked, instead, then input field is ignored and not sent. At this point, how can the model binding deal with posted data? The model binding layer is instructed to understand on as true, but it can't do much if no value for the *RememberMe* name is posted! The *CheckBox* helper silently appends an *INPUT* hidden element with the same *RememberMe* name and sets it to false. If the check box is checked, however, two values are posted for the same name, but in this case, the model binding layer only picks up the first.

Beyond this particular scenario, using HTML helpers over plain HTML or, better yet, tag helpers is primarily a matter of preference.

Comments

Last but not least are comments. You might not need them in production code, but you definitely need them in development code and you might need to use comments in Razor views. When you are working inside multiline code snippets using @{ ... }, you use the language syntax to place comments. When you want to comment a block of markup, you use the @* ... *@ syntax. Here's how:

```
@*
  <div> Some Razor markup </div>
*@
```

Nicely enough, Visual Studio detects comments and renders them with the configured color.

Layout Templates

In Razor, layout templates play the role of master pages. A layout template defines the skeleton that the view engine will render around any mapped view, thus giving a uniform look and feel to those sections of the site.

Each view can define its own layout template by simply setting the *Layout* property of the parent view class. The layout can be set to a hardcoded file or to any path that results from evaluating runtime conditions. As you saw in Chapter 5, you can use the *_ViewStart.cshtml* file to assign a default property to the *Layout* property —thus defining a default graphical template for all your views.

Guidelines for a Layout

Technically speaking, a layout template is in no way different from a view (or a partial view) and its content is parsed and processed by the view engine in just the same way. However, unlike most views (and all partial views), a layout template is a full HTML template starting with the *<html>* element and terminating with the *</html>* element.

> **Note** It is not required for a view to have the layout set as a distinct resource. In the end, layouts and regular views are treated in the same way by the Razor engine, which means a full HTML page view template wrapped by an HTML element is acceptable.

Because a layout file is a full HTML template, it should incorporate a comprehensive HEAD block in which meta information is provided (as well as favicons and commonly used CSS and JavaScript files). It's up to you to place script files in the HEAD section or at the end of the view body. The body of the template defines the layout for all the derived views. A typical layout template contains a header, a footer and perhaps a sidebar. The content displayed in those elements is inherited by all views and can either be statically set as plain localized text or can be bound from passed data. As we'll see in a moment, a layout page can receive data from the outside.

How many layout files should you have in a realistic application?

That's hard to say in general. For sure, you might want to have at least one layout. However, if all your views are full HTML views, you can blissfully live without layouts. A recommended rule for determining layouts is to have one for each macro area of the site. For example, you could have one layout for the home page, and you could then realistically have internal pages that are quite different. The number of internal pages depends on how those pages can be grouped. If your application needs to have a back office for admin users to enter data and configuration, well, that likely makes for another required layout.

> **Important** In any view, it is recommended you reference resources such as images, scripts, and stylesheets by using the tilde operator to refer to the root of the website. In ASP.NET Core, a tilde is expanded automatically by the Razor engine. Be aware that the tilde is only honored in the blocks of code parsed by the Razor engine. It won't work in a plain HTML file (with a *.html* extension), and it also won't work in all *<script>* elements of a Razor file. Either you express the path as a code block, or you use some JavaScript trick to fix the URL.

Passing Data to Layouts

Programmatically, a developer only references a view and its view model. In classic ASP.NET, the *View* method of the *Controller* class also has an overload that allows you to set the layout via code. That overload is not exposed in ASP.NET Core. When the view engine figures out that the view being rendered has a layout, the content of the layout is parsed first and then merged with the view template.

The layout can define the type of view model it expects to receive, but all that it really receives is the view model object—if any—passed to the actual view. For this reason, the view model of the layout view must ideally be a parent class of the view model used for the view. Hence, I suggest that for each layout you plan to have you define an ad hoc view model base class and derive specific view model classes for actual views just from there. See Table 6-2.

TABLE 6-2 Layouts and view model classes

View model	Layout	Description
HomeLayoutViewModel	*HomeLayout*	View model for the *HomeLayout* template
InternalLayoutViewModel	*InternalLayout*	View model for the *InternalLayout* template
BackofficeLayoutViewModel	*BackofficeLayout*	View model for the *BackofficeLayout* template

Better yet, all layout view model classes would inherit from a single parent class—for example, the *ViewModelBase* class we discussed in Chapter 5.

All this said, consider that a layout view—like any other view—can still be passed data via dependency injection and through dictionaries.

Defining Custom Sections

Any layout is forced to have at least one injection point for external view content. This injection point consists of a call to the method *RenderBody*. The method is defined in the base view class being used to render layouts and views. Sometimes, though, you need to inject content into more than one location. In this case, you define one or more named sections in the layout template and let views fill them out with markup.

```
<body>
    <div class="page">
     @RenderBody()
    </div>
    <div id="footer">
        @RenderSection("footer")
    </div>
</body>
```

Each section is identified by name and is considered required unless it is marked as optional. The *RenderSection* method accepts an optional Boolean argument that denotes whether the section is required. To declare a section optional, you do as follows:

```
<div id="footer">
    @RenderSection("footer", false)
</div>
```

The following code is functionally equivalent to the preceding code, but it's much better from a readability standpoint:

```
<div id="footer">
    @RenderSection("footer", required:false)
</div>
```

Note that *required* is not a keyword; more simply, it is the name of the formal parameter defined by the *RenderSection* method. (Its name shows up nicely thanks to IntelliSense.) There's no limitation on the number of custom sections you can use. A custom section can be used anywhere in the layout if, once populated in a view, the resulting HTML is valid.

If the view template doesn't include a section marked as required, then you get a runtime exception. Here's how to define content for a section in a view template:

```
@section footer {
    <p>Written by Dino Esposito</p>
}
```

You can define the content for a section anywhere in a Razor view template.

Partial Views

A partial view is a distinct piece of HTML that is contained in a view, but it is treated as an entirely independent entity. In fact, it is even legitimate to have a view written for one view engine and a referenced partial view that requires another view engine. Partial views are like HTML subroutines and serve two main scenarios: Having reusable UI-only HTML snippets and breaking up complex views into smaller and more manageable pieces.

Reusable HTML Snippets

Historically, partial views have been introduced as a way to have reusable pieces of HTML-based user interface. However, a partial view is just what the name says: A view, just smaller, built around a template and some passed or injected data. A partial view is reusable, but it is hardly a standalone HTML snippet.

To evolve from the level of a reusable template to the level of a standalone widget, a partial view lacks business logic. A partial view, in other words, is barely a rendering instrument. It is excellent to isolate banners and menus, maybe some tables and sidebars, but not autonomous web parts. For that, ASP.NET Core provides view components.

Breaking Up Complex Views

Overall, we find even more interesting the use of partial views as a way to break up large and complex forms into more manageable pieces. Large forms, especially multi-stepped forms, become more and more common, and without partial views, they can be problematic to express and handle.

From a user experience perspective, tabs are an excellent way to break up forms that are inevitably large and full of input fields. Large forms aren't only an issue for the user though. Let's consider the following tab-based forms in which tabs have been obtained using Bootstrap CSS classes.

```
<form class="form-horizontal" id="largeform"
    role="form" method="post"
    action="@Url.Action("largeform", "sample")">
    <div>
        <!-- Nav tabs -->
        <ul class="nav nav-tabs" role="tablist">
            @Html.Partial("pv_largeform_tabs")
            <li role="presentation" class="active">
                <a href="#tabGeneral" role="tab" data-toggle="tab">General</a>
            </li>
            <li role="presentation">
                <a href="#tabEmails" role="tab" data-toggle="tab">Emails</a>
            </li>
            <li role="presentation">
                <a href="#tabPassword" role="tab" data-toggle="tab">Password</a>
            </li>
        </ul>

        <!-- Tab panes -->
        <div class="tab-content">
            <div role="tabpanel" class="tab-pane active" id="tabGeneral">
                @Html.Partial("pv_largeform_general")
            </div>
            <div role="tabpanel" class="tab-pane" id="tabEmails">
                @Html.Partial("pv_largeform_emails")
            </div>
```

```
            <div role="tabpanel" class="tab-pane" id="tabPassword">
                @Html.Partial("pv_largeform_password")
            </div>
        </div>
    </div>
</form>
```

If you must write a form like this, without using partial classes, you will have the entire markup of a tab embedded in the main view. Given that each tab can be a simple view of its own, the amount of markup in a single place—to write, read, and edit—is overwhelming. Partial views used in this context are hardly reusable, but they serve you quite effectively.

Passing Data to Partial Views

The view engine treats a partial view like any other view. Therefore, a partial view receives data in the same way as a regular view or a layout. You can use a strongly typed view model class or dictionaries. However, if you don't pass any data in the call to the partial view, the partial view receives the same strongly typed view model passed to the parent view.

```
@Html.Partial("pv_Grid")
```

The content of the view dictionaries is always shared between the parent view and all its partial views. If the partial is passed its own view model, then it loses reference to the view model of the parent view.

Let's now consider sort of an edge case. Your parent view receives an array of data objects and loops through the list. Each data object then is passed to a partial view for actual rendering.

```
@foreach(var customer in Model.Customers)
{
    @Html.Partial("pv_customer", customer)
}
```

The rendering of the customer details is now completely offloaded to the *pv_customer* view which makes it eligible to be the only way in the application to render details of a customer. So far so good. What if you need to pass more information to the partial view that is not available in the customer data object it receives? You have a few options.

- First, you can refactor the classes involved so that the partial view receives all the required data. This approach, however, might compromise the overall reusability of the partial view.

- Second, you can use an anonymous type that joins the original data object plus additional data.

- Finally, you can pass any extra data via *ViewData*.

Razor Tag Helpers

Using HTML helpers, you can programmatically express the markup you wish to have without fully writing it. In a way, an HTML helper is a smart HTML factory you configure to emit some specific pieces of HTML. Internally, helpers are made of C# code, and externally, they are added to the Razor template as C# code snippets.

Tag helpers have ultimately the same effect as HTML helpers—they work as HTML factories—but provide a much more concise and natural syntax. In particular, you don't need any C# code to tie in tag helpers.

> **Note** Tag helpers are an ASP.NET Core-only feature. The closest you can get to tag helpers in classic ASP.NET MVC is with HTML helpers or, better yet, with HTML templated helpers.

Using Tag Helpers

Tag helpers are server-side code that can be bound to one or more markup elements and when run, can inspect the DOM of the element and possibly alter the markup being emitted. A tag helper is a C# class compiled to an assembly and requires a special view directive to be recognized.

Registering Tag Helpers

The *@addTagHelper* directive in a Razor view instructs the parser to link in the specified classes and process unknown markup attributes and elements against their content.

```
@addTagHelper *, YourTagHelperLibrary
```

The above syntax links in the current view as potential tag helpers all the classes in the *YourTagHelperLibrary* assembly. If you indicate a type name instead of the * symbol, then only that class out of the specified assembly will be picked up. If inserted in a *ViewImports.cshtml* file, the *@addTagHelper* directive will be automatically added to any Razor view being processed.

Attaching Tag Helpers to HTML Elements

At a first look, a tag helper can be seen as a custom HTML attribute or a custom HTML element with which the Razor parser deals. Here's how to use a sample tag helper.

```
<img src="~/images/app-logo.png" asp-append-version="true" />
```

And here's another example:

```
<environment names="Development">
    <script src="~/content/scripts/yourapp.dev.js" />
</environment>
<environment names="Staging, Production">
    <script src="~/content/scripts/yourapp.min.js" asp-append-version="true" />
</environment>
```

The assemblies registered as tag helpers tell the Razor parser which attributes and elements found in markup expressions should instead be processed server-side to generate the actual markup for the browser. Attributes and elements recognized as tag helpers are also emphasized in Visual Studio with a special color.

In particular, the *asp-append-version* tag helper modifies the bound element adding a timestamp to the URL of a referenced file so that the browser won't cache it. Here's the actual markup generated for the IMG element above.

```
<img src="/images/app-logo.png?v=yqomE4A3_PDemMMVt-umA" />
```

A version query string parameter is automatically appended, which is calculated as a hash of the file content. This indicates that whenever the file changes, a new version string will be generated, thus invalidating the browser's cache. This simple workaround fixes the long-standing problem of clearing the browser's cache during development whenever an external resource (such as an image, stylesheet, or script file) changes.

> **Note** No version string will be emitted if the referenced file doesn't exist. Instead, the *environment* tag helper conditionally outputs markup based on the currently detected ASP.NET Core hosting environment. Every tag helper is configured to bind to a particular HTML element. Multiple tag helpers can be attached to the same HTML element.

Built-in Tag Helpers

ASP.NET Core comes with a bag full of predefined tag helpers. All are defined in the same assembly that you likely would reference from the *_ViewImports.cshtml* file, which guarantees that built-in helpers are available to all Razor views.

```
@addTagHelper *, Microsoft.AspNetCore.Mvc.TagHelpers
```

Built-in tag helpers cover a range of functionalities. For example, there are some that affect the same HTML elements you can have in a Razor template: FORM, INPUT, TEXTAREA, LABEL, and SELECT. Many other helpers exist for validating messages to be displayed to users. All these system's tag helpers share the *asp-** name prefix. A full reference can be found at *http://docs.microsoft.com/en-us/aspnet/core/api/microsoft.aspnetcore.mvc.taghelpers*.

General Structure of Tag Helpers

To help make sense of the following sections covering some of the built-in tag helpers, it is useful to look first at the internal composition of tag helpers and the core information that characterizes them.

A tag helper class is identified by the HTML element or HTML elements to which it can refer. The tag helper class is mostly made of public properties and private methods that are used in the implementation of the actual behavior. Each public property may optionally be decorated with the name of the tag helper attribute to which it is associated. As an example, here's the declaration of the C# class for the anchor tag helper.

```
[HtmlTargetElement("a", Attributes = "asp-action")]
[HtmlTargetElement("a", Attributes = "asp-controller")]
[HtmlTargetElement("a", Attributes = "asp-area")]
[HtmlTargetElement("a", Attributes = "asp-fragment")]
[HtmlTargetElement("a", Attributes = "asp-host")]
[HtmlTargetElement("a", Attributes = "asp-protocol")]
[HtmlTargetElement("a", Attributes = "asp-route")]
[HtmlTargetElement("a", Attributes = "asp-all-route-data")]
[HtmlTargetElement("a", Attributes = "asp-route-*")]
public class AnchorTagHelper : TagHelper, ITagHelper
{
    ...
}
```

It reads like the tag helper can be associated only with A elements that have any of the listed attributes. In other words, if your Razor contains just a plain *<a href="...">...</a>* element with none of the above *asp-** attributes, then it will be emitted verbatim without further processing. Figure 6-1 shows that Visual Studio can detect which of the *asp-** attributes are actually supported by some registered tag helpers.

```
Index.cshtml* ☰ ✕
@model YouCore.Server.Models.HomeViewModel

<a asp-controller="Home"
    asp-action="Room"
    asp-hello="hello">Sample link</a>

<hr/>
```

FIGURE 6-1 Valid and invalid tag helper attributes

As you can see in the figure, Visual Studio detects that *asp-hello* is not a valid attribute for the A element on any of the registered tag helpers.

Anchor Tag Helpers

The anchor tag helper applies to the A element and allows you to specify the URL it points to with extreme flexibility. In fact, you can specify the target URL by breaking it up into area-controller-action components, by route name, and even specifying the segments of the URL, such as host, fragment, and protocol. Figure 6-1 shows how to use the anchor tag helpers.

> **Note** The helper class will throw an exception if both the *href* attribute and route attributes are specified.

Form Tag Helpers

The form tag helper supports attributes to set the action URL via a controller and action name or via a route name.

```
<form asp-controller="room" asp-action="book">
   ...
</form>
```

The Razor code above sets the *method* attribute to POST and the *action* attribute to the URL that results from the composition of the specified controller and action. Also, the form tag helper does an interesting and tricky thing; it injects a hidden field with a request verification token tailor-made to prevent cross-site request forgery (XSRF) attacks.

```
<form method="POST" action="/room/book"
   <input name="__RequestVerificationToken" type="hidden" value="..." />
   ...
</form>
```

Also, it adds a cookie with an encrypted version of the same value stored in the field. This represents a strong defense against XSRF attacks as long as you also decorate the receiving controller with a server-side attribute, as shown below.

```
[AutoValidateForgeryToken]
public class RoomController : Controller
{
   ...
}
```

The *AutoValidateForgeryToken* attribute will read the request validation cookie, decrypt it, and compare its value to the content of the *value* attribute of the request validation hidden field. If no match is found, an exception is thrown. Without the *AutoValidateForgeryToken* attribute, no double-check is performed. Typically, you might want to use the attribute at the controller level or, better yet, as a global filter. In this case, if you want to disable it only for some methods, you can use the *IgnoreValidateForgeryToken* attribute.

> **Note** In ASP.NET Core you also have a similar attribute named *ValidateForgeryToken*. The difference with *AutoValidateForgeryToken* is that the latter only checks POST requests.

Input Tag Helpers

The input tag helper binds an INPUT element to a model expression. The binding occurs through the *asp-for* attribute. Note that the *asp-for* attribute also works for the LABEL element.

```
<div class="form-group">
    <label class="col-md-4 control-label" asp-for="Title"></label>
    <div class="col-md-4">
        <input class="form-control input-lg" asp-for="Title">
    </div>
</div>
```

The *asp-for* attribute for the INPUT element generates *name, id, type,* and *value* attributes based on the expression. In the example, the value *Title* refers to a matching property on the bound view model. For the LABEL element, the *asp-for* attribute sets the *for* attribute and optionally, the content of the label. Here are the results.

```
<div class="form-group">
    <label class="col-md-4 control-label" for="Title">Title</label>
    <div class="col-md-4">
        <input class="form-control input-lg"
                type="text" id="Title" name="Title" value="...">
    </div>
</div>
```

The *value* property of the INPUT field gets the value generated by the expression. Note that you can also use complex expressions such as *Customer.Name*.

To determine the most appropriate type of field, the *asp-for* attribute also looks at data annotations possibly defined on the view model class. The affected attributes are never overridden if already specified in the markup. Also, based on data annotations, the *asp-for* attribute can generate HTML5 validation attributes reading from error messages and validation rules. These *data-** validation attributes are used by the validation tag helpers and also, if configured, by jQuery validation client-side validation.

Finally, it worth noting that if the view model structure changes and the tag helper expression is not updated, a compile-time error is produced.

Validation Tag Helpers

Validation tag helpers are of two types—validation of individual properties and summary. In particular, the validation message helper consumes the value of the *asp-validation-for* attribute on a SPAN element.

```
<span asp-validation-for="Email"></span>
```

The SPAN element is set with the corresponding HTML5 validation message that the *Email* INPUT field might have output. If any error messages should be rendered, they will be rendered as the body of the SPAN element.

```
<div asp-validation-summary="All"></span>
```

The validation summary helper, instead, consumes the *asp-validation-summary* attribute of the DIV elements. Its output is a UL element that lists all validation errors in the form. The value of the attribute determines which errors are listed. Feasible values are *All*, meaning that all errors are listed and *ModelOnly*, meaning that only model errors are listed.

Select List Tag Helpers

Particularly interesting is the tag helper for the SELECT element because it now solves a long-standing problem for web developers: Finding the most concise and effective way to bind an enumerated type to a drop-down list.

```
<select id="room" name="room" class="form-control"
        asp-for="@Model.CurrentRoomType"
        asp-items="@Html.GetEnumSelectList(typeof(RoomCategories))">
</select>
```

In the SELECT element, *asp-for* points to an expression to evaluate in order to find the selected item in the list. Instead, the *asp-items* tag provides the list of items. The new *Html.GetEnumSelectList* extension method takes an enumerated type and serializes it to a list of *SelectListItem* objects.

```
public enum RoomCategories
{
    [Display(Name = "Not specified")]
    None = 0,
    Single = 1,
    Double = 2
}
```

The nice touch is that if any element of the enumeration is decorated with the *Display* attribute, the rendered name is the specified text and not the literal value. Interestingly, the values of the options generated are the numeric values—not the names—of the enumerated entries.

Writing Custom Tag Helpers

Tag helpers help to keep the Razor template readable and concise. However, I would just use tag helpers to automate the writing of long, repetitive blocks of markup code rather than creating anything like a view-specific language. The more you do so, in fact, the more you drive yourself away from plain HTML.

Motivation for an Email Tag Helper

Suppose that a few of your views display email addresses as plain text. Wouldn't it be nice to make those strings clickable and pop up the Outlook new email window? In HTML, this is pretty easy to achieve. All you do is turn the text into an anchor and make it point to a *mailto* protocol string.

```
<a href="mailto:you@yourserver.com">you@yourserver.com</a>
```

In Razor, it would be something like this:

```
<a href="mailto:@Model.Email">@Model.Email</a>
```

It is not noticeably hard to read and maintain, but what if you also want to specify a default subject for the email and a body, a CC address, or the like? In this case, the code you need to write gets significantly more complex. You must check whether the subject is non-null and add it to the *mailto* protocol string; the same is required for any other attribute to process. You probably end up with a local *StringBuilder* variable to accumulate the final *mailto* URL. This code pollutes your view without adding significance because it is just boilerplate transformation of data into markup.

Planning the Tag Helper

A tag helper would make it easy to read and will hide from view (and from the view) the details of the transformation. You can now have the following:

```
<email to="@Model.Email.To"
       subject="@Model.Email.Subject">
   @Model.Email.Body
</email>
```

The tag helper class must be registered with the view, either in the view itself or for all views in the _ViewImports.cshtml_ file. Here's what you need.

```
@addTagHelper *, Your.Assembly
```

The new tag helper has a custom element and can be made even more sophisticated by adding extra properties such as CC.

Implementing the Tag Helper

A typical tag helper class inherits from _TagHelper_ and overrides the method _ProcessAsync_. The method is responsible for producing the output for any tag that is under the control of the helper.

As mentioned, to bind Razor elements to a helper, you use the _HtmlTargetElement_ attribute. The attribute contains the name of the element to which the helper will bind.

```
[HtmlTargetElement("email")]
public class MyEmailTagHelper : TagHelper
{
    public override async Task ProcessAsync(
              TagHelperContext context, TagHelperOutput output)
    {
        // Evaluate the Razor content of the email's element body
        var body = (await output.GetChildContentAsync()).GetContent();

        // Replace <email> with <a>
        output.TagName = "a";

        // Prepare mailto URL
        var to = context.AllAttributes["to"].Value.ToString();
        var subject = context.AllAttributes["subject"].Value.ToString();
        var mailto = "mailto:" + to;
        if (!string.IsNullOrWhiteSpace(subject))
                mailto = string.Format("{0}&subject={1}&body={2}", mailto, subject, body);

        // Prepare output
        output.Attributes.Clear();
        output.Attributes.SetAttribute("href", mailto);
        output.Content.Clear();
        output.Content.AppendFormat("Email {0}", to);
    }
}
```

```
<email to="@email" subject="@subject">
    Hello!
</email>
```

FIGURE 6-2 The sample tag helper in action in Visual Studio 2017

Figure 6-2 shows a sample Razor view using the helper. The markup emitted is the following.

```
<a href="mailto:dino.esposito@jetbrains.com&amp;subject=Talking about ASP.NET
Core&amp;body=Hello!">
    Email dino.esposito@jetbrains.com
</a>
```

Figure 6-3 shows the page in action.

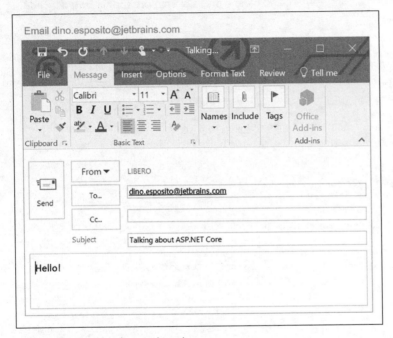

FIGURE 6-3 The sample page in action

If the name of the target element is not enough to restrict the elements under the effect of the tag helper, then you can add attributes.

```
[HtmlTargetElement("email", Attributes="to, subject")]
```

A tag helper decorated as above will apply only to *EMAIL* elements that have both the attributes specified and not null. If no tag helper matches the custom markup, the markup is emitted as is and each browser will deal with it in some way.

Tag Helpers vs. HTML Helpers

In ASP.NET Core, you have two similar tools to raise the abstraction level of the markup language in the Razor views: HTML helpers (also supported in classic ASP.NET MVC) and tag helpers. Both tools do the same job, and both provide an easier-to-use syntax for relatively complex and repetitive Razor tasks. However, an HTML helper is an extension method invoked programmatically.

```
@Html.MyDropDownList(...)
```

- An HTML helper incorporates—or generates programmatically—its markup. The markup, however, is hidden from the outside. Suppose now you need to edit a simple attribute of the internal markup—say, add a CSS class to some element. It's an easy task as long as the change is general and applies to all instances of the helper. If you want to be able to specify a different CSS attribute for each instance, then the CSS attribute must be exposed as an input parameter for the helper. Making this change has a significant effect both on the internal markup and the surrounding API.

- Tag helpers, instead, are just code around a markup right in the view. The code is only about how to manipulate the template being specified case by case.

Razor View Components

View components are a relatively new entry in the world of ASP.NET MVC. Technically, they are self-contained components that include both logic and view. In this regard, they're a revised version, and a replacement, of child actions as they appeared in classic ASP.NET.

Writing a View Component

In the context of a view, you reference view components via a C# block and pass them any input data that is required. Internally, the view component will run its own logic, process the data you passed in, and return a view ready for rendering.

Unlike tag helpers, ASP.NET Core doesn't have any predefined view components. Therefore, view components are created on a per-application basis.

Implementation of *ViewComponent*

The view component is a class that inherits from *ViewComponent* and exposes an *InvokeAsync* method whose signature matches the input data you might be passing from the view in Razor. Here's a reasonable layout for the view component core code.

```
public async Task<IViewComponentResult> InvokeAsync( /* input data */ )
{
    var data = await RetrieveSomeDataAsync(/* input data */);
    return View(data);
}
```

Within the view component class, you may have database or service references and might ask the system to inject dependencies for you. It's an entirely distinct piece of business logic that grabs data from where data lives and packages that up into a chunk of HTML.

Connecting Components to Razor Views

The view component class can be placed anywhere in the project, but all views used by view components are restricted to a specific location. In particular, you must have a *Components* folder that has one child folder for each view component. Typically, you place the *Components* folder under the *Views/ Shared* folder just to ensure full reusability of the components. If it makes sense to have multiple view components limited to just one controller, then it is okay to have a *Components* folder under the controller folder in *Views*.

The name of the view component folder is the name of the view component class. Note that if the class name ends with the *ViewComponent* suffix, then the suffix must be removed. This folder contains all Razor views being used. When you return from the *InvokeAsync* method, if no view name is specified then a *default.cshtml* file is assumed. The view is a regular Razor view with usual directives.

Invoking a View Component

To invoke a view component from within a view, you use the following code. Note that the *Component. InvokeAsync* method below can take any parameters, and those parameters are then passed to the *InvokeAsync* method of the internal implementation of the referenced component. The *Component.InvokeAsync* method is a placeholder for the markup being generated.

```
@await Component.InvokeAsync("LatestBookings", new { maxLength = 4 })
```

Note that a view component can also be invoked by a controller. In this case, the code to use is like the code shown below.

```
public IActionResult LatestBookings(int maxNumber)
{
    return ViewComponent("LatestBookings", maxNumber);
}
```

This approach is analogous to returning a partial view. In both cases, callers will receive an HTML fragment. The difference between a partial view and a view component is all in their internal implementation. A partial view is a plain Razor template that receives and incorporates data in the template. A view component receives input parameters, retrieves its data, and then incorporates it in the template.

The Composition UI Pattern

View components serve the purpose of help componentizing the view so that it results from the composition of distinct and self-made widgets. It's the "Composition UI" pattern that, despite the bold name, is ultimately a very intuitive concept.

Aggregating Data and UI Templates

Some views in the application should ideally result from the aggregation of data coming from different queries. In this context, a query is not necessarily a database query, but it is an operation that returns data shaped in the way the view requires. You can define a canonical view model object and have an application controller populate that with the data it gets out of several operations, possibly parallel operations. Let's consider the following view model for a dashboard view.

```
public class DashboardViewModel
{
    public IList<MonthlyRevenue> ByMonth { get; set; }
    public IList<EmployeeOfTheMonth> TopPerformers { get; set; }
    public int PercentageOfPeopleInTheOffice { get; set; }
}
```

As you can see, defining a canonical view model object aggregates three completely distinct pieces of information that the user wishes to see in the same view: the monthly revenues, the list of top performers and the percentage of people who checked into the office to date.

In general, the information can be located in the same database, or it can be spread across multiple databases and even multiple servers. So, in general, the application service will trigger three calls to get the data.

```
public DashboardViewModel Populate()
{
    var model = new DashboardViewModel();

    // Trigger the monthly revenue query
    model.ByMonth = RetrieveMonthlyRevenues(DateTime.Now.Year);

    // Trigger the top performers query
    model.TopPerformers = RetrieveTopPerformersRevenues(DateTime.Now.Year, DateTime.Now.Month);

    // Trigger the occupancy query
    model.PercentageOfPeopleInTheOffice = RetrieveOccupancy(DateTime.Now);

    return model;
}
```

In this approach, the retrieval of the data is centralized. The view will likely be made of three distinct partial views with each receiving one chunk of data.

```
<div>@Html.Partial("pv_MonthlyRevenues", Model.ByMonth)</div>
<div>@Html.Partial("pv_TopPerformers", Model.TopPerformers)</div>
<div>@Html.Partial("pv_Occupancy", Model.PercentageOfPeopleInTheOffice)</div>
```

Another approach consists of splitting this view into three smaller, independent pieces, each dedicated to one query task. A view component is just a partial view plus some dedicated query logic. The same view might then be expressed as shown below.

```
<div>@await Component.InvokeAsync("MonthlyRevenues", DateTime.Now.Year)</div>
<div>@await Component.InvokeAsync("TopPerformers", DateTime.Now)</div>
<div>@await Component.InvokeAsync("Occupancy", DateTime.Now)</div>
```

The controller responsible for rendering the dashboard view does not need to go through the application service, and it can just render the view. Rendering the view will then trigger components.

View Components vs. Child Actions

At first sight, view components look pretty similar to both partial views and child actions of classic ASP.NET MVC. ASP.NET Core has partial views but lacks child actions. Compared to a child action, a view component is faster because it doesn't go through the controller pipeline as do child actions. In particular, this means no model binding and no action filters.

How does a view component compare to a partial view?

Partial views are just templates that receive and render data; they have no back-end logic. They are typically codeless or just contain some rendering logic. A view component typically queries some database to get its data.

Impact of View Components

Having the view split into independent components is primarily a convenient way of organizing the work; splitting the view into independent components also can make the process of creating the view more parallel by having different developers taking care of distinct parts. However, view components are not necessarily a way to speed up the application.

Because each view component is rendered (and subsequently populated) independently, the database logic might result to be less than optimized. Unless the data lives in distinct and unrelated sources, multiple independent queries might involve multiple connections and multiple commands.

As a general rule, make sure that the resulting overall query logic is not hit by splitting the view into components. An example is the following. Let's say that the home page of a site must render a box with three most recent news headlines and another box with the last ten news with a photo, a headline, and an abstract. Distinct view components will require two distinct queries against the same database table. A centralized data retrieval process, instead, would probably go for just one query.

Summary

The Razor language in ASP.NET Core is essentially the same as in classic ASP.NET MVC. A couple of additional directives have been added to provide for new framework features—tag helpers and dependency injection. Also, view components have been added, which are a new flavor of components for reusable in-app HTML widgets. Beyond these changes, the Razor language works in ASP.NET Core similarly to how it worked in ASP.NET MVC.

This chapter completes our review of the ASP.NET Core application model. Starting in Chapter 7, "Design Considerations," we'll move toward cross-cutting concerns and touch on topics such as dependency injection, exception handling, and configuration.

PART III

Cross-cutting Concerns

Now that you're comfortable with ASP.NET Core projects and the MVC application model, we can turn to some of the real-world issues you'll face in building production solutions, including configuration, authentication, and data access.

Chapter 7, *Design Considerations*, introduces the key role of ASP.NET Core's native Dependency Injection (DI) infrastructure, and it addresses ubiquitous challenges such as managing global configuration data, handling errors and exceptions, and designing controllers.

Chapter 8, *Securing Your Application*, shows how to implement user authentication in ASP.NET Core, and use its new policy-based API to authorize users. While ASP.NET Core relies on familiar authentication concepts, experienced ASP.NET developers will find its implementation substantially different.

Finally, Chapter 9, *Access to Application Data*, takes a modern design-first approach to data access. Building on Eric Evans' influential innovations in Domain-driven Design (DDD), you'll master a modern pattern for an application backend that provides for persistence. Then, you'll put it to work with ASP.NET Core's facilities for reading and writing data. By the time you're done, you'll be prepared to handle data access, whether it involves NoSQL stores, the cloud, or pretty much anything else.

CHAPTER 7

Design Considerations

It takes two to make an accident.

—Francis Scott Fitzgerald, "The Great Gatsby"

This chapter covers a few cross-cutting concerns of all web applications such as global configuration data, patterns for dealing with errors and exceptions, the design of the controller classes, and modern features like dependency injection to pass data across layers of code. In the design of core components of an ASP.NET Core application, the native Dependency Injection (DI) infrastructure plays a fundamental role.

Without further ado, let's start taking a deeper look under the hood of the native DI infrastructure of the ASP.NET Core framework.

The Dependency Injection Infrastructure

DI is a development pattern widely used to make services available to code everywhere in the application. Whenever a code component (such as a class) needs to reference some external code (such as a service), you have two options.

- First, you create a fresh instance of the service component right in the calling code.

- Second, you expect to receive a valid instance of the service that someone else would create for you. Let's go with an illustrative example.

Refactoring to Isolate Dependencies

Suppose you have a class that acts as a wrapper around an external piece of functionality, such as a logger. In the code below, the class is tightly coupled with a specific implementation of the feature.

```
public class BusinessTask
{
    public void Perform()
    {
        // Get hold of the dependency
        var logger = new Logger();
```

```
        // Perform task
        ...

        // Use the dependency
        logger.Log("Done");
    }
}
```

If you move the class around, it will only work if the referenced component and all its dependencies are moved as well. As an example, if the logger uses, say, a database, then a connection to the database must be available anywhere the sample business class is used.

Decoupling Application Code from Dependencies

An old and wise principle of object-oriented design says you should always program to interfaces rather than to implementations. Applied to the previous code, this principle means we would extract an interface from the logger component and inject a reference to it into the business class.

```
public class BusinessTask
{
    private ILogger _logger;

    public BusinessTask(ILogger logger)
    {
        // Get hold of the dependency
        _logger = logger;
    }

    public void Perform()
    {
        // Perform task
        ...

        // Use the (injected) dependency
        _logger.Log("Done");
    }
}
```

The logger functionality, abstracted to the *ILogger* interface, is now injected via the constructor. From here, two main facts descend.

- First, the burden of instantiating the logger has been moved outside of the business class.

- Second, the business class can now transparently work with just any class of today and tomorrow that implements the given interface.

This is a basic form of dependency injection that sometimes is also referred to as *poor man's dependency injection* just to emphasize its bare-minimum, yet functional implementation.

Introducing DI Frameworks

A class designed to receive external dependencies moves the burden of creating all necessary instances to the calling code. However, if you use the DI pattern extensively, the amount of code to write before you can get an instance to inject can be significant. For example, the business class has a dependency on the logger and the logger, in turn, has a dependency on a data source provider. In turn, the data source provider might have another dependency and so forth.

To reduce the burden of similar situations, you can use a DI framework, which uses reflection or, more likely, dynamically compiled code to return the desired instance at the sole cost of a single line of code on your end. DI frameworks are sometimes referred to as Inversion-of-Control (IoC) frameworks.

```
var logger = SomeFrameworkIoC.Resolve(typeof(ILogger));
```

A DI framework essentially works by mapping an abstract type (commonly, an interface) to a concrete type. Whenever the occurrence of a known abstract type is requested programmatically, then the framework creates and returns an instance of the mapped concrete type. Note that the root object of a DI framework is commonly known as the *container*.

The Service Locator Pattern

Dependency injection is not the only possible pattern to invoke external dependencies in a loosely coupled way. An alternate pattern is called Service Locator. Here's how to retrieve the previous sample class to use Service Locator.

```
public class BusinessTask
{
    public void Perform()
    {
        // Perform task
        ...

        // Get the reference to the logger
        var logger = ServiceLocator.GetService(typeof(ILogger));

        // Use the (located) dependency
        logger.Log("Done");
    }
}
```

The *ServiceLocator* pseudo-class represents some infrastructure capable of creating a matching instance for the specified abstract type. The key difference between DI and Service Locator is that DI requires the surrounding code to be designed accordingly; signatures of the constructor and other methods may change. Service Locator is more conservative, but it also results in less readable code because a developer needs to investigate the entire source code to figure out dependencies. At the same time, Service Locator is an ideal choice when you are in the process of refactoring dependencies in a large existing codebase.

In ASP.NET Core, the role of the Service Locator is played by the *RequestServices* object in the HTTP context. Here's some sample code.

```
public void Perform()
{
    // Perform task
    ...

    // Get the reference to the logger
    var logger = HttpContext.RequestServices.GetService<ILogger>();

    // Use the (located) dependency
    logger.Log("Done");
}
```

Note that the sample code is assumed to be part of a controller class; therefore, *HttpContext* is meant to be a property of the base *Controller* class.

Generalities of the ASP.NET Core DI System

ASP.NET Core comes with its own DI framework that gets initialized right at the application startup. Let's review its most characterizing points.

Predefined Dependencies

When the container becomes available to application code, it already contains a few configured dependencies, as shown in Table 7-1.

TABLE 7-1 Abstract types mapped by default in the ASP.NET Core DI system

Abstract Type	Description
IApplicationBuilder	The type provides the mechanisms to configure the application's request pipeline
ILoggerFactory	The type provides the pattern for creating logger components
IHostingEnvironment	The type provides information about the web hosting environment which an application is running

In an ASP.NET Core application, you can inject any of the above types into any valid code injection points without any preliminary configuration. (More on injection points in a moment.) To be able to inject any other types, though, you must first go through a registration step.

Registering Custom Dependencies

You can register types with the ASP.NET Core DI system in either of two non-exclusive ways. Registering a type consists of letting the system know how to resolve an abstract type to a concrete type. The mapping can be statically set or determined dynamically.

A static mapping typically happens in the *ConfigureServices* method of the startup class.

```
public class Startup
{
    public void ConfigureServices(IServiceCollection services)
    {
```

```
        // Bind the concrete type CustomerService to the ICustomerService interface
        services.AddTransient<ICustomerService, CustomerService>();
    }
}
```

You use one of the *AddXxx* extension methods defined by the DI system to bind types. *AddXxx* extension methods for DI are defined on the *IServiceCollection* interface. The net effect of the code above is that any time an instance of a type that implements *ICustomerService* is requested, the system returns an instance of *CustomerService*. In particular, the method *AddTransient* ensures that a fresh new instance of the *CustomerService* type is returned every time. Other lifetime options exist, however.

Static resolution of abstract types is sometimes restrictive. What if, in fact, you need to resolve type T to different types depending on runtime conditions? This is where dynamic resolution comes into play; dynamic resolution allows you to indicate a callback function to resolve the dependency.

```
public void ConfigureServices(IServiceCollection services)
{
    services.AddTransient<ICustomerService>(provider =>
    {
        // Place your logic here to decide how to resolve ICustomerService.
        if (SomeRuntimeConditionHolds())
            return new CustomerServiceMatchingRuntimeCondition();

        else

            return new DefaultCustomerService();
    });
}
```

Realistically, you need to pass some runtime data to evaluate conditions. To retrieve the HTTP context from within the callback function, you resort to the service locator API.

```
public void ConfigureServices(IServiceCollection services)
{
    services.AddTransient<ICustomerService>(provider =>
    {
        // Place your logic here to decide how to resolve ICustomerService.
        var context = provider.GetRequiredService<IHttpContextAccessor>();
        if (SomeRuntimeConditionHolds(context.HttpContext.User))
            return new CustomerServiceMatchingRuntimeCondition();

        else ...
    });
}
```

Note You must call one of the *AddXxx* extension methods of *IServiceCollection* to add any of your types to the DI system as well as to bind any system abstract type to a different implementation.

Lifetime of a Dependency

In ASP.NET Core, there are a few different ways to request the DI system an instance of the mapped concrete type. Table 7-2 lists all of them.

TABLE 7-2 Lifetime options for DI-created instances

Method	Description
AddTransient	The caller receives a new instance of the specified type per call
AddSingleton	The caller receives the same instance of the specified type which was created the first time. Regardless of the type, every application gets its own instance
AddScoped	Same as *AddSingleton*, except that it is scoped to the current request

Note that by simply using an alternate overload of the *AddSingleton* method you can also indicate the specific instance to be returned for any successive calls. This approach is helpful when you need the object being returned to be configured with a certain state.

```
public void ConfigureServices(IServiceCollection services)
{
    // Singleton
    services.AddSingleton<ICustomerService, CustomerService>();

    // Custom instance
    var instance = new CustomerService();
    instance.SomeProperty = ...;

    services.AddSingleton<ICustomerService>(instance);
}
```

In this case, you first create the instance and store in it any state you wish, and then you pass it to *AddSingleton*.

Important It is key to notice that any components registered with a given lifetime can't depend on other components registered with a shorter lifetime. In other words, you should avoid injecting a component registered with a transient or scoped lifetime into a singleton. If you do so, you might run into application inconsistencies because the dependency upon the singleton makes the transient (or scoped) instance live well beyond its expected lifetime. This might not necessarily result in a visible bug in the application, but there is the risk that the wrong object (insofar as the application is concerned) is being worked on by the singleton. Generally, the problem exists whenever the lifetimes of chained objects are not the same.

Connecting to an External DI Framework

The DI system in ASP.NET Core is tailor-made to the needs of ASP.NET, so it might not offer all the features and functions you are familiar with in another DI framework. The nice thing about ASP.NET Core is that it allows you to plug in any external DI framework provided that the framework has been ported to .NET Core and a connector exists. The following code shows how to do that.

```
public IServiceProvider ConfigureServices(IServiceCollection services)
{
    // Configure the ASP.NET Core native DI system
    services.AddTransient<ICustomerService, CustomerService>();
    ...

    // Import existing mappings in the external DI framework
    var builder = new ContainerBuilder();
    builder.Populate(services);
    var container = builder.Build();

    // Replace the service provider for the rest of the pipeline to use
    return container.Resolve<IServiceProvider>();
}
```

When you plan to have an external DI framework in the application, the first thing you should do is change the signature of the *ConfigureServices* method in the startup class. Instead of being void, the method must return *IServiceProvider*. In the code above, the class *ContainerBuilder* is the connector for the specific DI framework we're trying to plug in (for example, Autofac). The method *Populate* imports all pending type mappings inside of Autofac, and then the Autofac framework is used to resolve the root dependency on *IServiceProvider*. This is the interface that all the rest of the pipeline will use internally to have dependencies resolved.

Aspects of the DI Container

In ASP.NET Core, the DI container returns *null* if asked to instantiate a type that has not yet been registered. If multiple concrete types have been registered for the same abstract type, the DI container returns an instance of the last registered type. If the constructor can't be resolved due to ambiguity or incompatible parameters, the DI container then throws an exception.

In case of sophisticated scenarios to handle, you can programmatically retrieve all concrete types registered for a given abstract type. The list is returned by the *GetServices<TAbstract>* method defined on the *IServiceProvider* interface. Finally, some popular DI frameworks let developers register a type based on keys or conditions. This scenario is not supported in ASP.NET Core. If that feature is crucial in your application, you might want to consider creating a dedicated factory class for the involved types.

Injecting Data and Services in Layers

Once a service has been registered with the DI system, all you need to do to use it is to request an instance in the necessary location. In ASP.NET Core, you can inject services into the pipeline—both through the *Configure* method and middleware classes—in controllers and views.

Injection Techniques

The primary way to inject a service into a component is via its constructor. Middleware classes, controllers, and views are always instantiated through the DI system, and subsequently, any additional parameter listed in the signature will be automatically resolved.

In addition to constructor injection, in controller classes, you can leverage the *FromServices* attribute to get an instance and, last but not least, the Service Locator interface. Note that the Service Locator interface is what you use when you need to check runtime conditions to resolve the dependency properly.

Injecting Services in the Pipeline

You can inject services into the startup class of an ASP.NET Core application. At this time, though, you can only proceed with constructor injection and only for the types listed in Table 7-1.

```
// Constructor injection
public Startup(IHostingEnvironment env, ILoggerFactory loggerFactory)
{
    // Initialize the application
    ...
}
```

Next up, as you proceed with configuring the pipeline with components that pre- and post-process the request, you can inject dependencies via the constructor of a middleware class (if you use any) or you can use the Service Locator approach.

```
app.Use((context, next) =>
{
    var service = context.RequestServices.GetService<ICustomerService>();
    ...
    next();
    ...
});
```

Injecting Services into Controllers

Inside of the MVC application model, service injection mostly occurs through the constructor of controller classes. Here's a sample controller.

```
public class CustomerController : Controller
{
    private readonly ICustomerService _service;

    // Service injection
    public CustomerController(ICustomerService service)
    {
        _service = service;
    }
    ...
}
```

Also, you can override the model binding mechanism to map method parameters to members.

```
public IActionResult Index(
        [FromServices] ICustomerService service)
{
    ...
}
```

The *FromServices* attribute causes the DI system to create and return an instance of the concrete type associated with the *ICustomerService* interface. Finally, in the body of controller methods, you can always refer to the HTTP context object and its *RequestServices* object to use the Service Locator API.

Injecting Services into Views

As seen in Chapter 5, "ASP.NET MVC Views," the *@inject* directive can be used in Razor views to force the DI system to return an instance of the specified type and bind it to the given property.

```
@inject ICustomerService Service
```

The net effect of the line above is that a property named "Service," which has been set to a DI-resolved instance of the *ICustomerService* type is made available in the Razor view. The lifetime of the assigned instance will depend on the configuration of the *ICustomerService* type in the DI container.

Collecting Configuration Data

Any realistic website is structured as a central engine connected to the outside world through HTTP-based endpoints. When ASP.NET MVC is used as the application model, those endpoints are implemented as controllers. As seen in Chapter 4, "ASP.NET MVC Controllers," controllers deal with incoming requests and generate outgoing responses. Reasonably, the behavior of the central engine that contains the logic behind the website is not entirely hard-coded but may contain some parametric information whose values are read from external sources.

In classic ASP.NET applications, the system support to grab configuration data was limited to a minimal API to read and write from the *web.config* file. At startup, developers typically collect all information into a global data structure callable from anywhere in the application. In ASP.NET Core, there's no *web.config* file anymore, but the framework offers an even richer and more sophisticated infrastructure for dealing with configuration data.

Supported Data Providers

The configuration of an ASP.NET Core application is based on a list of name-value pairs collected at runtime from a variety of data sources. The most common scenario for configuration of data is to have it read from a JSON file. However, many other options exist; Table 7-3 lists the most relevant options.

TABLE 7-3 Most common configuration data sources for ASP.NET Core

Data source	Description
Text files	Data is read from ad-hoc file formats including JSON, XML, and INI formats
Environment variables	Data is read from environment variables configured on the hosting server
In-memory dictionaries	Data is read from in-memory .NET dictionary classes

Also, the configuration API provides a built-in command-line argument data provider, which produces name-value configuration pairs right from command-line parameters. However, this option is not as common in ASP.NET applications because you have little control over the command line of the console application that fires up the web application. Command-line providers are more commonly used in console applications development.

JSON Data Provider

Any JSON file can become a data source for the configuration of the ASP.NET Core application. The structure of the file is completely up to you and can include any level of nesting. The search for the given JSON file begins in the content root folder as specified in the application startup.

As we'll see in more detail in a moment, the entire set of configuration data is built as a hierarchical document object model (DOM) and results from the union of data that might come from multiple data sources. This means you can use as many JSON files as needed in the building of the required configuration tree, and each file can have its own custom schema.

Environment Variables Provider

Any environment variables defined in the server instance are automatically eligible to be added to the configuration tree. All you have to do is programmatically append those variables to the tree. Environment variables are added as a single block. If you need filtering, then you'd better opt for an in-memory provider and add selected environment variables to the dictionary.

In-memory Provider

The in-memory provider is a plain dictionary of name-value pairs populated programmatically and added to the configuration tree. As a developer, you are entirely responsible for retrieving the actual values to store in the dictionary. Data passed through the in-memory provider can, therefore, be constant or read from any persistent data store.

Custom Configuration Providers

In addition to using predefined configuration data providers, you are also entitled to create your own provider. In this context, a provider is a class that implements the *IConfigurationSource* interface. Inside the implementation, however, you also need to reference a custom class that inherits from *ConfigurationProvider*.

A very common example of a custom configuration provider is one that uses an ad-hoc database table to read data. The provider ultimately hides the schema and layout of the database tables involved. To create a database-driven provider, you first create a configuration source object that is nothing more than a wrapper for a configuration provider.

```
public class MyDatabaseConfigSource : IConfigurationSource
{
    public IConfigurationProvider Build(IConfigurationBuilder builder)
    {
```

```
            return new MyDatabaseConfigProvider();
    }
}
```

A configuration provider is where the actual data retrieval is performed. The configuration provider contains and hides the details about the *DbContext* to use, the names of tables and columns and connection string. (The code snippet uses bits and pieces of Entity Framework Core, which we'll discuss in Chapter 9.)

```
public class MyDatabaseConfigProvider : ConfigurationProvider
{
    private const string ConnectionString = "...";

    public override void Load()
    {
        using (var db = new MyDatabaseContext(ConnectionString))
        {
            db.Database.EnsureCreated();
            Data = !db.Values.Any()
                        ? GetDefaultValues()
                        : db.Values.ToDictionary(c => c.Id, c => c.Value);
        }
    }

    private IDictionary<string, string> GetDefaultValues ()
    {
        // Pseudo code for determining default values to use
        var values = DetermineDefaultValues();

        return values;
    }
}
```

The sample code lacks an implementation for the *DbContext* class which is where you deal with the connection string, tables, and columns. In general, let's say that *MyDatabaseContext* is yet another piece of code you need to have around. The snippet using *MyDatabaseContext* refers to a database table named *Values*.

> **Note** If you find a way to pass *DbContextOptions* object as an argument to the provider, you can even manage to work with a rather generic EF-based provider. An example of this technique can be found at *http://bit.ly/2uQBJmK*.

Building a Configuration Document Object Model

Configuration data providers are necessary components to have but are not enough for actually retrieving and using parametric information within the web application. All the information that selected providers can supply must be aggregated in a single, possibly hierarchical, DOM.

Creating the Configuration Root

Configuration data is commonly built in the constructor of the startup class, as shown below. Note that injecting the *IHostingEnvironment* interface is necessary only if you're going to use it somewhere. Usually, you need to inject *IHostingEnvironment* only if you're setting the base path for locating JSON files or other configuration files.

```
public IConfigurationRoot Configuration { get; }
public Startup(IHostingEnvironment env)
{
    var dom = new ConfigurationBuilder()
        .SetBasePath(env.ContentRootPath)
        .AddJsonFile("MyAppSettings.json")
        .AddInMemoryCollection(new Dictionary<string, string> { { "Timezone", "+1" } })
        .AddEnvironmentVariables()
        .Build();

    // Save the configuration root object to a startup member for further references
    Configuration = dom;
}
```

The *ConfigurationBuilder* class is responsible for aggregating configuration values and building the DOM. The aggregated data should be saved within the startup class to be used later during the initialization of the pipeline. The next point to address is how to read the configuration data; the reference to the configuration root is simply the tool you leverage to access the actual values. Before we get to that, though, there are a few remarks to be made about text files used in the configuration.

Advanced Aspects of Configuration Files

As long as you create your own data provider, you can store configuration in any format you wish, and you can still bind stored data as name-value pairs to the standard configuration DOM. ASP.NET Core supports JSON, XML, and INI formats out of the box.

To add each to the configuration builder, you use an ad hoc extension method such as *AddJsonFile*, *AddXmlFile*, or *AddIniFile*. All methods share the same signature, which includes two extra Boolean parameters in addition to the file name.

```
// Extension method of the IConfigurationBuilder type
public static IConfigurationBuilder AddJsonFile(this IConfigurationBuilder builder,
    string path,
    bool optional,
    bool reloadOnChange);
```

The first Boolean argument indicates whether the file should be considered optional. If not, an exception is thrown if the file cannot be found. The second argument—*reloadOnChange*—indicates whether the file should be monitored for changes. If so, any time the file undergoes changes, then the configuration tree is automatically rebuilt to reflect those changes.

```
var builder = new ConfigurationBuilder()
    .SetBasePath(env.ContentRootPath)
    .AddJsonFile("MyAppSettings.json", optional: true, reloadOnChange: true);
Configuration = builder.Build();
```

In light of the remarks, this is a more resilient way to load configuration data from text files, whether JSON, XML, or INI.

> **Note** ASP.NET Core also supports environment-specific files for settings. This means that along with *MyAppSettings.json,* you can also have *MyAppSettings.Development.json* and perhaps *MyAppSettings.Staging.json.* You add all JSON files you might need, and the system picks up only the one that seems appropriate given the context. The current environment in which the application is running is determined by the value of the ASPNETCORE_ENVIRONMENT environment variable. In Visual Studio 2017, you can set it directly from the property page of the project. In IIS or Azure App Service, you just add it through the respective portals.

Reading Configuration Data

To read configuration data programmatically, you use the *GetSection* method on the configuration root object and pass it a path string to indicate exactly the piece of information you want to read. To delimit properties in a hierarchical schema, you use the : (colon) symbol. Suppose that the JSON file looks like this:

```
{
    "paging" : {
        "pageSize" : "20"
    },
    "sorting" : {
        "enabled" : "false"
    }
}
```

To read settings, you can proceed in many different ways as long as you know the path to value in the JSON schema. For example, *paging:pagesize* is the path string to read the page size. The path string you specify applies to the current configuration DOM and results from the aggregation of all defined data sources. A path string is always case-insensitive.

The simplest way to read settings is through the indexer API, as shown below.

```
// The returned value is a string
var pageSize = Configuration["paging:pageSize"];
```

It is important to note that by default, the setting is returned as a plain string and must be programmatically converted to its actual concrete type before further use. There's also a strongly typed API, though.

```
// The returned value is an integer (if conversion is possible)
var pageSize = Configuration.GetValue<int>("paging:pageSize");
```

The *GetSection* method lets you select an entire configuration subtree where you can act on using both the indexer and the strongly typed API.

```
var pageSize = Configuration.GetSection("Paging").GetValue<int>("PageSize");
```

Finally, you have available also a *GetValue* method and the *Value* property. Both would return the value of the setting as a string. Note that the *GetSection* method is a generic query tool on the configuration tree; it is not specific to JSON files only.

> **Note** The configuration API is designed to be read-only. However, this only means that you can't write back to the configured data source using an API. If you have another way to edit the content of the data source (i.e., programmatic overwrites of text files, database updates), then the system allows you reload the configuration tree. All you need to do is call the *Reload* method of the *IConfigurationRoot* object.

Passing Configuration Data Around

Reading configuration data punctually through path strings is not particularly friendly, though it represents a useful low-level tool. ASP.NET Core provides a mechanism to bind configuration data to strongly typed variables and members. Before we explore this point further, though, we should investigate ways to pass configuration data around to controllers and views.

Injecting Configuration Data

So far, we have used the configuration API from within the startup class. In the startup class, you configure the application's pipeline, which is a good place for reading back configuration data. More often, though, you need to read configuration data into controller methods and views. To make this happen, you have both an old approach and a new approach to follow.

The old approach consists of turning the *IConfigurationRoot* object into a global object visible from anywhere in the application. It works, but it's a legacy approach that is not recommended. The new approach consists of using the DI system to make the configuration root object available to controllers and views.

```
public class HomeController : Controller
{
    private IConfigurationRoot Configuration { get; }
    public HomeController(IConfigurationRoot config)
    {
        Configuration = config;
    }
    ...
}
```

Whenever an instance of the *HomeController* class is created, the configuration root is injected. However, to avoid receiving a null reference, you must first register the configuration root object created in the startup class with the DI system as a singleton.

```
services.AddSingleton<IConfigurationRoot>(Configuration);
```

You place this code in the *ConfigureServices* method of the startup class. Note that the *Configuration* object is just the configuration root object created in the constructor of the startup class.

Mapping Configuration to POCO Classes

In classic ASP.NET MVC, the best practice for dealing with configuration data entails that you load all your data once at startup into a global container object. The global object is accessible from controller methods, and its content can be injected as an argument into back-end classes such as repositories and even views. In classic ASP.NET MVC, the cost of mapping loose string-based data into the strongly typed properties of the global container is entirely on you.

In ASP.NET Core, instead, you can use the so-called Options pattern to automatically bind the name-value pairs from the configuration root DOM into the configuration container model. The Options pattern is the descriptive name for the following coding strategy.

```
public void ConfigureServices(IServiceCollection services)
{
    // Initializes the Options subsystem
    services.AddOptions();

    // Maps the specified segment of the configuration DOM to the given type.
    // NOTE: Configuration used below is the configuration root created
    //       in the constructor of the startup class
    services.Configure<PagingOptions>(Configuration.GetSection("paging"));
}
```

Once you have initialized the Options subsystem, you can then ask the subsystem to bind all the values read out of the specified section of the configuration DOM into the public members of the class used as the *Configure<T>* method argument. The binding follows the same rules used by the controller's model binding, and it recursively applies to nested objects. The binding silently fails if no binding is possible given the structure of the data and the binding object.

PagingOptions is a POCO class you create to store some (or even all) of the configuration settings. Here's a possible implementation:

```
public class PagingOptions
{
    public int PageSize { get; set; }
    ...
}
```

The overall behavior of the configuration API is analogous to how model binding works during the processing of a request at the controller level. The missing link for using the configuration's strongly typed object in controllers and views is found in how you inject it into the DI system. You must resort to the *IOptions<T>* abstract type.

Registering the *IOptions* type with the DI system is precisely the purpose of the *AddOptions* extension method. Therefore, all that remains to do is inject *IOptions<T>* wherever it is needed.

```
// PagingOptions is an internal member of the controller class
protected PagingOptions Configuration { get; set; }

public CustomerController(IOptions<PagingOptions> config)
{
    PagingOptions = config.Value;
}
```

If you extensively use the Options pattern in all your controllers, then you might want to consider moving the options property you see above to some base class and inherit your controller classes from there.

Finally, in a Razor view, all you do is use the *@inject* directive to bring in an instance of the *IOptions<T>* type.

The Layered Architecture

ASP.NET Core is a technology, but just like any technology, it shouldn't be used only as such. In other words, the best way to take advantage of a powerful technology is to put it in the context of a business domain. Hence, for a software technology, you won't go any further with complex applications without a sane and savvy architecture.

Visual Studio makes it easy to create your own controller class. It only requires you to right-click on a project folder and add a new class, even a POCO class. In a controller class, you'll typically have one method per user action that falls under the responsibility of the controller. How do you code an action method?

An action method is expected to collect input data and use it to prepare one or multiple calls to the middle tier of the application. Next, it receives computation or results and fills up a model that the view needs to receive. Finally, the action method sets up the response for the user agent. All this work might add up to several lines of code, making even a controller class with just a few methods quite a messy class. Getting input data is a problem mostly solved for you by the model binding layer. Ultimately, generating the response is just one call to a method that triggers the processing of the action result. The core of the action method is in the code that performs the task and prepares data for the view. Where does this code belong? Should it go right in the controller class?

The controller code is only the topmost part of the stack that can be easily mapped to the presentation layer. Underneath presentation, we can recognize a few other layers that altogether make for a compact application—easy to deploy to the cloud and scale. The inspiring pattern for designing controllers and their dependencies is the Layered Architecture pattern (see Figure 7-1).

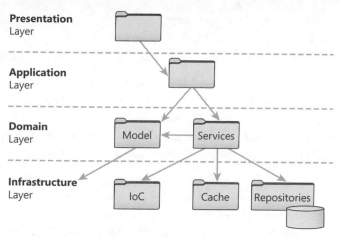

FIGURE 7-1 Visual representation of a layered architecture

Compared to the classic 3-tier architecture, the layered architecture counts a fourth section and has expanded the notion of the data access layer to encompass any other required piece of infrastructure, such as data access and many other cross-cutting concerns such as emails, logging, and caching.

The business layer of the classic 3-tier architecture has been broken into the application and domain layer. This is an attempt to clarify that there are two types of business logic: application and domain.

- The application logic is the orchestration of any tasks triggered by the presentation. The application layer is where any UI-specific transformation of data takes place.

- The domain logic is any core logic of the specific business that is reusable across multiple presentation layers. The domain logic is about business rules and core business tasks using a data model that is strictly business-oriented.

In an ASP.NET MVC application, the presentation layer is made of controllers and the application layer is made of controller-specific service classes that in literature go under the name of application services or worker services.

The Presentation Layer

The presentation layer funnels data to the rest of the system, ideally using a data model that well reflects the structure of the data in the screens. Generally speaking, each screen in the presentation that posts a command to the back end of the system groups data into an input model and receives a response using classes in a view model. Input and view models might coincide. At the same time, they might coincide with any data model being used in the back end to perform actual tasks. When a single entity can be used for input, logic, persistence, and view, this is an indicator that the application you're working with is particularly simple. Or it could mean that you've blissfully created a huge amount of technical debt.

The Input Model

In ASP.NET MVC, a user's clicks initiate a request that a controller class will handle. Each request is turned into an action mapped to a public method defined on a controller class. What about input data?

As usual, in ASP.NET, any input data is wrapped up in the HTTP request regardless of whether it's in the query string, in any form posted data, or perhaps in HTTP headers or cookies. Input data represents the data being posted for the server to take action. However you look at it, these are simply input parameters. Input data can be treated as loose values and variables, or it can be grouped into a class that acts as a container. The collection of input classes forms the overall input model for the application.

The input model carries data in the core of the system in a way that is identical to the expectations of the user interface. Employing a separated input model makes it easier to design the user interface in a very business-oriented way. The application layer will then take care of unpacking data and consuming it as appropriate.

The View Model

Any request will get a response, and more often than not, the response you get from ASP.NET MVC is an HTML view. In ASP.NET MVC, the creation of an HTML view is governed by the controller that invokes the system's back end and receives a response. The controller then selects the HTML template to use and passes the HTML template and data to an ad hoc system component—the view engine—which will mix template and data and produce the markup for the browser.

As we saw in Chapter 5, in ASP.NET MVC, there are a few ways to pass data to the view engine that will be incorporated in the resulting view. You can use a public dictionary such as *ViewData*, a dynamic object such as *ViewBag*, or a made-to-measure class that just collects all properties to pass. Any class you create to carry data to be incorporated into the response contributes to creating the view model. The application layer is the layer that receives input model classes and returns view model classes.

```
[HttpGet]
public IActionResult List(CustomerSearchInputModel input)
{
    var model = _applicationLayer.GetListOfCustomers(input);
    return View(model);
}
```

In the future, the ideal format for persistence will be different from the ideal format of presentation. The presentation layer is responsible for defining the clear boundaries of acceptable data, and the application layer is responsible for accepting and providing data in only those formats.

The Application Layer

The application layer is the entry point to the system's back end, and it is the point of contact between the presentation and back end. The application layer consists of methods bound in an almost one-to-one fashion to the use-cases of the presentation layer. We suggest you create a service class for each controller and have the controller action methods simply yield to the service class. Methods in the service class will receive classes in the input model and return classes from the view model. Internally, the service class will perform any due transformation to make data map nicely to the presentation and be ready for processing in the back end.

The primary purpose of the application layer is to abstract business processes as users perceive them and to map those processes to the hidden and protected assets of the application's back end. In an e-commerce system, for example, the user sees the shopping cart, but the physical data model might have no entities like the shopping cart. The application layer sits between the presentation and the back end, and the application does any necessary transformation.

When you make intensive use of the application layer, then your controllers suddenly will become fat-free controllers because they delegate all the orchestration work to the application layer. Last but not least, the application layer is completely agnostic of the HTTP context and fully testable.

The Domain Layer

The domain layer is the part of the business logic that is, for the most part, invariant to use-cases. A use-case—namely, an interaction between the user and the system—can sometimes be different depending on the device used to access the site or the version of the site. The domain logic provides pieces of code and workflows that are specific to the business domain and not specific to the application functionality.

The domain layer is made of two classes of families—domain models and domain services. In the domain model, you focus on classes that express business rules and domain processes. You should not aim to identify aggregations of data to persist; instead, any aggregation you identify should simply descend from business understanding and modeling. As Figure 7-2 shows, domain layer classes are persistence-agnostic. You only use domain model classes to perform business tasks in a way that is easier for you to code.

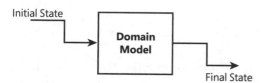

FIGURE 7-2 Classes in the domain model receive the state from the outside

The state is injected into a domain model class. For example, an Invoice class for a domain model knows how to deal with the invoice, but it receives the data to work on from the outside. The point of connection between the domain model and persistence layer is a domain service. A domain service is a class that sits on top of data access, brings data in, loads state into a domain model class, and takes the modified state out of the domain model class and puts it back into the data access layer.

The simplest and most illustrious example of a domain service is a repository. A domain service class typically holds a reference to the data access layer.

Important The idea of a domain model as described above is like the idea of a domain model that you find in Domain-driven Design (DDD). However, speaking pragmatically, the whole point of a domain model is business logic and behavior. Sometimes, modeling business rules through classes simplifies the design. This simplification is the added value of a domain model; certainly not the label "I do DDD" you can attach to your solution. For this reason, not all applications really need a domain model.

The Infrastructure Layer

The infrastructure layer is anything related to using concrete technologies, whether data persistence (O/RM frameworks like Entity Framework), external web services, specific security API, logging, tracing, IoC containers, email, caching, and more.

The most prominent component of the infrastructure layer is the persistence layer, which is nothing more than the old faithful data access layer, only extended to cover a few data sources other than plain relational data stores. The persistence layer knows how to read and/or save data and is made of repository classes.

Conceptually, a repository class is a class that only performs CRUD operations on persistence entities, such as Entity Framework entities. However, you can add any level of logic to the repository. The more logic you add to it the more it looks a like a domain service or an application service than a plain data access tool.

In summary, the point of the layered architecture is to set up a chain of dependencies that starts from the controller and reaches the bottom of the back end, passing through application services and consuming domain model classes, if any.

Dealing with Exceptions

In ASP.NET Core, you find many of the exception handling features found in classic ASP.NET MVC. You won't find anything that relates to sections of the *web.config* file, such as automatic redirects to error pages. However, the practices of ASP.NET Core exception handling are more or less the same as in classic ASP.NET.

In particular, ASP.NET Core offers exception handling middleware and controller-based exception filters.

Exception Handling Middleware

The exception handling middleware of ASP.NET Core offers a centralized error handler that conceptually matches the *Application_Error* handler of classic ASP.NET. The middleware captures any unhandled exceptions and uses your custom logic to route the request to the most appropriate error page.

There are two flavors of middleware tailor-made for two different audiences: developers and users. Reasonably, you might want to employ the user's page in production (or even in staging) and stick to the developer's page during development.

Error Handling in Production

Regardless of the middleware you choose, the way you configure it is always the same. You add the middleware to the pipeline using the *Configure* method of the startup class.

```
public class Startup
{
    public void Configure(IApplicationBuilder app)
    {
        app.UseExceptionHandler("/app/error");
        app.UseMvc();
    }
}
```

The *UseExceptionHandler* extension method receives a URL and places a new request for that URL right into the ASP.NET pipeline. In the end, the routing to the specified error page is not a canonical HTTP 302 redirect, but it has more of an internal prioritized request that the pipeline will process as usual.

From a developer's perspective, you "route" the user to a page that can figure out the most appropriate error message. In a way, error handling is decoupled from the main course of the application logic. At the same time, though, the internal nature of the error request gains the handling code full access to all the details of the detected exception. Note that in case of a classic redirect, the exception information would be lost unless you explicitly pass it around to the "next" request past the HTTP 302 response.

> **Note** The exception handling middleware should be placed at the very top of the pipeline to ensure that all possible exceptions that would not be caught by the application are detected.

Retrieving Exception Details

With the exception handling middleware properly configured, any unhandled exception would route the application flow to a common endpoint. In the above code snippet, the endpoint is the *Error* method on the *AppController* class. Here's a bare minimum implementation of the method. The most relevant segment is how to retrieve the exception information.

```
public IActionResult Error()
{
    // Retrieve error information
    var error = HttpContext.Features.Get<IExceptionHandlerFeature>();
    if (error == null)
        return View(model);
```

```
    // Use the information stored in the detected exception object
    var exception = error.Error;
    ...
}
```

Unlike classic ASP.NET, in ASP.NET Core, there's no intrinsic *Server* object with its popular *GetLastError* method. The *Features* object in the HTTP context is the official tool to retrieve uncleared exception information.

Capturing Status Codes

The code presented so far is sufficient to capture and handle any internal server errors (HTTP 500) that result from code execution. What if the status code is different? What if, for example, an exception occurs because the URL doesn't exist? To handle exceptions that would match to anything different from HTTP 500, you add another middleware.

```
app.UseStatusCodePagesWithReExecute("/app/error/{0}");
```

If a non-HTTP 500 exception is detected, the *UseStatusCodePagesWithReExecute* extension method routes the flow to the given URL. In light of this, the above error handling code should be revisited a bit.

```
public IActionResult Error(
    [Bind(Prefix = "id")] int statusCode = 0)
{
    // Switch to the appropriate page
    switch(statusCode)
    {
        case 404:
            return Redirect(...);
        ...
    }

    // Retrieve error information in case of internal errors
    var error = HttpContext.Features.Get<IExceptionHandlerFeature>();
    if (error == null)
        return View(model);

    // Use the information stored in the detected exception object
    var exception = error.Error;
    ...
}
```

In case of, say, an HTTP 404 error, it's up to you to redirect to a static page or view or to just adapt the error message in the same view served by the *Error* method.

Error Handling in Development

ASP.NET Core is extremely modular and nearly every feature you might want must be explicitly enabled. This holds true even for debugging error pages (classic ASP.NET developers used to call them "yellow pages of death"). To have actual messages and the stack trace unveiled in case of an exception, you should use yet another middleware.

```
app.UseDeveloperExceptionPage();
```

The middleware doesn't let you route to any custom page; it simply arranges on the fly a system error page that provides a snapshot of system status at the time of the exception (see Figure 7-3).

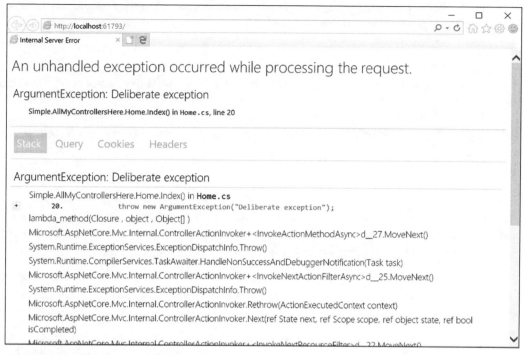

FIGURE 7-3 The developer's exception page

More often than not, you might want to switch between production and development exception handling middleware automatically. This is an easy win if you use the services of the hosting environment API.

```
Public void Configure(IApplicationBuilder app, IHostingEnvironment env)
{
    if (env.IsDevelopment())
    {
        app.UseDeveloperExceptionPage();
        app.UseStatusCodePagesWithReExecute("/app/error/{0}");
    }
    else
    {
        app.UseExceptionHandler("~/app/error");
        app.UseStatusCodePagesWithReExecute("/app/error/{0}");
    }
    ...
}
```

You use the *IHostingEnvironment* methods to detect the current environment and intelligently decide which exception middleware to turn on.

Exception Filters

As a general rule of good development, you should be using *try/catch* blocks around any piece of code that might possibly raise exceptions, such as remote web service or database calls. Also, you can use exception filters around controller code.

Setting Up an Exception Filter

Technically, an exception filter is an instance of a class that implements the *IExceptionFilter* interface, defined below.

```
public interface IExceptionFilter : IFilterMetadata
{
    void OnException(ExceptionContext context);
}
```

The filter is implemented in the *ExceptionFilterAttribute* and all its derived classes, including controller classes. This means that you can override the *OnException* method in any controller and use it as a catch-all handler for any exceptions that occur during the execution of a controller action or another filter attached to the controller or action method.

Exception filters can be configured to run globally, on a per-controller basis or even on a per-action basis. Exception filters are never called to handle exceptions outside the realm of a controller action.

> **Important** Exception filters won't let you catch model binding exceptions, route exceptions, and exceptions that would generate other than an HTTP 500 status code, most notably HTTP 404 but also authorization exceptions such as HTTP 401 and HTTP 403.

Handling Startup Exceptions

All the exception handling mechanisms examined so far operate in the context of the application pipeline. An exception, however, can also occur during the startup of the application well before the pipeline is fully configured. To capture startup exceptions, you must adjust the configuration of the *WebHostBuilder* class in *program.cs*.

In addition to all the settings we discussed in past chapters, you can add the *CaptureStartupErrors* setting, as shown below.

```
var host = new WebHostBuilder()
    ...
    .CaptureStartupErrors(true)
    .Build();
```

By default, the host silently exits when the startup process abruptly terminates because of an error. When *CaptureStartupErrors* is set to true, instead, the host will capture any exceptions from the startup class and attempts to display an error page. The page can be generic or detailed, based on the value of another setting you can add to the *WebHostBuilder* class.

```
var host = new WebHostBuilder()
    ...
    .CaptureStartupErrors(true)
    .UseSetting("detailedErrors", "true")
    .Build();
```

When the detailed-errors setting is enabled, the error page served has the same template as in Figure 7-3.

Logging Exceptions

In ASP.NET Core, exceptions processed through the *UseExceptionHandler* middleware are automatically logged, provided that at least one logger component is registered with the system. All logger instances pass through the system-provided logger factory, which is one of the few services added to the DI system by default.

Linking a Logging Provider

The ASP.NET Core Logging API is built on top of special components known as logging providers. A logging provider lets you send logs to one or more destinations such as the console, the Debug window, text files, a database, and the like. ASP.NET Core comes with a variety of built-in providers and also lets you plug in a custom provider.

A common way to link a logging provider to the system is via the extension methods on the *ILoggerFactory* service.

```
public void Configure(IApplicationBuilder app, ILoggerFactory loggerFactory)
{
    // Register two different logging providers
    loggerFactory.AddConsole();
    loggerFactory.AddDebug();
}
```

You can have as many logging providers as you wish in the same application. When adding a logging provider, you can also optionally add a log level, which means the provider will only receive messages with the appropriate relevance level.

Creating a Log

Logging providers work by storing messages in their respective destinations. A log is a related set of messages identified in some way (by name, for example). The code writes to a log through the services of the *ILogger* interface. You can create the logger in a couple of different ways.

First, you can create the logger right from the factory. The following code snippet shows how to create a logger and give it a unique name. Typically, the logger logs within the scope of a controller.

```
public class CustomerController : Controller
{
    ILogger logger;
```

```
    public CustomerController(ILoggerFactory loggerFactory)
    {
        logger = loggerFactory.CreateLogger("Customer Controller");
        logger.LogInformation("Some message here");
    }
}
```

The *CreateLogger* method gets the name of the log and creates it across registered providers. The *LogInformation* method is just one of the many methods that let you write to the log. The *ILogger* interface exposes one logging method for each supported log level, for example, (to eliminate fragment) *LogInformation* to output informational messages and *LogWarning* for more serious warning messages. Logging methods can accept plain strings, format strings, and even exception objects to serialize.

Alternatively, you can just resolve the *ILogger<T>* dependency through the DI system, thus bypassing the logger factory.

```
public class CustomerController : Controller
{
    ILogger Logger;

    public CustomerController(ILogger<CustomerController> logger)
    {
        Logger = logger;
    }

    // Use the internal member in the action methods
    ...
}
```

The log created here uses the full name of the controller class as a prefix.

Summary

To write an ASP.NET Core application, you must be acquainted with the DI system of the framework. It's a key change that makes you think more about the interface and concrete types. Programming to interfaces rather than implementations is old advice that holds true now. Interfaces are everywhere in ASP.NET Core, and they offer a way for developers to replace default functionalities with custom functionalities. The first example of interfaces used to pass data is configuration data. Another even more relevant example is the layered structure of the application code that stacks up controllers, application services, repositories, and optionally domain model classes.

What in past versions of ASP.NET was, for the most part, a best practice left to the discipline of individual teams and developers has been upgraded to the rank of common practice in ASP.NET Core. In ASP.NET Core, the quality of the resulting code is superior to any other versions of the framework because of the design. Most of the common best practices have been engineered right into the pillars of ASP.NET Core.

Another great example of common best practices engineered right in the framework will come in Chapter 8, which will discuss the API for securing access to an application.

CHAPTER 8

Securing the Application

There is no intelligence where there is no change and no need of change.

— *H. G. Wells, "The Time Machine"*

The security of web applications has many facets. First and foremost, in a web scenario, security relates to the act of ensuring the confidentiality of the data being exchanged. Second, it relates to avoiding tampering with the data thus ensuring that the integrity of the information is preserved as it travels end to end. Another aspect of web security is preventing injection of malicious code in the running application. Finally, security relates to building applications (and sections of an application) that only authenticated and authorized users can access.

In this chapter, we'll see how to implement user authentication in ASP.NET Core and explore the new policy-based API to deal with user authorization. Before we get there, though, a look at some infrastructure for security is in order.

Infrastructure for Web Security

The HTTP protocol was not designed with security in mind, but security was patched on it later. As obvious as it might sound, HTTP is not encrypted, which means third parties can still intercept and gather data that is being passed between two connected systems.

The HTTPS Protocol

HTTPS is the secured form of the HTTP protocol. By using it on a website, all communications between the browser and the website are encrypted. Any information going in and out of HTTPS pages is automatically encrypted in a way that ensures full confidentiality. Encryption is based on the content of a security certificate. The way in which data is sent depends upon the security protocols enabled on the web server, such as Transport Layer Security (TLS) and its predecessor, Secure Sockets Layer (SSL).

The first secure transportation protocol ever created was SSL, and it was created at Netscape back in 1995. It reached version 3.0 in a year, but it has not been updated since 1996. Clearly, SSL was an imperfect attempt at creating a secure protocol. TLS 1.0 was released in 1999, and it was designed to be incompatible with SSL 3.0 so that people would be forced to drop SSL and switch to TLS. In 2015, both SSL 2.0 and SSL 3.0 were deprecated. Today, it is highly recommended that you disable SSL 2.0 and SSL 3.0 in your web server configuration; only TLS 1.x should be enabled.

Dealing with Security Certificates

Quite often when talking about HTTPS and certificates, the expression *SSL certificate* is used. The expression seems to indicate that certificates are somewhat related to secure protocols. However, to be precise, certificates and protocols are different things. Hence, comparing SSL certificates to TLS certificates is a pointless argument.

The configuration of an HTTPS web server determines the secure protocols to use, and certificates only contain a pair of private/public encryption keys and bind the domain name and the identity of the owner.

As an end user, the major benefit of HTTPS is that when you visit the page of an HTTPS site—say, your online banking web site—you can be sure that the website claiming to be your bank's website really is your bank's website. In other words, the page you're viewing and interacting with is exactly the page it claims to be. As shocking as it might sound, this is not necessarily true for non-HTTPS pages. When HTTPS is not used, in fact, there's always the risk that the actual URL is fake or malicious, and that you're interacting with a page that only looks like the real page. For this reason, login pages should always be under HTTPS sites, and as a user, you should always be careful before signing in to a site from a non-HTTPS login page.

Applying Encryption to HTTPS

When your browser requests a web page located on an HTTPS connection, the website will initially react by returning the configured HTTPS certificate. The certificate contains the public key needed to arrange a secure conversation.

Next, the browser and the website will complete a handshake according to the rules of the configured protocols (typically TLS). If the browser trusts the certificate, it then generates a symmetric public/private key and shares the public key with the server.

Authentication in ASP.NET Core

User authentication is one of the most-changed parts in ASP.NET Core when compared to older versions of ASP.NET. However, the overall approach to authentication is still based on familiar concepts such as principal, login forms, and challenge and authorization attributes; however, the way you implement them is quite different. Let's explore the cookie authentication API as made available in ASP.NET Core, including the core facts of external authentication.

Cookie-based Authentication

In ASP.NET Core, user authentication involves the use of a cookie to track the identity of the user. Any users who attempt to visit a private page are redirected to a login page unless they carry a valid authentication cookie. The login page then collects credentials on the client side and verifies them on the server. If all is good, a cookie is emitted. The cookie travels with any subsequent requests from that user through the same browser until it expires. This workflow is not really different from any older versions of ASP.NET.

In ASP.NET Core, there are two major changes for those coming from an ASP.NET Web Forms and ASP.NET MVC background.

- First, there's no longer a *web.config* file, which means the configuration of the login path, cookie name, and expiration is specified and retrieved differently.

- Second, the *IPrincipal* object—the object used to model user identity—is based on claims rather than the sole plain username.

Enabling Authentication Middleware

To enable cookie authentication in a brand new ASP.NET Core application, you need to reference the *Microsoft.AspNetCore.Authentication.Cookies* package. The actual code entered into the application, however, is different in ASP.NET Core 2.0 compared to what it was in earlier versions of the same ASP.NET Core framework.

Authentication middleware is exposed as a service, and subsequently, it must be configured in the *ConfigureServices* method of the startup class.

```
public void ConfigureServices(IServiceCollection services)
{
    services.AddAuthentication(CookieAuthenticationDefaults.AuthenticationScheme)
        .AddCookie(options =>
        {
            options.LoginPath = new PathString("/Account/Login");
            options.Cookie.Name = "YourAppCookieName";
            options.ExpireTimeSpan = TimeSpan.FromMinutes(60);
            options.SlidingExpiration = true;
            options.AccessDeniedPath = new PathString("/Account/Denied");
            ...
        });
}
```

The *AddAuthentication* extension method gets a string as an argument that indicates the authentication scheme to use. You will go this route if you plan to support a single authentication scheme. Later, we'll see how to slightly tweak this code to support multiple schemes and handlers. The object returned by *AddAuthentication* must be used to call another method representing the authentication handler. In the example above, the *AddCookie* method instructs the framework to sign in and authenticate users via the configured cookie. Each authentication handler (cookie, bearer, and so on) has its own set of configuration properties.

In the *Configure* method, instead, you simply declare your intention to use authentication services as configured without specifying any further options.

```
public void Configure(IApplicationBuilder app)
{
    app.UseAuthentication();
    ...
}
```

There are a few names and concepts in the code snippet that deserve some further explanation—most notably, authentication schemes.

Cookie Authentication Options

Most of the information that classic ASP.NET MVC applications stored in the *<authentication>* section of the *web.config* file are now configured in code as middleware options. The snippet above listed some of the most common options you might want to choose. Table 8-1 provides more details about each option.

TABLE 8-1 Cookie authentication options

Option	Description
AccessDeniedPath	Indicates the path where an authenticated user will be redirected if the current identity doesn't have permission to view the requested resource. The option sets the URL the user must be redirected to instead of receiving a plain HTTP 403 status code.
Cookie	Container object of type *CookieBuilder* that contains properties of the authentication cookie being created.
ExpireTimeSpan	Sets the expiration time of the authentication cookie. Whether the time has to be intended as absolute or relative is determined by the value of the *SlidingExpiration* property.
LoginPath	Indicates the path where an anonymous user will be redirected to sign in with her own credentials.
ReturnUrlParameter	Indicates the name of the parameter being used to pass the originally requested URL that caused the redirect to the login page in case of anonymous users.
SlidingExpiration	Indicates whether the *ExpireTimeSpan* value is intended as an absolute or relative time. In the latter case, the value is considered as an interval, and the middleware will reissue the cookie if more than half the interval has elapsed.

Note that the value of path properties like *LoginPath* and *AccessDeniedPath* is not a string. In fact, *LoginPath* and *AccessDeniedPath* are of type *PathString*. In .NET Core, the type *PathString* differs from the plain *String* type because it provides correct escaping when building a request URL. In essence, it is a more URL-specific string type.

The overall design of the user authentication workflow in ASP.NET Core does allow an unprecedented amount of flexibility. Every single aspect of it can be customized at will. As an example, let's see how you can control the authentication workflow being used on a per-request basis.

Dealing with Multiple Authentication Schemes

It is interesting to notice that in past versions of ASP.NET, the authentication challenge was automatic and there was nearly nothing you could do about it. Automatic authentication challenge means that the system will automatically serve the configured login page as soon as it detects that the current user lacks proper identity information. In ASP.NET Core 1.x, the authentication challenge is automatic by default, but it is subject to your changes. In ASP.NET Core 2.0, settings to turn off automatic challenge have been dropped again.

In ASP.NET Core, however, you can register multiple and distinct pieces of authentication handlers and determine either algorithmically or via configuration which handler must be used for each request.

Enabling Multiple Authentication Handlers

In ASP.NET Core, you can choose from multiple authentication handlers such as cookie-based authentication, bearer authentication, authentication through social networks or an identity server, and whatever else you can ever think of and implement. To register multiple authentication handlers, you just list all the pieces one after the next in the *ConfigureServices* method of the ASP.NET Core 2.0 Startup class.

Each configured authentication handler is identified by a name. The name is just a conventional and arbitrary string you use in the application to refer to the handler. The name of the handler is known as the *authentication scheme*. The authentication scheme can be specified as a magic string, like Cookies or Bearer. However, for common cases, some predefined constants exist to limit typos when used in the code. If you use magic strings, then be aware that strings are treated as case-sensitive.

```
// Authentication scheme set to "Cookies"
services.AddAuthentication(options =>
{
    options.DefaultChallengeScheme = CookieAuthenticationDefaults.AuthenticationScheme;
    options.DefaultSignInScheme = CookieAuthenticationDefaults.AuthenticationScheme;
    options.DefaultAuthenticateScheme = CookieAuthenticationDefaults.AuthenticationScheme;
})
    .AddCookie(options =>
    {
        options.LoginPath = new PathString("/Account/Login");
        options.Cookie.Name = "YourAppCookieName";
        options.ExpireTimeSpan = TimeSpan.FromMinutes(60);
        options.SlidingExpiration = true;
        options.AccessDeniedPath = new PathString("/Account/Denied");
    })
    .AddOpenIdConnect(options =>
    {
        options.Authority = "http://localhost:6000";
        options.ClientId = "...";
        options.ClientSecret = "...";
        ...
    });
```

You simply concatenate handler definitions following a single call to *AddAuthentication*. At the same time, when multiple handlers are registered, you must indicate the default challenge, authentication and sign-in scheme of choice. In other words, you indicate which handler to use when the authentication is attempted on the presented token when the user is challenged to prove her identity at sign-in. In each handler, you can overwrite the sign-in scheme to meet your purposes.

Applying the Authentication Middleware

As in classic ASP.NET MVC, ASP.NET Core uses the *Authorize* attribute to decorate those controller classes or action methods subject to authentication.

```
[Authorize]
public class CustomerController : Controller
{
    // All action methods in this controller will
    // be subject to authentication except those explicitly
    // decorated with the AllowAnonymous attribute.
    ...
}
```

As pointed out in the code snippet, you can also use the *AllowAnonymous* attribute to mark a particular action method as anonymous and as such, not subject to authentication.

So the presence of the *Authorize* attribute on an action method restricts its use to only authenticated users. However, if multiple authentication middleware is available, which one should be applied? ASP.NET Core offers a new property on the *Authorize* attribute, which lets you choose the authentication scheme on a per request basis.

```
[Authorize(ActiveAuthenticationSchemes = "Bearer")]
public class ApiController : Controller
{
    // Your API action methods here
    ...
}
```

The net effect of this code snippet is that all public endpoints of the sample *ApiController* class are subject to the identity of the user as authenticated by the bearer token.

Modeling the User Identity

Any user logged into an ASP.NET Core application must be described in some unique way. In the early days of the web—when the ASP.NET Framework was first devised—the sole username was more than enough to uniquely identify a logged user. In older versions of ASP.NET, in fact, the username is all that gets saved in the authentication cookie and that models the user's identity.

There's a double level of information about users that is worth pointing out. Nearly all applications have some sort of users store in which all details about the users is saved. Data items in such a store have a primary key and many additional descriptive fields. When that user logs into the application, an authentication cookie is created, and some of the user-specific information is copied. At the very minimum, you must save in the cookie the unique value that identifies the user as it appears in the back end of the application. The authentication cookie, though, can also contain additional information strictly related to the security environment.

In summary, you typically have one entity in the domain and persistence layers that represents the user and a collection of name/value pairs that provide direct user information reading from the authentication cookie. These name/value pairs go under the name of *claims*.

Introducing Claims

In ASP.NET Core, claims are the content stored in the authentication cookie. All that you can store, as a developer, in an authentication cookie are claims—namely, name/value pairs. Compared to the past, there are many more pieces of information you can add to the cookie and read directly from there without fetching further data from the database.

You use claims to model the user identity. ASP.NET Core formalizes a long list of predefined claims, namely predefined key names aimed at storing certain well-known pieces of information. You are welcome to define additional claims. At the very end of the day, defining a claim is up to you and your application.

In the ASP.NET Core Framework, you find a *Claim* class that is designed around the layout below.

```
public class Claim
{
    public string Type { get; }
    public string Value { get; }
    public string Issuer { get; }
    public string OriginalIssuer { get; }
    public IDictionary<string, string> Properties { get; }

    // More properties
}
```

A claim has a property that identifies the type of the claim being made about the user. For example, the claim type is the role of the user in a given application. A claim also has a string value. For example, a value for the *Role* claim might be "admin." The description of a claim is completed by the name of an original issuer and also the name of the actual issuer in case the claim relays through intermediate issuers. Finally, a claim also can have a dictionary of additional properties to complement the value. All properties are read-only, and the constructor is the only way to push values. A claim is an immutable entity.

Using Claims in Code

Once the user has provided valid credentials (or, more generally, once the user has been bound to a known identity), the problem to solve is persisting key information about the recognized identity. As mentioned, in older versions of ASP.NET this was limited to storing the username. It's much more expressive in ASP.NET Core due to use of claims.

To prepare the user data to store in an authentication cookie, you typically proceed as follows:

```
// Prepare the list of claims to bind to the user's identity
var claims = new Claim[] {
    new Claim(ClaimTypes.Name, "123456789"),
    new Claim("display_name", "Sample User"),
    new Claim(ClaimTypes.Email, "sampleuser@yourapp.com"),
    new Claim("picture_url", "\images\sampleuser.jpg"),
    new Claim("age", "24"),
    new Claim("status", "Gold"),
    new Claim(ClaimTypes.Role, "Manager"),
    new Claim(ClaimTypes.Role, "Supervisor")
};
```

```
// Create the identity object from claims
var identity = new ClaimsIdentity(claims, CookieAuthenticationDefaults.AuthenticationScheme);

// Create the principal object from identity
var principal = new ClaimsPrincipal(identity);
```

You create an identity object—type *ClaimsIdentity*—from claims and create a principal object—type *ClaimsPrincipal*—from an identity object. When creating an identity, you also indicate the authentication scheme of choice (meaning you specify how to deal with claims). In the code snippet, the passed value of *CookieAuthenticationDefaults.AuthenticationScheme*—the string value of *Cookies*—indicates that claims will be stored in the authentication cookie.

There are a couple of things to notice in the above code snippet.

- First, the claim type is a plain string value, but many predefined constants exist for common types such as role, name, email. You can use your own strings or predefined strings exposed as constants out of the *ClaimTypes* class.

- Second, you can have multiple roles in the same list of claims.

Claim Assumptions

All claims are equal, but some claims are more equal than others. *Name* and *Role* are two claims that enjoy a (reasonable) special treatment from the ASP.NET Core infrastructure. Let's consider the following code:

```
var claims = new Claim[]
{
    new Claim("PublicName", userName),
    new Claim(ClaimTypes.Role, userRole),

    // More claims here
};
```

The list of claims has two elements—one named *PublicName* and one named *Role* (through the constant *ClaimTypes.Roles*). As you can see, no claim named Name exists. It's not an error, of course, as the list of claims is entirely up to you. However, having *Name* and *Role,* at least, is fairly common. The ASP.NET Core Framework provides an additional constructor for the *ClaimsIdentity* class that beyond the list of claims, and the authentication scheme also lets you indicate by name the claims in the given list that carry the identity's name and role.

```
var identity = new ClaimsIdentity(claims,
    CookieAuthenticationDefaults.AuthenticationScheme,
    "PublicName",
    ClaimTypes.Role);
```

The net effect of this code is that the claim named *Role* will be the role claim, as one would expect. Whether the provided list of claims contains a *Name* claim or not, the *PublicName* is the claim you should use as the name of the user.

The name and role are indicated in the list of claims because those two pieces of information will be used—mostly for backward compatibility with old ASP.NET code—to support the functions of the *IPrincipal* interface, such as *IsInRole* and *Identity.Name*. The roles specified in the list of claims will be automatically honored by the implementation of *IsInRole* in the *ClaimsPrincipal* class. Similarly, the name of the user defaults to the value of the claim appointed with the *Name* status.

In summary, *Name* and *Role* claims have default names, but you can override those names at will. The override takes place in one overloaded constructor of the *ClaimsIdentity* class.

Signing In and Signing Out

Having a principal object available is the necessary condition for signing in a user. The actual method that signs a user in, and in doing so creates the authentication cookie, is exposed by the HTTP context object under the name of *Authentication*.

```
// Gets the principal object
var principal = new ClaimsPrincipal(identity);

// Signs the user in (and creates the authentication cookie)
await HttpContext.SignInAsync(
        CookieAuthenticationDefaults.AuthenticationScheme,
        principal);
```

To be precise, the creation of the cookie during the sign-in process only happens if the authentication scheme is set to cookies. The exact sequence of operations that happen during the sign-in process depends on the handler for the selected authentication scheme.

The Authentication object is an instance of the *AuthenticationManager* class. The class has two more interesting methods: *SignOutAsync* and *AuthenticateAsync*. As the name suggests, the former method revokes the authentication cookies and signs the user out of the application.

```
await HttpContext.SignOutAsync(
        CookieAuthenticationDefaults.AuthenticationScheme);
```

When calling the method, you must indicate the authentication scheme from which you want to sign out. The *AuthenticateAsync* method instead just validates the cookie and checks to see if the user is authenticated. Also, in this case, the attempt to validate the cookie is based on the selected authentication scheme.

Reading Content of Claims

ASP.NET Core authentication is half a familiar world and half an unknown space—especially for those coming from years of classic ASP.NET programming. In classic ASP.NET, once the system has processed the authentication cookie, the username is easily accessible, and that's the only piece of information available by default. If more information about the user must be available, you create your own claims and serialize their content into the cookie, essentially creating your own principal object. Recently, support for claims has been added to classic ASP.NET. Using claims is the only way to work in ASP.NET Core. When you create your own principal, you make yourself responsible for reading the content of the claims.

The *ClaimsPrincipal* instance that you access programmatically via the *HttpContext.User* property has a programming interface to query for specific claims. Here's an example taken from a Razor view.

```
@if(User.Identity.IsAuthenticated)
{
    var pictureClaim = User.FindFirst("picture_url");
    if (pictureClaim != null)
    {
            var picture = pictureClaim.Value;
            <img src="@picture" alt="" />
    }
}
```

When rendering a page, you might want to show the avatar of the logged user. Assuming that this information is available as a claim, the code above shows the LINQ-friendly code to query for claims. The *FindFirst* method returns only the first of possibly multiple claims with the same name. If you want to take all of them, then you use the *FindAll* method instead. To read the actual value of the claim, you expand on the *Value* property.

> **Note** Once the login page credentials have been verified, you have the problem of getting hold of all the claims you want to persist in the cookie. Note that the more information you store in the cookie, the more user information you have available nearly for free. Sometimes, you can store a user key in the cookie, and once the sign-in begins, you use the key to retrieve the matching record from the database. This is more expensive but ensures the user information is always up to date, and it allows updates without logging the user out and in again when creating the cookie. The actual content for the claims should be read from locations you determine. For instance, claims content can come from a database, the cloud, or Active Directory.

External Authentication

External authentication refers to using an external and properly configured service to authenticate users coming to your website. In general terms, external authentication is a win-win situation. External authentication is good for end users who don't have to create one account for each website to which they intend to register. Also, external authentication is good for the developer who doesn't have to add critical boilerplate code and store and check the user's credentials for each website she sets up. Not just any website can serve as an external authentication server. An external authentication server requires the availability of specific features, but nearly any current social network can act as an external authentication service.

Adding Support for External Authentication Services

ASP.NET Core supports external authentication via identity providers from the ground up. Most of the time, all you do is install the appropriate NuGet package for the job. For example, if you want to allow your users to authenticate using their Twitter credentials, the first thing you do in your project is bring in the *Microsoft.AspNetCore.Authentication.Twitter* package and install the related handler:

```
services.AddAuthentication(TwitterDefaults.AuthenticationScheme)
  .AddTwitter(options =>
  {
      options.SignInScheme = CookieAuthenticationDefaults.AuthenticationScheme;
      options.ConsumerKey = "...";
      options.ConsumerSecret = "...";
  });
```

The *SignInScheme* property is the identifier of the authentication handler that will be used to persist the resulting identity. In this example, an authentication cookie will be used. To see the effects of the above middleware, add a controller method to trigger the Twitter-based authentication. Below is an example.

```
public async Task TwitterAuth()
{
   var props = new AuthenticationProperties
   {
      RedirectUri = "/"  // Where to go after authenticating
   };

   await HttpContext.ChallengeAsync(TwitterDefaults.AuthenticationScheme, props);
}
```

The internals of the Twitter handler knows which URL to contact to pass the application's identity (consumer key and secret) and enable a user's validation. If all goes well, the user is shown the familiar Twitter authentication page. If the user is already authenticated on the local device to Twitter, then she's only asked to confirm that it is okay to grant the given application permission to operate on Twitter on behalf of the user.

Figure 8-1 shows the confirmation page from Twitter that shows when a sample application attempts to authenticate a user.

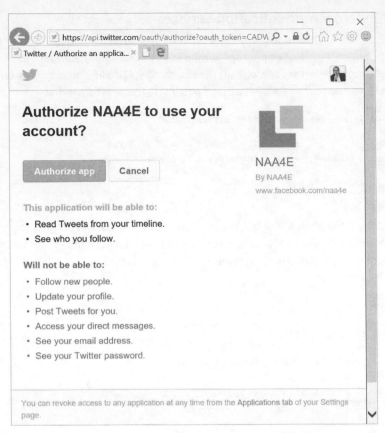

FIGURE 8-1 As a Twitter user, you're now authorizing the app to act on behalf of you

Next, once Twitter has successfully authenticated the user, the *SignInScheme* property instructs the application on what to do next. A value of "Cookies" is acceptable if you want a cookie from the claims returned by the external provider (Twitter, in the example). If you want to review and complete the information through, say, an intermediate form, then you have to break the process in two by introducing a temporary sign-in scheme. I'll get back to this more sophisticated scenario in a moment. For now, let's complete the tour of what happens in a simpler scenario.

The *RedirectUri* option indicates where to go once authentication has successfully completed. In such a simple scenario in which you only rely on the list of claims provided by the authentication service, you have no control over the data you know about each user who signs in to your system. The list of claims returned by default by the various social networks is not homogeneous. For example, if users connect through Facebook, you might have the user's email address. However, you might not have the email address if the user connects through Twitter or Google. It's not a big deal if you only support one social network, but if you support many of them—and the number might grow over time—then you have to set up an intermediate page to normalize information and ask users to enter all the claims you currently lack.

Figure 8-2 shows the workflow that sets up between the client browser, the web application, and the external authentication service when access is made to a protected resource that requires a login.

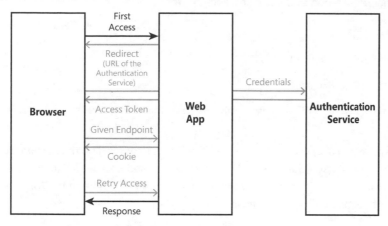

FIGURE 8-2 The full workflow, when access is made to a protected resource and authentication, is provided via an external service

This illustration shows three boxes representing the browser, the web application, and the authentication service. At the top, a bold arrow connects the box "Browsers" with the box "Web App." At the bottom, another arrow connects the box "Web App" with the box "Browsers." Other grayed arrows indicate the various steps of the process of authenticating users via an external service.

Requiring Completion of Information

To gather additional information after the external service has authenticated the user, you need to tweak a bit the service configuration. Essentially, you add another handler to the list, as shown below.

```
services.AddAuthentication(options =>
{
    options.DefaultChallengeScheme = CookieAuthenticationDefaults.AuthenticationScheme;
    options.DefaultSignInScheme = CookieAuthenticationDefaults.AuthenticationScheme;
    options.DefaultAuthenticateScheme = CookieAuthenticationDefaults.AuthenticationScheme;
})
    .AddCookie(options =>
    {
        options.LoginPath = new PathString("/Account/Login");
        options.Cookie.Name = "YourAppCookieName";
        options.ExpireTimeSpan = TimeSpan.FromMinutes(60);
        options.SlidingExpiration = true;
        options.AccessDeniedPath = new PathString("/Account/Denied");
    })
    .AddTwitter(options =>
    {
        options.SignInScheme = "TEMP";
        options.ConsumerKey = "...";
        options.ConsumerSecret = "...";
    })
    .AddCookie("TEMP");
```

When the external Twitter provider returns, a temporary cookie is created using the *TEMP* scheme. By setting the redirect path appropriately in the controller method that challenges the user, you have a chance to inspect the principal returned by Twitter and edit it further:

```
public async Task TwitterAuthEx()
{
    var props = new AuthenticationProperties
    {
        RedirectUri = "/account/external"
    };
    await HttpContext.ChallengeAsync(TwitterDefaults.AuthenticationScheme, props);
}
```

Twitter (or whatever service you use) will now redirect to the *External* method on the *Account* controller to complete your own workflow. When the *External* method is called back, it's all up to you. You might want to show an HTML form to collect additional information. In the building of this form, you might want to use the list of claims on the given principal.

```
public async Task<IActionResult> External()
{
    var principal = await HttpContext.AuthenticateAsync("TEMP");

    // Access the claims on the principal and prepare an HTML
    // form that prompts only for the missing information
    ...

    return View();
}
```

The user is then presented the form and fills it out; your form code validates the data and posts back. In the body of the controller method where you save the content of the completion form, you need to perform a couple of key steps before leaving. You retrieve the principal as shown above and then you sign in to the cookies scheme and sign out of the temporary *TEMP* scheme. Here's the code:

```
await HttpContext.SignInAsync(CookieAuthenticationDefaults.AuthenticationScheme, principal);
await HttpContext.SignOutAsync("TEMP");
```

At this point—and only at this point—the authentication cookie is created.

> **Note** In the previous sample code, *TEMP*, as well as *CookieAuthenticationDefaults.AuthenticationScheme*, are just internal identifiers; they can be renamed as long as they remain consistent throughout the application.

Issues of External Authentication

External authentication, such as via Facebook or Twitter, is sometimes cool for the users but not always. As usual, it is a matter of tradeoff. So, let's list a few challenges you have to face when using it in your applications.

First, users must log in to the social network or identity server of your choice. They might or might not love the idea of using existing credentials. In general, social authentication should always be provided as an option unless the application itself is so tightly integrated with a social network or so social itself to justify the reliance on the sole external authentication. Always consider that users might not have an account to the social network you're supporting.

From a development perspective, external authentication means that the effort to configure authentication is duplicated in each application. More often than not, you have to deal with user registration and fill up all required fields anyway, which means a lot of work as far as account management is concerned on your end. Finally, you have to maintain a link between the account in your local users store with an external account.

In the end, external authentication is not exactly a time-saver approach. It should be seen as a feature you offer to users of your application if justified by nature of the application itself.

Authenticating Users via ASP.NET Identity

So far, you have read about the fundamentals of user authentication in ASP.NET Core. An entire universe of features, however, lies behind user authentication. It usually goes under the name of membership system. A membership system doesn't simply manage the process of user authentication and identity data; it also deals with user management, password hashing, validation and reset, roles and their management and even more advanced functions such as two-factor authentication (2FA).

Building a custom membership system is not a huge task, but it's likely a repetitive task, and it's the classic wheel you have to reinvent every time, and for every application you build. At the same time, a membership system is not that easy to abstract into something that you can reuse across multiple applications with minimal overhead. Many attempts at it have been made over the years, and Microsoft itself counts a few of them. My personal take on membership systems is that if you're going to write and maintain multiple systems of the same complexity, you probably want to invest some time and build your own system with your own extensibility points. In other cases, the choice is between two extremes—a plain user authentication as discussed earlier in the chapter or ASP.NET Identity.

Generalities of ASP.NET Identity

ASP.NET Identity is a full-fledged, comprehensive, large framework that provides an abstraction layer over a membership system. As is, it is overkill if all you need is to authenticate users via plain credentials read out of a simple database table. At the same time, though, ASP.NET Identity is designed to decouple storage from the security layer. So, in the end, it provides a rich API with plenty of extensibility points for you to adapt things to your context while also including an API that often you only have to configure.

Configuring ASP.NET Identity means indicating the details of the storage layer (both relational and object-oriented) and the details of the identity model that best represents your users. Figure 8-3 illustrates the architecture of ASP.NET Identity.

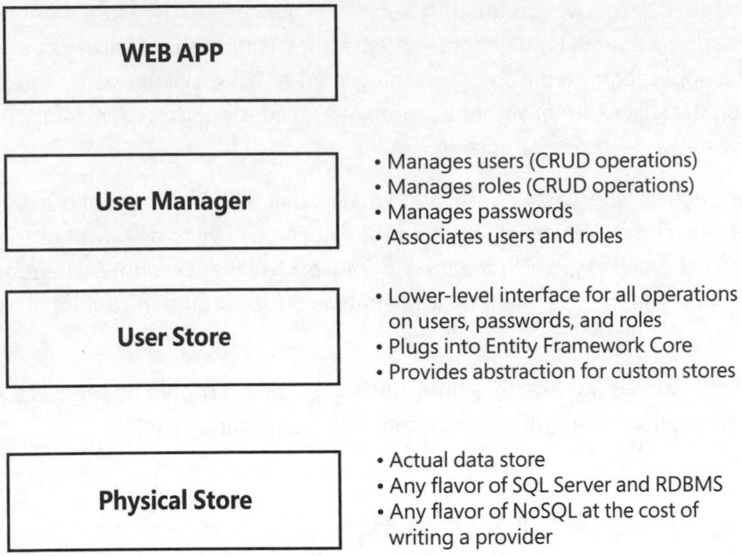

FIGURE 8-3 Overall architecture of ASP.NET Identity

The User Manager

The User Manager is the central console from which you conduct all of the operations supported by ASP.NET Identity. As mentioned, this includes an API to query for existing users, create new users, and update or delete users. The User Manager also provides methods to support password management, external logins, role management, and even more advanced features, such as user lockout, 2FA, emailing in case of need, and password strength validation.

In code, you invoke the above functions through the services of the *UserManager<TUser>* class. The generic type refers to the provided abstraction of the user entity. In other words, through the class, you can perform all coded tasks on the given model of the user.

User Identity Abstraction

In ASP.NET Identity, the model of the user identity becomes a parameter that you inject in the machinery, and it more or less works transparently because of the user identity abstraction mechanism and the underlying user store abstraction.

ASP.NET Identity provides a base user class that already contains many common properties you want to have on a user entity, such as a primary key, username, password hash, email address, and phone number. ASP.NET Identity also provides more sophisticated properties, such as email confirmation, lockout state, access failed count, and a list of roles and logins. The base user class in ASP.NET Identity is *IdentityUser*. You can use it directly or just derive your own class from it.

```
public class YourAppUser : IdentityUser
{
```

```
    // App-specific properties
    public string Picture { get; set; }
    public string Status { get; set; }
}
```

The *IdentityUser* class has some aspects hard-coded into the framework. The *Id* property is treated as the primary key when the class is saved to a database. This aspect can't be changed, even though I can hardly think of a reason for doing it. The primary key is rendered as a string by default, but even the type of the primary key has been abstracted in the design of the framework, so you can change it to your liking when deriving from *IdentityUser*.

```
public class YourAppUser : IdentityUser<int>
{
    // App-specific properties
    public string Picture { get; set; }
    public string Status { get; set; }
}
```

The *Id* property, in fact, is defined as follows:

```
public virtual TKey Id { get; set; }
```

> **Note** In older versions of ASP.NET Identity—for classic ASP.NET—the primary key was ren-
> dered as a GUID, and that has created a bit of an issue in some applications. In ASP.NET Core,
> you can use GUID if you want.

User Store Abstraction

The identity user class is saved to some persistence layer through the services of some storage API. The favorite API is based on Entity Framework Core, but the abstraction of the user store lets you plug in virtually any framework out there that knows how to store information. The main storage interface is *IUserStore<TUser>*. Here's an excerpt from it.

```
public interface IUserStore<TUser, in TKey> : IDisposable where TUser : class, IUser<TKey>
{
    Task CreateAsync(TUser user);
    Task UpdateAsync(TUser user);
    Task DeleteAsync(TUser user);
    Task<TUser> FindByIdAsync(TKey userId);
    Task<TUser> FindByNameAsync(string userName);
    ...
}
```

As you can see, the abstraction is a plain CRUD API on top of the identity user class. The query functionality is pretty basic because it only lets you retrieve users by name or ID.

However, a concrete ASP.NET Identity user store is much more than the *IUserStore* interface sug-gests. Table 8-2 lists storage interfaces for additional features.

TABLE 8-2 Some additional storage interfaces

Additional interface	Purpose
IUserClaimStore	The interface groups functions to store claims about the user. This is useful if you store claims as distinct pieces of information from the properties of the User entity itself.
IUserEmailStore	The interface groups functions to store email information, for example for password reset.
IUserLockoutStore	The interface groups functions to store lockout data to track brute force attacks.
IUserLoginStore	The interface groups functions to store linked accounts obtained through external providers.
IUserPasswordStore	The interface groups functions to store passwords and perform related operations.
IUserPhoneNumberStore	The interface groups functions to store phone information to use in 2FA.
IUserRoleStore	The interface groups functions to store role information.
IUserTwoFactorStore	The interface groups functions to store user information related to 2FA.

All those interfaces are implemented by the actual user store. If you create a custom user store—for example, one that targets a custom SQL Server schema or a custom NoSQL store—you are responsible for the implementation. ASP.NET Identity comes with an Entity Framework-based user store available through the *Microsoft.AspNetCore.Identity.EntityFrameworkCore* NuGet package. The store supports the interfaces listed in Table 8-2.

Configuring ASP.NET Identity

To start working with ASP.NET Identity, you first need to select (or create) a user store component and set up the underlying database. Assuming you opt for the Entity Framework user store, the first thing you must do is create a *DbContext* class in your application. The role of the *DbContext* class and all of its dependencies will be fully explained in Chapter 9, which is entirely devoted to Entity Framework Core.

In brief, a *DbContext* class represents the central console to access a database programmatically via Entity Framework. A *DbContext* class for use with ASP.NET Identity inherits from a system-provided base class (the *IdentityDbContext* class) and contains a *DbSet* class for users and other entities such as logins, claims, and emails. Here's how you lay out a class.

```
public class YourAppDatabase : IdentityDbContext<YourAppUser>
{
    ...
}
```

To configure the connection string to the actual database, you use normal Entity Framework Core code. More on this in a moment and then in Chapter 9.

In the *IdentityDbContext,* you inject the user identity class and also many other optional components. Here's the complete signature of the class.

```
public class IdentityDbContext<TUser, TRole, TKey, TUserLogin, TUserRole, TUserClaim> :
        DbContext
    where TUser : IdentityUser<TKey, TUserLogin, TUserRole, TUserClaim>
    where TRole : IdentityRole<TKey, TUserRole>
```

```
    where TUserLogin : IdentityUserLogin<TKey>
    where TUserRole : IdentityUserRole<TKey>
    where TUserClaim : IdentityUserClaim<TKey>
{
    ...
}
```

As you can see, you can inject the user identity, the role type, the primary key of the user identity, the type to use to link external logins, the type to use to represent user/role mappings, and the type to represent claims.

The final step to enable ASP.NET Identity is to register the framework with ASP.NET Core. This step occurs in the *ConfigureServices* method of the startup class.

```
public void ConfigureServices(IServiceCollection services)
{
    // Grab the connection string to use (or have it fixed)
    // Assume Configuration is set in the Startup class constructor (see Ch.7)
    var connString = Configuration.GetSection("database").Value;

    // Normal EF code to register a DbContext around a SQL Server database
    services.AddDbContext<YourAppDatabase>(options =>
            options.UseSqlServer(connString));

    // Attach the previously created DbContext to the ASP.NET Identity framework
    services.AddIdentity<YourAppUser, IdentityRole>()
            .AddEntityFrameworkStores<YourIdentityDatabase>();
}
```

Once the connection string to connect the database of choice is known, you use normal Entity Framework code to inject the *DbContext* of the given database in the ASP.NET Core stack. Next, you register the user identity role model, the role identity model, and the Entity Framework-based user store.

At configuration time, you also can indicate parameters for the authentication cookie to be created. Here's an example.

```
services.ConfigureApplicationCookie(options =>
{
    options.Cookie.HttpOnly = true;
    options.Cookie.Expiration = TimeSpan.FromMinutes(20);
    options.LoginPath = new PathString("/Account/Login");
    options.LogoutPath = new PathString("/Account/Logout");
    options.AccessDeniedPath = new PathString("/Account/Denied");
    options.SlidingExpiration = true;
});
```

Similarly, you can also change the cookie name and, in general, gain full control over the cookie.

Working with the User Manager

The *UserManager* object is the central object through which you use and administer the membership system based on ASP.NET Identity. You don't create an instance of it directly; an instance of it is silently registered with the DI system when you register ASP.NET Identity at startup.

```
public class AccountController : Controller
{
    UserManager<YourAppUser> _userManager;

    public AccountController(UserManager<YourAppUser> userManager)
    {
        _userManager = userManager;
    }

    // More code here
    ...
}
```

In any controller class where you need to use it, you just inject it in some way; for example, you could inject it through the constructor, as shown in the previous code snippet.

Dealing with Users

To create a new user, you call the *CreateAsync* method and pass to it the user object in use in the application with ASP.NET Identity. The method returns an *IdentityResult* value which contains a list of error objects and a Boolean property to denote success or failure.

```
public class IdentityResult
{
    public IEnumerable<IdentityError> Errors { get; }
    public bool Succeeded { get; protected set; }
}

public class IdentityError
{
    public string Code { get; set; }
    public string Description { get; set; }
}
```

There are two overloads for the *CreateAsync* method: one only takes the user object, and the other also accepts a password. The former method just doesn't set any password for the user. By using the method *ChangePasswordAsync,* you can set or change the password later.

When adding users to a membership system, you face the problem of determining how and where to validate the consistency of the data being added into the system. Should you have a user class that knows how to validate itself, or should you have validation deployed as a separate layer? ASP.NET Identity opted for the latter pattern. The interface *IUserValidator<TUser>* can be supported to implement any custom validator for the given type.

```
public interface IUserValidator<TUser>
{
    Task<IdentityResult> ValidateAsync(UserManager<TUser> manager, TUser user)
}
```

You create the class that implements the interface and then registers it with the DI system at application startup.

A user in the membership system can be deleted with a call to *DeleteAsync*. The method has the same signature as *CreateAsync*. To update the state of an existing user, instead, you have many predefined methods, such as *SetUserNameAsync*, *SetEmailAsync*, *SetPhoneNumberAsync*, *SetTwoFactorEnabledAsync*, and more. To edit claims, you have methods like *AddClaimAsync*, *RemoveClaimAsync*, and similar methods to deal with logins.

Every time you call a specific update method, a call to the underlying user store is performed. Alternatively, you can edit the user object in memory and then apply all changes in a batch mode using the *UpdateAsync* method.

Fetching Users

The ASP.NET Identity membership system provides two patterns for fetching user data. You can query the user object by parameter, whether ID, email, or username, or you can use LINQ. The following code snippet illustrates the use of a few query methods.

```
var user1 = await _userManager.FindByIdAsync(123456);
var user2 = await _userManager.FindByNameAsync("dino");
var user3 = await _userManager.FindByEmailAsync("dino@yourapp.com");
```

If the user store supports the *IQueryable* interface, you can build any LINQ query on top of the *Users* collections exposed from the *UserManager* object.

```
var emails = _userManager.Users.Select(u => u.Email);
```

If you only need a specific piece of information, such as the email or the phone number, then you can do it with a single API call—*GetEmailAsync*, *GetPhoneNumberAsync*, and the like.

Dealing with Passwords

In ASP.NET Identity, passwords are automatically hashed using the RFC2898 algorithm with ten thousand iterations. From a security perspective, it's an extremely safe way to store passwords. The hashing takes place through the services of the *IPasswordHasher* interface. As usual, you can replace the hasher with your own by adding a new hasher to the DI system.

To validate the strength of the password—and to refuse weak ones—you can rely on the built-in validator infrastructure and just configure it, or you can create your own. Configuring the built-in validators means setting minimum length and determining whether letters and/or digits are required. Here's an example:

```
public void ConfigureServices(IServiceCollection services)
{
    services.AddIdentity<YourAppUser, IdentityRole>(options=>
    {
        // At least 6 characters long and digits required
        options.Password.RequireUppercase = false;
        options.Password.RequireLowercase = false;
```

```
            options.Password.RequireDigit = true;
            options.Password.RequiredLength = 6;
      })
      .AddEntityFrameworkStores<YourDatabase>();
}
```

To use a custom password validator, you create a class that implements *IPasswordValidator* and register it with *AddPasswordValidator* at application startup after calling *AddIdentity*.

Dealing with Roles

At the end of the day, roles are just claims, and in fact, earlier in the chapter, we have seen that a predefined claim exists named *Role*. Speaking abstractly, a role is just a string with no permission and logic mapped to it that describes the role a user can play in the application. Mapping logic and permissions to roles is necessary to spice up the application and make it realistic. This responsibility, though, belongs to the developer.

However, in the context of a membership system, the intent of roles is much more specific. A membership system like ASP.NET Identity contains much of the work a developer should otherwise do herself to save and retrieve users and related information. Part of the work a membership system does is to map users to roles. In this context, a role becomes a list of things the user can or cannot do with the application. In ASP.NET Core and ASP.NET Identity, a role is a named group of claims saved in the user store.

In an ASP.NET Identity application claims, users, supported roles, and mappings between users and roles are stored separately. All operations that involve roles are grouped in the *RoleManager* object. Like the *UserManager* object, also *RoleManager* is added to the DI system when the call to *AddIdentity* is made at application startup. Likewise, you inject an instance of *RoleManager* in a controller via DI. Roles are stored in a distinct role store. In the EF scenario, it's simply a distinct table in the same SQL Server database.

Managing roles programmatically is nearly identical to managing users programmatically. Here's an example of how to create a role.

```
// Define the ADMIN role
var roleAdmin = new IdentityRole
{
    Name = "Admin"
};

// Create the ADMIN role in the ASP.NET Identity system
var result = await _roleManager.CreateAsync(roleAdmin);
```

In ASP.NET Identity, a role is ineffective until users are mapped to it.

```
var user = await _userManager.FindByNameAsync("dino");
var result = await _userManager.AddToRoleAsync(user, "Admin");
```

To add users to a role, you use the API of the *UserManager* class though. In addition to *AddToRoleAsync*, the manager features methods like *RemoveFromRoleAsync* and *GetUsersInRoleAsync*.

Authenticating Users

Authenticating users with ASP.NET Identity requires many steps because of the complexity and sophistication of the framework. Steps involve operations like validating credentials, handling failed attempts and locking users out, dealing with disabled users, and handling 2FA logic (if the feature is enabled). Then you must populate the *ClaimsPrincipal* object with claims and issue the authentication cookie.

All the steps are encapsulated in the API exposed by the *SignInManager* class. The sign-in manager is obtained via DI in the same way you have seen for *UserManager* and *RoleManager* objects. To perform all the steps of a login page, you use the *PasswordSignInAsync* method.

```
public async Task<IActionResult> Login(string user, string password, bool rememberMe)
{
    var shouldConsiderLockout = true;
    var result = await _signInManager.PasswordSignInAsync(
                         user, password, rememberMe, shouldConsiderLockout);
    if (result.Succeeded)
    {
        // Redirect where needed
        ...
    }
    return View("error", result);
}
```

The *PasswordSignInAsync* method takes the username and password (as clear text) and also a couple of Boolean flags to denote the persistence nature of the resulting authentication cookie and whether lockout should be considered.

 Note User lockout is an ASP.NET Identity built-in feature by means of which users can be disabled from logging into the system. The feature is controlled by two pieces of information—whether the lockout is enabled for the application and the lockout end date. You have ad hoc methods to enable and disable lockout, and you have ad hoc methods to set the lockout end date. A user is active either if the lockout is disabled or if the lockout is enabled, but the current date is past lockout end date.

The outcome of the sign-in process is summarized by the *SignInResult* type, which informs whether authentication was successful, 2FA is required, or if the user is locked out.

Authorization Policies

The authorization layer of a software application ensures that the current user is allowed to access a given resource, perform a given operation, or perform a given operation on a given resource. In ASP.NET Core, there are two ways to set up an authorization layer. You can use roles, or you can use policies. The former approach—role-based authorization—has been maintained from previous versions of the ASP.NET platform. Policy-based authorization instead is completely new to ASP.NET Core and quite powerful and flexible, too.

Role-based Authorization

Authorization is one step further than authentication. Authentication is about discovering the identity of a user to track its activity and only allow known users into the system. Authorization is more specific and is about defining requirements for users to call into predefined appllications' endpoints. Common examples of tasks subject to permissions and subsequently to the authorization layer include showing or hiding elements of the user interface, executing actions, or just flowing through to other services. In ASP.NET, roles are a common way to implement an authorization layer since the early days.

Technically speaking, a role is a plain string with no attached behavior. Its value, however, is treated as meta information by the ASP.NET and ASP.NET Core security layers. For example, both layers check roles for presence in the principal object. (See the method *IsInRole* in the identity object in the principal.) Beyond this, roles are used by applications to grant permissions to all users in that role.

In ASP.NET Core, the availability of role information in the claims of a logged user depends on the backing identity store. If you use social authentication, for example, you're never going to see roles at all. A user who authenticates through Twitter or Facebook won't bring any role information that might be significant for your application. However, your application might assign a role to that user based on internal and domain-specific rules.

In summary, roles are just meta information that the application—and only the application—can turn into permissions for doing or not doing certain things. The ASP.NET Core Framework only provides a bit of an infrastructure to persist, retrieve, and carry roles. The list of supported roles and mappings between users and roles is typically stored in the underlying membership system (whether custom or based on ASP.NET Identity) and is retrieved when the user credentials are validated. Next, in some way, the role information is attached to the user account and is exposed to the system. The *IsInRole* method on the identity object (*ClaimsIdentity* in ASP.NET Core) is the lever used to implement role-based authorization.

The *Authorize* Attribute

The *Authorize* attribute is the declarative way to secure a controller or just some of its methods.

```
[Authorize]
public class CustomerController : Controller
{
    ...
}
```

Note that if specified without arguments, the *Authorize* attribute only checks if the user is authenticated. In the code snippet above, all users who can successfully sign in to the system are equally enabled to call into any methods of the *CustomerController* class. To select only a subset of users, you use roles.

The *Roles* property on the *Authorize* attribute indicates that only users in any of the listed roles would be granted access to the controller methods. In the code below, both *Admin* and *System* users are equally enabled to call into the *BackofficeController* class.

```
[Authorize(Roles="Admin, System")]
public class BackofficeController : Controller
{
   ...

   [Authorize(Roles="System")]
   public IActionResult Reset()
   {
      // You MUST be a SYSTEM user to get here
      ...
   }

   [Authorize]
   public IActionResult Public()
   {
      // You just need be authenticated and can view this
      // regardless of role(s) assigned to you
      ...
   }

   [AllowAnonymous)]
   public IActionResult Index()
   {
      // You don't need to be authenticated to get here
      ...
   }
}
```

The *Index* method doesn't require authentication at all. The *Public* method just requires an authenticated user. The method *Reset* strictly requires a System user. All other methods you might have work with either an Admin or a System user.

If multiple roles are required to access a controller, you can apply the *Authorize* attribute multiple times. Alternatively, you can always write your own authorization filter. In the code below, only users who have the *Admin* and the *System* role will be granted permission to call into the controller.

```
[Authorize(Roles="Admin")]
[Authorize(Roles="System")]
public class BackofficeController : Controller
{
   ...
}
```

Optionally, the *Authorize* attribute also can accept one or more authentication schemes through the *ActiveAuthenticationSchemes* property.

```
[Authorize(Roles="Admin, System", ActiveAuthenticationSchemes="Cookies")]
public class BackofficeController : Controller
{
   ...
}
```

The *ActiveAuthenticationSchemes* property is a comma-separated string listing the authentication components the authorization layer will trust in the current context. In other words, it states that access to the *BackofficeController* class is allowed only if the user is authenticated through the *Cookies* scheme and has any of the listed roles. As mentioned, string values passed to the *ActiveAuthenticationSchemes* property must comply with the handlers registered with the authentication service at the startup of the application. Subsequently, an authentication scheme is essentially a label that selects a handler.

Authorization Filters

The information provided by the *Authorize* attribute is consumed by a predefined, system-provided authorization filter. This filter runs before any of the other ASP.NET Core filters because it is responsible for checking whether the user can perform the requested operation. If not, the authorization filter short-circuits the pipeline and cancels the current requests.

Custom authorization filters can be created, but you usually don't need to do it. It is preferable, in fact, to configure the existing authorization layer on which the default filter relies.

Roles, Permissions, and Overrules

Roles are an easy way to group the users of an application based on what they can or cannot do. Roles, however, are not very expressive; at least not enough for the needs of most modern applications. For example, consider a relatively simple authorization architecture: regular users of the site and power users authorized to access the back-office and to update the content. A role-based authorization layer can be built around two roles—user and admin. Based on that, you define which controllers and methods each group of users can access.

The problem is that in the real world, things are rarely so simple. In the real world, often you run into subtle distinctions of what a user can or cannot do within a given user role. You have roles, but you need to make exceptions and overrules. For example, among the users who can be given access to the back-office, some are only authorized to edit customer data, some should only work on contents, and some can do both. How would you render an authorization scheme like that of Figure 8-4?

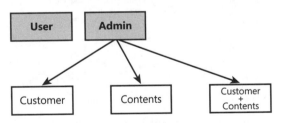

FIGURE 8-4 Roles and overrules to roles

This is an illustration made by a diagram of boxes and arrows. The box "User" and the box "Admin" have a gray background, and the box "Admin" has outbound arrows that connect it to other white boxes labeled "Customer," "Contents," and "Customer + Contents," respectively.

Roles are essentially flat concepts. How would you flatten out even a simple hierarchy like that shown in Figure 8-4? For example, you can create four different roles: *User, Admin, CustomerAdmin,* and *ContentsAdmin.* The *Admin* role will be the union of CustomerAdmin and ContentsAdmin.

It works, but when the number of overrules—which are strictly business specific—grows, the number of required roles will increase significantly.

The bottom line is that roles are not necessarily the most effective way to handle authorizations, though they are useful for backward compatibility and in very simple scenarios. For other situations, something else is required. Enter policy-based authorization.

Policy-based Authorization

In ASP.NET Core, the policy-based authorization framework is designed to decouple authorization and application logic. A policy is an entity devised as a collection of requirements. A requirement is a condition that the current user must meet. The simplest policy ever is that the user is authenticated. Another common requirement is that the user is associated with a given role. Another requirement is that the user has a particular claim or a particular claim with a particular value. In most general terms, a requirement is an assertion about the user identity that must be proven true for the user to be granted access to a given method.

Defining an Authorization Policy

You create a policy object using the following code:

```
var policy = new AuthorizationPolicyBuilder()
    .AddAuthenticationSchemes("Cookie, Bearer")
    .RequireAuthenticatedUser()
    .RequireRole("Admin")
    .RequireClaim("editor", "contents")
    .RequireClaim("level", "senior")
    .Build();
```

The builder object collects requirements using a variety of extension methods and then builds the policy object. As you can see, requirements act on the authentication status and schemes, the role, and any combination of claims read through the authentication cookie (or, if used, bearer token).

> **Note** Bearer tokens are an alternative to authentication cookies to carry information about the identity of a user. Bearer tokens are typically used by Web services invoked by non-browser clients, such as mobile applications. We'll tackle bearer tokens in Chapter 10, "Designing a Web API."

If none of the predefined extension methods for defining requirements work for you, then you can always resort to defining a new requirement through your own assertion. Here's how:

```
var policy = new AuthorizationPolicyBuilder()
    .AddAuthenticationSchemes("Cookie, Bearer")
    .RequireAuthenticatedUser()
    .RequireRole("Admin")
    .RequireAssertion(ctx =>
    {
```

```
        return ctx.User.HasClaim("editor", "contents") ||
            ctx.User.HasClaim("level", "senior");
    })
    .Build();
```

The *RequireAssertion* method takes a lambda that receives the *HttpContext* object and returns a Boolean value. The assertion is, therefore, a conditional statement. Note that if you concatenate *RequireRole* multiple times in the definition of the policy, then all roles must be honored by the user. If you want to express, instead, an OR condition then you have to resort to an assertion. In the above example, in fact, the policy allows users that are either editors of contents or senior users.

Once defined, policies must also be registered with the authorization middleware.

Registering Policies

The authorization middleware is first registered as a service in the *ConfigureServices* method of the startup class. In doing so, you configure the service with all required policies. Policies can be created through a builder object and added (or just declared) through the *AddPolicy* extension method.

```
services.AddAuthorization(options=>
{
    options.AddPolicy("ContentsEditor", policy =>
    {
        policy.AddAuthenticationSchemes(CookieAuthenticationDefaults.AuthenticationScheme);
        policy.RequireAuthenticatedUser();
        policy.RequireRole("Admin");
        policy.RequireClaim("editor", "contents");
    });
};
```

Each policy added to the authorization middleware has a name, and the name will be then used to reference the policy within the *Authorize* attribute on the controller class. Here's how you set a policy, instead of a role, to define permissions on a controller method.

```
[Authorize(Policy = "ContentsEditor")]
public IActionResult Save(Article article)
{
    ...
}
```

Through the *Authorize* attribute, you can set a policy declaratively and allow the authorization layer of ASP.NET Core to enforce it before the method executes. Alternatively, you can enforce the policy programmatically. Here's the necessary code.

```
public class AdminController : Controller
{
    private IAuthorizationService _authorization;
    public AdminController(IAuthorizationService authorizationService)
    {
        _authorization = authorizationService;
    }
```

```
public async Task<IActionResult> Save(Article article)
{
    var allowed = await _authorization.AuthorizeAsync(
        User, "ContentsEditor");
    if (!allowed.Succeeded)
        return new ForbiddenResult();

    // Proceed with the method implementation
    ...
}
}
```

As usual, the reference to the authorization service is injected via DI. The *AuthorizeAsync* method gets the principal object of the application and the policy name, and it returns an AuthorizationResult object with a *Succeeded* boolean property. When its value is false, you find the reason with *FailCalled* or *FailRequirements* of the *Failure* property. If the programmatic check of permissions fails, you should return a *ForbiddenResult* object.

> **Note** There's a subtle difference between returning *ForbiddenResult* or *ChallengeResult* when a permission check fails; the difference is even trickier if you consider ASP.NET Core 1.x. *ForbiddenResult* is a neat answer—you failed—and an HTTP 401 status code is returned. *ChallengeResult* is a milder kind of response. It ends up in a ForbiddenResult if the user is logged and redirects to the login page if not logged. However, starting with ASP.NET Core 2.0, *ChallengeResult* no longer redirects non-logged users to the login page. Hence, the only reasonable way to react to failed permissions is through *ForbiddenResult*.

Policies in Razor Views

So far, we have seen policy checking in controller methods. You can also perform the same checks in Razor views, especially if you're using Razor pages as discussed in Chapter 5, "ASP.NET MVC Views."

```
@{
    var authorized = await Authorization.AuthorizeAsync(User, "ContentsEditor")
}
@if (!authorized)
{
    <div class="alert alert-error">
        You're not authorized to access this page.
    </div>
}
```

For the previous code to work, you must first inject the dependency on the authorization service.

```
@inject IAuthorizationService Authorization
```

Using the authorization service in a view can help hide segments of the user interface not within reach of the current user.

> **Important** Showing or hiding user interface elements (links to secured pages, for example) only based on authorization permission checks isn't enough to be secure. Doing so works as long as you also do permission checks at the controller method level. Keep in mind that controller methods are the only way to gain access to the back end of a system, and people can always try to access a page directly by typing the URL in the browser. A hidden link is not completely secure. The ideal method is to check permissions at the gate, and the gate is the controller level. The only exception is starting with ASP.NET Core 2.0, you use Razor pages.

Custom Requirements

The stock requirements cover claims and authentication and provide a general-purpose mechanism for customization based on assertions. You can create custom requirements, too. A policy requirement is made of two elements—a requirement class that just holds data and an authorization handler that will validate the data against the user. You create custom requirements if you fail expressing the desired policy with stock tools.

As an example, let's say we want to extend the ContentsEditor policy by adding the requirement that the user must have at least three years of experience. Here's a sample class for a custom requirement.

```
public class ExperienceRequirement : IAuthorizationRequirement
{
    public int Years { get; private set; }
    public ExperienceRequirement(int minimumYears)
    {
        Years = minimumYears;
    }
}
```

A requirement must have at least one authorization handler. A handler is a class of type *AuthorizationHandler<T>* where *T* is the requirement type. The code below illustrates a sample handler for the *ExperienceRequirement* type.

```
public class ExperienceHandler : AuthorizationHandler<ExperienceRequirement>
{
    protected override Task HandleRequirementAsync(
        AuthorizationHandlerContext context,
        ExperienceRequirement requirement)
    {
        // Save User object to access claims
        var user = context.User;
        if (!user.HasClaim(c => c.Type == "EditorSince"))
            return Task.CompletedTask;

        var since = int.Parse(user.FindFirst("EditorSince").Value);
        if (since >= requirement.Years)
            context.Succeed(requirement);

        return Task.CompletedTask;
    }
}
```

The sample authorization handler reads the claims associated with the user and checks for a custom *EditorSince* claim. If not found, it just returns without doing anything. Success is returned only if the claim exists and the claim contains an integer value not less than the specified number of years. The custom claim is expected to be a piece of information linked in some way to the user—for example, a column in the Users table—saved to the authentication cookie. However, once you hold a reference to the user, you can always find the username from the claims and run a query against a database or external service to learn the number of years of experience and use the information in the handler.

Note Admittedly, the above example would have been a bit more realistic had the EditorSince value held a *DateTime* and calculated if a given number of years have passed since the user began as an Editor.

An authorization handler calls the method *Succeed* indicating that the requirement has been successfully validated. If the requirement didn't pass then the handler doesn't need to do anything and can just return. However, if the handler wants to determine the failure of a requirement, regardless of that fact that other handlers on the same requirement may succeed, it then calls the method *Fail* on the authorization context object.

Important In general, calling *Fail* from a handler should be considered an exceptional situation. An authorization handler, in fact, generally succeeds or does nothing because a requirement can have multiple handlers, and another one might succeed. Calling *Fail* remains an option for crucial situations when you want to stop any other handler from succeeding, no matter what. Also, note that even when *Fail* is called programmatically, the authorization layer evaluates every other requirement because handlers may have side effects like logging.

Here's how you add a custom requirement to the policy. Because this is a custom requirement, you have no extension method, and you must proceed through the *Requirements* collection of the policy object.

```
services.AddAuthorization(options =>
{
    options.AddPolicy("AtLeast3Years",
        policy => policy
                .Requirements
                .Add(new ExperienceRequirement(3)));
});
```

Also, you also must register the new handler with the DI system under the scope of the *IAuthorizationHandler* type.

```
services.AddSingleton<IAuthorizationHandler, ExperienceHandler>();
```

As mentioned, a requirement can have multiple handlers. When multiple handlers are registered with the DI system for the same requirement in the authorization layer, it suffices that at least one succeeds.

In the implementation of the authorization handler, it might sometimes be necessary to inspect request properties or route data.

```
if (context.Resource is AuthorizationFilterContext)
{
    var url = mvc.HttpContext.Request.GetDisplayUrl();
    ...
}
```

In ASP.NET Core, the *AuthorizationHandlerContext* object exposes a *Resource* property set to the filter context object. The context object is different depending on the framework involved. For example, MVC and SignalR send their own specific context object. Whether you cast the value held in the *Resource* property depends on what you need to access. For example, the *User* information is always there, so you don't need to cast for that. However, if you want MVC-specific details, such as routing or URL and request information, then you have to cast.

Summary

Securing an ASP.NET Core application passes through two layers—authentication and authorization. Authentication is the step aimed at associating an identity to the requests coming from a particular user agent. Authorization is aimed at checking whether that identity can perform the operations it is requesting in some way.

Authentication passes through a basic API centered on the creation of an authentication cookie and can also rely on the services of a dedicated framework that provides a highly customizable membership system—ASP.NET Identity. Authorization comes in two flavors. One is traditional role-based authorization, which works in the same way it works in classic ASP.NET MVC. The other is policy-based authentication, which is a new approach that makes for a richer and more expressive permission model. A policy is a collection of requirements based on claims and custom logic based on any other information that can be injected from the HTTP context or external sources. A requirement is associated with one or more handlers, and a handler is responsible for the actual evaluation of the requirement.

While discussing ASP.NET Identity, we touched on some database-related objects and concepts. In the next chapter, we'll just tackle data access in ASP.NET Core.

CHAPTER 9

Access to Application Data

If you hide your ignorance, no one will hit you and you'll never learn.

— *Ray Bradbury, "Fahrenheit 451"*

More than a decade ago, Eric Evans introduced Domain-driven Design (DDD), and one statement he made in his seminal book shook the pillars of software development. Essentially, he said that persistence should be the last—although not the least—concern of an architect in the design of the system. In this chapter, we'll start from there to try to make sense of data access in modern web applications and to develop a relatively generic pattern for an effective application back end. Persistence is clearly part of the application back end and, regardless of the abstraction layer you intend to have on top, persistence is obviously made of a framework to read and write data from some persistent store, possibly located on a remote server on some cloud platform. More and more applications use NoSQL stores and quite a few use two distinct stacks to deal with data—command and query.

Discussing data access in the context of a modern ASP.NET Core application is not simply a matter of going through the nitty-gritty details of a data access library. The vision you'll get in this chapter is design-first rather than technology-first. So, we'll first try to capture the essence of a general-purpose pattern for the application back end—inspired by the DDD well-known *Layered Architecture* pattern— and then end up reviewing the data access options for actual reads and writes of application data. In this regard, we'll tackle the key capabilities of Entity Framework Core.

Toward a Relatively Generic Application back end

In the suggested Layered Architecture pattern, Evans revisits the canonical 3-tier architecture— presentation, business, data—introducing two key changes. The first change is that he moves the focus on the concept of a layer rather than a tier. A layer refers to a logical separation between application components whereas a tier refers to physically distinct applications and servers. The second change is in the number of layers recognized in the schema. The layered architecture is based on four layers— presentation, application, domain, and infrastructure.

Compared to the canonical 3-tier schema, you see that the business tier has been split into two segments—application logic and domain logic—and the data tier has been renamed to a much more generic infrastructure layer. (See Figure 9-1.)

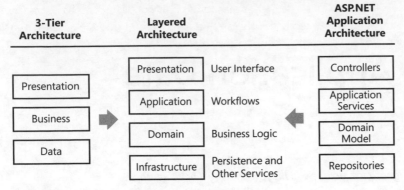

FIGURE 9-1 3-tier and Layered Architecture compared

It's easy to see from the figure how the various pieces of an ASP.NET application map to the layers of the Layered Architecture. Of the layers in Figure 9-1, only components in the infrastructure are expected to know about database details such as location and connection string. The rest of the system should ideally be designed agnostic of the actual schema of persisted data. All that the topmost application layers see is data just shaped as they need it to be. Hence, persisted data is still crucial for any application to work, but all that any application should know is how to read and write the data it needs. These details can, and should, be hidden as much as possible.

Monolithic Applications

In a classic bottom-up design—a design philosophy that has been in large use for decades—the first sign of understanding of the system you give to the outside world is the data model. Everything else is built on top of that including processes and, more than everything else, user interface and experience.

In a monolithic application, data travels from the bottom of the persistence up to the front end and back. The data goes through a couple of transformation points that adapt data collected in the user interface to the storage needs and adjust that stored data in the back end for display purposes (see Figure 9-2).

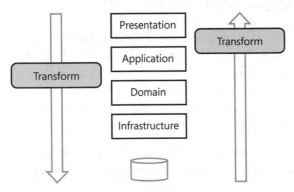

FIGURE 9-2 Shapes of data in a monolithic application

As you can easily guess from the figure, data goes through a couple of distinct paths: From storage to front end and from front end back to storage. Shouldn't we consider breaking the application stack in two? Wouldn't treating the command stack and the read stack independently be more effective for development? This question has led to NoSQL stores as well as XML and JSON support in classic RDBMS systems. This is just what Command and Query Responsibility Segregation (CQRS) pattern is making. A separation between the command and the query stack makes it easier to deal with those real-world situations in which data is ideally stored in one way and read in another way.

Though not strictly a necessity, Layered Architecture combined with CQRS provides a starting design point that probably represents the best fit for most cases today (see Figure 9-3).

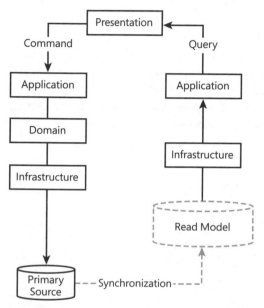

FIGURE 9-3 Layered Architecture pattern combined with CQRS design

The CQRS Approach

The moment you open your mind to having two distinct stacks—one for reading and one for updating the state of your application—a number of possible implementation scenarios unveil. No scenario is just perfect for everyone. The *one-size-fits-all* pattern doesn't work here, but the general idea of CQRS can have benefits for everyone.

Any seasoned developer can remember how problematic it was to work out the ideal data model that could combine the principles of relational data modeling with the intricacies of actual views required by end users. A single application stack forces you to have a single data model that is persistence-oriented but adapted to effectively serve the needs of the front end. Especially when combined with the additional abstraction layer of a methodology like Domain-driven Design, the design of the back end (business logic and data access logic) easily becomes an entangled mess.

In this regard, CQRS adds simplicity by breaking the design problem into two smaller problems and helping to find the right design solution for each problem without external constraints. This is, however, the epiphany of a new vision of the application architecture. The nice thing about having distinct stacks is that you can easily use separate object models for implementing commands and queries. If required, you can have a full domain model for commands but plain data transfer objects tailor-made for the presentation, perhaps simply materialized from SQL queries. Also, when you need multiple presentation front ends (for example web, mobile web, and mobile applications), all you do is create additional read models. The complexity results from the summation of individual complexities rather than from the Cartesian product of all. This is just what Figure 9-3 tries to communicate.

Working with Distinct Databases

The separation of the back end into distinct stacks simplifies design and coding and sets the ground for an unparalleled scalability potential. At the same time, it raises issues that should be carefully considered at the architecture level. How can you keep the two stacks in sync so that the data commands write is read back consistently? Depending on the business problem you're trying to solve, a CQRS implementation can be based on one or two databases. If a shared database is used, then getting the right projection of data for the query purpose is just extra work in the read stack performed on top of plain queries. A shared database, at the same time, ensures classic ACID consistency.

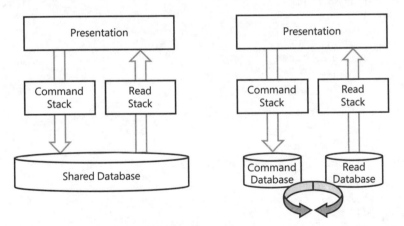

FIGURE 9-4 Comparing CQRS architectures using shared and distinct databases for command and query stacks

When it comes to performance or scalability, you can consider using different persistence endpoints for the command and read stacks. As an example, the command stack might have an event store, a NoSQL document store, or perhaps a non-durable store such as an in-memory cache. The synchronization of command data with read data might happen asynchronously or even be scheduled periodically depending on how stale data (and on how stale that data is) affects the presentation. In case of distinct databases, the read database is often a plain relational database that just offers one (or more) projection of the data (see Figure 9-4).

When Is CQRS Appropriate?

CQRS is not a comprehensive approach to the design of an enterprise-class system. CQRS is simply a pattern that guides you in architecting a specific bounded context of a possibly larger system. The CQRS architectural pattern was devised primarily to solve performance issues in highly concurrent business scenarios where handling commands synchronously and performing data analysis was getting more and more problematic. Many seem to think that outside the realm of such collaborative systems, the power of CQRS diminishes significantly. As a matter of fact, the power of CQRS shines in collaborative systems because it lets you address complexity and competing resources in a much smoother way. There's more to it than meets the eye, I think.

CQRS can sufficiently pay the architecture bill even in far simpler scenarios, where the plain separation between query and command stacks leads to simplified design and dramatically reduces the risk of design errors. Put another way, CQRS lowers the level of skills required to implement even quite a sophisticated system. Using CQRS makes doing a good job regarding scalability and cleanliness an affordable effort for nearly any team.

> **Note** Using CQRS with a clean and full separation of stacks (for example, using distinct databases) straightens the road ahead to using events as the primary source of data. Using events as the primary source of data means that the command stack just records what has happened (for example, a new customer has been added to the system) without necessarily updating the current list of customers. Getting the up-to-date list of customers is the responsibility of the read stack, and to preserve performance, out-of-band synchronization can be added so that every recorded event triggers an update on the read stack that keeps all of the data snapshots necessary to the application up to date.

Inside the Infrastructure Layer

In a realistic application back end, the infrastructure layer is anything related to using concrete technologies, including data persistence (O/RM frameworks like Entity Framework), external web services, specific security API, logging, tracing, IoC containers, caching, and more. The most prominent component of the infrastructure layer is the persistence layer—nothing more than the old faithful data access layer only possibly extended to cover a few data sources other than plain relational data stores. The persistence layer knows how to read and/or save data and is made of repository classes.

The Persistence Layer

If you use the classic approach of storing the current state of the system, then you're going to have one repository class per each relevant group of entities. By a group of entities, I mean entities that always go together, such as orders and order items. (This concept is referred to as *aggregates* in DDD jargon.) The structure of a repository can be CRUD-like, meaning you have Save, Delete, and Get methods on a generic type T, and you work with predicates to query ad hoc sections of data. Nothing, however, really prevents you from giving your repository an RPC style with methods that reflect actions—reads, deletes or insertions—that serve the purpose of the business. I usually summarize this by saying that there's no wrong way to write a repository.

Caching Layers

Not all data you have in a system changes at the same rate. In light of this, it makes little sense to ask the database server to read unchanged data every time a request comes in. At the same time, in a web application, requests come in concurrently. Many requests might hit the web server each second, and many of those concurrent requests might request the same page. Why shouldn't you cache that page, or at least the data it consumes?

Even though all systems are supposed to work without a cache, very few applications can survive a second or two without data caching. On a high-traffic site, a second or two can make the difference. In many situations, caching has become an additional layer built around ad hoc frameworks (actually, in-memory databases) such as Memcached, ScaleOut, or NCache. At the same time, in-memory solutions are not free of issues either because they might trigger more frequent and longer garbage collection operations on longer-lived objects of generation 2. In edge cases, this could lead to timeouts.

External Services

Another scenario for the infrastructure layer is when data is only accessible through web services. A good example of this scenario is when the web application lives on top of some CRM software or has to consume proprietary company services. In general, the infrastructure layer is responsible for wrapping external services as appropriate. Architecturally speaking, today, we really have to think of an infrastructure layer rather than as a plain data access layer that wraps up a relational database.

Data Access in .NET Core

When it comes to data access in an ASP.NET Core application, the first option that often comes to mind is using Entity Framework Core (EF Core). For sure, EF Core is the new entry specifically created from the ashes of canonical Entity Framework 6.x to offer a primary choice of an O/RM to developers. The remainder of this chapter will cover the basic and most common tasks one would likely perform with EF Core. Before we get there, though, it is interesting to skim the other options you have as far as data access is concerned. And you'll be surprised at how many different options you might have.

Entity Framework 6.x

Entity Framework 6.x (EF6) is the old faithful O/RM framework we used for quite a few years to code data access tasks in .NET applications. EF6 is only partially compatible with the new .NET Core platform. In other words, you are welcome to use EF6 in your .NET Core projects but doing that forces you to compile your .NET Core code against the full .NET Framework. The issue is that EF6 doesn't fully support .NET Core. The net effect is that using EF6 from within your ASP.NET Core application doesn't give you any of the cross-platform features you might have heard about. An ASP.NET Core application compiled against the full .NET Framework (and then possibly reusing some existing EF6 code) is restricted to run under Windows.

> **Note** When running under Windows, an ASP.NET Core application can be hosted under IIS, but it can also be hosted in a Windows service and run on top of Kestrel. It would be quite efficient even though you lose the higher-level services of IIS. At the same time, though, you don't always need those services. As usual, it is a matter of trade-offs.

Wrapping Up EF6 Code in a Separate Class Library

The recommended way to use EF6 in an ASP.NET Core application is to put all the classes, including DB context and entity classes, in a separate class library project and make it target the full framework. Next, a reference to this project will be added to the new ASP.NET Core project. This additional step is required because ASP.NET Core projects don't support all the functionality that you can programmatically trigger from within the EF6 context class. Hence, direct use of the EF6 context class inside of ASP.NET Core projects is not supported.

> **Important** Realistically, using an intermediate class library is not a limitation. In fact, the primary reason for using EF6 in an ASP.NET Core (or just .NET Core) project is to reuse existing code rather than to use a familiar old API. Existing code is likely already isolated in a separate class library. However, even if you're writing fresh EF6 code, keeping it well isolated from the main body of the project is an excellent design choice that would make it easy in the future to replace the framework for data access and use a fully supported cross-platform API like EF Core or any other of the options described in this chapter.

Retrieving the Connection String

The way in which EF6 context classes retrieve their connection string is not completely compatible with the newest and totally rewritten configuration layer of ASP.NET Core. Let's consider the following common code fragment.

```
public class MyOwnDatabase : DbContext
{
    public MyOwnDatabase(string connStringOrDbName = "name=MyOwnDatabase")
        : base(connStringOrDbName)
    {

    }
}
```

The application-specific Db context class receives the connection string as an argument or retrieves it from the *web.config* file. In ASP.NET Core, there's nothing like a *web.config* file, so the connection string either becomes a constant or should be read through the .NET Core configuration layer and passed in.

Integrating EF Context with ASP.NET Core DI

Most of the ASP.NET Core data access examples you find on the web show how to inject the DB context into all layers of the application via Dependency Injection (DI). You can inject the EF6 context in the DI system as you would do with any other service. The ideal scope is per-request, which means the same instance is shared by all possible callers within the same HTTP request.

```
public void ConfigureServices(IServiceCollection services)
{
    // Other services added here
    ...

    // Get connection string from configuration
    var connString = ...;
    services.AddScoped<MyOwnDatabase>(() => new MyOwnDatabase(connString));
}
```

With the above configuration in place, you can now inject even an EF6 DB context directly into a controller or, more likely, into a repository class.

```
public class SomeController : Controller
{
    private readonly MyOwnDatabase _context;

    public SomeController(MyOwnDatabase context)
    {
        _context = context;
    }

    // More code here
    ...
}
```

The above code snippet—injecting a DB context into a controller class—is fairly common in articles and documentation, but it is not something I recommend you do for the simple reason that it inevitably leads to fat controllers and one big layer of code that from the input level goes straight to the data access. I'd rather use the DI pattern in a repository class or not use the DI pattern at all for DB context classes.

ADO.NET Adapters

In ASP.NET Core 2.0, Microsoft has brought back some components of the old ADO.NET API, specifically *DataTable* objects, data readers, and data adapters. While always supported as a constituent part of the .NET Framework, the ADO.NET classic API was progressively abandoned in recent years in the development of new applications in favor of Entity Framework. Because of this, it was sacrificed in the design of the .NET Core API 1.x and then brought back by popular demand in version 2.0. As a result, in ASP.NET 2.0 applications, you can write data access code to manage connections, SQL commands, and cursors just as you could at the beginning of the .NET era.

Issuing Direct SQL Commands

In ASP.NET Core, the ADO.NET API has nearly the same programming interface it has in the full .NET Framework, and it has the same programming paradigms. First and foremost, you can gain full control over each command by managing the connection to the database and creating the command and its parameters programmatically. Here's an example:

```
var conn = new SqlConnection();
conn.ConnectionString = "...";
var cmd = new SqlCommand("SELECT * FROM customers", conn);
```

Once ready, the command must be issued through an open connection. A few more lines of code are required to achieve this.

```
conn.Open();
var reader = cmd.ExecuteReader(CommandBehavior.CloseConnection);

// Read data and do any required processing
...
reader.Close();
```

The connection is automatically closed when you close the reader because of the close-connection behavior requested when the data reader was opened. The *SqlCommand* class can execute the command through a variety of methods, as explained in Table 9-1.

TABLE 9-1 Execute methods of a *SqlCommand* class

Execute Method	Description
ExecuteNonQuery	Executes the command but returns no value. Ideal for non-query statements such as UPDATEs.
ExecuteReader	Executes the command and returns a cursor that points to the beginning of the output stream. Ideal for query commands.
ExecuteScalar	Executes the command and returns a single value. Ideal for query commands returning a scalar value such as MAX or COUNT.
ExecuteXmlReader	Executes the command and returns an XML reader. Ideal for commands that return XML content.

The methods in Table 9-1 offer a variety of options to grab the results of any SQL statement or stored procedure you want to execute. Here's an example that shows how to go through the records of a data reader.

```
var reader = cmd.ExecuteReader(CommandBehavior.CloseConnection);
while(reader.Read())
{
    var column0 = reader[0];             // returns an Object
    var column1 = reader.GetString(1)    // index of the column to read

    // Do something with data
}
reader.Close();
```

Note The ADO.NET API in .NET Core is identical to the API you have in the .NET Framework and doesn't support more recent development in the SQL Server area, such as native JSON support in SQL Server 2016 and newer. For example, there's nothing like *ExecuteJsonReader* method to parse JSON data to a class.

Loading Data in Disconnected Containers

Using a reader is ideal if you need to process a long response while keeping the amount of memory at a minimum. Otherwise, it is preferable to load the results of a query into a disconnected container such as a *DataTable* object. There are a few facilities for this.

```
conn.Open();
var reader = cmd.ExecuteReader(CommandBehavior.CloseConnection);
var table = new DataTable("Customers");
table.Columns.Add("FirstName");
table.Columns.Add("LastName");
table.Columns.Add("CountryCode");
table.Load(reader);
reader.Close();
```

A *DataTable* object is the in-memory version of a database table with schema, relations, and primary keys. The easiest way to fill one is getting a data reader cursor and loading the entire content in the declared columns. Mapping happens by column index, and the actual code behind the *Load* method is very close to the loop presented earlier. From your end, though, it only takes a method, but still leaves on you the responsibility of managing the state of the database connection. For this reason, in general, the safest approach you can take is to use the Dispose pattern and create the database connection within a C# *using* statement.

Fetching via Adapters

The most compact way to fetch data into in-memory containers is through data adapters. A data adapter is a component that sums up the entire query process. It is made of a command object, or just the select command text, and a connection object. It takes care of opening and closing the connection for you and packages all results of the query (including multiple result sets) into a *DataTable* or a *DataSet* object. (A *DataSet* is a collection of *DataTable* objects.)

```
var conn = new SqlConnection();
conn.ConnectionString = "...";
var cmd = new SqlCommand("SELECT * FROM customers", conn);
var table = new DataTable();
var adapter = new SqlDataAdapter(cmd);
adapter.Fill(table);
```

Again, if you are familiar with the ADO.NET API, you'll find it back in .NET and ASP.NET Core 2.0 as it was originally. This guarantees that one more piece of legacy code can be ported to other platforms. Beyond that, support for ADO.NET gives another chance to use the more advanced capabilities of SQL

Server 2016, such as JSON support and history of updates, in .NET Core and ASP.NET Core. For those features, in fact, you have no ad hoc support from either EF6 or EF Core.

Using Micro O/RM Frameworks

An O/RM framework does the dirty and praiseworthy job of querying rows of data and mapping them to the properties of an in-memory object. Compared to *DataTable* objects discussed above, an O/RM loads the same low-level data into a strongly-typed class rather than a generic table-oriented container. When it comes to O/RM frameworks for the .NET Framework, most developers think of Entity Framework or perhaps NHibernate. Those are the most popular frameworks but also the most gigantic. For an O/RM framework, the attribute of gigantic relates to the number of features it supports, ranging from mapping capabilities to caching, and from transactionality to concurrency. The support for the LINQ query syntax is crucial in a modern O/RM for .NET. It makes for a long list of features that inevitably impacts the memory footprint and even the performance of single operations. That's why a few people and companies have recently started using micro O/RM frameworks. A few options exist for ASP.NET Core applications.

Micro O/RM vs. Full O/RM

Let's face it. A micro O/RM does the same basic job of a full O/RM, and most of the time, you don't really need a fully-fledged O/RM. Want an example? Stack Overflow, one of the most trafficked websites on the planet, doesn't use a full O/RM. Stack Overflow even managed to create their own micro O/RM just for performance reasons. That being said, my personal feeling is that most applications use Entity Framework only because it's part of the .NET Framework and because it makes writing a query a matter of C# code instead of SQL. Productivity does matter, and in general terms, I tend to consider the use of a full O/RM a more productive choice because of the number of examples and features, including internal optimization of commands to ensure a sufficient trade-off all the time.

If a micro O/RM can have a much smaller memory footprint, then it is essentially because it lacks features. The question is whether any of the missing features affect your application. The primary missing features are second-level caching and built-in support for relationships. Second-level caching refers to having an additional layer of cache managed by the framework that persists results for a configured amount of time across connections and transactions. Second-level caching is supported in NHibernate but not in Entity Framework (although some workarounds make it possible in EF6 and an extension project exists for EF Core). This is to say that second-level caching is not a big discriminant between micro and full O/RM frameworks. Much more relevant is the other missing feature—support for relationships.

When you write a query, say in EF, you can include in the query any foreign-key relationship regardless of the cardinality. Expanding the results of a query to joined tables is part of the syntax and doesn't require building the query through a different and more articulated syntax. You usually don't get this with a micro O/RM. In a micro O/RM, this is precisely the point where you make the trade-off. You can have faster performance of the operation at the cost of spending more time writing a more complex query that requires more advanced SQL skills. Alternatively, you can skip over the SQL skills and let the system do the work for you. This extra service from the framework comes at the cost of memory footprint and overall performance.

Also, a full O/RM can provide designers and/or migration facilities that not everybody likes and uses that contribute to making the image of the full O/RM more gigantic.

Sample Micro O/RMs

The Stack Overflow team opted for creating a tailor-made mini O/RM—the Dapper framework—taking on the responsibility of writing super optimized SQL queries and adding themselves tons of external caching layers. The Dapper framework is available at *http://github.com/StackExchange/Dapper*. The framework shines at executing SELECT statements against a SQL database and mapping the data returned to objects. Its performance is nearly identical to using a data reader—which is the fastest way to query data in .NET, but it can return a list of in-memory objects.

```
var customer = connection.Query<Customer>(
        "SELECT * FROM customers WHERE Id = @Id",
        new { Id = 123 });
```

The NPoco Framework works along the same guidelines, and even the code is only minimally different from Dapper. The NPoco framework is available at *http://github.com/schotime/npoco*.

```
using (IDatabase db = new Database("connection_string"))
{
    var customers = db.Fetch<Customer>("SELECT * FROM customers");
}
```

The family of micro O/RM grows every day, and many others exist for ASP.NET Core, such as Insight. Database (*http://github.com/jonwagner/Insight.Database*) and PetaPoco, which is supplied as a single big file to integrate into your application (*http://www.toptensoftware.com/petapoco*).

The key thing about micro O/RM, however, is not so much which one you should use but whether you use a micro O/RM instead of a full O/RM.

> **Note** According to the numbers released by Stack Overflow engineers on the Dapper home page (*http://github.com/StackExchange/Dapper*), performance-wise, Dapper can be up to 10 times faster than Entity Framework on a single query. It's a huge difference, but not necessarily sufficient to have everyone decide to use Dapper or another micro O/RM. That choice depends on the number of queries you run and the skills of the developers writing them, as well as which alternatives you have to improve performance.

Using NoSQL Stores

The term NoSQL means many things and points to many different products. In the end, NoSQL can be summarized by saying that it's the data storage paradigm of choice when you don't want—or don't need—relational storage. All in all, there's just one use-case when you really want to use a NoSQL store: When the schema of the records changes but the records are logically related.

Think of a form or a questionnaire to fill and store in a multi-tenant application. Each tenant can have its own list of fields, and you need to save values for a variety of users. Each tenant form might be different, but the resulting records are all logically related and should ideally go in the same store. In a relational database, you have very few options other than creating a schema that is the union of all possible fields. But even in this case, adding a new field for a tenant requires altering the schema of the table. Organizing data by rows rather than by column poses other problems, such as the performance hit every time the query for a tenant crosses the SQL page size. Again, it depends on the specific application usage but, the fact is, schema-less data is not ideal for a relational store. Enter NoSQL stores.

As mentioned, there are many ways to catalog NoSQL stores. For this book, I prefer to simply split them into physical and in-memory stores. In spite of physical/memory contrast, the distinction is pretty thin. NoSQL stores are mostly used as a form of cache and less frequently as the primary data store. When they're used as the primary data store, it's usually because the application has an event-sourcing architecture.

Classic Physical Stores

A physical NoSQL store is a schemaless database that saves .NET Core objects to disk and offers functions to fetch and filter them. The most popular NoSQL store is probably MongoDB, which goes hand in hand with Microsoft's Azure DocumentDB. Interestingly, applications written to use the MongoDB API can be made to write to a DocumentDB database simply by changing the connection string. Here's instead a sample query written for DocumentDB.

```
var client - new DocumentClient(azureEndpointUri, password);
var requestUri = UriFactory.CreateDocumentCollectionUri("MyDB", "questionnaire-items");
var questionnaire = client.CreateDocumentQuery<Questionnaire>(requestUri)
        .Where(q => q.Id == "tenant-12345" && q => q.Year = 2018)
        .AsEnumerable()
        .FirstOrDefault();
```

The major benefit of a NoSQL store is the ability to store differently shaped, but related, data and scale storage and easy query capabilities. Other physical NoSQL databases are RavenDB, CouchDB, and CouchBase, which is particularly suited for mobile applications.

In-memory Stores

In-memory stores are essentially large-cache applications that work as key-value dictionaries. Even though they do back up content, they are perceived as being large chunks of memory in which applications park data for quick retrieval. An excellent example of an in-memory store is Redis (*http://redis.io*).

To understand the relevance of such frameworks, think again of Stack Overflow's publicly documented architecture. Stack Overflow (*www.stackoverflow.com*) uses a customized version of Redis as an intermediate second-level caching to maintain questions and data for a long period without the need to re-query from the database. Redis supports disk-level persistence, LRU-eviction, replication, and partitioning. Redis is not directly accessible from ASP.NET Core, but it can be done through the ServiceStack API (see *http://servicestack.net)*.

Another in-memory, NoSQL database is Apache Cassandra, which is accessible in ASP.NET Core via the DataStax driver.

EF Core Common Tasks

If you intend to remain in the realm of a full O/RM for ASP.NET Core, the choice is limited to the new, tailor-made version of Entity Framework, known as EF Core. EF Core supports a provider model through which it lets you work with a variety of relational DBMS, specifically SQL Server, Azure SQL Database, MySQL, and SQLite. For all these databases, EF Core has a native provider. Also, an in-memory provider exists, which is good for testing purposes. For PostgreSQL, you need an external provider from *http://npgsql.org*. An Oracle provider for EF Core is expected by early 2018.

To install EF Core in an ASP.NET Core application, you need the *Microsoft.EntityFrameworkCore* package plus specific packages for the database provider you intend to use (SQL Server, MySQL, SQLite, or something else).The most common tasks you would perform are listed below.

Modeling a Database

EF Core only supports the Code First approach, meaning that it requires a set of classes to describe the database and contained tables. This collection of classes can be coded from scratch or reverse-engineered via tooling from an existing database.

Defining the Database and the Model

In the end, a database is modeled after a class derived from *DbContext*. This class contains one or more collection properties of type *DbSet<T>* where *T* is the type of records in the table. Here's the structure of a sample database.

```
public class YourDatabase : DbContext
{
    public DbSet<Customer> Customers { get; set; }
}
```

The *Customer* type describes the records of the *Customers* table. The underlying physical, relational database is expected to have a table named *Customers* whose schema matches the public interface of the *Customer* type.

```
public class EntityBase
{
    public EntityBase()
    {
        Enabled = true;
        Modified = DateTime.UtcNow;
    }

    public bool Enabled { get; set; }
    public DateTime? Modified { get; set; }
}
public class Customer : EntityBase
{
    [Key]
    public int Id { get; set; }

    public string FirstName { get; set; }
    public string LastName { get; set; }
}
```

While laying out the public interface of the *Customer* class, you can still use common object-oriented techniques and use base classes to share common properties across all tables. In the example, *Enabled* and *Modified* are two properties automatically added to all tables whose mapped classes inherit from *EntityBase*. Also, note that any class that will generate a table must have a primary key field defined. For example, you can do that via the *Key* attribute.

> **Important** The schema of the database and the mapped classes must always be kept in sync; otherwise, exceptions are thrown by the EF Core. This means that even adding a new nullable column to a table might be an issue. At the same time, also adding a public property to one of the classes might be a problem. In this case, though, the *NotMapped* attribute saves you from getting an exception. The fact is that EF Core tends to suppose you interact with the physical database only through its migration scripts. Migration scripts are the official way to keep the model and database in sync. However, migrations are mostly a developer thing while often the database is a property of the IT department. In this case, migrations between the model and the database can only be manual.

Injecting the Connection String

In the code presented above, there's nothing that shows the physical link between your code and a database. How would you inject the connection string? Technically, a *DbContext*-derived class is not fully configured to work against a database until the provider is indicated and all the information to run it—most notably the connection string. You can set the provider overriding the *OnConfiguring* method of the *DbContext* class. The method receives an option builder object with an extension method for each of the natively supported providers: for SQL Server, SQLite plus a test-only in-memory database. To configure SQL Server (including SQL Express and Azure SQL Database), you proceed as follows.

```
public class YourDatabase : DbContext
{
    public DbSet<Customer> Customers { get; set; }

    protected override void OnConfiguring(DbContextOptionsBuilder optionsBuilder)
    {
        optionsBuilder.UseSqlServer("...");
    }
}
```

The parameter to *UseSqlServer* must be the connection string. If it is acceptable that the connection string is a constant, you just type it where you see the ellipsis in the code snippet above. More realistically, instead, you want to use different connection strings based on the environment—production, staging, development, and the like. In this case, you should find a way to inject it.

Because the connection string doesn't change dynamically (and if it changes, it's a very special situation that well deserves to be treated differently), the first option that comes to mind is adding a global static property to the *DbContext* class to be set with the connection string.

```
public static string ConnectionString = "";
```

Now the *ConnectionString* property is silently passed to the *UseSqlServer* method in the *OnConfiguring* method. The connection string is typically read from the configuration files and set at the application startup.

```
public void Configure(IApplicationBuilder app, IHostingEnvironment env)
{
    YourDatabase.ConnectionString = !env.IsDevelopment()
        ? "production connection string"
        : "development connection string";

    // More code here
}
```

Similarly, you can employ different JSON configuration files for production and development and store there individual connection strings to use. This approach is also probably easier from a DevOps perspective because the publish script just picks up the right JSON file by convention. (See Chapter 2, "The First ASP.NET Core Project.")

Injecting the *DbContext* Object

If you search for EF Core articles, including the official Microsoft documentation, you see many examples showing code along the following guidelines.

```
public void ConfigureServices(IServiceCollection services)
{
    var connString = Configuration.GetConnectionString("YourDatabase");
    services.AddDbContext<YourDatabase>(options =>
        options.UseSqlServer(connString));
}
```

The code adds the *YourDatabase* context object to the DI subsystem so that it can be retrieved from anywhere in the application. While adding the context, the code also fully configures it for the scope of the current request and, in the example, to use the SQL Server provider on a given connection string.

Alternatively, you can create instances of the database context yourself and give them the lifetimes you want (for instance, singleton, or scoped) and inject only the connection string in the context. The static property discussed above is an option. Here's another one.

```
public YourDatabase(IOptions<GlobalConfig> config)
{
    // Save to a local variable the connection string
    // as read from the configuration JSON file of the application.
}
```

As discussed in Chapter 7, "Design Considerations," you can apply the Options pattern and load global configuration data from a JSON resource into a class and inject that class via DI into the constructor of classes.

> **Note** Of the many ways to inject the connection string, which one should you choose? Personally, I go with the static property because it is simple, direct, and easy to understand and figure out. My second favorite approach is injecting configuration into the *DbContext*. As far as injecting the fully configured *DbContext* into the DI system, that scares me because it could lead developers to call *DbContext* anywhere they might need it, thus defeating any effort to separate concerns.

Automatically Creating the Database

The overall process of modeling a database and mapping it to classes is a bit different than in EF6; the code required to create a database (if it doesn't already exist) also is. In EF Core, this step must be explicitly requested and is not a consequence of the base of a database initializer component. If you want a database to be created, place the following two lines of code in the startup class in the *Configure* method:

```
var db = new YourDatabase();
db.Database.EnsureCreated();
```

The *EnsureCreated* method creates the database if it does not exist (and skips otherwise). Loading initial data to the database is also under your full programmatic control. A common pattern is to expose a public method—the name is up to you—out of the *DbContext* class and calling it right after *EnsureCreated*.

```
db.Database.SeedTables();
```

Inside the initializer, you can either call the EF Core methods directly or repositories if you have them defined.

Note Scaffolding tasks such as reverse-engineering an existing database or migrating changes from classes to the database can be controlled via many command line tools. More details can be found here: *http://docs.microsoft.com/en-us/ef/core/get-started/aspnetcore/existing-db*.

Working with Table Data

Reading and writing data with EF Core is, for the most part, just the same as in EF6. Once the database has been correctly created or reverse-engineered from an existing database, then queries and updates work the same way. Some differences exist in the EF6 and EF Core API, but overall, I think the best approach is to try to do things the same as in EF6 and focus on exceptions only when, and if, they occur.

Fetching a Record

The following code shows how to fetch a record by its primary key. The approach is more general, indeed, and shows how to fetch a record by conditions.

```
public Customer FindById(int id)
{
    using (var db = new YourDatabase())
    {
        var customer = (from c in db.Customers
                        where c.Id == id
                        select c).FirstOrDefault();
        return customer;
    }
}
```

Two things are more relevant than the code itself.

■ First, the code is encapsulated in a method exposed by a repository class. A repository class is a wrapper class that uses a fresh instance of a *DbContext*, or an injected copy (it's up to you), to expose database-specific operations.

■ The second relevant thing is that the code above is a sort of a monolith. It opens a connection to the database, retrieves its data and closes the connection. It all happens in the context of a single transparent database transaction. If you need to run two different queries, consider that two calls to a repository method will open/close connections to the database twice.

If the business process you're coding requires two or more queries from the database, you might want to try to concatenate them in a single transparent transaction. The scope of the *DbContext* instance determines the scope of a system-created database transaction.

```
public Customer[] FindAdminAndSupervisor()
{
    using (var db = new YourDatabase())
    {
```

```
        var admin = (from c in db.Customers
                    where c.Id == ADMIN
                    select c).FirstOrDefault();
        var supervisor = (from c in db.Customers
                    where c.Id == SUPERVISOR
                    select c).FirstOrDefault();
        return new[] {admin, supervisor};
    }
}
```

In this case, the two records are retrieved via distinct queries, but in the same transaction and over the same connection. Another interesting use-case is when the overall query is built piecemeal. Let's say that one method fetches a chunk of records, and the output is then passed to another method to restrict further the result set based on runtime conditions. Here's some sample code:

```
// Opens a connection and returns all EU customers
var customers = FindByContinent("EU");

// Runs an in-memory query to select only those from EAST EU
if (someConditionsApply())
{
    customers = (from c in customers where c.Area.Is("EAST") select c).ToList();
}
```

In the end, you get just what you need, but the use of memory is less than optimal. Here's a better way to do it.

```
public IQueryable<Customer> FindByContinent(string continent)
{
    var customers = (from c in db.Customers
                    where c.Continent == continent
                    select c);

    // No query is actually run at this point! Only the formal
    // definition of the query is returned.
    return customers;
}
```

Not calling *FirstOrDefault* or *ToList* at the end of the query expression doesn't actually run the query; instead, it simply returns the formal description of it.

```
// Opens a connection and returns all EU customers
var query = FindByContinent("EU");

// Runs an in-memory query to select only those from EAST EU
if (someConditionsApply())
{
    query = (from c in query where c.Area.Is("EAST") select c;
}

var customers = query.ToList();
```

The second filter now simply edits the query adding an additional *WHERE* clause. Next, when *ToList* is called, the query is run once and gets all customers from Europe which are also located in the East.

Dealing with Relationships

The following code defines a one-to-one relationship between two tables. The *Customer* object refers to a *Country* object in a Countries table.

```
public class Customer : EntityBase
{
    [Key]
    public int Id { get; set; }
    public string FirstName { get; set; }
    public string LastName { get; set; }

    [ForeignKey]
    public int CountryId { get; set; }
    public Country Country { get; set; }
}
```

That's enough for the database to define a foreign-key relationship between the tables. When querying customer records, you can easily have the *Country* property expanded through an underlying JOIN statement.

```
var customer = (from c in db.Customers.Include("Country")
                where c.Id == id
                select c).FirstOrDefault();
```

Because of the *Include* call, now the returned object has the *Country* property filled out with a JOIN statement on the configured foreign key. The string you pass to *Include* is the name of the foreign-key property. Technically, in a query statement, you can have as many *Include* calls as you need. However, the more you have, the graph of objects you return with subsequent additional memory consumption also grows.

Adding a Record

Adding a new record requires some code to add an object in memory and then persisting the collection to disk.

```
public void Add(Customer customer)
{
    if (customer == null)
      return;
    using (var db = new YourDatabase())
    {
        db.Customers.Add(customer);
        try
        {
            db.SaveChanges();
        }
        catch(Exception exception)
        {
            // Recover in some way or expand the way
            // it works for you, For example, only catching
            // some exceptions.
        }
    }
}
```

Nothing more than this is required, as long as the object being passed is fully configured and populated in all required fields. A good approach for a data access layer is that you validate objects from a business perspective in the application layer (in the service class invoked from the controller) and either assume everything is okay in the repository or throw an exception if anything goes wrong. Alternatively, in the repository method, you can also repeat some checks just to make sure everything is okay.

Updating a Record

In EF Core updating, a record is a two-step operation. First, you query for the record to update and then, in the context of the same *DbContext*, you update its state in memory and persist changes.

```
public void Update(Customer updatedCustomer)
{
    using (var db = new YourDatabase())
    {
        // Retrieve the record to update
        var customer = (from c in db.Customers
                        where c.Id == updatedCustomer.Id
                        select c).FirstOrDefault();
        if (customer == null)
            return;

        // Make changes
        customer.FirstName = updatedCustomer.FirstName;
        customer.LastName = updatedCustomer.LastName;
        customer.Modified = DateTime.UtcNow;
        ...

        // Persist
        try
        {
            db.SaveChanges();
        }
        catch(Exception exception)
        {
            // Recover in some way or expand the way
            // it works for you, For example, only catching
            // some exceptions.
        }
    }

}
```

Updating the fetched record with the posted record can be boring code to write. While nothing is faster than manually copying field-to-field, reflection or advanced tools like AutoMapper can be a time-saver. Also, having a single line of code to clone an object is helpful. Having said that, though, consider that updating a record is primarily a business operation rather than a plain database operation, and the two things coincide only in trivial applications. The point here is that depending on business conditions, some fields should never be updated or should get system-calculated values. More, sometimes updating a record is not enough and other operations should be performed in the context of the same business transaction. This is to say that having a single update method where you blindly copy properties from source object to target object is a much less common scenario than it might seem at first. I'll return to this in a moment, talking about transactions.

Deleting a Record

Deleting a record is like updating a record. Also, in this case, you have to retrieve the record to delete, remove it from the in-memory collection of the database and then update the physical table.

```
public void Delete(int id)
{
    using (var db = new YourDatabase())
    {
        // Retrieve the record to delete
        var customer = (from c in db.Customers
                        where c.Id == id
                        select c).FirstOrDefault();
        if (customer == null)
            return;
        db.Customers.Remove(customer);

        // Persist
        try
        {
            db.SaveChanges();
        }
        catch(Exception exception)
        {
            // Recover in some way or expand the way
            // it works for you, For example, only catching
            // some exceptions.
        }
    }
}
```

There are two remarks to make about deletions. First, deletions also are business operations, and very rarely, business operations require destroying data. More often than not, deleting a record is a matter of logically deleting it, which would turn the delete operation into an update. The implementation of the delete operation as done in EF6 and EF Core might seem overwhelming, but it leaves room for applying any required logic.

If you really need to physically remove records from the database, regardless of whether cascading options have been configured at the database level, you can just go with a plain SQL statement.

```
db.Database.ExecuteSqlCommand(sql);
```

In general, I encourage you (and your customers) to carefully consider a physical deletion of records. The future of development blinks at event sourcing, and one of the pillars of event sourcing is that databases are *append-only* structures.

Dealing with Transactions

In real-world applications, most of the database operations are part of a transaction, and sometimes, they are part of a distributed transaction. By default, if the underlying database provider supports transactions, all changes that go with a single call to *SaveChanges* are then processed within a transaction. This means that if any of the changes fail, the entire transaction is rolled back so that none of the attempted changes are physically applied to the database. In other words, *SaveChanges* either does all the work it was called to do or nothing.

Explicit Control of Transactions

In cases when you can't drive all changes through a single call to *SaveChanges,* you can define an explicit transaction through an ad hoc method on the *DbContext* class.

```
using (var db = new YourDatabase())
{
    using (var tx = db.Database.BeginTransaction())
    {
        try
        {
            // All database calls including multiple SaveChanges calls
            ...

            // Commit
            tx.Commit();
        }
        catch(Exception exception)
        {
            // Recover in some way or expand the way
            // it works for you, For example, only catching
            // some exceptions.
        }
    }
}
```

Again, note that not all database providers may support transactions. However, that's not the case with providers of popular databases such as SQL Server. What happens when the provider doesn't support transactions depends on the provider itself—it can either throw an exception or just do nothing.

Sharing Connections and Transactions

In EF Core, when creating an instance of the *DbContext* object, you can inject a database connection and/or a transaction object. The base classes for both objects are *DbConnection* and *DbTransaction*.

If you inject the same connection and transaction to two different *DbContext* objects, the effect is that all operations across those contexts will happen in the same transaction and over the same database connection. The following code snippet shows how to inject a connection in a *DbContext*.

```
public class YourDatabase : DbContext
{
    private DbConnection _connection;
    public YourDatabase(DbConnection connection)
    {
        _connection = connection;
    }

    public DbSet<Customer> Customers { get; set; }
```

```
protected override void OnConfiguring(DbContextOptionsBuilder optionsBuilder)
{
    optionsBuilder.UseSqlServer(_connection);
}
}
```

To inject a transaction scope, instead, you proceed as below:

```
context.Database.UseTransaction(transaction);
```

To get a transaction object from within a running transaction, you use the *GetDbTransaction* method. Have a look at *http://docs.microsoft.com/en-us/ef/core/saving/transactions* for more information.

> **Note** Some support for *TransactionScope* has been added to .NET Core 2.0, but I suggest you check carefully to ensure that it works for the scenarios with which you intend to use it before you embark on serious development. The class is there, but for the time being, the behavior doesn't seem the same as you might expect from the version in the full .NET Framework that, by the way, allowed you to enlist together relational transactions and file system and/or Web service operations.

A Word on Async Data Processing

The entire set of methods in EF Core that trigger database operations also have an async version: *SaveChangesAsync*, *FirstOrDefaultAsync*, and *ToListAsync* to name just the most commonly used methods. Should you use them? What kind of benefit are they really providing? And what's the point of async processing in an ASP.NET Core application?

Asynchronous processing is not, per se, faster than synchronous processing. An async call has, instead, a much more intricate execution flow than a synchronous call. In the context of web applications, asynchronous processing is mostly about not having threads blocked while waiting for a synchronous call to return instead of processing the next requests. The entire application is, therefore, more responsive because it can take and serve more requests. From here comes the sense of improved speed, and more importantly, increased scalability.

The C# language used the *async/await* keywords to turn any apparently synchronous code into asynchronous code in a very simple way. However, with great power comes great responsibility: be always aware of the cost to spawn additional threads to process workloads that might not require this asynchronicity. Remember that you are not dealing with parallelism here but forwarding the workload to another thread while the current one returns back to the pool to process more incoming requests. You get more scalability but maybe with a possibly slight speed impact.

Async Processing in ASP.NET Core Applications

Let's say you mark a controller method as asynchronous. The code downloads content from a website and tracks the thread ID before and after the async operation.

```
public async Task<IActionResult> Test()
{
    var t1 = Thread.CurrentThread.ManagedThreadId.ToString();
    var client = new HttpClient();
    await client.GetStringAsync("http://www.google.com");
    var t2 = Thread.CurrentThread.ManagedThreadId.ToString();
    return Content(string.Concat(t1, " / ", t2));
}
```

The net effect you obtain can be summarized as in Figure 9-5.

FIGURE 9-5 Thread ID before and after an async operation

As the figure shows, the request was served by different threads before and after the async break-point. The request for the specific page is not really benefiting from the async implementation, but the rest of the site would enjoy it. The reason is that no ASP.NET thread was busy waiting for an I/O operation to complete. Thread #9 returns to the ASP.NET pool to serve any new incoming request right after asking the .NET thread pool to call the *GetStringAsync* asynchronous operation. When this async method completed, the first available thread from the pool was picked up. It could have been thread #9 again, but not necessarily. In a highly trafficked site, the number of requests that can arrive in the seconds a long operation takes to complete can keep high or sink the level of responsiveness of the site.

Async Processing in Data Access

To cause a thread to return to the pool and be ready to serve another request, it is necessary for the thread to wait for an async operation. The wording of this syntax might be confusing: when you see **await MethodAsync** appears, it means that the current thread pushes the call to MethodAsync to the .NET thread pool and returns. The code following the MethodAsync call will happen on any available thread after the method returns. Calling into a web service, as in the code snippet below, is a possibility. Another possibility is to call asynchronously into some database via EF Core.

Let's consider a common scenario. Say you have a web application made of some static content, views are relatively quick to render, and a few views run significantly slower because of required long database operations.

Imagine that you get a number of concurrent requests that exhaust the thread pool. A number of those requests need to hit the database, and subsequently, all those threads are used to process a request but are actually idle, waiting for the database query to come back. Your system can't serve more requests, and the CPU is nearly at 0 percent! It might seem that turning database access into async code would solve the problem. Again, it depends.

First and foremost, we're talking about refactoring large portions of the data access layer. Whatever way you look at it, it's not a walk in the park. But let's assume you do it. Second, what you really achieve is that more threads come back to the pool ready to take on other incoming requests. What if those requests need to hit the database to be processed? By turning your data access code to async mode, you only gained the ability to clog the database even more! You turned to async because your database was too slow to respond to incoming requests, and all that you did was send more queries to the database. This is not exactly a way to solve the problem. Adding a cache between the web server and the database would be a much better solution. Again, take the time to measure your distributed application performances under load and update your code and architecture if needed.

On the other hand, this is not the only scenario. It could even be that the more requests you can serve by turning async are for static resources or quick pages. In this case, your site would provide users with a much more responsive experience and provide better scalability.

Which Server Would You Like to Slow Down?

In some ways, it seems to me that when the site is slow to respond because of long-running (not CPU-bound) operations, you should make a decision about which server is acceptable to slow down—the web server or the database server.

Generally speaking, the ASP.NET thread pool can handle many more simultaneous requests than a database server. Performance counters will tell you if the problem is the actual HTTP traffic that's too high for the IIS configuration or if the web server is fine, but it's the database that is having a hard time. There are settings in the IIS/ASP.NET configuration that can increase the number of requests and threads per CPU. If numbers show that quick requests are sacrificed in the queue, simply raising that number can be faster than turning the code to async.

If numbers tell you that the bottleneck is the database that gets too many requests for queries that take too long to complete, then you need to review the overall architecture of the back end or just manage to use caching or simply try to make queries more efficient.

Architectural changes in the back end could, for example, mean offloading the request to an external queue and have the queue call you back when done. A long-running query—whatever "long" means to your application—is better treated as a fire-and-forget operation. I realize that this approach might require a completely different, message-based architecture. That's, however, the real key to scale up. Asynching everything is not a guarantee of super performance, but it is not a performance killer either. Do not delude yourself thinking it just works and fixes everything.

Summary

ASP.NET Core applications have many ways to access data. EF Core is not the only option, but it is an O/RM specifically designed for the .NET Core platform and to work well with ASP.NET Core. As we have seen in the chapter, you can use ADO.NET as well as micro O/RM to create your data access layer. My best advice is to treat the data access layer as a separate layer in depending not directly from the presentation but from an application layer where you concentrate all the workflows.

Frontend

In Part IV, we turn to your application's front end, introducing technologies and complementary frameworks for building usable and modern presentation layers.

Chapter 10, *Designing a Web API*, shows how to build true Web APIs with ASP.NET Core to return JSON, XML, or other data. With these techniques, you can solve ubiquitous problems in modern application scenarios where diverse clients continually invoke remote backends to download data or request processing.

In Chapter 11, *Posting Data from Client Side*, you'll learn how to post data in ASP.NET Core using JavaScript without the overhead of old-fashioned full-page form refreshes. Next, in Chapter 12, *Client-side Data Binding*, we'll cover techniques for refreshing content in a browser directly via JavaScript without reloads. You'll walk through downloading and dynamically replacing portions of an HTML page and setting up JSON endpoints that can be queried for fresh data to regenerate HTML layouts entirely on the client side.

Chapter 13, *Building Device-friendly Views*, completes our tour of web application front ends. You'll learn how to overcome the difficult challenge of delivering native-like web application experiences on iPhone or Android by simulating native widgets through rich component controls that output mixtures of JavaScript and HTML5.

CHAPTER 10

Designing a Web API

We've got to live, no matter how many skies have fallen.

— D.H. Lawrence, "Lady Chatterley's Lover"

In the context of ASP.NET Core, the term "web API" finally gets its real meaning without ambiguity and need to explain the contours further. A web API is a programmatic interface made of a number of publicly exposed HTTP endpoints that typically (but not necessarily) return JSON or XML data to callers. A web API fits nicely in what today appears to be a fairly common application scenario: a client application needs to invoke some remote back end to download data or request processing. The client application can take many forms including a JavaScript-intensive web page, a rich client, or a mobile application. In this chapter, we'll see what it takes to build a web API in ASP.NET Core. In particular, we'll focus on the philosophy of the API—whether REST-oriented or procedure-oriented—and on how to secure it.

Building a Web API with ASP.NET Core

At its core, a web API is a collection of HTTP endpoints. That means in ASP.NET Core, an application equipped with a terminating middleware that parses the query string and figures out the action to take is a minimal, but working, web API. More likely, though, you would build a web API using controllers to better organize functions and behavior. There are two major approaches to the design of the API. You can expose endpoints that refer to actual business workflows and actions under your total control, or you can define business resources and use the entire HTTP stack—headers, parameters, status codes, and verbs—to receive input and return output. The former approach is procedure-oriented and is usually labeled as RPC, short for Remote Procedure Call. The other approach is inspired by REST philosophy.

The REST approach is more standard and in general, more recommended for a public API that is part of the enterprise business. If customers are using your API, then you might want to expose it according to a set of generally accepted and known design rules. If the API exists only to serve a limited number of clients—mostly under the same control of the API creators—no real difference exists between using the RPC or the REST design route. Let's ignore REST principles for the moment and focus on what it takes to expose HTTP JSON endpoints in ASP.NET Core.

Exposing HTTP Endpoints

Even though you could embed some request processing logic right in the terminating middleware, the most common approach is using controllers. Overall, going through controllers and the MVC application model saves you the burden of dealing with routes and binding of parameters. As we'll see later, though, ASP.NET Core also is flexible enough to accommodate scenarios where the server structure is minimal and does its dirty job quickly and without ceremony.

Returning JSON from the Action Method

To return JSON data, all you do is create an ad hoc method in a new or existing *Controller* class. The sole specific requirement for the new method is returning a *JsonResult* object.

```
public IActionResult LatestNews(int count)
{
    var listOfNews = _service.GetRecentNews(count);
    return Json(listOfNews);
}
```

The *Json* method ensures that the given object is packaged in a *JsonResult* object. Once returned from the controller class, the *JsonResult* object is processed by the action invoker, which is when the actual serialization takes place. That's all of it. You retrieve the data you need, you package it up into an object, and pass it on to the *Json* method. Done. Or, at least, it's done if the data is fully serializable.

The actual URL to invoke the endpoint can be determined through the usual routing approaches—conventional routing and/or attribute routing.

Returning Other Data Types

Serving other data types doesn't require a different approach. The pattern is always the same—retrieve data and serialize it to a properly formatted string. The *Content* method on the base controller class allows to you serialize any text using a second parameter to instruct the browser about the intended MIME type.

```
[HttpGet]
public IActionResult Today(int o = 0)
{
    return Content(DateTime.Today.AddDays(o).ToString("d MMM yyyy"), "text/plain");
}
```

To return the content of a server file, for example, a PDF file for download, you can proceed as follows.

```
public IActionResult Download(int id)
{
    // Locate the file to download (whatever that means)
    var fileName = _service.FindDocument(id);

    // Reads the actual content
    var bytes = File.ReadAllBytes(fileName);
    return File(bytes, "application/pdf", fileName);
}
```

If the file is located on the server (for example, your application is hosted on-premise), then you can locate it by name. If the file was uploaded to a database or Azure blob storage, then you retrieve its content as a stream of bytes and still pass the reference to the appropriate overload of the *File* method. Setting the correct MIME type is up to you. The third parameter of the *File* method refers to the name of the downloaded file. (See Figure 10-1.)

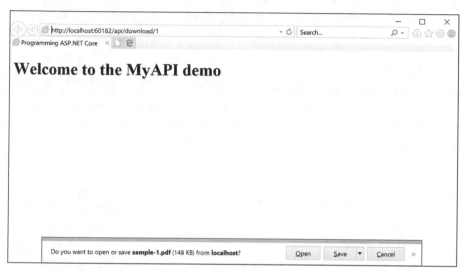

FIGURE 10-1 Downloading a file from a remote endpoint

Requesting Data in a Particular Format

In the previous examples, the return type of the endpoint was fixed and determined by the running code. It's fairly common, instead, that the same content can be requested by different clients, each with its own preferred MIME type. I run into this situation quite often. Most of the services I write for a particular customer just return data formatted as JSON. This serves the needs of the corporate developers consuming the services from within .NET, mobile, and JavaScript applications. Sometimes, however, some endpoints are consumed also by Flash applications that, for a number of reasons, prefer to process data as XML. An easy way to solve the issue is to add a parameter to the endpoint URL that using any convention that works for you knows the desired output format. Here's an example.

```
public IActionResult Weather(int days = 3, string format = "json")
{
    // Get weather forecasts for the specified number of days for a given city
    var cityCode = "...";
    var info = _weatherService.GetForecasts(cityCode, days, "celsius");

    // Return data as requested by the user
    if (format == "xml")
        return Content(ForecastsXmlFormatter.Serialize(info), "text/xml");
    return Json(info);
}
```

The *ForecastsXmlFormatter* is a custom class that just returns a custom handmade XML string written to any schema that works in the particular context.

Restricting to Verbs

In all the examples considered so far, the code that handles the request is a controller method. Hence, you can use all of the programmatic features of a controller action method to control the binding of the parameters and, more importantly, the HTTP verbs and/or necessary headers or cookies to trigger the code. The rules are the same routing rules we explored in Chapter 3. For example, the code below restricts the endpoint api/weather to be invoked over a GET request only.

```
[HttpGet]
public IActionResult Weather(int days = 3, string format = "json")
{
    ...
}
```

In much the same way, you apply restrictions on the referrer URL and/or same-origin security policies for JavaScript clients.

Important It is key to note that in this section of the chapter, I'm just trying to show very simple but still effective ways to solve common problems of a web API. More structured solutions exist for design and security, and I will cover those later in this chapter.

File Servers

Before we reconsider the crucial aspects of the design of an API and add some security to it, let's briefly look back at an example presented in Chapter 2—a mini website.

Terminating Middleware to Catch Requests

In Chapter 2, we introduced the terminating middleware and discussed some interesting use cases for it. The code below is a reprint of one of the examples presented in the chapter.

```
public void Configure(IApplicationBuilder app,
          IHostingEnvironment env,
          ICountryRepository country)
{
```

```
    app.Run(async (context) =>
    {
        var query = context.Request.Query["q"];
        var listOfCountries = country.AllBy(query).ToList();
        var json = JsonConvert.SerializeObject(listOfCountries);
        await context.Response.WriteAsync(json);
    });
}
```

The method *Run*—the terminating middleware—catches any requests that are not handled otherwise. For example, it catches requests that don't go through any of the configured controllers. As is, whatever the actual endpoint will be, the code above checks for a specific query string parameter (named *q*) and filters the internal list of countries by that value. You can refactor the code to be, for example, a file server.

Terminating Middleware to Catch Only Some Requests

By design, the terminating middleware catches any requests unless it is restricted to some specific URLs. To restrict the valid URLs, you can use the *Map* middleware method.

```
public void Configure(IApplicationBuilder app)
{
    app.Map("/api/file", DownloadFile);
}

private static void DownloadFile(IApplicationBuilder app)
{
    app.Run(async context =>
    {
        var id = context.Request.Query["id"];
        var document = string.Format("sample-{0}.pdf", id);
        await context.Response.SendFileAsync(document);
    });
}
```

Because of the *Map* method, every time the incoming request points to the */api/file* path the code attempts to find an *id* query string parameter. From there, it then builds a file path and returns the content to the caller.

What we managed to have is a very thin file server that can intelligently retrieve paths to stored images and serve them back with the minimal amount of code that is legitimately possible to have.

Designing a RESTful Interface

Our first run over the whole topic of exposing JSON and data endpoints to external HTTP callers unveiled a couple of facts. First, exposing endpoints is really easy and is in no way different from exposing the common pieces of a website. Instead of returning HTML, you return JSON or whatever else. Second, when you expose an API instead of a website, some aspects of the server code deserve more attention and a deeper forethinking.

In the first place, you might want to be very clear and consistent about what each endpoint requires and what it provides. It's not simply a matter of documenting URLs and JSON schemas. It's also a matter of setting strict rules as far as how HTTP verbs and headers are accepted and handled, and how status codes are returned. Also, you might want to put an authorization layer on top of the API that authenticates callers and checks their permissions on the various endpoints.

REST is a very common approach to unify the way public APIs are exposed to clients. ASP.NET Core controllers just support some extra features to make the output as RESTful as possible.

REST at a Glance

The core idea behind REST is that the web application—mostly a web API—works entirely based on the full set of capabilities of the HTTP protocol, including verbs, headers, and status codes. REST is a shorthand name for *Representational State Transfer,* which means the application will handle requests in the form of HTTP verbs (GET, POST, PUT, DELETE, and HEAD) acting on resources. In REST, a resource is nearly identical to a domain entity and is represented by a unique URI.

> **Note** REST is a sort of CRUD over the web done against resources identified by URI rather than database entities identified by primary keys. REST defines operations through HTTP verbs in much the same way CRUD does via SQL statements.

REST has been around for a while even though it was obfuscated in the beginning by another service concept—SOAP, which is short for Simple Object Access Protocol. REST was defined by Roy Fielding in 2000 and SOAP was formulated more or less at the same time. A deep philosophical difference separates REST and SOAP.

- SOAP is about accessing objects hidden behind a web façade and is about invoking actions on them. SOAP is about exposing the programmability of a set of objects and is essentially about performing remote procedure calls (RPC).

- REST is about acting directly on objects through basic core operations—the HTTP verbs.

Given this foundational difference, SOAP only uses a small subset of HTTP verbs in its implementation—GET and POST.

Intended Meaning of HTTP Verbs

HTTP verbs have easy to remember, mostly self-explanatory meanings. They apply the basic create-read-update-delete CRUD semantics of database to web resources. A web resource, in the end, is the business entity you access via the web API. If the business entity is, say, a booking, then a POST command on the URI of the particular booking will add a new one into the system. The details of a REST-compliant request, whether a POST, PUT, GET, or whatever, will be detailed later when ASP.NET Core controller classes get into the game. Table 10-1 lists and comments on the HTTP verbs.

TABLE 10-1 HTTP verbs

HTTP Verb	Description
DELETE	Issues the request for deleting the addressed resource, whatever that means for the back end. The actual implementation of the "delete" operation belongs to the application and could be either something physical or logical.
GET	Issues the request for getting the current representation of the addressed resource. The use of additional HTTP headers can fine-tune the actual behavior. For example, the *If-Modified-Since* header mitigates the request by expecting a response only if changes have occurred since the specified time.
HEAD	Same as GET, except that only metadata of the addressed resource are returned, not the body. This command is primarily used to check whether a resource exists.
POST	Issues the request for adding a resource when the URI is not known in advance. The REST response to this request returns the URI of the newly created resource. Again, what "adding a resource" actually means for the back end is the responsibility of the back end.
PUT	Issues the request for making sure that the state of the addressed resource is in line with provided information. It's the logical counterpart of an update command.

Each of those requests is expected to have a well-known layout regarding what comes in (verbs and headers) and what comes out (status code and headers.)

Structure of a REST Request

Let's just go through the verbs listed in Table 10-1 and find out more about the suggested template of a request. (See Table 10-2.)

TABLE 10-2 Schema of REST requests

HTTP Verb	Request	Response in case of success
DELETE	All the parameters that allow for identification of the resource. For example, the unique integer identifier of the resource. http://apiserver/booking/12345 With the above request, you intend to delete the booking resource whose ID is 12345.	There are various options for the response. ■ Void response. ■ Status code 200 or 204. ■ Status code 202 to indicate that request was successfully received and accepted but will be enacted later.
GET	All the parameters that allow for identification of the resource, plus optional headers such as *If-Modified-Since*.	Status code 200. The body of the response contains information about the state of the addressed resource.
HEAD	Same as above.	Status code 200. The body is empty, and the metadata of the resource is returned as HTTP headers.
POST	Any data relevant to the operation. The POST operation creates a new resource, so there's no identifier to be passed.	There are a few things to notice for a successful POST operation. ■ Status code 201 (created) but also a status code of 200 or 204 is acceptable. ■ The body of the response contains any information valuable to the caller. ■ The Location HTTP header is set to the URI of the newly created resource.

HTTP Verb	Request	Response in case of success
PUT	All the parameters that allow for identification of the resource, plus any data relevant to the operation.	There are various options for the response. ■ Status code is 200 or 204. ■ The void response is also acceptable.

A status code of 200 indicates the success of whatever operation was attempted. In general, a successful operation might require that the URI of the addressed resource is returned. This is acceptable, for example, for a successful POST that returns the URI of the newly created resource. It is arguably acceptable, instead, for a DELETE because the URI you would return points to a resource that should no longer exist. To indicate success with no response, you can either send a 200 and an optional empty body or, more precisely, a 204, which just means success and empty response. Choosing 200 or 204 depends on the verb but is also, to some extent, an arbitrary decision of the API designer.

In case of errors, you return 500 or a more specific error code. If the resource can't be found, you return 404. If not authorized, you return 401 or more specific codes.

To REST or Not to REST?

As I see things, REST is primarily a matter of philosophy. Philosophy is generally good in life, but its concrete usefulness also depends on the context. It's hard to be a philosopher when you're in a save-or-sink situation. At the same time, a good philosophy might reduce your likelihood of being in a save-or-sink situation.

This is to say that REST is ultimately up to you, the web API designer.

REST gives you a way to be clean and tidy in the organization of the API. At the same time, if you're only partially clean and tidy in the actual implementation, well, that's an issue as well that removes all the good you might have done elsewhere.

REST is not the absolute good, per se, and RPC is not the absolute evil, per se. The good or evil of REST depends on the context. For example, if you're planning a public API for customers to buy licenses, or just widely use it, then the cleaner and tidier you are the better. In my business, I have plenty of web services that run the business and big public events, and none of them is REST. However, it works, but we mostly use those web services internally or with partners.

Going with RPC is perhaps more natural because it's inherently business-driven. REST requires quite a bit of forethinking and discipline from a development perspective. REST is not a magic wand, though.

Compared to RPC, REST has two other factors to consider.

■ One is hypermedia, namely the idea that HTTP responses also return an additional field (named _links) with further action that can be taken after the response is received. Hypermedia, therefore, provides information to the client on what it could potentially do next.

■ Another aspect of REST that could have a positive impact on the client side is that REST expects that HTTP responses declare their cacheablility.

REST in ASP.NET Core

Before ASP.NET Core, Microsoft had something called the Web API framework specifically designed to build web APIs with full programming support for RESTful web APIs. The Web API framework was not fully integrated with the underlying ASP.NET pipeline in the sense that once routed to the framework, a request had to go through a dedicated pipeline. Using Web API in the context of an ASP.NET MVC 5.x application might or might not be a valid decision. You can achieve the same goals using plain ASP.NET MVC 5.x controllers, even RESTful interfaces, but you don't get built-in facilities for being RESTful. Being RESTful then is up to you; matching the requirements of Table 10-2 is up to you and your extra code.

In ASP.NET Core, there's nothing like a distinct and dedicated web API framework. There are only controllers with their set of action results and helper methods. If you want to build a web API, you just return JSON, XML, or whatever else as discussed earlier. If you want to build a RESTful API, you just get familiar with another set of action results and helper methods.

RESTful Action Results

In Chapter 4, "ASP.NET MVC Controllers," you already faced the full list of web API-related action result types. Here, I have included a table of action results, grouping them by the core action performed (Table 10-3).

TABLE 10-3 Web API-related *IActionResult* types

Type	Description
AcceptedResult	Returns a 202 status code and sets the URI to check to be informed about the ongoing status of the request.
BadRequestResult	Returns a 400 status code.
CreatedResult	Returns a 201 status code along with the URI of the resource created set in the *Location* header.
NoContentResult	Returns a 204 status code and null content.
OkResult	Returns a 200 status code.
UnsupportedMediaTypeResult	Returns a 415 status code.

As you can see, the action result types prepare a response that is in line with the typical REST behavior as described earlier in Table 10-2. A few types in the table have sibling types that offer a slightly different behavior. For example, there are three variations of action results for the 202 and 201 status codes.

In addition to *AcceptedResult* and *CreatedResult*, you find *xxxAtActionResult* and *xxxAtRouteResult* types. The difference is in how the types express the URI to monitor the status of the accepted operation and the location of the resource that was just created. The *xxxAtActionResult* type expresses the URI as a pair of controller and action strings, whereas the *xxxAtRouteResult* type uses a route name.

For a few other action result types, there's an *xxxObjectResult* variation. Good examples are *OkObjectResult* and *BadRequestObjectResult*. The difference is that object result types also let you append an object to the response. So *OkResult* just sets a 200 status code, but *OkObjectResult* sets a 200 status code and appends an object of your choice. A common way to use this feature is to return a *ModelState* dictionary updated with the detected error when a bad request comes. Another example could be a *NotFoundObjectResult* that could set the current time of the request.

Finally, another interesting distinction is between *NoContentResult* and *EmptyResult*. Both return an empty response but *NoContentResult* sets a status code of 204 whereas *EmptyResult* sets a 200 status code.

Skeleton of Common Actions

Let's review some possible code for a REST API based on the controllers of ASP.NET Core. The sample controller features a resource that represents the news, and the code shows how to possibly code GET, DELETE, POST, and PUT actions.

```
[HttpPost]
public CreatedResult AddNews(News news)
{
    // Do something here to save the news
    var newsId = SaveNewsInSomeWay(news);

    // Returns HTTP 201 and sets the URI to the Location header
    var relativePath = String.Format("/api/news/{0}", newsId);
    return Created(relativePath, news);
}


[HttpPut]
public AcceptedResult UpdateNews(Guid id, string title, string content)
{
    // Do something here to update the news
    var news = UpdateNewsInSomeWay(id, title, content);
    var relativePath = String.Format("/api/news/{0}", news.NewsId);
    return Accepted(new Uri(relativePath));
}


[HttpDelete]
public NoContentResult DeleteNews(Guid id)
{
    // Do something here to delete the news
    // ...

    return NoContent();
}


[HttpGet]
public ObjectResult Get(Guid id)
{
    // Do something here to retrieve the news
    var news = FindNewsInSomeWay(id);

    return Ok(news);
}
```

All return types are derived from *IActionResult,* and actual instances are created using ad hoc helper methods exposed by the *Controller* base class. It is interesting to note that compared to the former

Web API, in ASP.NET Core, controller helper methods simplify the work by capturing most of the common REST chores. In fact, if you look into the source code of the *CreatedResult* class, you see the following code:

```
// Invoked from the base class ObjectResult
public override void OnFormatting(ActionContext context)
{
    if (context == null)
        throw new ArgumentNullException("context");
    base.OnFormatting(context);
    context.HttpContext.Response.Headers["Location"] = (StringValues) this.Location;
}
```

In Web API, you had to write most of this code yourself. ASP.NET Core does a better job of making controller classes RESTful. The source code of Web API-related classes in ASP.NET Core can be inspected looking at the *http://github.com/aspnet/Mvc/blob/dev/src/Microsoft.AspNetCore.Mvc.Core* folder.

Content Negotiation

Content negotiation is a feature of ASP.NET Core controllers that was not supported by ASP.NET MVC 5 controllers and was introduced specifically for the needs of the Web API framework. In ASP.NET Core, it's built into the engine and is available to developers. As the name suggests, content negotiation refers to a silent negotiation taking place between the caller and the API. The negotiation regards the actual format of returned data.

Content negotiation is taken into account if the incoming request contains an *Accept* header that advertises the MIMEs the caller can understand. The default behavior in ASP.NET Core is serializing any returned object as JSON. In the following code, for example, the *News* object would be serialized as JSON unless content negotiation determines a different format.

```
[HttpGet]
public ObjectResult Get(Guid id)
{
    // Do something here to retrieve the news
    var news = FindNewsInSomeWay(id);

    return Ok(news);
}
```

If the controller detects an *Accept* header, it goes through the types listed in the header content until it finds a format it can provide. The scan follows the order in which MIME types appear. If no type is found that the controller can support, then JSON is used.

Note that content negotiation is triggered if the incoming request contains an *Accept* header and the response sent back by the controller is of type *ObjectResult*. If you serialize the controller response via, say, the *Json* method, no negotiation will ever take place regardless of the headers sent.

> **Note** Another action result type, *UnsupportedMediaTypeResult*, appears to have some relationship to content negotiation. Processing this action result would return a 415 HTTP status code, meaning that *Content-Type* header—another HTTP other than *Accept*—was sent to describe the content of the request. For example, the *Content-Type* header indicates the actual format of an image file being uploaded. If the controller doesn't support that content type (for example, a PNG is uploaded that the server doesn't support), then a 415 code might be returned. Given this, the *UnsupportedMediaTypeResult* type is not really related to content negotiation.

Securing a Web API

Securing a web application is simpler than securing an API exposed over HTTP. A web application is consumed by web browsers, and web browsers can easily deal with cookies. In ASP.NET Core, the *Authorize* attribute on action methods instructs the runtime that only authenticated users can invoke the method. In ASP.NET Core (and in any sort of web applications), cookies are the primary way to store and forward information about the identity of the user. When it comes to an API over the web, there are additional scenarios to consider. The client can be a desktop application or, more likely, a mobile application. Suddenly, cookies are no longer an effective way to secure an API while keeping it widely usable by the largest possible number of clients.

Overall, I'd split the security options for a web API into two big camps: *simple-but-to-some-extent-effective* methods and *best practice* methods.

Planning Just the Security You Really Need

Security is a serious matter, isn't it? So why would you ever consider anything that is less than a best practice? The reason is that security doesn't mean the same to everyone. Security is a nonfunctional requirement whose relevance changes based on the context. I have in-production web APIs with no authorization layer at all—APIs that anyone can call if only they could figure out the URLs. I also have other web APIs that implement a very basic layer of access control, which are sufficient for the vast majority of thinkable scenarios. Finally, I also have a couple of web APIs with which I use best practice access control.

The tradeoff between *simple-but-to-some-extent-effective* methods and *best practice* methods is how long it takes and much it costs to have best practice security in place. The relevance of the data you hold and share via the API is crucial to your decision. A read-only API that shares public or non-sensitive data is much less problematic from an access control perspective.

In this regard, I'd love to share an anecdote from one of the ASP.NET MVC classes I taught recently. In the middle of the ASP.NET MVC security module of the class, one of the attendees asked why on earth did he need all the mess I was describing about principals, roles, claims, tokens, and the like. I gently noted that it all depended on the relevance of the data. The answer made me laugh, but it just helped to nail the point down. "The most that can happen in my application," he said, "is that one user views the photos of someone else's cows. Not really a big deal." I couldn't agree more!

 Important Using the *Authorize* attribute on action methods subject to access control works on a web API, but it only lets users connecting through web browser clients to prove their identity. If users come to the API via a mobile or desktop application, you must find a way to support cookies. Windows does have some APIs for the purpose, and in mobile applications, you can make the connection through some dedicated frameworks that basically use a web view to deal with cookies. The whole point of securing an API is finding a unified approach that is not cookie-based and still guarantees detection of the identity.

Simpler Access Control Methods

Let's review a few options to add an access control layer on top of your web API. None is perfect, but none is entirely ineffective either.

Basic Authentication

The simplest approach to incorporate access control in the web API is to use the Basic authentication built into the web server. Basic authentication is based on the idea that user credentials are packaged in every request.

Basic authentication has pros and cons. It is supported by major browsers, it is an Internet standard, and it is simple to configure. The downside is that credentials are sent with every request and, worse yet, they are sent as clear text.

Basic authentication expects that credentials are sent to be validated on the server. The request is then accepted only if credentials are valid. If credentials are not in the request, an interactive dialog box is displayed. Realistically, basic authentication also requires some ad hoc middleware to check credentials against accounts stored in some database.

 Note Basic authentication is simple and quite effective if combined with a layer that does custom validation of credentials. To overcome the limitation of credentials sent as clear text, you should always implement a Basic authentication solution over HTTPS.

Token-based Authentication

The idea is that the web API receives an access token—typically a GUID or an alphanumeric string—validates it and serves the request if the token is not expired and is valid for the application. There are various ways to issue a token. The simplest is that tokens are issued offline when a customer contacts the company to license the API. You create the token and associate it with a particular customer. From that point forward, the customer is responsible for the abuse or misuse of the API, and server-side methods work only if they recognize the token.

The web API back end needs to have a layer that checks tokens. You can add this layer as plain code to any method or, better yet, configure it to be a piece of the application middleware. Tokens can be appended to the URL (for example, as query string parameters) or embedded in the request as an HTTP header. None of these approaches is perfect, and no approach exists that is safer. In both cases, the value of the token can be spied on. Using a header is preferable because an HTTP header is not immediately visible in the URL.

To make the defense stronger, you might want to use some strict expiration policy on the tokens. All in all, though, the strength of this approach is that you always know who is responsible for the abuse or misuse of the API and can stop them from disabling the token at any time.

Additional Access Control Barriers

Also (or as an alternative to the previous approaches), you can still serve only requests coming from a given URL and/or IP address(es). From within a controller method, you can check the IP address from which the request comes using the following expression:

```
var ip = HttpContext.Connection.RemoteIpAddress;
```

Note, though, that getting the IP address when the application is behind a load balancer (for example, Nginx) might be more problematic and some fallback logic that checks and handles the *X-Forwarded-For* HTTP header might be required.

The originating URL is usually set in the *referer* HTTP header that indicates the last page the user was on before placing the request. You can state that your web API serves certain requests only if the *referer* header contains a fixed value. HTTP headers, though, can be set easily by ad hoc robots.

In general, techniques like checking the IP address and/or HTTP headers like *referer* and even *user-agent* are primarily ways to raise the bar higher and higher.

Using an Identity Management Server

In general, an identity management server is a server that sits in the middle of many applications and components and outsources identity services. In other words, instead of having the authentication logic in-house, you configure such a server and expect it to do the job. In the context of Web API, an identity server can provide a single sign-on between configured, related APIs and access control. In the ASP.NET Core space (but also in the classic ASP.NET space), a popular choice is Identity Server, version 4 for ASP.NET Core. (See *http://www.identityserver.com*.) Identity Server is an open-source product and implements both OpenID Connect and OAuth protocols. In this regard, it qualifies as an excellent tool to delegate access control to keep your web API secure. In the rest of the chapter, we'll be referring to Identity Server 4 for ASP.NET Core.

Note The advantage of using an identity server to control the access to a web API is that you still mark action methods with the *Authorize* attribute, but no cookies are used to present the user's identity. The web API receives (and checks) an authorization token that comes as an HTTP header. The content of the token is set by the selected Identity Server instance once configured with the users' data enabled to access the web API. Because no cookies are involved, a web API protected with Identity Server can easily serve mobile applications, desktop applications, and any present or (why not?) future HTTP client.

Preparing the Ground for Identity Server v4

Figure 10-2 shows the overall picture of how Identity Server interacts with your web API and its enabled clients.

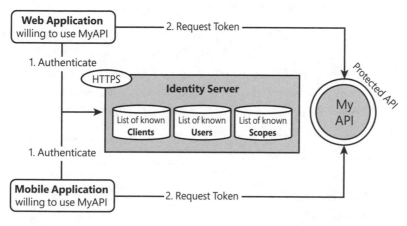

FIGURE 10-2 The big picture of a web API protected with Identity Server

Identity Server must be a dedicated, self-hosted application, which in ASP.NET Core, you can decide to expose directly through Kestrel or via a reverse proxy. In any case, you need a well-known HTTP address to reach out the server. To be fair, you need a well-known HTTPS address to contact the server. HTTPS adds privacy to whatever is exchanged over the wire. Identity Server provides access control, but realistically, you always want to have HTTPS on top of an identity server.

Figure 10-2 shows that Identity Server is preferably a separate application from the API. To fully demonstrate it, we're going to have three distinct projects—one to host Identity Server, one to host the sample web API, and one to simulate a client application.

Building a Host Environment for Identity Server

To host Identity Server, start creating a fresh new ASP.NET Core project and add the *IdentityServer4* *NuGet* package. If you're already using ASP.NET Identity (see Chapter 8), then you might want to add also *IdentityServer4.AspNetIdentity*. Additional packages might be required, depending on the actual features you turn on. The startup class looks like below (the Config methods are explained later on).

```
public class Startup
{
    public void ConfigureServices(IServiceCollection services)
    {
        services.AddIdentityServer()
            .AddDeveloperSigningCredential()
            .AddInMemoryApiResources(Config.GetApiResources())
            .AddInMemoryClients(Config.GetClients());
    }

    public void Configure(IApplicationBuilder app, IHostingEnvironment env)
    {
        app.UseDeveloperExceptionPage();
        app.UseIdentityServer();

        app.Run(async (context) =>
        {
            await context.Response.WriteAsync(
                "Welcome to Identity Server - Pro ASP.NET Core book");
        });
    }
}
```

Figure 10-3 shows the home page you see. As is, the server has no endpoints and no user interface, but adding an admin user interface to change configuration aspects is up to you. An AdminUI service for Identity Server 4 has been released as an add-on. (See *http://www.identityserver.com*).

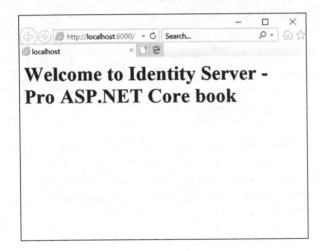

FIGURE 10-3 The Identity Server instance up and running

Let's find out more about the configuration parameters of the server and specifically clients, API resources, and signing credentials.

Adding Clients to Identity Server

The list of clients refers to client applications allowed to connect to Identity Server and access the resources and the APIs protected by the server. Each client application must be configured for what it can be allowed to do and how it can do it. For example, a client application can be limited to call only into a segment of an API. At a minimum, you might want to configure a client application with an ID and a secret as well as a grant type and scopes.

```
public class Config
{
    public static IEnumerable<Client> GetClients()
    {
        return new List<Client>
        {
            new Client
            {
                ClientId = "contoso",
                ClientSecrets = {
                    new Secret("contoso-secret".Sha256())
                },
                AllowedGrantTypes = GrantTypes.ClientCredentials,
                AllowedScopes = { "weather-API" }
            }
        };
    }
    ...
```

You might be familiar with IDs and secrets if you've ever tried to work with a social network API. For example, to access Facebook data, you first create a Facebook application that is fully identified by a couple of strings—ID and secret, as they're named in Identity Server. The grant type indicates how a client will be allowed to interact with the server. A client application can have multiple grant types. It should be noted that a client application here is not the same as running an actual application. Actually, a *client application*, as discussed here, is an OpenID Connect and OAuth2 concept. For example, a concrete mobile application and an actual website can use the same client application to access Identity Server.

If you intend to protect a web API, you typically use *ClientCredentials*, which means that a request token is not necessary for the individual user; a request token is only necessary for the client application. In other words, as the web API owner, you grant access to a client application and all of its individual users. In general, though, Identity Server can be used to perform access control on a per-user basis, which creates the need for multiple grant types and even multiple grant types for the same client application. For more information on scenarios that go beyond protecting a web API in a server-to-server communication, you might want to check *http://docs.identityserver.io/en/release/topics/grant_types.html*.

When the *ClientCredentials* option is used, the resulting flow is exactly like that in Figure 10-2. The actual application that needs to call the protected API first sends a token request to the Identity Server token endpoint. In doing so, the actual application uses the credentials (ID and secret) of one of the configured Identity Server clients. If authentication is successful, the actual application gets an access token back that represents the client to pass on to the web API. (More on this later in the chapter.)

Adding API Resources to Identity Server

In general, an API resource refers to the resources (for example, a web API) you want to protect from unauthorized access. Concretely, an API resource is just the label that identifies your web API within Identity Server. An API resource is made of a key and a display name. Through API resources, a client application sets its scope in much the same way you declare the claims of the user you intend to access in Facebook applications. Declaring the API resources of interest prevents the client application from accessing any web API, or a portion of a web API, not in scope. When registering with Identity Server, a web API declares the resources it handles.

```
public class Config
{
    public static IEnumerable<ApiResource> GetApiResources()
    {
        return new List<ApiResource>
        {
            new ApiResource("fun-API",
            "My API just for test and fun"),
            new ApiResource("weather-API",
                "My fabulous weather API"),
        };
    }
...}
```

In the code above, Identity Server is configured to support two resources—*fun-API* and *weather-API*. The client application defined earlier is interested only in *weather-API*.

Persistence of Clients and Resources

In the example discussed here, we're using statically defined clients and resources. While this might even be the case in some deployed applications, it's not much realistic indeed. It could make sense in a closed environment when you control all components in the game and can recompile and redeploy API, server, and actual applications when something must change, and a new resource or a new client is required.

More likely, clients and resources are loaded from some persistent store. This can be achieved in a couple of ways. One entails that you write your own code to retrieve clients and resources and pass them as in-memory objects to Identity Server. The second way leverages the built-in infrastructure of Identity Server.

```
services.AddIdentityServer()
    .AddDeveloperSigningCredential()
    .AddConfigurationStore(options =>
    {
        options.ConfigureDbContext = builder =>
            builder.UseSqlServer("connectionString...",
                sql => sql.MigrationsAssembly(migrationsAssembly));
    })
    ...
```

If you go this way, you need migrations to pass the schema of the database that will then be silently created. To create migrations assembly, you need to run ad hoc commands bundled with the additional NuGet package *IdentityServer4.EntityFramework* that you need to install, too. Finally, note that Identity Server also gives you a chance to plug in caching components for performance reasons. In this case, it suffices that the plugged components implement a given interface regardless of the actual underlying technology used for saving data.

> **Note** For a comprehensive view of the various options you have as far as persistence and signing are concerned, see *http://docs.identityserver.io/en/release/quickstarts/8_entity_framework.html*.

Signing Credentials

In the startup code above, you have seen the *AddDeveloperSigningCredential* method used to create a temporary key to sign tokens being sent back as proof of identity. If you look at the project after the first run, you see a JSON file added named *tempkey.rsa*.

```
{"KeyId":"c789...","Parameters":{"D":"ndm8...",...}}
```

While this might be good to try out, it definitely needs to be replaced with a persistent key or certificate for production scenarios. Realistically, at some point, you want to switch to *AddSigningCredential*, perhaps after checking the current environment. The *AddSigningCredential* method adds a signing key service that retrieves the same key information that *AddDeveloperSigningCredential* creates on the fly from a persistent store. The method *AddSigningCredential* can accept the digital signature in a variety of formats. It can be an object of type *X509Certificate2* or a reference to a certificate from the certificate store.

```
AddIdentityServer()
    .AddSigningCredential("CN=CERT_SIGN_TEST_CERT");
```

It can also be an instance of the *SigningCredentials* class or *RsaSecurityKey*.

> **Note** For a comprehensive view of the various options you have as far as signing is concerned, see *http://docs.identityserver.io/en/release/topics/crypto.html*.

Adapting the Web API to Identity Server

At this point, the server is up and running and ready to control access to our API. However, the web API still lacks a layer of code that connects it to the Identity Server. To add authorization via Identity Server, you need to take two steps. First, you add the *IdentityServer4.AccessTokenValidation* package. The package adds the necessary middleware to validate the tokens coming from Identity Server. Second, you configure the service as below.

```
public void ConfigureServices(IServiceCollection services)
{
    // Configure the MVC application model
    services.AddMvcCore();
    services.AddAuthorization();
    services.AddJsonFormatters();
```

```
        services.AddAuthentication(IdentityServerAuthenticationDefaults.AuthenticationScheme)
            .AddIdentityServerAuthentication(x =>
            {
                x.Authority = "http://localhost:6000";
                x.ApiName = "weather-API";
                x.RequireHttpsMetadata = false;
            });
}
```

Note that the MVC application model configuration used in the code snippet is the absolute minimum you need. The authentication scheme is *Bearer,* and the *Authority* parameter points to the URL of the Identity Server in place. The *ApiName* parameter refers to the API resource the web API implements, and *RequireHttpsMetadata* establishes that HTTPS is not required to discover the API endpoint.

Also, you simply place all your APIs that are not intended to be public under the umbrella of the *Authorize* attribute. User information can be inspected through the *HttpContext.User* property. That's all there is to it! When the access token is presented to the web API, the Identity Server's access token validation middleware will investigate it and match the audience scope of the incoming request to the value of the *ApiName* property. (See Figure 10-4.) If no match is found, an unauthorized error code is returned.

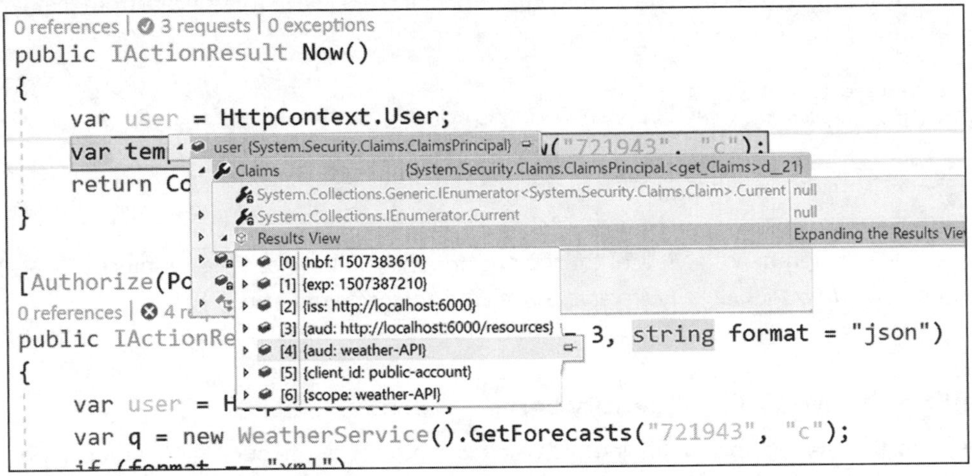

FIGURE 10-4 Inspecting the content of the *HttpContext.User* object in Visual Studio

Let's see now what it takes to actually call into the API.

Putting It All Together

In force of the security layer, callers of the web API must now provide some credentials to connect. Connection takes place in two steps. First, a caller attempts to get a request token from the configured Identity Server endpoint. In doing so, the caller provides credentials. Credentials must match those of a client application registered with Identity Server. Second, if credentials are recognized, an access token is issued, which must be passed to the web API. Here's the code.

```
// Obtains the actual URL to request the token from the instance of Identity Server.
// By default, it is <server-URL>/connect/token.
var disco = DiscoveryClient.GetAsync("http://localhost:6000").Result;

// Attempts to get an access token to call the web API. ID and secret of
// the client application to use must be provided.
var tokenClient = new TokenClient(disco.TokenEndpoint,
                                  "public-account", "public-account-secret");
var tokenResponse = tokenClient.RequestClientCredentialsAsync("weather-API").Result;
if (tokenResponse.IsError) { ... }
```

The classes used in the code above require that the *IdentityModel* NuGet package is added to your client application project. Finally, while placing the call to the web API, the access token must be appended as an HTTP header.

```
var http = new HttpClient();
http.SetBearerToken(tokenResponse.AccessToken);
var response = http.GetAsync("http://localhost:6001/weather/now").Result;
if (!response.IsSuccessStatusCode) { ... }
```

If you're licensing the API to a customer, all you have to do is 1) provide the credentials of the client application you created in Identity Server to call into the web API, and 2) provide the name you have chosen for the API resource. You could also create a client application for each customer and append additional claims to each request or run some authorization code in web API methods to check the identity of the actual caller and make decisions about that.

Summary

A web API is a common element in most applications today. A web API is used to provide data to an Angular or MVC front end as well as to provide services to mobile or desktop applications. In a web-to-web scenario, security can be easily implemented through cookies, but a bearer-based approach clears any dependencies from cookies, thus making the API easy to call from whatever HTTP client is used.

An identity management server is an application that sits in between a web API (but also a web application) and its callers and provides authentication, in much the same way social networks can do. The underlying protocols are just the same—OpenID Connect and OAuth2. Identity Server is an open-source product you can set up in your own environment and configure to act as your authentication and authorization server.

CHAPTER 11

Posting Data from the Client Side

It matters not what someone is born, but what they grow to be.
—*J. K. Rowling, "Harry Potter and the Goblet of Fire"*

Admittedly, the problem of posting data to a web server from an HTML form has always been a no-brainer. HTML does it all for you, and all you must learn is how to cope with the basic syntax of HTML. As far as forms are concerned, the HTML syntax hasn't changed at all since the early days up to HTML5. In this chapter, we face reality. Reality says that it is much less acceptable for an end user to sustain a classic HTML form than it was a few years ago. Having the browser carry on the posting of a form means that a full page refresh will occur. This might be acceptable for a login form, for example, but not for a form that just aims at posting some content without the immediate need for the user to jump to a different page.

In this chapter, we'll fully dissect HTML forms starting with an overview of the HTML syntax and then moving forward to employ some client-side JavaScript code to perform the actual posting of the form content. Using JavaScript to carry on the operation poses additional problems, such as dealing with the feedback of the ongoing server-side operation and refreshing portions of the current view.

Organizing HTML Forms

The content of an HTML form is automatically posted by the browser when one of the submit buttons it contains is pushed. The browser automatically scans the input fields within the boundaries of the FORM element, serializes their content to a string, and sets up an HTTP command to the target URL. The type of the HTTP command (commonly POST) and the target URL are set via attributes on the HTML FORM element. The code behind the target URL—a controller action method in an ASP.NET MVC application—processes the posted content and typically serves back a new HTML view. Any feedback about the processing of the posted data is incorporated into the returned page. Let's briefly review syntax and issues of HTML forms.

Defining an HTML Form

An HTML form is made of a collection of INPUT elements whose values are streamlined to a remote URL when one of submit buttons is pushed. A form can have one or more submit buttons. If no submit button is defined, then the form can't be posted unless it's done through ad hoc script code.

```
<form method="POST" action="@Url.Action(action, controller)">
    <input type="text" value="" />
    ...
    <button type="submit">Submit</button>
</form>
```

You can have as many INPUT elements as you need in a form, and each is characterized by the value of its *type* attribute. Feasible values are *text*, *password*, *hidden*, *date*, *file*, and many others. The *value* attribute of an INPUT element contains the content to display initially and the content to upload when the submit button is pushed.

The FORM element has no user interface except the content produced by the child INPUT elements. Any style you need must be added via CSS, and any layout you want to have must be added inside or around the FORM element, as it best suits you. There's nothing really new or fancy about HTML forms, but a few side problems originate when you try to use forms beyond any basic usage. All in all, there are three relevant programming aspects with forms in the MVC application model.

- If multiple submit buttons exist in the form, how would you easily detect which button was used to post the form?

- How do you organize the form layout when too many input fields are necessary?

- How do you refresh the screen after the form has been submitted and the content is processed?

Let's delve deeper into these.

Multiple Submit Buttons

Sometimes the content of the form can be submitted to trigger a few different actions on the server. How would you understand the intended action on the server? If you use a single submit button, then you have to find a way to add somewhere else in the form enough information for the MVC controller to figure out the intended task to perform. Otherwise, you can just place multiple submit buttons in the form.

In this case, though, the target URL is always the same regardless of the clicked button and, again, you're left with the problem of letting the server know which action you want to be taken. Let's see how to pack this information in the BUTTON element itself.

```
<form class="form-horizontal">
<div class="form-group">
    <div class="col-xs-12">
        <button name="option" value="add" type="submit">ADD</button>
        <button name="option" value="save" type="submit">SAVE</button>
        <button name="option" value="delete" type="submit">DELETE</button>
    </div>
</div>
</form>
```

By design, browsers post the name of the submit button along with the value of the element. Most of the time, though, *name* and *value* attributes are not set for submit buttons. Omitting those attributes might be acceptable when a single button can post the form, but having them becomes crucial when multiple submit buttons exist. How should you set *name* and *value* attributes? In the context of the MVC application model, any posted data is processed by the model binding layer. Once you are aware of this, you can give all the submit buttons the same name and store a unique value in the value attribute that can be used on the server to figure out the next action.

Better yet, you can associate the values set in the *value* attribute to the elements of an *enum* type, as is shown below.

```
public enum Options
{
    None = 0,
    Add = 1,
    Save = 2,
    Delete = 3
}
```

Figure 11-1 shows the effect of using such an HTML code when posting forms with multiple submit buttons.

```
1 reference
public class DemoController : Controller
{
    private readonly HomeService _service;
    0 references
    public DemoController(HomeService service)
    {
        _service = service;
    }


    0 references
    public IActionResult Multiple(string input, Options option)
    {                                                    option Save
        var model = _service.GetHomeViewModel();  ≤ 6,773ms elapsed
        return View(model);
    }
}
```

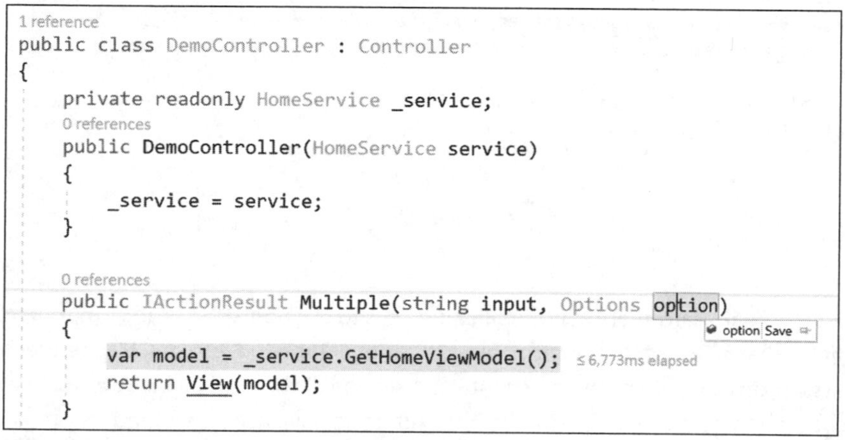

FIGURE 11-1 The value of the submit button is mapped to any corresponding value of an enum type

Large Forms

Often, the number of input fields needed in a form is overwhelmingly high. A long, scrollable HTML form is a solution, but it is arguably the most effective in terms of user experience. First and foremost, users have to move up and down between fields, which means they sometimes lose their focus and forget what they just typed. Also, mistyped values are a problem. Even worse, problems arise when the order in which data must be entered is quite strict, and some data entries influence later entries. For these reasons, a single, huge form is never a good idea. How would you break large forms into smaller and more manageable pieces?

The idea here is to introduce tabs in the body of the HTML form. The body of the FORM element can contain any HTML except child forms. So, the simplest and most effective trick is to use tabs to group related input fields and hide all others from view. This way is much simpler for the user because

she can focus on just a few things at a time. When it comes to posting the form content, nothing is really different because grouping input controls may give users the feeling of multiple forms.
In reality, the FORM container is a form, and because of this, there is a single collection of input fields
to be posted.

```
<form method="post" action="...">
    <div id="wizard">
        <!-- Tabstrip -->
        <ul class="nav nav-tabs" role="tablist">
            <li role="presentation" class="active">
                <a href="#personal" role="tab" data-toggle="tab">You</a>
            </li>
            <li role="presentation">
                <a href="#hobbies" role="tab" data-toggle="tab">Hobbies</a>
            </li>
            :
        </ul>

        <!-- Tab panes -->
        <div class="tab-content">
            <div role="tabpanel" class="tab-pane active" id="personal">
                <!-- Input fields -->
            </div>
            <div role="tabpanel" class="tab-pane" id="hobbies">
                <!-- Input fields -->
            </div>
            :
        </div>
    </div>
</form>
```

The simplest way to break a large form into smaller pieces is to use Bootstrap's tab component. You
split all the input fields that would go in the form into a number of tabs and let Bootstrap render them.
Users will see a classic tabstrip where each pane contains a section of the original input form. In this
way, users can focus on a small chunk of information at a time and have nearly no need to scroll the
browser window up and down.

The list of submit buttons can be placed wherever it most suits you. For example, you can place
them on the same line as tabs, perhaps next to the right edge of the viewport. Here's some Bootstrap
markup for a form submit button within a tabstrip.

```
<ul>
<li> ... </li>
<li> ... </li>
<li> ... </li>
<button class="btn btn-danger pull-right">SAVE</button>
</ul>
```

Figure 11-2 shows the visual effect of a large, tabbed form.

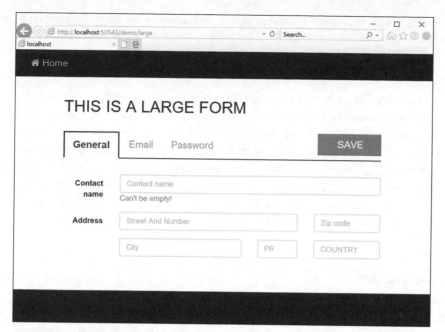

FIGURE 11-2 Tabbed input forms

Note All tabs are freely accessible as if the form were just one long list of input fields. If you want to enforce rules and make the experience look a lot more like a guided wizard, then I recommend you look into some jQuery plugins before you start creating your own infrastructure. You could start with the Twitter Bootstrap Wizard plugin.

As mentioned, data is posted in the usual way, and it is captured in the usual way by the MVC model binding layer. Client-side validation takes place in the usual way, too. However, in this case, you now have the problem of giving feedback to users about erroneous input fields. Say the user goes to the **Password** tab and enters some invalid data. Next, she moves to the **Email** tab, types some acceptable data and clicks **Save**. The validation would fail on the currently invisible tab, so any visual feedback you might have rendered is not immediately visible to the user. In this case, I suggest you find a way to intercept the validation error and add an icon to the tab so that the user understands where the invalid input was entered. (I'll return to this later.)

The Post-Redirect-Get Pattern

There are issues in server-side web development that have existed since the early days, and a definitive solution that is unanimously accepted has never been found. One of these issues is how to deal with the response of a POST request, whether it is a regular HTML view, a JSON packet, or an error. The problem of dealing with a POST response doesn't much affect entirely client-side applications in which the POST request is issued and managed via JavaScript from the client. In light of this, many developers call this a false problem that only old-school developers might have. However, if you're here and MVC is your application model of choice, then chances are that your solution is not entirely made of client-side interactions. That means discussing the Post-Redirect-Get pattern—the recommended way of dealing with form posts—is worth the cost.

> **Note** The *Post-Redirect-Get* pattern is also illuminating from the perspective of CQRS, Command-Query Responsibility Segregation, an emerging pattern for essentially keeping the query and command stack of an application separated to develop, deploy, and scale them independently. In a web application, a form post is handled by the command stack, but presenting some visual response to the user pertains to the query stack. Hence, the post request ends when it is done with all tasks, and the user interface is updated in some other way. Again, the Post-Redirect-Get pattern offers one way to refresh the user interface in full respect of command-query stack separation.

Formalizing the problem

Let's consider a user that submits a form from within a web page. From the browser's perspective, that's a plain HTTP POST request. On the server, the request is mapped to a controller method that typically renders back a Razor template. As a result, the user receives some HTML and feels happy. Everything works just fine, so where's the problem?

There are two issues. One is the misalignment between the displayed URL that reflects the form action (hence, something like "save" or "edit") and the view in front of the user, which is a "get" action. The other issue is related to the last action tracked by the browser.

All browsers track the last HTTP command the user requested and reiterate that command when the user presses F5 or selects the **Refresh** menu item. In this case, the last request is an HTTP POST request. Repeating a post might be a dangerous action because the POST is typically an action that alters the state of the system. To be safe, the operation needs be an idempotent operation (that is, it doesn't change the state if executed repeatedly). To warn users about the risk of refreshing after a post, all browsers display a well-known message as in Figure 11-3.

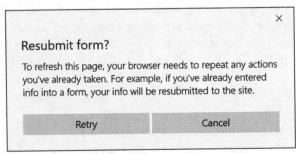

FIGURE 11-3 Sample warning message from Microsoft Edge when a POST is reiterated

Such windows have existed for years, and they didn't prevent the diffusion of the web, but they're ugly to see. Getting rid of those windows, though, is not as easy as it might seem. To eliminate the risk of getting such messages, the entire flow of server-side web operations should be revisited, and this ends up creating new types of problems.

Addressing the Problem

The Post-Redirect-Get (PRG) pattern consists of a small set of recommendations aimed at guaranteeing that each POST command actually ends with a GET. It resolves the F5 refresh problem and promotes neat separation between command and query HTTP actions.

The problem originates from the fact that in a typical web interaction, a POST that renders back some user interface is followed by an implicit GET. The PRG pattern just suggests you make this GET explicit through a redirect or another client request that has the same effect as a redirect. Here's some concrete code.

```
[HttpGet]
[ActionName("register")]
public ActionResult ViewRegister()
{
    // Display the view through which the user will register
    return View();
}
```

To register, the user fills out and submits the form. A new request comes in as a POST and is handled by the following code:

```
[HttpPost]
[ActionName("register")]
public ActionResult PostRegister(RegisterInputModel input)
{
    // Alters the state of the system (i.e., register the user)
    ...

    // Queries the new state of the system for UI purposes.
    // (This step is an implicit GET)
    return View()
}
```

As written here, the method *PostRegister* alters the state of the system and reports it back through an internal, server-side query. For the browser, it was only a POST operation with some HTML response. Applying the PRG pattern to this code requires just one change: In the POST method, instead of returning the view, you redirect the user to another page. For example, you might want to redirect to the GET method of the same action.

```
[HttpPost]
[ActionName("register")]
public ActionResult PostRegister(RegisterInputModel input)
{
    // Alters the state of the system (i.e., register the user)
    ...
    // Queries the new state of the system for UI purposes.
    // (This step is NOW an explicit GET via the browser)
    return RedirectToAction("register")
}
```

As a result, the last tracked action is a GET, and this eliminates the F5 issue. But there's more. The URL displayed on the browser's address bar is now a lot more significant.

The PRG pattern is the approach to follow if you're creating a classic server application with full page refreshes after each request. A more modern alternative that doesn't have the issues of POST/GET being fused is to post the content of the form via JavaScript.

Posting Forms Via JavaScript

If posting is a browser-led operation, then the output returned by the target URL is displayed to the user without filters. If posting is conducted via JavaScript instead, your client-side code has the great chance to control the entire operation and manage things so that users can have a very smooth experience.

Regardless of the specific framework you use—whether it's plain jQuery or a much more sophisticated framework—the steps to take to post an HTML form can be summarized as below:

- Collect the data to post from the input fields of the form.

- Serialize individual field values into a stream of data that can be packaged into an HTTP request.

- Prepare and run the Ajax call.

- Receive response, check for errors, and adjust the user interface accordingly.

There's no need, however, for handcrafting all the steps above. All browsers expose an API to script the FORM element as it is coded in the local DOM. Therefore, all we do is write some JavaScript code to have the browser post the form out-of-band and handle the response accordingly.

Uploading the Form Content

The correct body of an HTTP request that carries form content is defined in the HTML standard papers. It's the string given by the concatenation of input names and related values. Each name/value pair is joined to the next by the & symbol.

```
name1=value1&name2=value2&name3=value3
```

There are many ways to create such a string. You can do it yourself by reading values from DOM elements and creating the string, but using jQuery facilities is faster and more reliable.

Serializing the Form

In particular, the jQuery library offers the *serialize* function, which takes a FORM element, loops through the child INPUT elements, and returns the final string.

```
var form = $("#your-form-element-id");
var body = form.serialize();
```

Another option in jQuery is the *$.param* function. The function produces the same output as *serialize* except that it accepts a different type of input. Whereas *serialize* can only be called on a form and it automatically scans the list of input fields, *$.param* requires an explicit array of name/value pairs but produces the same output.

Once you have the content to serialize you only have to place the HTTP request. Note that browsers also offer the *submit* method on the FORM element of their DOM. The effect is different from placing an HTTP call. The *submit* method produces the same effect as pushing the button—a browser-led upload of the form content with a subsequent full-page refresh. If you manage your own HTTP call instead, you're in total control of the workflow.

Placing the HTTP Request

To place an HTTP request, you use jQuery again. A form is uploaded using the HTTP verb specified by the *method* attribute of the form HTML element. The target URL instead is identified by the content of its *action* attribute. Here's a sample AJAX call you can use to upload the content of an HTML form.

```
var form = $("#your-form-element-id");
$.ajax({
    cache: false,
    url: form.attr("action"),
    type: form.attr("method"),
    dataType: "html",
    data: form.serialize(),
    success: success,
    error: error
});
```

The jQuery *ajax* function allows you to pass in two callbacks to handle the success or failure of the request. It is worth noting that success or failure refers to the status code of the response and not to the business operation behind the physical HTTP request. In other words, if your request triggers a command that fails but your server code swallows the exception and returns an error message in an HTTP 200 response, the error callback will never be triggered. Let's have a look at a possible ASP.NET MVC endpoint getting invoked via Ajax and JavaScript.

```
public IActionResult Login(LoginInputModel credentials)
{
    // Validate credentials
    var response = TryAuthenticate(credentials);
    if (!response.Success)
        throw new LoginFailedException(response.Message);
    var returnUrl = ...;
    return Content(returnUrl);
}
```

In this case, if the authentication fails, an exception is thrown, meaning that the status code of the request becomes HTTP 500, which will invoke the error handler. Otherwise, the next URL is returned where you want the user to be redirected after a successful login. Note that as this method is invoked via Ajax, any redirect to another URL can only take place via JavaScript from the client side.

```
window.location.href = "...";
```

The post of the form is invoked in the *click* handler of the form buttons. To prevent the browser from posting the form automatically upon clicking, you might want to change the button *type* attribute to a button instead of submit.

```
<button type="button" id="myForm">SUBMIT</button>
```

The *click* handler can perform additional tasks before and after the post of the form, including giving users some feedback.

Giving Users Feedback

The callback handlers, whether for the success or error case, receive all data the controller method returned, and they are responsible for displaying that data. Displaying that data might require unpacking and splitting the data across the various pieces of the HTML user interface. If the form post was successful, you might want to show users a reassuring message like, "The operation completed successfully." Even more importantly, if the form post resulted in a functional failure, then you might want to provide details that typically indicate that some input data was incorrect. It is up to you whether the messages (success or failure) are hardcoded or determined on the server in a context-sensitive manner. If they're generated on the server, though, you might want to define a serializable data structure to be returned, which contains the outcome of the operation and also provides a description of what has happened. I like to use something like this:

```
public class CommandResponse
{
    public bool Success { get; set; }
    public string Message { get; set; }
}
```

Should messages stay on screen indefinitely until the next operation is attempted? Error messages might reasonably remain on screen until the next submission but, at some point, must be removed. You can remove error message just before you submit the form again. Things are different for a successful message. It's important to show a confirmation message, but the message must not be invasive nor should it be around for too long. I'd avoid modal popups here, and would rather bind the message to a timer so that it first appears as a piece of text interspersed with the regular user interface and is then dismissed a few seconds later without any user intervention.

A middle ground is to display the message in a DIV that looks like an alert box and gives users a chance to dismiss it by simply clicking a button. When I take this route, I typically use the Bootstrap alert class to style the container of the message and use the following chunk of JavaScript in the global layout so that it automatically applies to all alert boxes and makes them easily dismissible.

```
$(".alert").click(function(e) {
    $(this).hide();
});
```

Note that dismissible alert boxes are also supported natively by Bootstrap, but I find this trick quicker to write and easier for users because they can click or touch anywhere to dismiss the message. Figure 11-4 shows error messages after a form post was attempted via JavaScript.

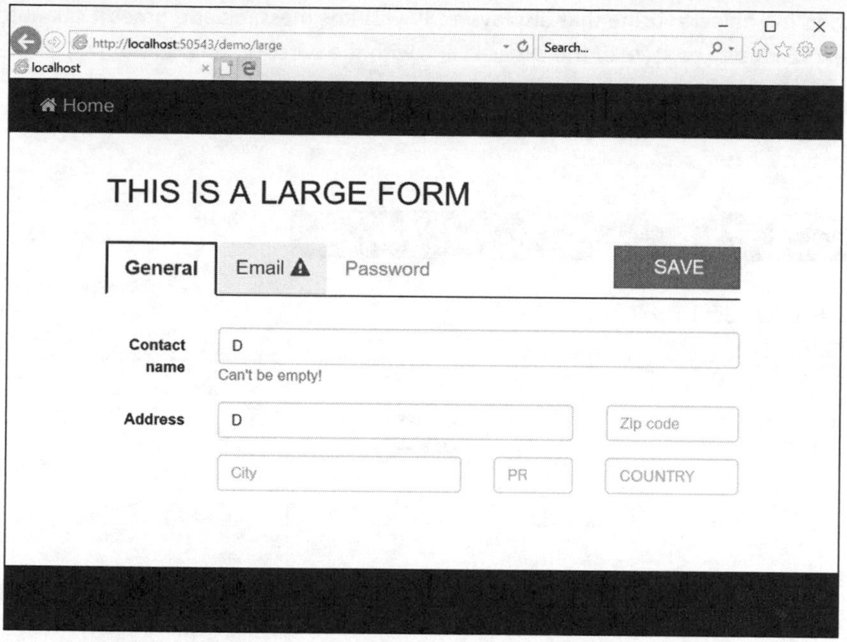

FIGURE 11-4 Error messages in a client-side managed HTML form

The feedback for the user is orchestrated from within the client page. Here's some sample code. For more details—specifically for the details of the JavaScript libraries being used to support the described behavior—refer to the sample code that comes with this book. (See *http://github.com/despos/progcore*.) In particular, look at the file *ybq-core.js* in the Ch11 folder.

```
Ybq.postForm("#large-form",
    function(data) {
        var response = JSON.parse(data);
        Ybq.toast("#large-form-message",
                response.message,
                response.success);
});
```

The *postForm* function is just a wrapper that contains the Ajax snippet presented earlier:

```
var form = $("#your-form-element-id");
$.ajax({
    cache: false,
    url: form.attr("action"),
    type: form.attr("method"),
    dataType: "html",
    data: form.serialize(),
    success: success,
    error: error
});
```

The *toastr* method is a helper routine that displays a DIV with the message and times it out automatically after a few seconds. The style of the DIV is in line with the outcome (success or fail) of the operation. (See Figure 11-5.)

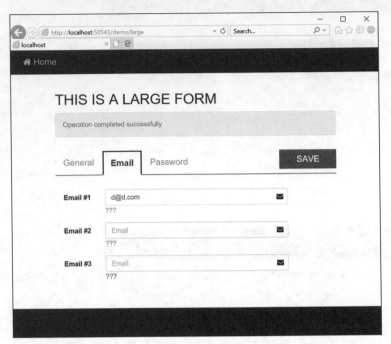

FIGURE 11-5 Error messages in a client-side managed HTML form

Note In ASP.NET Core, the *Json* method that serializes objects back to the client is smart enough to serialize honoring the JavaScript casing conventions. In light of this, when the above *CommandResponse* type is serialized back, C# properties like *Success* and *Message* become JavaScript properties named *success* and *message*. (This is different from what happens in MVC 5.x.)

Refreshing Portions of the Current Screen

When you post the form and the operation completes successfully, sometimes you need to refresh some portions of the current user interface. If the form posts via the browser, then the PRG pattern ensures the new page is entirely redrawn from scratch with fresh and up-to-date information. This is not the case when you post the form content from the client side using JavaScript.

Updating Small Pieces of the User Interface

Sometimes the parts of the current user interface to be updated are small and, more importantly, the new content can be figured out from the content of the form. In this case, all you do is save the small pieces of new content to some local variables and use them to update the involved DOM elements. In this context, a small piece of the user interface is anything as simple and compact as a string or a number.

```
Ybq.postForm("#large-form",
    function(data) {
        // Deserialize the received response
        var response = JSON.parse(data);

        // Update the UI
        if (response.success) {
            var name = $("#contactname").val();
            $("#public-name").html(name);
        }

        // Give feedback about the overall operation
        Ybq.toast("#large-form-message",
                response.message,
                response.success);
});
```

In the example, we're assuming that the view contains some text label named *public-name* that is set to the name of the contact in the form.

Calling Back the Server for Partial Views

Other times, refreshing the user interface might not be that simple. Refreshing the text of a label is no big deal, but sometimes a full piece of HTML is required. This HTML chunk can be arranged on the client side, but unless you're using some client-side data binding library (more on this in the next chapter), it only introduces a possible double point of failure. Basically, you have some code on the server and some code on the client to generate the same HTML output at different times. This means that any change you could make to the actual style or layout must be applied in two different places, using two different languages.

In these cases, it could be more reliable to call back the server and have it serve back just the chunk of HTML you're looking for. This helps to componentize the user interface. In Chapter 5, "ASP.NET MVC Views," we also discussed view components. I'd say that if the chunk of HTML is complex enough, you could implement it as a view component and order it to refresh. Sometimes, you can make it a partial view and just add a new action method to some controller that simply returns the partial view as modified by the current state of the system. Here's an example.

```
[HttpGet]
public IActionResult GetLoginView()
{
    // Get any necessary data
    var model = _service.GetAnyNecessaryData();
    return new PartialView("pv_loginbox", model);
}
```

The method is invoked via Ajax and returns the current state of some user interface portion. All it does is gather the data necessary to populate the HTML and pass it to the Razor view engine for populating the partial view. The client application receives an HTML string and just updates an HTML element (most likely, a DIV) using the jQuery *html* method.

Uploading Files to a Web Server

In HTML, files are pretty much treated like any other type of input in spite of the deep difference that exists between files and primitive data. As usual, you start by creating one or more INPUT elements with the *type* attribute set to *file*. The native browser user interface allows users to pick a local file, and then the content of the file is streamlined with the rest of the form content. On the server, the file content is mapped to a new type—the *IFormFile* type—and enjoys a much more uniform treatment from the model binding layer than in previous versions of MVC.

Setting Up the Form

To pick up a local file and select it for upload, you don't strictly need more than the following markup.

```
<input type="file" id="picture" name="picture">
```

While this code must be found somewhere in HTML pages for user interface reasons, it usually is hidden from view. This allows applications to provide a much nicer user interface while still preserving the ability to bring up the local explorer window.

A common trick is to hide the INPUT element and display some nice user interface to invite users to click. Next, the handler of the click just forwards the click event to the hidden INPUT element.

```
<input type="file" id="picture" name="picture">
<div onclick="$('#picture').click()">image not available</div>
```

For the form content to be uploaded correctly, the *enctype* attribute also must be specified with the fixed value of *multipart/form-data*.

FIGURE 11-6 Hidden INPUT file element

Processing File Content on the Server

In ASP.NET Core, file content is abstracted to the *IFormFile* type, which mostly preserves the same programming interface of the *HttpPostedFileBase* type you might have used in MVC 5 applications.

```
public IActionResult UploadForm(FormInputModel input, IFormFile picture)
{
    if (picture.Length > 0)
    {
        var fileName = Path.GetFileName(picture.FileName);
        var filePath = Path.Combine(_env.ContentRootPath, "Uploads", fileName);
        using (var stream = new FileStream(filePath, FileMode.Create))
        {
            picture.CopyTo(stream);
        }
    }
}
```

Note that the *IFormFile* reference can also be added to the *FormInputModel* complex type because model binding would easily and happily map the content by name like it does for primitive and complex data types. The code above sets a file name from the current content root folder and creates a server copy of the file with the original name of the uploaded file. If multiple files are uploaded, you simply reference an array of *IFormFile* types.

If you're posting the form via JavaScript, then you'd better replace the form serialization code we've seen above with the following snippet:

```
var form = $("#your-form-element-id");
var formData = new FormData(form[0]);
form.find("input[type=file]").each(function () {
    formData.append($(this).attr("name"), $(this)[0].files[0]);
});
$.ajax({
    cache: false,
    url: form.attr("action"),
    type: form.attr("method"),
    dataType: "html",
    data: formData,
    success: success,
    error: error
});
```

The code ensures that all input files are being serialized.

Issues with File Uploads

The above code is guaranteed to work for small files, even though it is hard to define what "small" means in general terms. Let's say that you can always start with this code unless you know before-hand you're going to upload files as large as 30 megabytes. In this case, and in any case in which you experience some delays on the web server related to the size of the file, you might want to consider streaming the content of the files. Detailed instructions can be found at *http://docs.microsoft.com/ en-us/aspnet/core/mvc/models/file-uploads*.

This is only the first issue you might have these days when it comes to file uploads. Another issue is the need for a highly dynamic and interactive user interface. Users might expect that visual feedback is provided about the progress of the upload operation. Also, when the file to upload is an image (say, the photo of a registered user) users might even expect a preview and the ability to cancel the previously selected image and leave the field blank. All these operations are possible but are not free of effort. You could consider using some ad hoc component such as Dropzone.js. (See *http://dropzonejs.com*)

Another issue is related to how you save a copy of the uploaded file on the server. The code shown above creates a new file on the server. Note that the above code will throw an exception if any of the referenced folders don't exist. This approach was more than OK for years but is losing appeal the more the cloud model gains relevance. If you store uploaded files locally to a web application hosted in an Azure App Service, your application will work transparently as multiple instances of the same App Service will share the same storage. The problem with uploaded files is that in general it is better keeping them off the main server. Until the cloud exploded, there was not much else you could do other than storing files locally or perhaps in a database. With the cloud, you have cheap blob storage that can be used to store files even beyond the storage limits of a classic App Service configuration. Also, the traffic to the files is, in part, diverted from your main server.

The code above can be rewritten to save the uploaded image to an Azure blob container. To do that, you need an Azure storage account.

```
// Get the connection string from the Azure portal
var storageAccount = CloudStorageAccount.Parse("connection string to your storage account");

// Create a container and save the blob to it
var blobClient = storageAccount.CreateCloudBlobClient();
var container = blobClient.GetContainerReference("my-container");
container.CreateIfNotExistsAsync();
var blockBlob = container.GetBlockBlobReference("my-blob-name");
using (var stream = new MemoryStream())
{
    picture.CopyTo(stream);
    blockBlob.UploadFromStreamAsync(stream);
}
```

The Azure blob storage is articulated in containers, and each container is bound to an account. Within a container, you can have as many blobs as you wish. A blob is characterized by a binary stream and a unique name. To access the Azure blob storage, you can also use a REST API, so the blob storage is accessible also outside the web application.

 Note To test the Azure blob storage, you use the Azure blob simulator, which allows you to play locally with the API of the platform.

Summary

Today applications can hardly afford the burden of full page refreshes when the user performs any action. While quite a few websites that are built around the old-fashioned approach still exist, that does not excuse not trying to make a better one. Outside the realm of ASP.NET Core, you can have an Angular application which would perform any data access tasks by calling remote services and refreshing the user interface locally. Whether through Angular (or analogous frameworks) or by using plain JavaScript in Razor views, you should aim to make the user interface a bit smoother and fluid.

In this chapter, we focused on how to post data to the server from the client side using JavaScript code. In the next chapter, we'll see the options we must render to HTML whatever we bring down to the client page from remote servers.

CHAPTER 12

Client-side Data Binding

Our great mistake is to try to exact from each person virtues which he does not possess, and to neglect the cultivation of those which he has.

—Marguerite Yourcenar, "Memoirs of Hadrian"

The term *data binding* refers to the ability of a visual component to be programmatically updated with fresh data. The canonical example is a text box that is assigned a default text to show for the user to edit. Data binding is therefore just what the name suggests—a way to bind data to a visual component in software. HTML elements—input fields but also DIV and text elements such as P and SPAN elements—are visual components. Client-side data binding refers to the techniques you can adopt to refresh the content of a browser-displayed web page directly via JavaScript and without reloading the page from the web server.

In this chapter, we'll review and compare a few techniques that can be used to update the user interface and better reflect the state of the application. The simplest approach consists in downloading chunks of updated HTML from the server. Those segments just dynamically replace existing segments of HTML, thus serving up a partial rendering of the currently displayed page. Another approach entails having a JSON-based set of endpoints that can be queried for fresh data to regenerate the HTML layout entirely on the client side in JavaScript.

Refreshing the View via HTML

There is no doubt that a full refresh of a webpage that is quite rich with graphics and media can be significantly slow and cumbersome for users. This is precisely why Ajax and partial rendering of pages became so popular. At the other extreme of page rendering, we find the concept of a Single Page Application (SPA). At its core, an SPA is an application made of one (or a few) minimal HTML pages incorporating a nearly empty DIV populated at runtime with a template and data downloaded from some server. On the way from server-side rendering to the full client-side rendering of SPAs, I suggest we start with an HTML partial rendering approach.

Preparing the Ground

The idea is that any page is first served entirely from the server and downloads as a single chunk of HTML. Next, any interaction between the user and the controls within the page is arranged via Ajax calls. The invoked endpoint performs any command or query and returns any response as pure HTML.

Returning HTML is less efficient than returning plain JSON data because HTML is made of layout information and data whereas in a JSON stream, the amount of extra information is limited to the schema and, on the average, is smaller than HTML layout data. This said, downloading plain server-side rendered HTML is much less intrusive and doesn't require additional skills or learning an entirely new programming paradigm. Still, a bit of JavaScript is required, but it is limited to using familiar DOM properties such as *innerHTML* or just a few core jQuery methods.

Defining Refreshable Areas

An area of a page that is subject to dynamic refresh must be easily identifiable and well isolated from the rest of the page. Ideally, it is a DIV element with a known ID.

```
<div id="list-of-customers">
    <!-- Place here any necessary HTML -->
</div>
```

Once any fresh HTML has been downloaded for the DIV, it only takes a line of JavaScript to update it, as shown below.

```
$("#list-of-customers").html(updatedHtml);
```

From a Razor perspective, a refreshable area is fully rendered with a partial view. Not only would a partial view help componentize the resulting page favoring reuse and separation of concerns, but it would also make it far easier to refresh portions of the page from the client without a full page reload.

```
<div id="list-of-customers">
    @Html.Partial("pv_listOfCustomers")
</div>
```

The missing link is a controller action method that performs some query or command action and then returns HTML generated by the partial view.

Putting It All Together

Let's say you have a sample page that renders a list of customer names. Any user authorized to view the page can click a side button to delete the current row. How would you code that? The old-way approach entails linking the button to a URL where a POST controller method would perform the operation and then redirect back to a GET page that renders the page with up-to-date data. It works, but it takes a chain of requests (Post-Redirect-Get) and, more importantly, causes a full-page reload. For heavy pages—nearly every realistic website page is heavy—it is definitely cumbersome.

A refreshable area allows the user to click a button and have some JavaScript place the POST request and serve back some HTML. The same handler that places the initial request for deleting the customer would receive a fragment of HTML to stick on top of the existing table of customers.

The Action Method

The controller action method is nothing special, except that it returns a partial view result instead of a full view result. Such a method exists only to edit a given view. To skip unwanted calls, you might even decorate the method with a couple of custom filter attributes, as below.

```
[AjaxOnly]
[RequireReferrer("/home/index", "/home", "/")]
[HttpPost]
[ActionName("d")]
public ActionResult DeleteCustomer(int id)
{
    // Do some work
    var model = DeleteCustomerAndReturnModel(id);

    // Render HTML back
    return PartialView("pv_listOfCustomers", model);
}
```

AjaxOnly and *RequireReferrer* are custom filters (see companion source code) that run the method only if the request comes via Ajax and from any of the given referrers. The other two attributes set the need for a POST call and an action name of *d*.

The Response from the Method

Placing the call via Ajax, the browser would receive an HTML fragment and use it to replace the content of the refreshable area. Here's some sample code you would bind to the click of a button.

```
<script type="text/javascript">
    function delete(id) {
        var url = "/home/d/";
        $.post(url, { id: id })
          .done(function (response) {
                // In this context, the parameter "response" is the
                // method response. Hence, it is the fragment of HTML
                // returned by the action method via PartialView().
                $("#listOfCustomers").html(response);
        });
    }
</script>
```

For the user, the experience is quite nice. She clicks, for example, an item on a list and the list refreshes instantaneously to reflect changes. The effect is shown in Figure 12-1. In the figure, the screen on the left captures the user clicking the delete button for one of the rows, and the screen on the right shows the list of customers minus the deleted row.

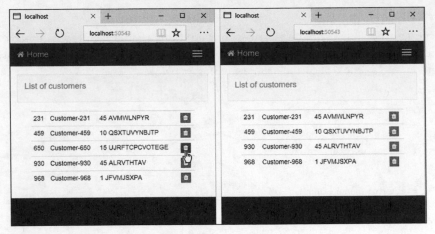

FIGURE 12-1 Partial refresh of the page after an update

For the user, the experience is quite nice. For example, she clicks an item on a list, and the list refreshes instantaneously to reflect changes.

Limitations of the Technique

The technique works beautifully, but it is limited to updating one HTML fragment at a time. Whether this is really a limitation depends on the nature—and the actual content—of the view. More realistically, a web view can have two or more fragments that need to be updated after a server operation. As an example, consider the page shown in Figure 12-2.

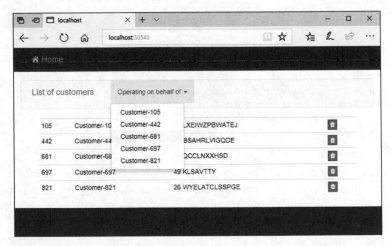

FIGURE 12-2 A web page with two related HTML fragments to update

The page has two related fragments that need be updated when a customer is deleted. You don't just want to update the table to remove the deleted customer; you also need to refresh the drop-down list. Obviously, you can have two methods on the controller with each returning a distinct fragment. That would require some additional code, as shown below.

```
<script type="text/javascript">
    function delete(id) {
        var url = "/home/d/";
        $.post(url, { id: id })
          .done(function (response) {
              $("#listOfCustomers").html(response);
              $.post("home/dropdown", "")
               .done(function(response) {
                   $("#dropdownCustomers").html(response);
               });
          });
    }
</script>
```

After receiving the first response, you make a second Ajax call to request the second HTML fragment. Again, it works, but it probably can be done better.

Introducing the Multiple View Action Result Type

A controller method returns a type that implements the *IActionResult* type or, more likely, inherits from *ActionResult*. The idea is to create a custom action result type that returns multiple HTML fragments combined into a single string with each fragment separated by a conventional separator. The technique has two major advantages. First, a single HTTP request is made for as many HTML fragments as needed. Second, the workflow is simpler. The logic to determine which parts of the view should be updated lives on the server and the client just receives an array of HTML fragments. The client still needs to contain the UI logic necessary to stick every fragment where it belongs. This aspect, though, can be further lessened by building a custom framework around it that declaratively links a fragment to its HTML element in the client DOM. Let's have a look at the C# class for the custom action result type.

```
public class MultiplePartialViewResult : ActionResult
{
    public const string ChunkSeparator = "---|||---";

    public IList<PartialViewResult> PartialViewResults { get; }

    public MultiplePartialViewResult(params PartialViewResult[] results)
    {
        if (PartialViewResults == null)
            PartialViewResults = new List<PartialViewResult>();
        foreach (var r in results)
            PartialViewResults.Add(r);
    }

    public override async Task ExecuteResultAsync(ActionContext context)
    {
        if (context == null)
            throw new ArgumentNullException(nameof(context));

        var services = context.HttpContext.RequestServices;
        var executor = services.GetRequiredService<PartialViewResultExecutor>();

        var total = PartialViewResults.Count;
        var writer = new StringWriter();
```

```
            for (var index = 0; index < total; index++)
            {
                var pv = PartialViewResults[index];
                var view = executor.FindView(context, pv).View;
                var viewContext = new ViewContext(context,
                    view,
                    pv.ViewData,
                    pv.TempData,
                    writer,
                    new HtmlHelperOptions());
                await view.RenderAsync(viewContext);

                if (index < total - 1)
                    await writer.WriteAsync(ChunkSeparator);
            }

            await context.HttpContext.Response.WriteAsync(writer.ToString());
        }
}
```

The action result type holds an array of *PartialViewResult* objects and executes them one after the other, accumulating HTML markup in an internal buffer. When done, the buffer is flushed to the output stream. The output of each *PartialViewResult* object is separated using a conventional, but arbitrary, substring.

The interesting part is how you use this custom action result type from a controller method. Let's rewrite the *DeleteCustomer* action method.

```
[AjaxOnly]
[RequireReferrer("/home/index", "/home", "/")]
[HttpPost]
[ActionName("d")]
public ActionResult DeleteCustomer(int id)
{
    // Do some work
    var model = DeleteCustomerAndReturnModel(id);

    // Render HTML back
    var result = new MultiplePartialViewResult(
            PartialView("pv_listOfCustomer", model),
            PartialView("pv_onBehalfOfCustomers", model));
    return result;
}
```

The constructor of the *MultiplePartialViewResult* class accepts an array of *PartialViewResult* objects, so you can add as many as you have to the call.

Finally, the HTML code in the client page also changes slightly.

```
<script type="text/javascript">
    function delete(id) {
        var url = "/home/d/";
        $.post(url, { id: id })
          .done(function (response) {
              var chunks = Ybq.processMultipleAjaxResponse(response);
```

```
        $("#listOfCustomers").html(chunks[0]);
        $("#dropdownCustomers").html(chunks[1]);
    });
  }
</script>
```

The *Ybq.processMultipleAjaxResponse* JavaScript function is a short piece of code that just splits the received string on the conventional separator. The code is easy, as shown below. Figure 12-3 illustrates the effects.

```
Ybq.processMultipleAjaxResponse = function (response) {
    var chunkSeparator = "---|||---";
    var tokens = response.split(chunkSeparator);
    return tokens;
};
```

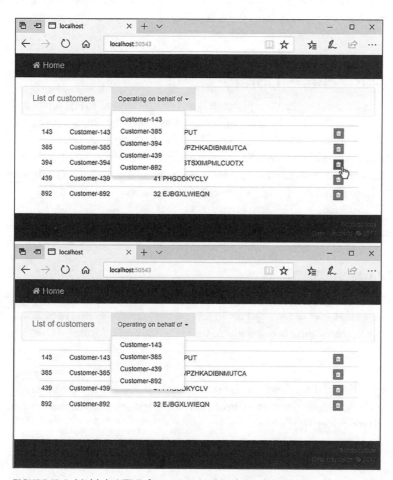

FIGURE 12-3 Multiple HTML fragments updated simultaneously

Refreshing the View via JSON

An SPA application is built on top of an HTML template and uses directives to instruct the runtime on how to modify the DOM. A directive usually takes the form of an HTML attribute that some embedded JavaScript module will process. Directives can be quite complex and include chainable formatters and filters. Also, directives might sometimes need to refer to core language operations, such as checking a condition or running a loop. A framework like Angular takes the approach of building applications from the client side quite far away from the quick and dirty problem of rebuilding an HTML template dynamically to make it display fresher data.

At the very end of the day, when refreshing a section of a page, Angular builds a string dynamically and displays it using DOM commands. The same, however, can be done using a much smaller framework that embeds an HTML template in the page and knows how to fill it out with bound data. Beyond this basic point, the difference between a huge framework like Angular and a handmade string builder is just quantity of features.

Introducing the Mustache.JS Library

Mustache is a logic-less syntax for creating text templates. It is not strictly limited to HTML; it can be used to generate any text, such as HTML, XML, any configuration files, and (why not) source code in the language of your choice. In a nutshell, Mustache can produce whatever text can be obtained by expanding tags in a template to incorporate provided values. Mustache is logic-less for the simple reason that it doesn't support control flow statements such as IF statements or loops. To some extent, what it does is conceptually close to using a *String.Format* call in C# code.

Around the Mustache template, there is the Mustache.JS library that essentially takes some JSON data and expands tags in the provided template.

Key Aspects of the Mustache Syntax

The Mustache syntax for text templates to be filled out is centered around two main types of tags: variables and sections. There are more types of tags, but those are the two most relevant types. For more information, check out *http://mustache.github.io*. A variable takes the following form:

```
{{ variable_name }}
```

The tag is a placeholder for data in the bound context that can be mapped to the variable name. The mapping happens recursively, meaning that the current context is traversed up to the top, and if no match is found, nothing is rendered. Here's an example:

```
<p>
  <b>{{ lastname }}</b>,
  <span>{{ firstname }}</span>
</p>
```

Now assume that the above template is bound to the following JavaScript object:

```
{
  "firstname": "Dino",
  "lastname": "Esposito"
}
```

The final result is below.

```
<p>
  <b>Esposito</b>,
  <span>Dino</span>
</p>
```

By default, any text is rendered in the template in its escaped form. If you want unescaped HTML instead, you just add an extra pair of curly brackets: *{{{ unescaped }}}*.

Mustache sections render a given chunk of text multiple times, once for each data element found in a bound collection. A section starts with a # symbol and ends with a / symbol in much the same way an HTML element ends. The string following the # symbol is the value of the key and is used to identify the data to bind and subsequently determines the final output.

```
<ul>
  {{ #customers }}
    <li>{{ lastname }}</li>
  {{ /customers }}
</ul>
```

Bound to a JavaScript object with a child collection named *customers* where each member has a *lastname* property, the template can return something as below.

```
<ul>
  <li>Esposito</li>
  <li>Another</li>
  <li>Name</li>
  <li>Here</li>
</ul>
```

The value of the section can also be a JavaScript function. In this case, the function will be invoked and passed to the body of the template.

```
{{ #task_to_perform }}
  {{ book }} is finished.
{{ /task_to_perform }}
```

In this case, *task_to_perform* and *book* are both expected to be members of the bound JavaScript object.

```
{
  "book": "Programming ASP.NET Core",
  "task_to_perform": function() {
    return function(text, render) {
      return "<h1>" + render(text) + "</h1>"
    }
  }
}
```

The final output is some HTML that wraps the phrase "Programming ASP.NET Core is finished" in an H1 element.

Finally, the caret (^) symbol before the section key indicates that the following template should be used in case of inverted values of the key. The common scenario for the caret is to render some content in case of empty collections.

```
{{ #customers }}
  <b>{{ companyname }}</b>
{{ /customers }}
{{ ^customers }}
  No customers found
{{ /customers }}
```

Although far from being comprehensive, the Mustache syntax covers the most common data binding scenarios. Let's see how to attach JSON data to a template programmatically.

Passing JSON to the Template

You embed a Mustache template in a Razor view (or a plain HTML page) using a variation of the classic SCRIPT element.

```
<script type="x-tmpl-mustache" id="template-details">
   <!-- Mustache template goes here -->
</script>
```

The *type* attribute is set to *x-tmpl-mustache,* and this prevents the template from being treated by the browser. You also give the SCRIPT element a unique ID for retrieving the content of the template programmatically.

```
<script type="text/javascript">
    var template = $('#template-details').html();
    Mustache.parse(template);   // optional, speeds up future uses
</script>
```

The template variable contains the inner content of the SCRIPT element, namely the source of the Mustache template. Here's an example that returns information about a given country.

```
<script id="template-details" type="x-tmpl-mustache">
    <div class="panel panel-primary">
        <div class="panel-heading">
            <h3 class="panel-title">
                {{Results.Name}}
            </h3>
        </div>
        <div class="panel-body">
            <div class="col-xs-8">
                <p>Capital is <strong>{{Results.Capital.Name}}</strong></p>
                <p>Phone international prefix is <strong>+{{Results.TelPref}}</strong></p>
            </div>
            <div class="col-xs-4">
                <button id="btnGeo"
                        type="button"
```

```
                    class="btn btn-info"
                    data-toggle="collapse"
                    data-target="#geo">
                More
            </button>
            <div id="geo" class="collapse pull-right">
            </div>
        </div>
    </div>
</div>
</script>
```

As an example, consider a page that lists a few countries and provides a link for each to drill down.

```
<table class="table table-condensed">
    @foreach (var c in Model.CountryCodes)
    {
        <tr>
            <td>@c</td>
            <td>
                <button class="btn btn-xs btn-info"
                        onclick="i('@c')">
                    <span class="fa fa-chevron-right"></span>
                </button>
            </td>
        </tr>
    }
</table>
```

Clicking the button runs the following JavaScript function:

```
<script type="text/javascript">
function i(id) {
    var url = "/home/more/";
    $.getJSON(url, { id: id })
        .done(function (response) {
            var rendered = Mustache.render(template, response);
            $("#details").html(rendered);
        });
}
</script>
```

The *template* expression is the Mustache template calculated earlier once and pre-parsed to speed up successive calls. You obtain the final HTML markup with the call to the *Mustache.render* method.

Putting It All Together

Figure 12-4 shows a sample page in action. By clicking on the country button, users will place a remote call to an endpoint that retrieves further details about the countries and returns it as JSON data. The data is then bound to the view through a Mustache template.

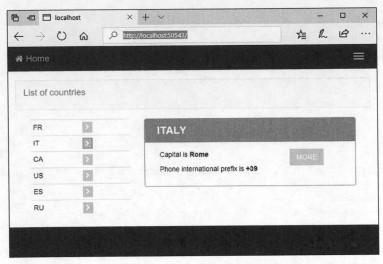

FIGURE 12-4 Client-side templates used to render the details of the selected country

Introducing the KnockoutJS Library

The Mustache library only supports direct binding variables and logic-less templates. In other words, you have neither conditional expressions nor more sophisticated loops for navigating through bound collections via sections in Mustache. Another library you might want to look into is KnockoutJS.

Key Aspects of the KnockoutJS Library

KnockoutJS differs from Mustache for two main reasons. First, it is not based on a separate template. Second, it supports a far richer binding syntax. In KnockoutJS, there's no separate template turned into HTML and then inserted into the main DOM. In KnockoutJS, the template is the HTML of the final view. To express its richer syntax, however, KnockoutJS uses its own set of HTML custom attributes.

Another crucial aspect of the library is the MVVM (Model-View-View-Model) pattern for binding data to the layout. Most of the MVVM pattern is also recognizable in the Mustache approach to programming, but in KnockoutJS, it is much clearer. In KnockoutJS, you take a JavaScript object and apply it to a selected segment of the DOM. If the DOM is decorated with the proper attributes, then contained data is applied. In KnockoutJS, though, data binding is bidirectional, which means JavaScript code is applied to the DOM. Also, any changes applied to the DOM (such as when a bound input text box is edited) are copied back to the mapped properties of the JavaScript object.

Binding Mechanism

KnockoutJS has one global method to attach data to a section of the DOM. The method is called *applyBindings*, and it takes two input parameters. The first is the JavaScript object that carries the data. The other parameter is optional, and it refers to the root object of the DOM where data must be attached. Data binding takes place through a variety of expressions, as in Table 12-1.

TABLE 12-1 Most relevant binding commands in KnockoutJS

Command Binding	Description
Attr	Binds the value to the specified HTML attribute of the parent element. `<a data-bind="attr:{ href:actualLink }">Click me</a>` The *actualLink* expression identifies a valid expression (property or function) on the bound object.
Css	Binds the value to the *class* attribute of the parent element. `<h1 data-bind="css:{ superTitle:shouldHilight }"></h1>` The *shouldHilight* expression identifies a valid Boolean expression on the bound object. If true, the specified CSS class will be added to the current value of the *class* attribute.
event	Binds the value to the specified event of the parent element. `<button data-bind="event:{click:doSomething}">Click me</button>` The *doSomething* expression identifies a function to be invoked when the element is clicked.
Style	Binds the value to the *style* attribute of the parent element. `<h1 data-bind="style:{ color:textColor }"></h1>` The *textColor* expression identifies a valid expression on the bound object that can be assigned to the specified style attribute.
Text	Binds the value to the body of the parent element. `<span data-bind="text:lastName"></span>` The *lastName* expression identifies a valid expression on the bound object that can be assigned as the content of the element.
Value	Binds the value to the *value* attribute of the parent element. `<input type="text" data-bind="value:lastName"></input>` The *lastName* expression identifies a valid expression on the bound object that can be assigned as the value of the input field.
Visible	Sets the visibility of the parent element. `<div data-bind="visible:shouldBeVisible"> ... </div>` The *shouldBeVisible* expression identifies a valid Boolean expression on the bound object.

All binding commands are used within the data binding expression, which takes the form below:

```
<h1 data-bind="command:binding" />
```

The *data-bind* attribute takes an expression of the form *command:actual_binding_value*. The command part identifies the part of the parent element that will be affected. The actual binding value refers to the expression that, once evaluated, produces the actual value. Multiple bindings can be combined in the same assignment made to the *data-bind* attribute. In this case, they will be separated by a comma. A few more binding commands exist but they follow the same pattern shown in Table 12-1. Commands not mentioned in the table are just specific binding for specific HTML attributes or events. Find out more on *http://knockoutjs.com*.

Observable Properties

Observable properties are a rather advanced feature of the KnockoutJS library that provides change notifications for bound properties. Once the property of a JavaScript object has been populated with an observable value, any UI element that is bound to it will be automatically updated every time the value changes. And because of the two-way nature of KnockoutJS, data binding any changes made through the UI is immediately reflected to in-memory JavaScript objects.

```
var author = {
    firstname : ko.observable("Dino"),
    lastname : ko.observable("Esposito"),
    born: ko.observable(1990)
};
```

Observables are subject to a slightly different syntax for reading and writing values.

```
// Reading an observable value
var firstName = author.firstname();

// Writing an observable value
author.firstname("Leonardo");
```

Observable values can also be computed expressions, as shown below.

```
author.fullName = ko.computed(function () {
    return author.firstname() + " " + person.lastname();
});
```

Once bound to a UI element, computed expressions are updated automatically every time any of the linked observables change.

Control Flow

KnockoutJS has two main constructs to control the flow of operations: the *if* command and the *foreach* command. The former implements conditions whereas the latter is about repeating a template for all the elements in a bound collection. Here's how to use the *if* command.

```
<div data-bind="if: customers.length > 0">
    <!-- List of customers here -->
</div>
```

The body of the DIV element is rendered only if the *customers* collection is not empty. You can also use the version *ifnot*, which renders any output only if the negated condition is true.

The foreach command repeats the child template for each element bound to it. The following code shows how to populate a table.

```
<div id="listOfCountries">
    <table class="table table-condensed" data-bind="foreach:countryCodes">
        <tr>
            <td><span data-bind="text:$data"></span></td>
        </tr>
    </table>
</div>
```

This is a very basic way of using KnockoutJS. To populate the table, you need a JavaScript call that gets a JSON collection.

```
<script type="text/javascript">
    var initUrl = "/home/countries";
    $.getJSON(initUrl,
        function (response) {
            ko.applyBindings(response);
        });
</script>
```

This code runs at page loading and downloads some JSON from a site endpoint. The JSON, as returned from the server, is passed to the Knockout template. In this case, *countryCodes* is a property of the JSON returned. The endpoint is the same used in the Mustache example. The *countryCodes* property is a simple array of strings. When there's no property to bind other than direct values, you use the *$data* expression.

Putting It All Together

Using KnockoutJS requires a significantly different mindset than when using Mustache or basic server-side data binding. Albeit a client-side binding library, Mustache is much closer to the classic server-side oriented vision of rendering than KnockoutJS. The core differences are in the richness of the syntax and the rich support for the MVVM model.

With KnockoutJS, everything takes place on the client side, and the view model you bind to data must be rendered on the client as a JavaScript object. However, the rich support for the MVVM model requires that the JavaScript object contains both data and behavior. Every event handler you bind needs to reference a method on the view model. How would you get an instance of the object? The most convenient way is to define the object on the client side in a SCRIPT block referenced from the Razor view. Let's take the previous example one step further.

```
<script type="text/javascript">
    function CountryViewModel(codes) {
        this.countries = $.map(codes, function(code) { return new Country(code); });
    }
    function Country(code) {
        this.code = code;
        this.showCapital = function() {
            var url = "/home/more/";
            $.getJSON(url, { id: code })
                .done(function (response) {
                    alert(response.Results.Capital.Name);
                });
        }
    }
</script>
```

The SCRIPT block defines a *CountryViewModel* wrapper object and a *Country* helper object. The raw data to populate both objects comes from the same server endpoint we used earlier for the Mustache example.

```
<script type="text/javascript">
    var initUrl = "/home/countries";
    $.getJSON(initUrl,
        function (response) {
```

```
                var model = new CountryViewModel(response.countryCodes);
                ko.applyBindings(model);
        });
    </script>
```

The above JavaScript code is responsible for triggering the actual page filling. The list of country codes downloaded is wrapped in a *CountryViewModel* object, and it is applied to the entire page DOM through KnockoutJS. Internally, the wrapper object creates a list of *Country* objects, one per country code. The additional step is because we expect the user interface to produce a table of clickable elements, but the click handler is subject to receive a bound value—the country code. Hence, the click handler must be data-bound, and with KnockoutJS, the click handler must be a member of the bound object. Purposely, the *Country* object offers a *showCapital* method that reads the current country code from the internal state of the object. Here's the final shape of the KnockoutJS-enabled Razor view.

```
<table class="table table-condensed" data-bind="foreach:countries">
    <tr>
        <td data-bind="text:code"></td>
        <td>
            <button class="btn btn-info" data-bind="event:{click:showCapital}">
                <i class="fa fa-chevron-right"></i>
            </button>
        </td>
    </tr>
</table>
```

The *countries* property is an array of Country objects, and the *foreach:countries* command loops for each bound object create a TR element. The first TD element shows the country code—the property *code*—directly in the body of the element. The second TD contains a BUTTON element whose click handler is bound to the *showCapital* method of the bound item. (See Figure 12-5.)

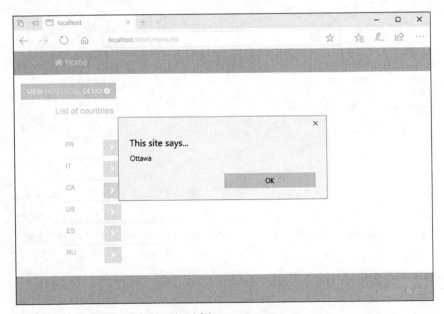

FIGURE 12-5 The KnockoutJS version of the country page

The Angular Way to Building Web Apps

Around the time in which the KnockoutJS library came out (this was a few years ago), the first version of another, more comprehensive library was released—the Angular library. Today, Angular 4 is available, but it is now much more than just a library for conveniently binding data to HTML elements. Today, Angular is a full-fledged framework for building web applications using HTML and JavaScript. Nicely enough, Angular also supports using TypeScript, which ultimately compiles to JavaScript.

Angular is made of multiple libraries to cover anything from data binding to routing and navigation and from HTTP to dependency injection and unit testing. The way you devise the application is unique and quite different from classic ASP.NET development. In Visual Studio 2017, you find a built-in template for building an Angular application. If you go through it and then explore the source code generated, you'll see a completely different architecture made of two types of modules: Angular modules and JavaScript modules. Angular modules more or less compare to ASP.NET MVC areas, whereas JavaScript modules are pieces of functionality you add, and I'd say more or less compare to NuGet packages you bind. Also, you have components that compare to ASP.NET view components or, more loosely, to Razor views. Within components, you have templates and data binding through a syntax that provides a set of facilities comparable to the MVVM model of KnockoutJS.

Angular strictly depends on NodeJS and npm. Outside Visual Studio 2017, you also need to use Angular CLI to generate the skeleton of a new project. Overall, Angular still delivers a web application, but it does so through a completely different experience and through a completely different programming approach. There are many resources for Angular development. The starting point, though, is *https://angular.io*.

Summary

Today, applications can hardly afford the burden of full-page refreshes when the user performs relevant operations. A decade ago, the (re)discovery of Ajax sparked a whole new world of techniques and a framework that culminated with client-side data binding. Overall, modern web applications have two substantial ways to do client-side data binding. One is maintaining a server-side, ASP.NET-friendly structure and enriching individual views with more dynamic rendering. The other is to choose a completely different framework and play by another set of rules.

In this chapter, we explored only the first route and provided three different levels of solutions. First, we went through the dynamic download of server-side–arranged chunks of HTML. Second, we integrated a minimal client-side JavaScript library (MustacheJS). Third, we upgraded to a full-fledged client-side data binding library such as KnockoutJS.

The other route to client-side data binding entails opting for a non-ASP.NET framework such as Angular. Not that Angular can't be integrated with ASP.NET as the hosting environment—in fact, you find Angular templates in Visual Studio 2017 and plenty of examples and courseware on Angular with ASP.NET Core. However, building an Angular application requires a completely different set of skills, practices, and techniques that can hardly be covered in due depth in a single chapter.

With the next chapter, we'll complete our look at the front end of web applications and discuss ways to build device-friendly views.

CHAPTER 13

Building Device-friendly Views

How much of the nose on your face can you see, unless someone holds a mirror up to you?

—Isaac Asimov, "I, Robot"

Users who connect to your web application through a device usually have high expectations when it comes to their experiences. Ultimately, they expect websites to provide an experience close to that of native iPhone or Android analogous app. This means, for example, having popular widgets, such as pick-lists, sideway menus, and toggle switches. Most of these widgets don't exist as native elements of HTML and must be simulated by using rich components controls that output a mix of JavaScript and markup each time. Twitter Bootstrap and jQuery plugins do a fantastic job, but that's not enough, and anyway, some work is required every time on your end. However, as we've seen in Chapter 6, ASP.NET Core tag helpers can significantly help smoothing this issue by raising the abstraction level of the markup you write and turning it under the hood into the necessary HTML and JavaScript.

Responsive web design (and, again, ultimately the grid system of Twitter Bootstrap) is another powerful tool that can reduce the burden of having a dedicated mobile app for a given site. The quick rule is, do not have a mobile application until the business loudly demands it. Until then, though, do not ignore how you offer your services through devices (mostly smartphones and tablets). If you have ignored devices since the early days, then you might even never reach the point in which business would loudly demand a native app.

Adapting Views to the Actual Device

The bottom line is that creating a website making the best possible use of HTML, CSS, and JavaScript is one thing. It is quite another, instead, to make a device-friendly website that looks like a native application or, at the very minimum, behaves as such. And it grows to be an even bigger problem when you consider that a device-friendly website is sometimes expected to have only a subset of the features compared to the full site and even different use-cases.

The good news, though, is that some of the development issues can be lessened by making good use of HTML5.

The Best of HTML5 for Device Scenarios

On the average, browsers mounted on devices offer great support for HTML5 elements, sometimes significantly better than desktop browsers. This means that at least on devices that fall under the umbrella of "smartphones" or "tablets," you can default to HTML5 elements without worrying about workarounds and shims. Two aspects of HTML5 are particularly relevant for device-friendly development: input types and geolocation.

New Input Types

There's quite a bit of difference between dates, numbers, or even email addresses, not to mention predefined values. However, current HTML doesn't seem to support much more than plain text as input. Therefore, developers are responsible for preventing users from typing unwanted characters by implementing client-side validation of the entered text. The jQuery library has several plugins that simplify the task, but this just reinforces the point—input is a delicate matter.

HTML5 comes with a plethora of new values for the attribute type of the *INPUT* element. Also, the *INPUT* counts several new attributes mostly related to these new input types. Here are a few examples:

```
<input type="date" />
<input type="time" />
<input type="range" />
<input type="number" />
<input type="search" />
<input type="color" />
<input type="email" />
<input type="url" />
<input type="tel" />
```

What's the real effect of these new input types? The intended effect—though not completely standardized yet—is that browsers provide an ad hoc UI so that users can comfortably enter a date, time, or number.

Desktop browsers do not always honor these new input types, and the experience they provide is not always uniform. Things are much better in the mobile space. First and foremost, users typically browse the web with the default browser on mobile devices. Consequently, the experience is always uniform and specific to the device.

In particular, input fields like *email*, *url*, and *tel* push mobile browsers on smartphones to automatically adjust the input scope of the keyboard. Figure 13-1 shows the effect of typing in a *tel* input field on an Android device: the keyboard defaults to numbers and phone-related symbols.

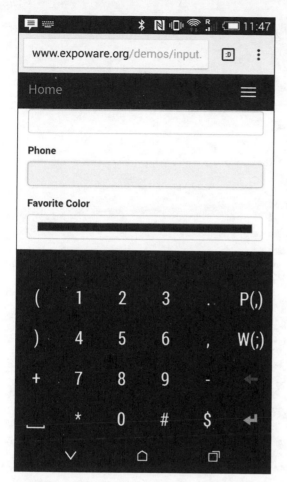

FIGURE 13-1 The *tel* input field on an Android smartphone

Today, not all browsers provide the same experience, and although they mostly agree on the user interface associated with the various input types, still some key differences exist that might require developers to add custom JavaScript polyfills. As an example, let's consider the *date* type. No version of Internet Explorer or Safari offers any special support whatsoever for dates. Also, in this case, things go much better with mobile devices, as the screenshot in Figure 13-2 demonstrates.

FIGURE 13-2 The *date* input field on an Android smartphone

In general, mobile browsers on recent smartphones are quite respectful of HTML5 elements, and therefore, developers should be ready to use proper input types.

Geolocation

Geolocation is an HTML standard that is widely supported by both desktop and mobile browsers. As mentioned, sometimes the mobile version of a website needs to have ad hoc use-cases that users won't find on the full version of the site. When this happens, it's quite likely that geolocation of users is involved in the mobile-only versions. Here's some sample code.

```
<script type="text/javascript"
        src="http://maps.googleapis.com/maps/api/js?sensor=true"></script>
<script type="text/javascript">
    function initialize() {
    navigator.geolocation.getCurrentPosition(
```

```
            showMap,
            function(e) {alert(e.message);},
            {enableHighAccuracy:true, timeout:10000, maximumAge:0 });
    }

    function showMap(position) {
        var point = new google.maps.LatLng(
                position.coords.latitude,
                position.coords.longitude);
        var myOptions = {
                zoom: 16,
                center: point,
                mapTypeId: google.maps.MapTypeId.ROADMAP
        };
        var map = new google.maps.Map(document.getElementById("map_canvas"), myOptions);
        var marker = new google.maps.Marker({
                position: point,
                map: map,
                title: "You are here" });
    }
</script>
<body onload="initialize()">
  <div id="map_canvas" style="width:100%; height:100%"></div>
</body>
```

This page asks for user permission about geolocation and then shows the exact geographical position of the device on a map.

> **Note** Geolocation is subject to browser policies that usually work on a per-site basis. Also, note that Google Chrome only supports Google Maps functions on secure sites (HTTPS). The above example, therefore, might not work for the map part, but you can always grab the latitude and longitude instead.

Feature Detection

Responsive Web Design (RWD) sprung to life from lateral thinking that says detecting devices is hard. Another option is to grab a few snippets of basic information available on the client side (for example, the size of the browser window), set up ad hoc style sheets, and let the browser reflow content in the page accordingly. This thinking led to feature detection and brought about the creation of a popular library—Modernizr—and the equally popular website, *http://caniuse.com*.

What Modernizr Can Do for You

The idea behind feature detection is simple and, to some extent, even smart. You don't even attempt to detect the actual capabilities of the requesting device, which is known to be cumbersome, difficult, and even poses serious issues as far as maintainability of the solution is concerned.

Equipped with a feature-detection library, you decide what to display based only on what you can detect programmatically on the device. Instead of detecting the user agent, and blindly assuming that such devices don't support a given feature, you just let an ad hoc library like Modernizr find out for you whether the feature is actually available on the current browser, regardless of the host device. (See *http://modernizr.com*).

For example, instead of maintaining a list of the browsers (and related user agent strings) that support date input fields, you just check with Modernizr if date input fields are available on the current browser. Here's some illustrative script code.

```
<script type="text/javascript">
Modernizr.load({
    test: Modernizr.inputtypes.date,
    nope: ['jquery-ui.min.js', 'jquery-ui.css'],
    complete: function () {
        $('input[type=date]').datepicker({
            dateFormat: 'yy-mm-dd'
        });
    }
});
</script>
```

You tell Modernizr to test the date input type, and if the test fails, you download jQuery UI files and run the *complete* callback function to set up the jQuery UI date picker plugin for all INPUT elements in the page of type date. This allows you to blissfully use HTML5 markup in your page regardless of the effect on end users.

```
<input type="date" />
```

Feature detection offers the significant plus that you, as a developer, have just one site to design and maintain. The burden of adapting content responsively is pushed to graphical designers or ad hoc libraries, such as Modernizr.

What Modernizr Can Do for You

Modernizr consists of a JavaScript library with some code that runs when the page loads and checks whether the current browser can offer certain HTML5 and CSS3 functionalities. Modernizr exposes its findings programmatically so that the code in the page can query the library and intelligently adapt the output.

Modernizr does a great job, but the job it performs doesn't cover the entire range of issues you face when optimizing a website for mobile users. Modernizr is limited to what you can programmatically detect as JavaScript functions, which might or might not be exposed out of *navigator* or *window* browser objects.

In other words, Modernizr is not able to tell you about the form factor of the device or whether the device is a smartphone, tablet, or a smart TV. When browsers eventually expose the user's device type, Modernizr will be able to add this service too. By applying some logic to the results you can get from Modernizr, you can "reliably guess" whether the browser is mobile or desktop. You can hardly go beyond that point, though.

Therefore, if you really need to do something specific for smartphones and/or tablets, Modernizr is of not much help.

The major strength of feature detection, which we can summarize as "one *site* fits all," is also likely to be the major weakness. Is just one site what you really want? Do you really want to serve the "same" site to smartphones, tablets, laptops, and smart TVs? The answer to these questions invariably is specific to each business. In general terms, it can only be a resounding, "It depends."

Enter client-side, lightweight device detection via user agent strings.

Client-side Device Detection

Optimizing a website for mobile devices doesn't usually mean allowing users to have the same experience as a native app on their favorite platforms. A mobile website is very rarely specific to iOS or Android operating systems. A mobile website, instead, is devised and designed in such a way any mobile browser can give users a good experience.

Currently, sniffing the user agent string is the only reliable way to determine whether the device is a desktop computer or less powerful type of device, such as a phone or tablet.

Handmade User Agent Sniffing

There a few online resources that provide some heuristics to detect mobile browsers. They use a combination of two core techniques: analysis of the user agent string and cross-checking of some of the properties of the browser's *navigator* object. In particular, you might want to take a look at the following URLs for more information:

- *http://www.quirksmode.org/js/detect.html*

- *http://detectmobilebrowsers.com*

In particular, the script you find on the second website uses a tricky regular expression to check for a long list of keywords known to be related to mobile devices. The script works and is available for a variety of web platforms, including plain JavaScript and ASP.NET. It has two nontrivial drawbacks, though.

One drawback is the date of the last update you find on the web page. Last time I checked, it was dated 2014. It might be better by the time you read this, yet it leaves unaltered the perception that keeping the regular expression up to date is expensive and must be done frequently. Not to mention that the script for ASP.NET is a plain Web Forms script based on VBScript and is incompatible with ASP.NET Core.

The other drawback is that the script only attempts to tell you whether the user agent is known to identify a mobile device as opposed to a desktop device. It lacks logic, and it lacks programming power to identify more specifically the class of the requesting device and its known capabilities.

If you're looking for a free client-side solution to sniff user agent strings, then I suggest you look at WURFL.JS. (See *http://wurfl.io*.) Among other benefits, WURFL.JS is not based on any regular expressions; it's your responsibility to keep it up to date.

Using WURFL.JS

In spite of the name, WURFL.JS is not a static JavaScript file you can host on-premises or upload to your cloud site. More precisely, WURFL.JS is an HTTP endpoint you link to your web views through a regular SCRIPT element.

To get the WURFL.JS services, therefore, you only need to add the following line to any HTML views you have that need to know about the actual device.

```
<script type="text/javascript" src="//wurfl.io/wurfl.js"></script>
```

The browser knows nothing about the nature of the WURFL.JS endpoint. The browser just attempts to download and execute any script code it can get from the specified URL. The WURFL server that receives a request uses the user agent of the calling device to figure out its actual capabilities. The WURFL server relies on the services of the WURFL framework—a powerful device data repository and a cross-platform API used by Facebook, Google, and PayPal.

The net effect of calling the aforementioned HTTP endpoint is to inject a tailor-made JavaScript object into the browser DOM. Here's an example of what you get:

```
var WURFL = {
    "complete_device_name":"iPhone 7",
    "is_mobile":false,
    "form_factor":"Smartphone"
};
```

The server-side endpoint receives the user agent string sent with the request and thoroughly analyzes it. The server-side endpoint then selects three pieces of information and arranges a JavaScript string to return.

Table 13-1 provides the list of WURFL.JS properties.

TABLE 13-1 WURFL.JS Properties

Property	Description
complete_device_name	Descriptive name for the detected device. The name includes vendor information and device name (e.g., iPhone 7).
form_factor	Indicates the class of the detected device. It's one of the following strings: Desktop, App, Tablet, Smartphone, Feature Phone, Smart-TV, Robot, Other non-Mobile, or Other Mobile.
is_mobile	If true, it indicates that the device is not a desktop device.

Figure 13-3 shows WURFL.JS in action on a public test page you can find at *http://www.expoware .org/demos/device.html*.

FIGURE 13-3 Device detection with WURFL.JS

Regarding performance, WURFL.JS is fairly efficient; it does a lot of caching and doesn't really check any user agent it receives. While in development, though, you can switch off the cache by adding *debug=true* to the URL.

> **Important** The WURFL.JS framework is free to use as long as the website is publicly available. If used in production, though, it might become a bottleneck in case of high volumes of traffic. In this case, you might want to consider a commercial option that reserves more bandwidth and also gives you access to a longer list of device properties. For more information, check out *http://www.scientiamobile.com*.

Mixing Client-side Detection and Responsive Pages

WURFL.JS can be used in many different scenarios including browser personalization, enhancing analytics, and the optimization of advertising. Further, if you are a front-end developer and implementing device detection on the server side is not an option for you, WURFL.JS is your savior. For more examples, check out the WURFL.JS documentation at *http://wurfl.io*.

Let's briefly consider a few scenarios where you want to use client device detection. One scenario is downloading images of size and content that are appropriate for the device. You can go with code like this:

```
<script>
   if (WURFL.form_factor == "smartphone") {
      $("#myImage").attr("src", "...");
   }
</script>
```

Similarly, you can use the WURFL object to redirect to a specific mobile site if the requesting device looks like a smartphone:

```
<script>
    if (WURFL.form_factor == "smartphone") {
        window.location.href = "...";
    }
</script>
```

WURFL.JS gives you clues about the actual device, but for the time being, there's no way to mix CSS media queries and external information such device-specific details. A responsive design driven by actual user agents rather than media query parameters is still possible, but it's entirely on your own. The most common way to use WURFL.JS is within the context of Bootstrap or any other RWD solutions. You get the device details, and via JavaScript, you enable or disable specific features or download ad hoc content.

 Note In the companion code that comes with this book, you will find an example that uses WURFL.JS to figure out which area of the website to point users. The example is a simple proof-of-concept, but it might be enlarged to consider a scenario in which most of the site is a classic RWD site except for a few areas that are duplicated based on the form-factor of the device.

Client Hints Coming Soon

Client Hints is the colloquial name of a draft that is emerging, which will provide a unified, standard way for browsers and servers to negotiate content. Client Hints is inspired by the widely used *Accept-** HTTP headers. With each request, the browser sends in a few extra headers; the server reads those headers and can use them to adapt the content being returned.

At the current stage of the draft, you can have a header suggesting the desired width of the content and the client's maximum download speed. These two pieces of information could be enough to make the server aware of most critical situations we face today: small screen devices over slow connections. In most cases, in fact, it's not even crucial to know if it's a smartphone or another type of device. Today, and even more so in the future, responsive content would likely be a good approximation except for very slow connections and very low-resolution devices, including old iPhone devices. Client Hints goes in this direction. The following code shows a very simple way to include some client hints in a web view. This meta tag is an alternative to using HTTP response headers for servers to advertise their support for client hints.

```
<meta http-equiv="Accept-CH" content="DPR, Viewport-Width, Width">
```

Some early documentation about Client Hints and prospective headers being defined for exchange is available at *http://httpwg.org/http-extensions/client-hints.html*.

Device-friendly Images

High-quality and effective images are a necessary burden to nearly any website. However, serving images to devices is problematic because of the ratio between the necessary size of the image and the computing power of the device (to say nothing of the network). Serving device-friendly images means essentially two things: serving images of an appropriate size in bytes and appropriately cropped and/or resized to remain relevant in the context in which they are used. In other words, serving an appropriate image is both a matter of quantity (of bytes) and quality (art direction).

The PICTURE Element

In HTML5, a new element for rendering images makes its debut—the PICTURE element. You can think of it as a superset of the old familiar *IMG* element. Here's the syntax.

```
<picture>
    <source media="(min-width: 481px)" srcset="~/content/images/poppies_md.jpg"
            class="img-responsive">
    <source media="(max-width: 480px)" srcset="~/content/images/poppies_xs.jpg"
            class="img-responsive">
    <img src="~/content/images/poppies.jpg" alt="Poppies"
         class="img-responsive">
</picture>
```

Instead of having one image that is scaled up or down based on the viewport width, multiple images can be specified to appear at given breakpoints. Because each determined breakpoint can have its own image, images can be designed to better address the needs of art direction. In Figure 13-4, you see the effect of the previous code in Microsoft Edge. The debug bar at the top shows the current width of the screen. At 480 pixels wide, you see an XS image that is centered around the old country building. At 481 pixels wide, the image changes to offer a landscape view of the poppy field.

FIGURE 13-4 The PICTURE element in Microsoft Edge

The same original image was adapted to serve the XS and MD breakpoints. Note that although XS and MD suffixes seem to recall Bootstrap's breakpoints, there's no relationship between those breakpoints and Bootstrap's. Only the value of the *media* attribute on the *source* child node of the PICTURE element sets the conditions for the browser to switch images.

The PICTURE element is gaining traction, but it is not supported across the entire spectrum of browsers. However, it works on more recent versions of Google Chrome, Opera, and Microsoft Edge, meaning that you can use it in your websites with limited concerns. For developers and administrators, the PICTURE element raises the non-secondary issue of maintaining multiple copies of the same image to be used depending on the current screen size. For a site with many images that are frequently updated, this can be a real problem.

Another option for multi-resolution images is using the ImageEngine platform. Unlike the PICTURE element, the ImageEngine platform doesn't pose any compatibility issues.

The ImageEngine Platform

ImageEngine is a commercial image resizing tool exposed as a service. (See *http://wurfl.io*.) It is particularly well-suited for device-friendly scenarios where it can significantly reduce the image payload of views, thus reducing the load time. The platform operates as a sort of Content Delivery Network because it sits between your server application and the client browser, serving images intelligently on behalf of the server.

The primary purpose of the ImageEngine platform is to reduce the traffic generated by images. In this regard, it presents itself as an ideal tool for mobile websites. However, ImageEngine is not limited to that. First and foremost, you can serve resized images to any device, regardless of type. Second, you can use ImageEngine as an online resizer tool with a URL-based programmatic interface. Finally, you can use ImageEngine as your smart image—only CDN and save yourself the burden of maintaining multiple versions of the same image to speed up the load time on various screen sizes.

Resizing Images Automatically

To use ImageEngine, you first need to get an account. The account identifies you with a name and helps the server keep your traffic distinct from other users. Before you create an account, though, you can play with the test account. In a Razor view, you display images on web pages as below:

```
<img src="~/content/images/autumn.jpg">
```

When you use ImageEngine, you replace it with the following markup.

```
<img src="//try.imgeng.in/http://www.yoursite.com/content/images/autumn.jpg">
```

Once you have your account, you simply replace *try* with your account name. If the account name is *contoso*, then the URL of the image becomes:

```
<img src="//contoso.imgeng.in/http://www.yoursite.com/content/images/autumn.jpg">
```

In other words, you need to pass the full URL of your original image to the ImageEngine back end so that the image can be silently downloaded and cached. ImageEngine supports a number of parameters including cropping and sizing to given dimensions. ImageEngine not only resizes images to the size it reckons ideal for the device, but it can also accept specific suggestions, as in Table 13-2. Parameters are inserted in the resulting URL.

TABLE 13-2 URL parameters of the ImageEngine tool

URL Parameter	Description
w_NNN	Sets the desired width of the image in pixels. Sample URL: //contoso.imgeng.in/w_200/IMAGE_URL
h_NNN	Sets the desired height of the image in pixels. Sample URL: //contoso.imgeng.in/h_200/IMAGE_URL
pc_NN	Sets the desired percentage of reduction for the image. Sample URL: //contoso.imgeng.in/pc_30/IMAGE_URL
m_XXX	Sets the resize mode of the image. Feasible values are: box (default), cropbox, letterbox, and stretch. Sample URL: //contoso.imgeng.in/m_cropbox/w_300/h_300/IMAGE_URL
f_XXX	Sets the desired output format of the image. Feasible values are: png, jpg, webp, gif, and bmp. By default, the image is returned in the original format. Sample URL: //contoso.imgeng.in/f_webp/IMAGE_URL

Note that width/height and percentage are mutually exclusive. If none is indicated, the image is resized to the dimensions suggested by the detected user agent. Multiple parameters can be combined as segments of the URL. For example, the URL below resizes the image in a 300x300 cropping appropriately from the center of the image in case the original dimensions don't return a square. The order of parameters is unimportant.

```
//contoso.imgeng.in/w_300/h_300/m_cropbox/IMAGE_URL
```

Figure 13-5 shows the benefits of using ImageEngine. When the page is served to a smartphone, the size is different from the original. The two IMG elements in the sample page refer to the same physical image through ImageEngine and are served directly.

```
<img id="img1" src="http://try.imgeng.in/http://www.expoware.org/images/tennis1.jpg" />
<img id="img2" src="http://www.expoware.org/images/tennis1.jpg" />
```

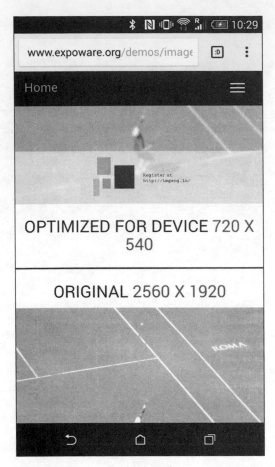

FIGURE 13-5 ImageEngine in action

Compared to the upcoming PICTURE element, ImageEngine doesn't let you serve really different images so if art direction is involved, you really need to host and serve physically different images which can be further preprocessed via ImageEngine. If you don't have art direction concerns, though, ImageEngine saves you the burden of resizing manually and saves bandwidth.

Device-oriented Development Strategies

So far, we have discussed quick client-side techniques to improve the rendering of pages, and behavior thereof, on various devices. Let's extend the landscape to the entire website and review the approaches you can take to serve content effectively to devices.

Client-centric Strategies

So far, most of the content has revolved around JavaScript improvements to the page document object model. Let's just summarize the options.

Responsive HTML Templates

If you start today with a brand-new website, I'd recommend you use Bootstrap to have a responsive template for all your views. Using a responsive HTML template ensures that your views display nicely when the user resizes the desktop browser window and that you have a basic coverage of mobile users. At the very minimum, in fact, mobile users will receive the same views that desktop users receive when they resize the browser.

It might not be ideal from a performance perspective, but if devices are new and fast enough, and connectivity is not really bad, the effect is acceptable. I wouldn't recommend this route for the website in which mobile interactivity is a core part of the business; but, in most cases, it just works.

When it comes to Bootstrap, and more in general to RWD, the primary issue you face is the definition of breakpoints—that is, the width of the screen that triggers a change of the view. Bootstrap has its own set of breakpoints that go under the suffixes of XS, SM, MD, and LG. Each breakpoint corresponds to a fixed width in pixels. It mostly works, but it's far from perfect. In particular, the Bootstrap system of breakpoints doesn't properly treat smartphones and small-screen devices. The XS suffix is triggered at 768 pixels, which is way too wide for a smartphone. In Bootstrap 4, however, a new breakpoint is added that sets the width of smallest recognized devices around 500 pixels. Again, this is not perfect, but it is a much better compromise.

The alternative is not to use Bootstrap at all, or you could create a completely custom grid system that replaces the Bootstrap's grid with application-specific measures.

Add Client-side Enhancements

If you have time and budget, you might want to improve the quality of responsive views and optimize the way certain parts of it (for example, images) are handled, and enable some mobile-specific features if you detect appropriate devices. This step goes in the general direction of offering the best possible user experience and encompasses both feature and device detection. The following demo shows how to optimize the apparently trivial task of picking a date so that the experience is ideal, regardless of the device.

```
<div class="col-xs-6">
    REGULAR DATE-PICKER<br />
    <input type="text" class="form-control" date>
</div>
<div class="col-xs-6">
    DEVICE-SPECIFIC DATE-PICKER<br />
    <input type="text" class="form-control" id="mdate">
</div>
```

The two similar INPUT fields above are modified via JavaScript. The one with the custom *date* attribute is attached to a date-picker plugin. The other, instead, has its *type* attribute changed to *date* only if the detected device is a smartphone or a feature phone. (Tablets, for example, will get the date-picker plugin.)

```
<script>
    // Blindly uses a date-picker.
    // For example, https://uxsolutions.github.io/bootstrap-datepicker
```

```
    $("input[date]").datepicker({
        // More configuration
    });

    // Datepicker or native
    if (WURFL.form_factor === "Smartphone" ||
        WURFL.form_factor === "Feature Phone") {
        $("#mdate").attr("type", "date");
    } else {
        $("#mdate").datepicker();
    }
</script>
```

FIGURE 13-6 Date-pickers are not really comfortable to use on smartphones

As Figure 13-6 shows, date-picker components are not particularly comfortable to use on smart-phones. They might be acceptable on tablets, but for small screen devices, the native picker is much better. However, a dynamic change of the value of the *type* attribute is necessary to distinguish between a native and a programmatic date picker, and detection of the device is necessary. This is one of most concrete examples of client-side enhancements.

Routing to Views

Earlier in the chapter, I hinted at a technique that downloads appropriate HTML depending on the requesting user agent. Using WURFL.JS, you can detect the form factor of the browser and download the most appropriate content from your server. This entails that every view (or just most critical views) are available in multiple copies, for example, a version for smartphones and a version for desktop browsers. Here's some code that determines the content of the page programmatically based on the detected device.

```
<html>
<head>
    <meta charset="utf-8" />
    <meta name="viewport" content="width=device-width, initial-scale=1.0">
    <title>DEVICE DISCOVERY</title>
    <link href="content/styles/bootstrap.min.css" rel="stylesheet" type="text/css" />
    <script src="content/scripts/jquery-3.1.1.min.js"></script>
    <script src="content/scripts/bootstrap.min.js"></script>
    <script src="//wurfl.io/wurfl.js?debug=true"></script>

    <script type="text/javascript">
        var formFactor = WURFL.form_factor;
        var agent = WURFL.complete_device_name;
        window.addEventListener("DOMContentLoaded", function () {
            $("#title").html(formFactor + "<br>" + agent);
        });
    </script>
    <script type="text/javascript">
        var url = "/screen/default";
        $(document).ready(function () {
            switch (formFactor) {
            case "Smartphone":
                    url = "/screen/smartphone";
                break;
            case "Tablet":
                    url = "/screen/tablet";
                break;
            }
            $.ajax({
                url: url,
                cache: false,
                dataType: "html",
                success: function(data) {
                    $("#body").html(data);
                }
            });
        });
    </script>
</head>
<body>

<!-- Some more content here -->

<div class="text-center text-warning">
    <div id="title"></div>
</div>
```

```
<div id="body">
    <div class="text-center">
        <span>LOADING ...</span>
    </div>
</div>
<!-- Some more content here -->

</body>
</html>
```

The final blocks of script in the *HEAD* section update the header of the page (using the plain DOM API) and the actual content (using the jQuery API). The use of different APIs is only meant to show that you are not dependent on any API for page updates. Based on the detected form factor, the page connects to a site-specific endpoint and requests the chunk of HTML that is most appropriate. Figure 13-7 shows the view you get on a tablet. (Note that the figure has been obtained using the Microsoft Edge emulator to pass an Apple iPad user agent string.)

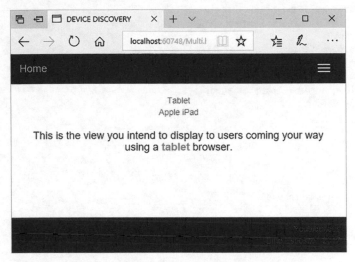

FIGURE 13-7 Tablet-specific view of the sample page

The technique discussed here is effective in the sense that it can deliver the multi-view benefits you want, but it is not strictly effective in terms of flexibility and manageability of the solution. You still need to create and maintain multiple copies of the same view, and you must update all of them when something needs to change. For years, I've been a fan of mobile-specific views but in the long run, it became too much work, and RWD (and Bootstrap as the herald of it) is probably the best compromise you can get if time and budget are serious constraints.

Server-centric Strategies

One easy way to improve the previous approach—still keeping it subject to multiple versions of the same logical view—is performing the device detection on the server. Also, pure server-side detection is not free from issues.

Server-side Detection

At the very end of the day, server-side detection consists of analyzing the user agent string sent by the browser. In theory, it can be as easy as running the user agent string through a regex expression. However, given the huge number of devices today—user agents and edge cases—if device detection is crucial and it is preferable to have it on the server, then you must be ready to pay for a professional service.

> **Note** The framework I use is WURFL OnSite, but other options exist, such as Device Atlas. At the time of this writing, with ASP.NET Core 2.0 released, the major problems with all device detection server frameworks is the lack of support for .NET Core.

While waiting for server frameworks to be ported to .NET Core, the realistic options you have are listed in Table 13-3.

TABLE 13-3 Server-side detection options from within ASP.NET Core applications

API	Description
WURFL OnSite .NET API WURFL Cloud .NET API	■ Within an ASP.NET Core application compiled for the full .NET Framework. ■ Wrapping the API in a microservice (standalone web service) and invoking it from ASP.NET Core via HTTP. For more information, see *http://www.scientiamobile.com*.
Device Atlas .NET API	Same as above.
WURFL InFuze module	WURFL InFuze is an IIS extension module that adds configured device properties to each request via HTTP headers. In this regard, it is completely independent of the version of the .NET Framework. See *http://www.scientiamobile.com*.

The bottom line is that server-side detection provides the nicest experience for users because they get the most appropriate selection of content and layout automatically and in the fastest way. With server-side detection, in fact, no unused data is ever downloaded, and no additional requests are placed for ad hoc views. The problem is the maintenance of the site and the proliferation of configuration parameters and partial views.

If offering an ad hoc experience is crucial for the business, then having an ad hoc mobile site is still a valid option to consider.

Redirecting to Mobile Websites

Suppose now you have two websites—the full site, whether responsive or not, and the mobile site, sometimes referred to in the literature as an *m-site*. How would you reach them? The real world is full of examples that approach this problem in different ways, while still achieving good business results.

I believe we might all agree that having a single public URL for the website would be great. Users have only to remember the *www* thing and the software does the magic of silently switching to the most appropriate content available. Companies who don't do so—we might agree—might be facing some business pain. You can think of having some very basic and simple device detection that redirects to a physically separated website under a different URL. In this case, you don't strictly need to know all details of a device but just a rough heuristic that it is a mobile device or not.

From a development perspective, you can consider the ad hoc mobile website as a different project. Having it as a different project is a great achievement because you can develop it with ad hoc technologies and frameworks, outsource it to external companies, have different people work on it, and have it done at any later time. Also, the mobile site can be added anytime.

Summary

A server-side solution is inherently more flexible than a purely client-side, RWD-based solution because it allows you to check the device before you send anything down the wire. In this way, the website can intelligently decide the most appropriate content. In practice, though, serving device-specific views is never an easy thing and the core issue is not the mechanism used to detect the underlying device. The problem is cost.

Device detection doesn't mean serving a different version of pages for each browser or device. It more realistically means maintaining at most three or four collections of views for most common form factors: desktops, smartphones, tablets, legacy phones, or perhaps very large screens. Multiple pages are a cost, no doubt.

The approach that sounds the most reasonable today consists of having a default responsive solution and a separate smartphone-specific website with just the use-cases that are relevant to mobile users. You can achieve this by deploying two distinct websites and using some client-side detection to redirect. Another option is to use a server-side approach, which gives you more control over the behavior and also scales a lot more easily and flexibly in case you decide to be open to more form factors.

Either way, as a developer, you can't neglect the user experience on mobile devices, and you can't even conclude that a responsive template is all you need. Responsive design is just one answer, and probably, it's not even entirely correct.

The ASP.NET Core Ecosystem

You're now well-prepared to build modern solutions with ASP.NET Core. Before we conclude, it's time to widen our view of the development lifecycle. This final Part V explores crucial issues concerning the ASP.NET Core runtime pipeline, application deployment, and moving from older ASP.NET frameworks.

Chapter 14, *The ASP.NET Core Runtime Environment*, takes a deeper look at the internal architecture of the ASP.NET Core runtime environment, its Kestrel server, and the core middleware. These fundamentally new technologies establish a cross-platform runtime that is fully decoupled from the web server environment.

Chapter 15, *Deploying an ASP.NET Core Application*, guides you through ASP.NET Core's more diverse application deployment options: not just Windows Server or Microsoft Azure app services, but also Linux on-premise machines, third-party cloud environments such as Amazon Web Services (AWS), and Docker containers.

Finally, in Chapter 16, *Migration and Adoption Strategies*, I'll help you parse the tradeoffs you face in moving to ASP.NET Core. I'll help you assess ASP.NET Core's value in the very different scenarios of greenfield development and brownfield development, as well as many projects that fit in between. I'll also introduce some practical tools and techniques for planning your transition[md]including opportunities to move toward microservices and containers.

CHAPTER 14

The ASP.NET Core Runtime Environment

Conscience does make cowards of us all; and thus the native hue of resolution is sicklied over with the pale cast of thought.

—*William Shakespeare, "Hamlet"*

In Chapter 2, "The First ASP.NET Core Project," we opened the ASP.NET Core machine hood and had our first look at it. In doing so, we learned that the runtime environment and the pipeline through which any requests pass is quite different from what is found in past versions of ASP.NET. Also, the new ASP.NET Core runtime environment is empowered by a system-provided, embedded Dependency Injection (DI) infrastructure that silently watches, as a ghost friend, over all the steps of processing an incoming request.

In this chapter, we take it further and explore more in depth the internal architecture of the ASP.NET Core runtime environment and its components, primarily the Kestrel server and request middleware.

The ASP.NET Core Host

At its core, an ASP.NET Core application consists of a standalone console application that sets up the host environment for the actual application model, most likely an MVC application model. The host is responsible for configuring a server that listens for incoming HTTP requests and passes requests to the processing pipeline. The following code shows the default implementation of the host program of a typical ASP.NET Core application as it results from the standard Visual Studio 2017 templates. The following source code is written in the *program.cs* file of an ASP.NET Core project.

```
public class Program
{
    public static void Main(string[] args)
    {
        BuildWebHost(args).Run();
    }

    public static IWebHost BuildWebHost(string[] args) =>
        WebHost.CreateDefaultBuilder(args)
            .UseStartup<Startup>()
            .Build();
}
```

Let's find out more about the web host component and the other, simpler, options you have to start the host.

The *WebHost* Class

WebHost is a static class that provides two methods for creating instances of classes exposing the *IWebHostBuilder* interface with predefined settings. The class also comes with many methods to quickly start the environment passing just the URL to listen to and a delegate for the behavior to implement. Again, this is the living proof of the extreme flexibility of the ASP.NET Core runtime, as we'll see in the next example.

Configuring the Behavior of the Host

The *Start* methods on the *WebHost* class allow you to set up a web application in a variety of ways. One of the most interesting is the overload that sets up the application around a plain lambda function.

```
using (var host = WebHost.Start(
    app => app.Response.WriteAsync("Programming ASP.NET Core")))
{
    // Wait for the host to end
    ...
}
```

All the application does is run the specified function, regardless of the URL invoked. The instance returned by the *Start* method of the *WebHost* class is of type *IWebHost* and represents an already started host environment for the application. Inside the *WebHost.Start* method, the following pseudo-code runs:

```
public static IWebHost Start(RequestDelegate app)
{
    var defaultBuilder = WebHost.CreateDefaultBuilder();
    var host = defaultBuilder.Build();

    // This line actually starts the host
    host.Start();
    return host;
}
```

Note that the *Start* method runs the host in a non-blocking manner, which means the host needs some additional instruction to continue listening for incoming requests. Here's an example. (See Figure 14-1.)

```
    ic static void Main(string[] args)

    using (var host = WebHost.Start(
        app => app.Response.WriteAsync("Programming ASP.NET Core")))
        {
            // Wait for the host to end
            Console.WriteLine("Courtesy of 'Programming ASP.NET Core'\n====");
            Console.WriteLine("Use Ctrl-C to shut down the host...");
            host.WaitForShutdown();
        }
}
```

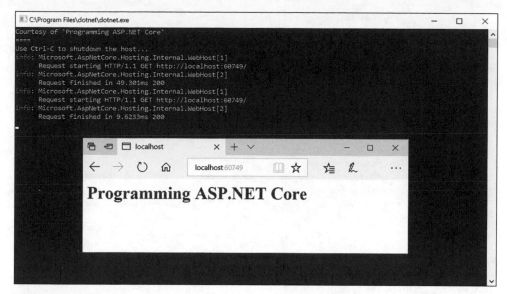

FIGURE 14-1 The host in action

By default, the host listens for incoming requests on port 5000. As you can see from the figure, the logger is automatically turned on even though no apparent line in our user-level code is turned it on. This means that the host receives some default configuration. The *WebHost.CreateDefaultBuilder* method is internally called by the Start method and is responsible for the receipt of the default configuration. Let's find out more about the default settings.

The Default Settings

In ASP.NET Core 2.0, the method *CreateDefaultBuilder* (defined as a static method on the *WebHost* class) creates and returns an instance of the host object. All the *Start* methods defined on *WebHost* end up calling the default builder internally. Here's what happens when the default web host builder is invoked.

```
public static IWebHostBuilder CreateDefaultBuilder(string[] args)
{
    return new WebHostBuilder()
            .UseKestrel()
            .UseContentRoot(Directory.GetCurrentDirectory())
            .ConfigureAppConfiguration(
              (Action<WebHostBuilderContext, IConfigurationBuilder>) ((context, config) =>
                {
                    var env = context.HostingEnvironment;
                    config.AddJsonFile("appsettings.json", true, true)
                        .AddJsonFile(string.Format("appsettings.{0}.json",
                                    env.EnvironmentName), true, true);
                    if (env.IsDevelopment())
                    {
                        var assembly = Assembly.Load(new AssemblyName(env.ApplicationName));
                        if (assembly != null)
                            config.AddUserSecrets(assembly, true);
                    }
```

```
            config.AddEnvironmentVariables();
            config.AddCommandLine(args);
        }))
    .ConfigureLogging(
        (Action<WebHostBuilderContext, ILoggingBuilder>) ((context, logging) =>
        {
            logging.AddConfiguration(context.Configuration.GetSection("Logging"));
            logging.AddConsole();
            logging.AddDebug();
        }))
    .UseIISIntegration()
    .UseDefaultServiceProvider(
        (Action<WebHostBuilderContext, ServiceProviderOptions>) ((context, options) =>
        {
            options.ValidateScopes = context.HostingEnvironment.IsDevelopment()));
        }
}
```

In summary, the default builder does six different things, as outlined in Table 14-1.

TABLE 14-1 Actions taken by the default builder

Action	Description
Web server	Adds Kestrel as the embedded web server of the ASP.NET Core pipeline.
Content root	Sets the current directory as the root folder for any file-based content accessed by the web application.
Configuration	Adds a few configuration providers: *appsettings.json*, environment variables, command line arguments, and user secrets (only in development mode).
Logging	Adds a few logging providers: those defined in the *logging* section of the configuration tree as well as the console and debug loggers.
IIS	Enables integration with IIS as the reverse proxy.
Service provider	Configures the default service provider.

It is key to note that all those operations always occur outside your control whenever you call one of the methods on the *WebHost* class to fire up the host for the web application. If you want to shape up a custom collection of settings for the host, please read on. Before we look into a custom host configuration, however, let's first look into the options you have to actually run the host and make it listen to incoming calls.

> **Tip** To investigate the source code of a class in Visual Studio, I use ReSharper, which includes dotPeek that does the actual decompile work as soon as you press F12. Without ReSharper, dotPeek—a free tool—can still be configured in Visual Studio to act as a symbol server. More information can be found here: *http://bit.ly/2AnTOvK*. ILSpy is another in-place decompiler that can be freely used in Visual Studio, and it is available on the marketplace.

Starting the Host

Whenever you create a host through any of the methods exposed by the *WebHost* class, you receive an already-started host that is already listening on the configured addresses. As mentioned, the *Start* method used by default launches the host in a non-blocking manner, but other options exist, too.

The *Run* method starts the web application and then blocks the calling thread until the host is shut down. The *WaitForShutdown* method, instead, blocks the calling thread until the application shutdown is triggered manually, for example via Ctrl+C.

Custom Hosting Settings

Using the default host builder is easy and delivers a host with most of the features you still want to have. You can further extend the host with additional aspects such as the startup class and the URLs to listen to. Or you can have a host that features fewer capabilities than the default host.

Manually Creating the Web Host

The following code shows how to create a brand-new host from scratch.

```
var host = new WebHostBuilder().Build();
```

The *WebHostBuilder* class has a number of extension methods to add features. At the very minimum, you need to specify the in-process HTTP server implementation to be used. This web server listens for HTTP requests and forwards them to the application wrapped up in friendly *HttpContext* packages. Kestrel is the default and the most commonly used web server implementation. To enable Kestrel, you call the *UseKestrel* method.

To make your web application compatible with IIS hosting, you also need to enable the feature through the *UseIISIntegration* extension method. Finally, you might want to specify the content root folder and the startup class to use to finalize the configuration of the runtime environment.

```
var host = new WebHostBuilder()
            .UseKestrel()
            .UseIISIntegration()
            .UseContentRoot(Directory.GetCurrentDirectory())
            .Build();
```

Two more aspects of the application must be specified at this point. One is the loading of the application settings, and the other is the terminating middleware. In ASP.NET Core 2.0, you can use the new *ConfigureAppConfiguration* method to load application settings, as in the code snippet shown above. Instead, you use the *Configure* method to add the terminating middleware, namely the code that will process any incoming requests.

```
var host = new WebHostBuilder()
            .UseKestrel()
            .UseIISIntegration()
```

```
            .UseContentRoot(Directory.GetCurrentDirectory())
            .Configure(app => {
                app.Run(async (context) => {
                    var path = context.Request.Path;
                    await context.Response.WriteAsync("<h1>" + path + "</h1>");
                });
            })
            .Build();
```

Application settings, terminating middleware, and the various optional middleware components can also be more comfortably specified in the startup class. And the startup class is just another relevant parameter you pass to the web host builder instance via the *UseStartup* method.

```
var host = new WebHostBuilder()
            .UseKestrel()
            .UseIISIntegration()
            .UseContentRoot(Directory.GetCurrentDirectory())
            .UseStartup<Startup>()
            .Build();
```

Functionally speaking, the above code snippet delivers a number of capabilities sufficient to run an ASP.NET Core 2.0 application.

Locating the Startup Class

The startup class can be specified in a number of ways. The most common is to use the generic version of the *UseStartup<T>* extension method where type *T* identifies the startup class. This is demonstrated by the previous code snippet.

You can also use a non-generic form of *UseStartup* and pass the .NET type reference as an argument.

```
var host = new WebHostBuilder()
            .UseKestrel()
            .UseIISIntegration()
            .UseContentRoot(Directory.GetCurrentDirectory())
            .UseStartup(typeof(MyStartup))
            .Build();
```

Finally, you can also specify the type of the startup by the assembly name.

```
var host = new WebHostBuilder()
            .UseKestrel()
            .UseIISIntegration()
            .UseContentRoot(Directory.GetCurrentDirectory())
            .UseStartup(Assembly.Load(new AssemblyName("Ch14.Builder")).FullName)
            .Build();
```

If you choose to pass *UseStartup* an assembly name, then it is assumed the assembly contains a class named *Startup* or *StartupXxx* where *Xxx* matches the current hosting environment (*Development*, *Production*, or whatever else).

Application Lifetime

In ASP.NET Core 2.0, three application lifetime events are supported for developers to perform startup and shutdown tasks. The *IApplicationLifetime* interface defines the host events you can hook up in the code.

```
public interface IApplicationLifetime
{
    CancellationToken ApplicationStarted { get; }
    CancellationToken ApplicationStopping { get; }
    CancellationToken ApplicationStopped { get; }
    void StopApplication();
}
```

As you can see, in addition to started, stopping, and stopped events, the interface also features a proactive *StopApplication* method. You add event handling code in the *Configure* method of the startup class.

```
public void Configure(IApplicationBuilder app, IApplicationLifetime life)
{
    // Configures a graceful shutdown of the application
    life.ApplicationStarted.Register(OnStarted);
    life.ApplicationStopping.Register(OnStopping);
    life.ApplicationStopped.Register(OnStopped);

    // More runtime configuration here
    ...
}
```

The *ApplicationStarted* event reaches your code when the host is up and running and waiting for a programmatically controlled termination. The *ApplicationStopping* event indicates that a programmatic shutdown of the application has started, but some requests might still be in the queue. The host is essentially about to shut down. Finally, the *ApplicationStopped* event is triggered when no more pending requests are in the queue. The actual shutdown of the host will take place as soon as the processing of the event terminates.

The *StopApplication* method is the interface method that starts the programmatic shutdown of the web application host. The method is also silently called if you press Ctrl+C from the *dotnet.exe* launcher console window. If you use the following code, then the expected output is shown in Figure 14-2.

```
private static void OnStarted()
{
    // Perform post-startup activities here
    Console.WriteLine("Started\n=====");
    Console.BackgroundColor = ConsoleColor.Blue;
}

private static void OnStopping()
{
    // Perform on-stopping activities here
    Console.BackgroundColor = ConsoleColor.Black;
    Console.WriteLine("=====\nStopping\n=====\n");
}
```

```
private static void OnStopped()
{
    // Perform post-stopped activities here
    var defaultForeColor = Console.ForegroundColor;
    Console.ForegroundColor = ConsoleColor.Red;
    Console.WriteLine("Stopped.");
    Console.ForegroundColor = defaultForeColor;
    Console.WriteLine("Press any key.");
    Console.ReadLine();
}
```

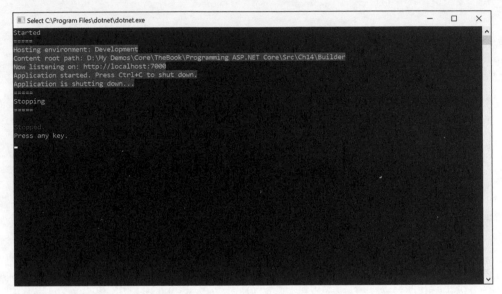

FIGURE 14-2 Application lifetime events

As you can see, lifetime events wrap around any activity of web application.

Other Settings

The web host can be further customized by a collection of additional settings that fine-tune some minor aspects of the behavior. Table 14-2 lists them all.

TABLE 14-2 Additional settings of a web host

Extension method	Description
CaptureStartupErrors	Boolean value to control the capture of startup errors. The default value is *false* unless the overall configuration sets Kestrel running behind IIS. If errors are not captured, then any exceptions will result in the host exiting. If errors are being captured, then startup exceptions are swallowed, but the host still attempts to start the configured web server.
UseEnvironment	Sets the application running environment programmatically. The method takes a string that matches predefined environments such as Development, Production, Staging, or any other environment name that makes sense for the application. Normally, the environment name is read from an environment variable (*ASPNETCORE_ENVIRONMENT*) and, when using Visual Studio, environment variables, might be set through the user interface or in the *launchSettings.json* file.

Extension method	Description		
UseSetting	The universal method used to set options directly through an associated key. When setting a value with this method, the value is set as a string (in quotes) regardless of the type. The method can be used to configure at least the following settings:		
	DetailedErrorsKey	Boolean value indicating whether detailed errors should be captured and reported. The default is *false*.	
	HostingStartupAssembliesKey	Semi-colon delimited string of additional assembly names to be loaded at startup. The default is the empty string.	
	PreventHostingStartupKey	Prevents the automatic loading of startup assemblies including the application's assembly. The default is *false*.	
	ShutdownTimeoutKey	Specifies the number of seconds the web host will wait before shutting down. The default is 5 seconds. Note that the same setting can be set using the *UseShutdownTimeout* extension method. The wait gives the web host time to fully process requests.	

	The property names are expressed as properties of the *WebHostDefaults* enumeration.
	
	`WebHost.CreateDefaultBuilder(args)`
	`    .UseSetting(WebHostDefaults.DetailedErrorsKey, "true");`		

UseShutdownTimeout	Specifies the amount of time to wait for the web host to shut down. Default is 5 seconds. The method accepts a *TimeSpan* value.		

You might be wondering why such an extremely detailed level of control on the web host configuration is possible. You also might be wondering why configuration of application settings can be done in the *program.cs* at the web host level, far before the application actually starts. The answers are twofold. First, is completeness. Second, is the ability to facilitate integration tests. Having a great deal of flexibility in the setup of the web host lets you easily create duplicate projects in which all is the same, but the host and the configuration of the host can be arranged to match a given integration scenario.

In this section, I deliberately skipped one more configuration parameter: the list of URLs the web server will listen for in incoming requests. I'll discuss this in the next section, which is dedicated to the selection and configuration of the ASP.NET Core embedded web server.

Note When it comes to expressing the configuration of the web host, the order of settings is important, but overall, it obeys a basic rule: the last setting wins. Hence, if you, say, indicate multiple startup classes then no errors are thrown, but simply the last setting specified takes precedence.

The Embedded HTTP Server

An ASP.NET Core application needs an in-process HTTP server to run. The web host fires up the HTTP server and makes it listen to any configured ports and URLs. The HTTP server is expected to capture incoming requests and push them through the ASP.NET Core pipeline where the configured middleware will process it. Figure 14-3 presents the overall architecture.

FIGURE 14-3 The HTTP Server in the ASP.NET Core runtime architecture

The diagram in the figure shows a direct connection between the ASP.NET Core internal HTTP server and the Internet space. In reality, such a direct connection is optional. You can choose, in fact, to put a reverse proxy in the middle to just shield the internal HTTP server from being accessed from the open Internet. (I'll return to this in a moment.)

Selection of the HTTP Server

The internal HTTP server of Figure 14-3 comes in two flavors. It can be based on Kestrel or on a kernel-level driver named *http.sys*. In both cases, the implementation will listen on a configured set of ports and URLs, and it will dispatch any incoming requests to the ASP.NET Core 2.0 pipeline.

Kestrel vs. *Http.sys*

The most common choice for the ASP.NET Core 2.0 internal HTTP server is Kestrel, which is a cross-platform web server based on *libuv*. In particular, *libuv* is a cross-platform asynchronous I/O library. When you create a new ASP.NET Core project from within Visual Studio, the templates deliver code using Kestrel as the web server. The most interesting aspect of Kestrel is that it is supported on all platforms and versions that .NET Core supports.

An alternative to Kestrel is using *http.sys*, namely a Windows-only HTTP server that relies on the services of the old faithful Windows *http.sys* kernel driver. In general, you might always want to use Kestrel except for a few specific situations. Up until the release of version 2.0, Kestrel was not recommended for scenarios where no reverse proxy had to be used to shield the application from public Internet access. In this regard *http.sys* represents a more reliable choice (though limited to the Windows platform) because it is based on a much more mature technology. Also, *http.sys* is Windows specific and supports features not available—by design—in Kestrel, such as Windows authentication.

To further reinforce the point about the robustness of *http.sys*, you should consider that the same IIS runs as an HTTP listener on top of *http.sys*. However, the future is well laid out. Kestrel is cross-platform and will be increasingly improved as a robust enough web server capable of sustaining the open Internet without the barrier of a reverse proxy. My recommendation is to use Kestrel, unless you have evidence that Kestrel doesn't work well for you. The following code shows how to enable *http.sys* in an ASP.NET Core application.

```
var host = new WebHostBuilder().UseHttpSys().Build();
```

When Kestrel is not fit, then you go with a reverse proxy outside Windows (for example, Nginx or Apache). Under Windows, instead, you can choose *http.sys* directly or IIS.

Specifying URLs

The internal HTTP server can be configured to listen on a variety of URLs and ports. You specify this
information through the *UseUrls* extension method defined on the web host builder type.

```
var host = new WebHostBuilder()
              .UseKestrel()
              .UseUrls("...")
              ...
              .Build();
```

The *UseUrls* method indicates the host addresses with ports and protocols on which the server
should listen for incoming requests. If multiple URLs are to be specified, you separate them with semi-
colons. By default, the internal web server is instructed to listen on the local host on port 5000. You use
the * wildcard to indicate that the server should listen for requests on any hostname using the specified
port and protocol. As an example, the following code is acceptable, too.

```
var host = new WebHostBuilder()
              .UseKestrel()
              .UseUrls("http://*:7000")
              ...
              .Build();
```

Note that an ASP.NET Core internal HTTP server is characterized by the *IServer* interface. This
means that in addition to Kestrel and *http.sys,* you could even create your own custom HTTP server by
implementing the interface. The *IServer* interface provides members to configure endpoints to which
the server should listen for requests. By default, the list of URLs to listen to is taken from the web host.
However, you can force the server to accept the list of URLs through its own API. You can do that by
using the *PreferHostingUrls* web host extension method.

```
var host = new WebHostBuilder()
              .UseKestrel()
              .PreferHostingUrls(false)
              ...
              .Build();
```

The *hosting.json* File

The use of the *UseUrls* method—or even the use of the server's specific API for endpoints—presents
one relevant drawback: The names of the URLs are hardcoded in the source code of the application and
require a new compile step to be changed. To avoid that, you can load the HTTP server configuration
from an external file, the *hosting.json* file.

The file must be created in the root of the application's folder. Here's an example that shows how to
set the server's URLs.

```
{
  "server.urls": "http://localhost:7000;http://localhost:7001"
}
```

To force loading the *hosting.json* file, you add it to the application settings via a call to *AddJsonFile*.

Configuring a Reverse Proxy

Originally, the Kestrel server was not designed to be exposed to the open Internet, meaning that a reverse proxy was required on top of it for security reasons and as a way to protect the application from possible web attacks. Starting with ASP.NET Core 2.0, though, a thicker defense barrier was added, resulting in more configuration options to take into account.

> **Note** In addition to security reasons, one scenario that requires a reverse proxy is when you have multiple applications that share the same IP and port running on the same server. Kestrel doesn't simply support this scenario; once configured to listen on a port; Kestrel handles all traffic coming through regardless of the host header.

Reasons for Using a Reverse Proxy

Whether the application behind Kestrel is designed to be exposed to the public Internet or only to an internal network, you can configure the HTTP server to work with or without a reverse proxy. In general terms, a reverse proxy is a proxy server that retrieves resources on behalf of a client from one or more servers. (See Figure 14-4.)

FIGURE 14-4 The reverse proxy scheme

A reverse proxy completely shields the actual web server (in our case, the Kestrel server) from requests coming from the various user agents. The reverse proxy is usually a full-fledged web server that captures incoming requests and serves them to the back-end server after some preliminary work. The user agents are completely unaware of the actual server behind the proxy, and insofar as they are concerned, they're really connecting to the actual server.

As previously mentioned, the primary reason for having a reverse proxy is security and the ability to prevent potentially harmful requests from even reaching the actual web server. Another reason for having a reverse proxy is that an additional layer of server helps set up the most appropriate load balancing configuration. You can configure an IIS (or perhaps Nginx server) to be the load balancer and maintain control over the number of actual servers connected to an ASP.NET Core installation. For example, during long generation-2 garbage collector operations, one process is not capable of processing requests, so the traffic on the same server could be handled by other instances of the application. Another scenario in which a reverse proxy is helpful is when it simplifies the SSL setup. In fact, only the reverse proxy requires the SSL certificate. After that, any communication with your application server can take place using plain HTTP. Finally, using a reverse proxy can provide a smoother install of an ASP.NET Core solution onto an existing server infrastructure.

> **Important** ASP.NET Core was designed from the ground up to use its own HTTP server to ensure consistent behavior across multiple platforms. While IIS, Nginx, and Apache can all be used as reverse proxies, each of them requires its own environment, which would have required some sort of a provider model built into ASP.NET Core. The team has therefore decided to expose a common standalone façade out of ASP.NET Core that other web servers can plug into at the cost of some additional configuration work or writing additional plugins.

Configuring IIS as a Reverse Proxy

Both IIS and IIS Express can be used as a reverse proxy for ASP.NET Core. When this happens, the ASP.NET Core application runs in a process separate from the IIS worker process. At the same time, though, the IIS process needs an ad hoc module to bridge the IIS worker process and the ASP.NET Core process. This extra component is known as the ASP.NET Core ISAPI module.

The ASP.NET Core module takes care of starting the ASP.NET Core application and forwards HTTP requests to it. Also, it blocks at the gate any request that could configure a denial of service attack or a request whose body is too long or that could time out. Furthermore, the module is also responsible for restarting the ASP.NET Core application when it crashes or when the IIS worker process detects conditions for a restart.

As a developer, you need to ensure that the ASP.NET Core module is installed on the IIS machine. Also, you need to place a call to the *UseIISIntegration* web host extension method while configuring the host of the ASP.NET Core application.

Configuring Apache as a Reverse Proxy

The exact way in which an Apache web server is configured to run as a reverse proxy depends on the actual Linux operating system. However, some general guidance can be provided. Once Apache is properly installed and working, the configuration files are located under the */etc/httpd/conf.d/* directory. There you create a new file with a *.conf* extension with content analogous to the following:

```
<VirtualHost *:80>
        ProxyPreserveHost On
        ProxyPass / http://127.0.0.1:5000/
        ProxyPassReverse / http://127.0.0.1:5000/
</VirtualHost>
```

In the example, the file sets Apache to listen for any IP address, using port 80, and all requests received through the machine 127.0.0.1 port 5000. Communication is bidirectional because *ProxyPass* and *ProxyPassReverse* are specified. This step is sufficient to enable forwarding of requests but not to have Apache manage the Kestrel process. To have Apache manage the Kestrel process, you need to create a *service file*, which is a text file that fundamentally tells Apache what to do for certain detected requests.

```
[Unit]
    Description=Programming ASP.NET Core Demo

[Service]
    WorkingDirectory=/var/progcore/ch14/builder
    ExecStart=/usr/local/bin/dotnet /var/progcore/ch14/builder.dll
    Restart=always

    # Restart service after 10 seconds in case of errors
    RestartSec=10
    SyslogIdentifier=progcore-ch14-builder
    User=apache
    Environment=ASPNETCORE_ENVIRONMENT=Production

[Install]
    WantedBy=multi-user.target
```

Note that the specified user (if different from *apache*) must be created first and given ownership for files. Finally, the service must be enabled from the command line. More details can be found at *https://docs.microsoft.com/en-us/aspnet/core/publishing/apache-proxy*. The instructions you find are also very similar to configure Nginx as a reverse proxy.

Kestrel Configuration Parameters

In ASP.NET Core 2.0, the public programming interface of Kestrel has gotten significantly richer. You can now easily configure it to support HTTPS, bind to sockets and endpoints, and filter incoming requests.

Binding to Endpoints

Kestrel provides its own API to bind to URLs for listening for incoming requests. You configure those endpoints calling the method *Listen* on the *KestrelServerOptions* class.

```
var ip = "...";
var host = new WebHostBuilder()
            .UseIISIntegration()
            .UseKestrel(options =>
            {
                options.Listen(IPAddress.Loopback, 5000);
                options.Listen(IPAddress.Parse(ip), 7000);
            });
```

The *Listen* method accepts an instance of type *IPAddress*. Any IP address can be parsed to an instance of the class through the method *Parse*. Predefined values are *Loopback* for the local host, *IPv6Any* for all IPv6 address, or *Any* for just any network address.

Under Nginx, you can also bind to a Unix socket for improved performance.

```
var host = new WebHostBuilder()
            .UseIISIntegration()
```

```
            .UseKestrel(options =>
            {
                options.ListenUnixSocket("/tmp/progcore-test.sock");
            });
```

In the end, there are three ways to let Kestrel know about its listening endpoints: You can use the *UseUrls* extension method, the *ASPNETCORE_URLS* environment variable, or the *Listen* API. *UseUrls* and the environment variable provide a programming interface that is not specific to Kestrel, and that can be used with custom (or alternate) HTTP servers. Note, though, that these more generic binding methods suffer some limitations. In particular, you can't use SSL with these methods. Also, if both the *Listen* API and these methods are used, then the *Listen* endpoints will take priority. Finally, note that if you use IIS as the reverse proxy, then URL bindings hardcoded in IIS will override both the *Listen* endpoints and endpoints set through *UseUrls* or the environment variable.

Switching to HTTPS

It then turns out that to enable Kestrel to work over HTTPS, you can only specify endpoints using the *Listen* API. Here's a quick example of how it could work.

```
var host = new WebHostBuilder()
            .UseIISIntegration()
            .UseKestrel(options =>
            {
                options.Listen(IPAddress.Loopback, 5000, listenOptions =>
                {
                    listenOptions.UseHttps("progcore.pfx");
                });
            }
        });
```

To enable HTTPS, you just add a third parameter to the *Listen* method and use it to indicate the path to the certificate.

Filtering Incoming Requests

In ASP.NET Core 2.0, the Kestrel web server has become stronger in the sense that it now supports more configuration options to automatically filter out incoming requests that exceed preset constraints. In particular, you can set a maximum number of client connections, a maximum body size for requests, and a data rate.

```
var host = new WebHostBuilder()
            .UseIISIntegration()
            .UseKestrel(options =>
            {
                options.Limits.MaxConcurrentConnections = 100;
                options.Limits.MaxRequestBodySize = 10 * 1024;
                options.Limits.MinRequestBodyDataRate =
                    new MinDataRate(bytesPerSecond: 100, gracePeriod: TimeSpan.FromSeconds(10));
                options.Limits.MinResponseDataRate =
                    new MinDataRate(bytesPerSecond: 100, gracePeriod: TimeSpan.FromSeconds(10));
            }
        });
```

All the settings set above apply to any requests for the entire application.

There's virtually no limit to the number of concurrent connections, but setting a limit is recommended.

 Note Requests that are upgraded from HTTP (or HTTPS) to another protocol (likely WebSockets) are no longer counted against the total of concurrent connections.

By default, the maximum request body size is set to more than 30 million bytes (around 28 MB). Whatever default is set, it can be overridden through the *RequestSizeLimit* attribute on an action method. Alternatively, it can also be overridden through a middleware interceptor, as we'll see in a moment.

Note that Kestrel sets a minimum data rate to 240 bytes per second. If the request doesn't send enough bytes for more than the established grace period (set to 5 seconds by default), then the request is timed out. You are welcome to adjust your own minimum and maximum data rate and related grace period.

The primary reason for these limits is to make Kestrel more robust and better able to face denial of service attacks when facing the public Internet without the protection of a reverse proxy. These limits, in fact, are usual defense barriers against flood attacks for a web server.

The ASP.NET Core Middleware

Every request that hits the ASP.NET Core application is subject to the action of the configured middleware before it can reach the portion of code that will actually process it and generate a response. The term middleware refers to the software components assembled in a sort of a chain referred to as the application pipeline.

Pipeline Architecture

Each component in the chain can do work before and/or after the request is processed to generate a response and can decide in total liberty whether to pass the request to the next component in the pipeline. (See Figure 14-5.)

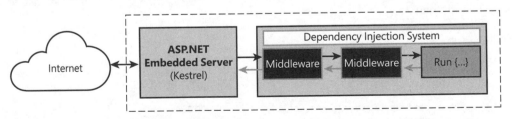

FIGURE 14-5 The ASP.NET Core pipeline

As in the figure, the pipeline results from the composition of middleware components. The chain of components ends with a special component known as the *terminating middleware*. The terminating middleware is the component that triggers the actual processing of the request and the turning point of the loop. Middleware components are invoked in the order they have been registered to pre-process the request. At the end of the loop, the terminating middleware runs, and after that, the same middleware components are given a chance to post-process the request but in the reverse order. (See Figure 14-5.)

Structure of a Middleware Component

A middleware component is a piece of code fully represented by the request delegate. The request delegate takes the form below.

```
public delegate Task RequestDelegate(HttpContext context);
```

In other words, it is a function that receives an *HttpContext* object and does some work. Depending on the way a middleware component is registered with the application pipeline, it can process all incoming requests or just selected requests. The default way to register a middleware component is the following:

```
app.Use(async (context, next) =>
{
    // First chance to process the request. No response has been generated for
    // request yet.
    <Perform pre-processing of the request>

    // Yields to the next component in the pipeline
    await next();

    // Second chance to process the request. When here, the request's response
    // has been generated.
    <Perform post-processing of the request>
});
```

You can use flow control statements, such as conditional statements, in the chunks of code running before and after the forward pass to the next component in the pipeline. Middleware components can take multiple forms. The request delegate discussed earlier is just the simplest.

As we'll see later in the chapter, middleware components can be packaged in classes and bound to extension methods. Hence, any method we call in the *Configure* method of the startup class is likely a middleware component.

The Importance of the Next Middleware

Invoking the *next* delegate is optional, but you should be very well aware of the consequences of not calling it. If any middleware component omits to call the *next* delegate, the entire pipeline for that request is short-circuited and the default terminating middleware might not be invoked at all.

Whenever a middleware component returns without yielding to the *next* middleware, the response generation process ends there. Therefore, a middleware component that does not yield to the next component is acceptable as long as it takes the responsibility of completing the generation of the response for the current request.

A couple of illustrative examples of middleware components that short-circuit the request are *UseMvc* and *UseStaticFiles*. The former parses the current URL, and if it can be matched to one of the supported routes, it passes the control to the corresponding controller to generate and return the response. The latter does the same if the URL corresponds to a physical file located in a configured web path.

Instead, if you're writing your own middleware component as a third-party extension, you might want to be very careful about what you do, meaning you might want to be a good citizen who plays by the rules. On the other hand, if the business logic of your component strictly requires you short-circuit the request, then you must fully document the behavior.

Registering Middleware Components

A middleware component can be added to the application's pipeline in a number of ways, as illustrated in Table 14-3.

TABLE 14-3 Methods to register a middleware component

Method	Description
Use	An anonymous method passed as an argument that is invoked on any requests.
Map	An anonymous method passed as an argument that is invoked only on a given URL.
MapWhen	An anonymous method passed as an argument that is invoked only if a given Boolean condition is verified for the current request.
Run	An anonymous method passed as an argument that is set to be the terminating middleware. If no terminating middleware is found, no response is generated.

Note that the method *Run* can be called multiple times, but only the first one is processed. This is because the Run method is where the request processing ends and where the flow of the pipeline chain is inverted. The inversion takes place the first time that the running middleware is found. Any running middleware defined after the first is just never reached.

```
public void Configure(IApplicationBuilder app)
{
    // Terminating middleware
    app.Run(async context =>
    {
        await context.Response.WriteAsync("Courtesy of 'Programming ASP.NET Core'");
    });

    // No errors, but never reached
    app.Run(async context =>
    {
        await context.Response.WriteAsync("Courtesy of 'Programming ASP.NET Core' repeated");
    });
}
```

Middleware components are registered in the *Configure* method of the startup class. The order in which the methods in Table 14-3 appear sets the order in which code is run.

> **Note** The *Run* terminating middleware can be used as a catch-all route in applications using the MVC model. As mentioned, *UseMvc* short-circuits incoming requests, redirecting them to the identified controller action method. However, if no route is configured for a given request, then the request proceeds through the rest of the pipeline until it finds a terminating middleware, if any.

Writing Middleware Components

Let's see some examples of inline middleware components, namely middleware code expressed through anonymous methods. Before the end of the chapter, we'll also see how to pack middleware code in reusable elements.

The *Use* Method

Here's a basic usage of the *Use* method to register a middleware component. The method simply wraps the actual output of the request processing into a BEFORE/AFTER log message. (See Figure 14-6.)

FIGURE 14-6 Demonstrating middleware components

Here's the necessary code. The *SomeWork* class in the demo just returns the current time through the method *Now*.

```
public void Configure(IApplicationBuilder app)
{
    app.Use(async (context, nextMiddleware) =>
    {
        await context.Response.WriteAsync("BEFORE");
        await nextMiddleware();
        await context.Response.WriteAsync("AFTER");
    });

    app.Run(async (context) =>
    {
        var obj = new SomeWork();
        await context
            .Response
            .WriteAsync("<h1 style='color:red;'>" + obj.Now() + "</h1>");
    });
}
```

You use middleware to perform some nontrivial tasks or to configure the environment to measure. Here's another example.

```
app.Use(async (context, nextMiddleware) =>
{
    context.Features
        .Get<IHttpMaxRequestBodySizeFeature>()
        .MaxRequestBodySize = 10 * 1024;
    await nextMiddleware.Invoke();
});
```

Here the code uses the information within the HTTP context to set the maximum body size for all requests. Taken as is, the code is not really interesting. If we're going to set a maximum body size for all requests, then we'd be better off doing it at the Kestrel level. However, the middleware infrastructure allows us to alter the state of the request only for certain requests.

The *Map* Method

The *Map* method works as the *Use* method works except that the execution of the code is subject to the incoming URL.

```
app.Map("/now", now =>
{
    now.Run(async context =>
    {
        var time = DateTime.UtcNow.ToString("HH:mm:ss (UTC)");
        await context
            .Response
            .WriteAsync("<h1 style='color:red;'>" + time + "</h1>");
    });
});
```

The code above runs only if the requested URL is */now*. Therefore, the *Map* method allows branching the pipeline based upon the path. (See Figure 14-7.)

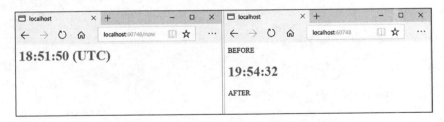

FIGURE 14-7 Different effects because of different middleware components

If you combine the two preceding pieces of middleware, the order in which you register them can change the output. In general, *Map* calls are placed earlier in the pipeline.

> **Note** Middleware components are the conceptual counterpart of HTTP modules in classic ASP.NET. However, the *Map* method sets a key difference with HTTP modules. HTTP modules, in fact, have no way to filter URLs. When writing an HTTP module, you have to check the URL yourself and decide whether to process or ignore the request. There's no way to register the module only for certain URLs.

The *MapWhen* Method

The *MapWhen* method is a variation of *Map* that uses a generic Boolean expression instead of a URL path. The following example triggers the specified only if the query string expression contains a parameter named *utc*.

```
app.MapWhen(
    context => context.Request.Query.ContainsKey("utc"),
    utc =>
    {
        utc.Run(async context =>
        {
            var time = DateTime.UtcNow.ToString("HH:mm:ss (UTC)");
            await context
                .Response
                .WriteAsync("<h1 style='color:blue;'>" + time + "</h1>");
        });
    });
```

Dealing with HTTP Response

Middleware components are a delicate piece of code because of a basic rule of the HTTP protocol. Writing to the output stream is a sequential operation. Therefore, once the body of the response has been written (or just started to be written), HTTP response headers cannot be added. This is because, in an HTTP response, headers appear before the body.

As long as all the middleware code is made of inline functions under the total control of the team, this is not necessarily a big issue, and any issues with the response headers can be fixed easily. What about, instead, if you're writing a third-party middleware component that others can use? In this case, your component must be able to run in different runtime environments. What if the business logic of your components requires altering the response body?

The moment your code starts writing to the output stream, it stops other following components from adding HTTP response headers. At the same time, if you need to add an HTTP header, then other components might occasionally block you. To solve the issue, the *Response* object in ASP.NET Core exposes a *OnStarting* event. The event fires just before the first component attempts to write to the output stream. Hence, if your middleware needs to write a response header, then all you do is register a handler for the *OnStarting* event and append the header from there.

```
app.Use(async (context, nextMiddleware) =>
{
    context.Response.OnStarting(() =>
    {
        context.Response.Headers.Add("courtesy", "Programming ASP.NET Core");
        return Task.CompletedTask;
    });

    await nextMiddleware();
});
```

So far in the chapter, we have discussed inline middleware, However, in the previous chapters, we have met many ad hoc extension methods that can be called within the *Configure* method of the startup class. For example, we have used *UseMvcWithDefaultRoute* to configure the MVC application model and *UseExceptionHandler* to configure exception handling. These were all middleware components. The different form is because those middleware pieces of code are packaged into reusable classes. Let's see how to package our own middleware into reusable classes.

> **Note** Adding response headers in the *OnStarting* handler works most of the time, but some edge cases need to be mentioned. In particular, sometimes you might need to wait for the entire response to be generated before you can decide which headers to add, as well as their content. In this case, you might consider creating a sort of in-memory buffer around the *Response.Body* property that receives all the writings without physically populating the response output stream. When all middleware components have completed, it copies everything back. The idea is well illustrated here: *https://stackoverflow.com/questions/43403941*.

Packaging Middleware Components

Unless you just need some quick processing to take place during the preliminary handling of an HTTP request, it is always a good idea to package up middleware into reusable classes. The actual code you would write for the *Use* or *Map* methods won't change; it is just being wrapped up.

Creating a Middleware Class

A middleware class is a plain C# class with a constructor and a public method named *Invoke*. No base class and no known contract is required. The system invokes the class dynamically. The code below demonstrates a middleware class that attempts to determine if the requesting device is a mobile device.

```
public class MobileDetectionMiddleware
{
    private readonly RequestDelegate _next;

    public MobileDetectionMiddleware(RequestDelegate next)
    {
        _next = next;
    }
```

```
public async Task Invoke(HttpContext context)
{
    // Parse the user-agent to "guess" if it's a mobile device.
    var isMobile = context.IsMobileDevice();
    context.Items["MobileDetectionMiddleware_IsMobile"] = isMobile;

    // Yields
    await _next(context);

    // Provide some UI only as a proof of existence
    var msg = isMobile ? "MOBILE DEVICE" : "NOT A MOBILE DEVICE";
    await context.Response.WriteAsync("<hr>" + msg + "<hr>");
}
}
```

The constructor receives the *RequestDelegate* pointer to the next middleware component in the configured chain and saves it to an internal member. The *Invoke* method contains, instead, just the code you would pass to the *Use* method, where you register the middleware inline. The signature of the *Invoke* method must match the signature of the *RequestDelegate* type.

The example above scans the user-agent HTTP header to find out whether the requesting device is a mobile device. In the demo, *IsMobileDevice* is a quite naive extension method on the *HttpContext* class that simply uses a regular expression to locate some mobile-flavored substrings. I would be very careful before using this code in production. It doesn't fail with most devices, but it might miss the point with quite a few of them. (In general, device detection is quite a serious matter, so you might want to consider ad hoc libraries for the job. See Chapter 13, "Building Device-friendly Views.")

For our purposes, however, it works nicely. In particular, it shows a trick to enable middleware components to share information in the context of the same request. Right after having figured out whether the requesting device is mobile or not, the middleware saves the Boolean answer to an aptly created entry in the *Items* dictionary on the *HttpContext* instance. The *Items* dictionary is shared in memory throughout the request processing, meaning that any middleware components can check it and use the findings for internal reasons. For this to work, though, it is required that middleware components are aware of each other. The net effect of the mobile detection middleware is to store in the *Items* dictionary a Boolean value denoting whether the device is considered a mobile device. Note that the same information can be accessed programmatically from any place in the application—say, a controller method—where you have access to the *HttpContext* object.

Registering a Middleware Class

To add middleware expressed through a class, you need to use a slightly different method from the *IApplicationBuilder* abstraction. Hence, in the *Configure* method of the startup class, you use the following code:

```
public void Configure(IApplicationBuilder app)
{
    // Other middleware configured here
    ...
```

```
    // Attach the mobile-detection middleware
    app.UseMiddleware<MobileDetectionMiddleware>();

    // Other middleware configured here
    ...
}
```

The *UseMiddleware<T>* method registers the specified type as a middleware component.

Registering via Extension Methods

Although not strictly required from a purely functional point of view, it is common practice to define an extension method to hide the use of *UseMiddleware<T>*. The effect is the same, but the readability of the code is improved.

```
public static class MobileDetectionMiddlewareExtensions
{
    public static IApplicationBuilder UseMobileDetection(this IApplicationBuilder builder)
    {
        return builder.UseMiddleware<MobileDetectionMiddleware>();
    }
}
```

Writing an extension method to the *IApplicationBuilder* type only takes a few lines of code and only requires hiding the direct call to *UseMiddleware<T>* behind a friendlier-named method. Here's the final version of the startup class when the extension method defined above is used.

```
public void Configure(IApplicationBuilder app)
{
    // Other middleware configured here
    ...

    // Attach the mobile-detection middleware
    app.UseMobileDetection();

    // Other middleware configured here
    ...
}
```

Although the name of the extension method is arbitrary, it is conventionally given a name in the form *UseXXX* where *XXX* is the name of middleware class.

Summary

If you look at ASP.NET Core from the perspective of an application, you won't see many changes compared to classic ASP.NET MVC. ASP.NET Core supports the same MVC application model but does that on top of a completely different runtime environment. ASP.NET Core doesn't support the Web Forms application model, but this is not a plain business decision—it is a purely technical matter instead.

The new ASP.NET Core runtime is designed from the ground up to be cross-platform and decoupled from the web server environment. To achieve the supreme goal of running on multiple platforms, ASP.NET Core introduces its own host environment and an interface that bridges it to the actual host. In this context, a key role is played by the *dotnet.exe* tool which is actually connected to the web server and forwards calls to the ASP.NET Core pipeline where Kestrel—the internal HTTP server—receives and processes requests.

In this chapter, we first analyzed the host server architecture with a particular focus on Kestrel, and then we moved to look into middleware components. Middleware components form the internal request pipeline, namely the chain that processes any incoming requests. Although conceptually compatible with classic ASP.NET HTTP modules, middleware components have a different structure and are invoked through a different workflow.

In the next chapter, we investigate the deployment of ASP.NET Core applications and the necessary steps to accommodate a platform-independent application onto a specific one.

CHAPTER 15

Deploying an ASP.NET Core Application

Sometimes it's a little better to travel than to arrive.

—Robert Pirsig, "Zen and the Art of Motorcycle Maintenance"

Writing an ASP.NET Core application requires the creation and editing of a variety of files, not all of which are really necessary to put the application live on a production or staging server. Hence, the very first step on the way to deploying an ASP.NET Core application is publishing it to a local folder so that all necessary files are compiled, and only those files that need be moved to the live environment are isolated somewhere. The list of deployable files usually includes code files compiled to DLLs plus static and configuration files.

Classic ASP.NET applications could only be deployed to IIS under a Windows server operating system and more recently to a Microsoft Azure app service. For ASP.NET Core applications, you have more choices, including a Linux on-premise machine or another cloud environment such as Amazon Web Services (AWS) or even a Docker container.

In this chapter, we'll explore the various deployment options and the most relevant configuration issues. First, however, let's see what it takes to publish an ASP.NET Core application.

Publishing the Application

I recommend you start your understanding of the deployment model with a basic publish step, especially if you are new to ASP.NET development or if you are new to the ASP.NET MVC application model. (I assume you have a strong ASP.NET Web Forms background.)

Publishing from within Visual Studio

To start out, let's assume you have a complete, fully tested application ready for deployment. As an example, you can take the *SimplePage* application in the companion source code included with the book (see *https://github.com/despos/ProgCore/tree/master/Src/Ch15*). Figure 15-1 presents the Visual Studio menu item where you start the publishing process.

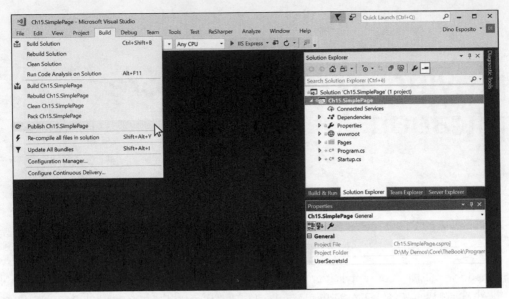

FIGURE 15-1 Ready to publish an ASP.NET Core application

Choosing the Publishing Target

Right after you click on the Publish item from the Build menu in Visual Studio, you are presented another view to choose the destination of the files being published. (See Figure 15-2.)

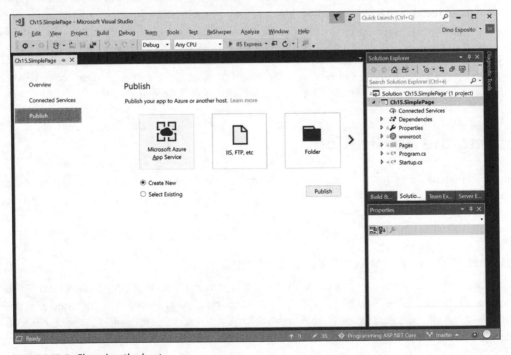

FIGURE 15-2 Choosing the host

You have a few possible destinations for the application files, summarized in Table 15-1. Note that the list of options is a bit longer than what Figure 15-2 shows; on the right edge of the view, there's a scrolling arrow to see more options.

TABLE 15-1 Supported publish hosts in Visual Studio 2017

Host	Description
Microsoft Azure App Service	The application will be published to a new or existing Microsoft Azure App Service.
Microsoft Azure Virtual Machine	The application will be published to an existing Microsoft Azure virtual machine.
IIS	The application will be published to the specified IIS instance via FTP, WebDeploy, or by a direct copy of the necessary files.
Folder	The application will be published to the given file system folder on the local machine.
Import profile	The application will be published using the information saved to a *.publishsettings* file.

To form an idea about the files really necessary to publish, let's choose the Folder option.

Be aware that you'll only see what's in Figure 15-2 if the project doesn't yet contain a publish profile. The moment you act on any of the presented destinations, a publish profile is created, and the page defaults to the last used profile and offers to create a new one.

The Publish Profile File

The publish profile is a *.pubxml* XML file saved under the *Properties/PublishProfiles* folder of the project. This file should not be checked into the source control because it depends on the *.user* project file which, in turn, can contain sensitive information. Both files are for use only on the local machine.

The *.pubxml* file is an MSBuild file and is automatically invoked during the build process in Visual Studio. The file can be edited to tailor-make the expected behavior. A typical change involves including or excluding project files from deployment. For more information, check out *https://docs.microsoft. com/en-us/aspnet/core/publishing/web-publishing-vs*.

Publishing Files to a Local Folder

Figure 15-3 shows the interface you're presented when you choose to publish to a folder. The actual folder that will receive the files is selected in the text box.

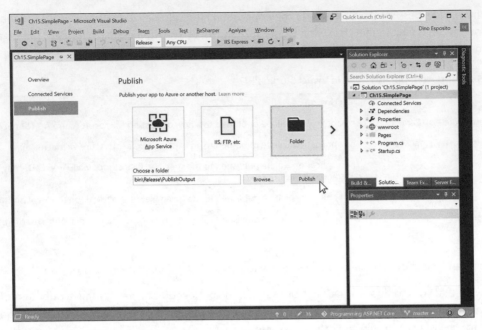

FIGURE 15-3 Publishing to a local folder

The publish procedure will compile from scratch the application in Release mode and copy all bina-ries to the specified folder. It also automatically creates a publish profile file for future repeats of the operation. (See Figure 15-4.)

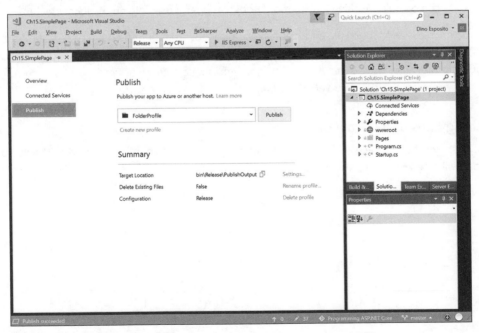

FIGURE 15-4 Report after publishing files. Note the link to create a new profile

If you inspect the folder, for the sample project, you find the *WWWROOT* folder and the binaries. Note that the sample project has no views; it uses Razor Pages instead. At any rate, Figure 15-5 shows no evidence of a folder with view files, whether Pages or Views. In both cases, Razor views are precompiled into a DLL. Precompiled views are enabled by default in the project templates for ASP.NET Core 2.0 created by Visual Studio 2017. To change it back to dynamically compiled views, you need to add the following line to the CSPROJ file of the project.

```
<PropertyGroup>
    <TargetFramework>netcoreapp2.0</TargetFramework>
    <MvcRazorCompileOnPublish>false</MvcRazorCompileOnPublish>
</PropertyGroup>
```

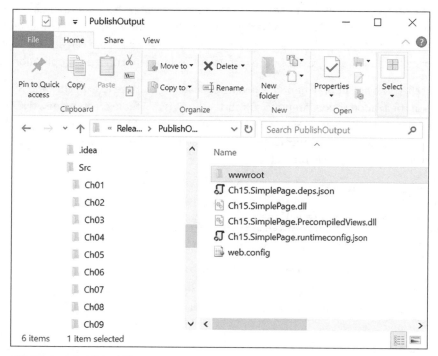

FIGURE 15-5 Published files

As you can see, the publish folder of the application only contains application binaries, including any third-party dependencies. The primary DLL file can be launched by using the *dotnet* utility from the command line or configuring the host web server environment to do the same.

The key thing to notice here is that the published files configure a portable, framework-dependent form of deployment. In other words, for the application to run correctly, the .NET Core framework libraries for the target platform must be available on the server.

Publishing Self-contained Applications

Publishing a portable application has been the norm for the entire lifetime of the ASP.NET platform. The size of deployment is small and limited to the sole application binaries and files. On the server, multiple applications share the same framework binaries. With .NET Core, the alternative to a portable deployment is to publish self-contained applications.

When a self-contained application is published, the .NET Core binaries for the specified runtime environment are also copied over. This makes the size of the deployment significantly larger. For the sample application discussed here, the size of a portable deployment is less than 2 MB, but it can grow up to 90 MB for a self-contained install that targets a generic Linux platform.

The upside of self-contained applications, however, is that the application has everything it needs to run regardless of the version(s) of the .NET Core Framework installed on the server. At the same time, you should be aware that deploying several self-contained applications to a system can absorb large amounts of disk space because the entire .NET Core Framework is duplicated on a per-application basis.

To support the self-contained deployment of a given application, you have to explicitly add the runtime identifiers of the platforms you intend to support. When Visual Studio creates a new .NET Core project, this information is missing and results in a portable deployment. To enable self-contained deployment, you have to manually edit the *.csproj* project file and add a *RuntimeIdentifiers* node to it. Here's the *.csproj* content for the sample project.

```
<Project Sdk="Microsoft.NET.Sdk.Web">
  <PropertyGroup>
    <TargetFramework>netcoreapp2.0</TargetFramework>
    <RuntimeIdentifiers>win10-x64;linux-x64</RuntimeIdentifiers>
  </PropertyGroup>
  <ItemGroup>
    <None Remove="Properties\PublishProfiles\FolderProfile.pubxml" />
  </ItemGroup>
  <ItemGroup>
    <PackageReference Include="Microsoft.AspNetCore.All" Version="2.0.0" />
  </ItemGroup>
  <ItemGroup>
    <DotNetCliToolReference
        Include="Microsoft.VisualStudio.Web.CodeGeneration.Tools" Version="2.0.0" />
  </ItemGroup>
  <ItemGroup>
    <Folder Include="Pages\Shared\" />
    <Folder Include="Properties\PublishProfiles\" />
  </ItemGroup>
</Project>
```

The current project is enabled to deploy on Windows 10 and generic Linux x64 platforms. The monikers to be used in the *RuntimeIdentifiers* node are taken from an official catalog you find documented here: *https://docs.microsoft.com/en-us/dotnet/core/rid-catalog*.

At this point, when publishing the application to a folder, the wizard offers you to select the target platform from the settings of the publish profile. Figure 15-6 presents the two versions of the view for portable and self-contained scenarios.

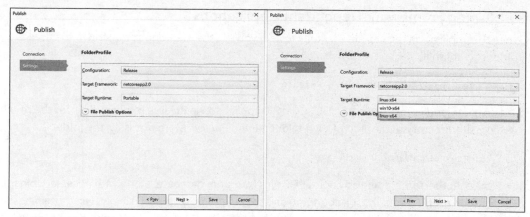

FIGURE 15-6 Portable versus runtime-specific publishing

Once you have captured in a folder the files to publish, you have only to upload them to the final destination. If you choose another publish option (such as an Azure App Service), then the upload happens transparently.

Publishing Using CLI Tools

The same operations you can perform from within Visual Studio 2017 can be performed from the command line using CLI tools. When working from the command line, you can use an IDE editor of your choice to write code. If you use Visual Studio Code, you can open a command console via the Integrated Terminal item under the **View** menu. (See Figure 15-7.)

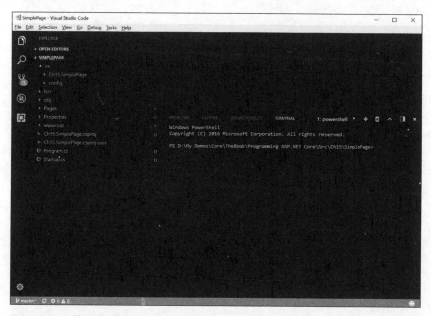

FIGURE 15-7 The Visual Studio Code terminal

Publishing Framework-Dependent Applications

Once the application is complete and fully tested, you use the following command in the *CSPROJ* folder to publish it.

```
dotnet publish -f netcoreapp2.0 -c Release
```

The command compiles the ASP.NET Core 2.0 application in Release mode and places the resulting files in a subdirectory of the project's *Bin* folder named *Publish*. More precisely, the folder is

```
\bin\Release\netcoreapp2.0\publish
```

Note that the *dotnet* tool also copies PDB files (program database) along with necessary binaries. PDB files are useful primarily for debugging and should not be distributed. However, those files should be saved somewhere because they could come in handy the moment you need to debug the Release build of your application because of unpredictable exceptions, errors, or other misbehavior.

Publishing Self-contained Applications

For self-contained applications, the command line to use is only slightly different. Basically, you add the runtime identifier to the same command line you would use for publishing a framework-dependent application.

```
dotnet publish -f netcoreapp2.0 -c Release -r win10-x64
```

The command line above would publish the files for a Windows x64 platform. The total size is more than 96 MB. The target folder where the files will go is:

```
\bin\Release\netcoreapp2.0\win10-x64\publish
```

To indicate the runtime identifier, you use the official ID taken from the .NET Core catalog at *https://docs.microsoft.com/en-us/dotnet/core/rid-catalog*.

 Note If the application being published has dependencies on third-party components, then you should make sure the dependencies are added to the *<ItemGroup>* section of the *.csproj* file, and the actual files are available in the local NuGet cache before publishing.

Deploying the Application

The publish step is necessary to isolate the files to be copied. From within Visual Studio, you have plenty of tools to publish files locally or directly to IIS or Microsoft Azure. Other options, such as deploying to a Linux on-premise machine or another cloud platform (such as Amazon Web Services) require specific upload and configuration work.

Let's see more in detail what's required to fully deploy an application to IIS, Azure, and a Linux machine.

Deploying to IIS

As is true with classic ASP.NET applications, Any ASP.NET Core application runs out of the IIS core process and out of any instance of the IIS worker process (*w3wp.exe*). Technically, an ASP.NET Core application doesn't even need a web server on the forefront. If we deploy the application to IIS (or Apache) it is because we have reasons (primarily, security and load balancing) to put on a façade on top of the embedded ASP.NET Core native web server.

The Hosting Architecture

As mentioned, a classic ASP.NET application is hosted inside of an application pool, represented by an instance of the IIS *w3wp.exe* worker process. Some .NET facilities built into IIS take care of creating an application-specific instance of the *HttpRuntime* class. This object is used to receive requests captured by the *http.sys* driver and to forward them to the appropriate website allocated in the application pool.

Figure 15-8 outlines the IIS hosting architecture for an ASP.NET Core application. An ASP.NET Core application is a plain console application loaded through the *run* command of the *dotnet* launcher tool. ASP.NET Core applications are never loaded and fired up from within an IIS worker process. Instead, they are triggered via an additional IIS native ISAPI module known as the ASP.NET Core Module. This module ultimately invokes *dotnet* to trigger the console application.

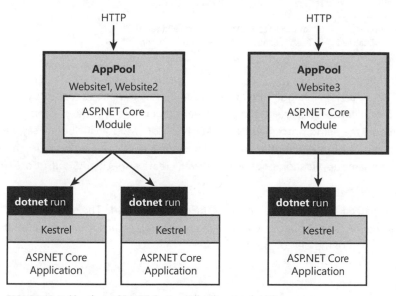

FIGURE 15-8 Hosting ASP.NET Core applications under IIS

As a result, to host ASP.NET Core applications on an IIS machine, you first need to install the ASP.NET Core ISAPI module.

> **Note** The ASP.NET Core ISAPI module only works with Kestrel. If you use *HttpSys* in ASP.NET Core 2.0 (or *WebListener* in ASP.NET Core 1.x), it just won't work. For more information, see *https://docs.microsoft.com/en-us/aspnet/core/fundamentals/servers/aspnet-core-module*. The link also provides download details.

Configuration of the ASP.NET Core Module

All that the ASP.NET Core module does is ensure that the application is properly fired up when the first request for the application comes in. Also, it makes sure that the process stays in memory and is reloaded if the application crashes and the pool is restarted.

You might have noticed that the publish wizard also creates a *web.config* file. This file does not affect the actual behavior of the application, but it serves the sole purpose of configuring the ASP.NET Core module under IIS. Here's a sample.

```xml
<?xml version="1.0" encoding="utf-8"?>
<configuration>
  <system.webServer>
    <handlers>
      <add name="aspNetCore" path="*" verb="*"
           modules="AspNetCoreModule" resourceType="Unspecified" />
    </handlers>
    <aspNetCore processPath="dotnet" arguments=".\Ch15.SimplePage.dll"
                stdoutLogEnabled="false" stdoutLogFile=".\logs\stdout" />
  </system.webServer>
</configuration>
```

The configuration file adds an HTTP handler for any verbs and paths that filters requests through the code written in the module. The wildcard on the path means that only any requests going through the application pool are being processed by the ASP.NET Core module including, say, ASPX requests. For this reason, it is recommended that you don't mix applications relying on different ASP.NET frameworks in the same application pool or, better yet, create a specific ASP.NET Core set of application pools.

The *aspNetCore* entry, instead, provides arguments for the module to work. The entry states that the module has to run *dotnet* on the specified application main DLL, plus some logging configuration. This *web.config* file must be part of the deployment.

Note To be successfully hosted under IIS, an ASP.NET Core application must configure the web host with a call to *UseIISIntegration* extension method. The method checks some environment variables that might have been set by the ASP.NET Core Module. If no variables are found, the method is a no-op. For this reason, you might want to always have a call to it, regardless of where you actually end up hosting the application.

Final Touches to the IIS Environment

If you deploy an ASP.NET Core application to IIS, then you intend to use IIS as a reverse proxy. This means that you don't expect any request processing work being done by IIS other than forwarding the traffic as is. For this reason, you can configure the application pool so that it doesn't use managed code and subsequently doesn't instantiate any .NET runtime. (See Figure 15-9.)

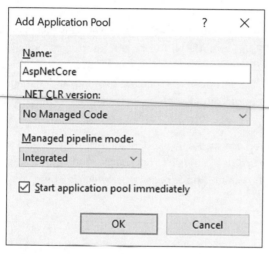

FIGURE 15-9 Creating an ad hoc application pool

Another aspect of the IIS configuration you might want to focus on is the identity behind the application pool–hosted the ASP.NET Core application. By default, the identity of any new application pool is set to *ApplicationPoolIdentity*. This is not the real account name, but a moniker that corresponds to a local machine account aptly created by IIS and named after the application pool.

Hence, should you need to define access control rules for a given resource (such as a server file or folder), then be aware that the real account name, as shown previously in Figure 15-9, is *IIS APPPOOL\AspNetCore*. This said, you are not forced in any way to take the default account. By using the usual IIS interface, you can change the identity behind the application pool at any time to any user account.

Deploying to Microsoft Azure

In an alternative to deploying on-premise to a server machine equipped with IIS, you can host your ASP.NET Core application on Microsoft Azure. There are several ways to host a website on Azure. The most common and recommended for ASP.NET Core application is to use an App Service. Under some particular circumstances, you should look at Service Fabric or even at hosting on an Azure Virtual Machine. This latter option is the closest you will get to the hosting scenario we've considered so far—hosting on-premise under IIS.

Let's find out more about the various options.

Using an Azure App Service

The Azure App Service (AAS) publish target is the first option that the Visual Studio 2017 publish wizard offers, as shown in Figure 15-2. A new App Service can be created, or you can even publish to an existing App Service.

AAS is a hosting service that can accommodate plain web applications and web APIs such as REST APIs and mobile back ends. It is not limited to ASP.NET and ASP.NET Core, but it supports a variety of other web environments such as Node.js, PHP, and Java on both Windows and Linux. AAS provides built-in security, load balancing, high-availability, SSL certificates, application scaling, and management. Furthermore, it can be combined with continuous deployment from GitHub and Visual Studio Team Services (VSTS).

AAS charges you by the computer resources you use, as determined by the App Service plan you choose. AAS also niftily integrates with the Azure WebJobs service to add background job processing to your web application. Figure 15-10 shows the Create App Service page, which is where you start when publishing to AAS. (See Figure 15-10.)

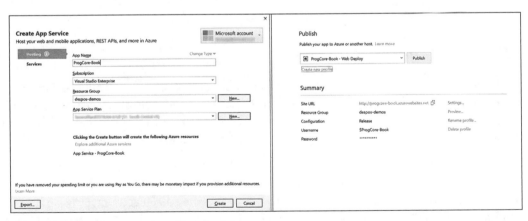

FIGURE 15-10 Creating a new Azure App Service

By clicking **Publish**, Visual Studio will use WebDeploy to upload all necessary files to AAS. The application will be up and running in a matter of (a few) minutes. Figure 15-11 shows a sample application that is up and running.

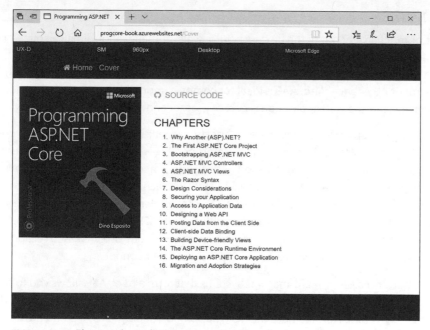

FIGURE 15-11 The sample application now up and running

Once published, the AAS dashboard allows you to set application settings entries (for example, all data you would take from user secrets during development) and performs any necessary fine-tuning.

To gain access to the physical files of the application, most notably Razor views or pages if not precompiled, you can use the App Service Editor service. In this way, you gain read/write access to the deployed files and can even make edits on the fly. (See Figure 5-12.)

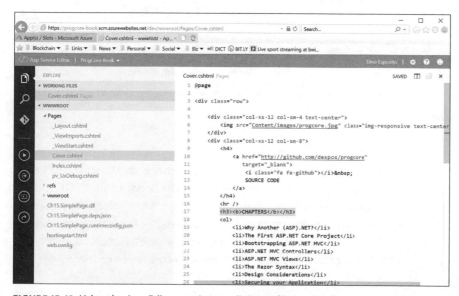

FIGURE 15-12 Using the App Editor service to edit Razor files on the fly

Using Service Fabric

AAS provides a lot of functionality out of the box, such auto-scale, authentication, limit call rates, and easy integration with additional software services, such Azure Active Directory, Application Insights, and SQL. Using AAS is trivially easy and ideal for many teams, especially teams with limited site administering and deployment experience. Also, AAS is ideal for compact, monolithic, and nearly stateless applications. What if, instead, the web application is part of a larger and distributed system?

In this case, you likely end up with a microservice architecture in which some of the nodes are good to be deployed as AAS but are also subject to be strictly interoperable with other nodes. Azure Service Fabric (ASF) just makes the composition of application nodes easier. Imagine a scenario where your application needs two different data stores (relational and NoSQL), caching, and maybe a service bus. Without ASF, every node is independent and dealing with, say, fault tolerance is up to you. Worse yet, fault tolerance must be dealt with for every service you publish. With ASF, cache and everything else will be co-located with the main application, providing for faster access but also increased reliability and simplified deployment—single shot instead of multiple shots, one per node.

ASF is probably a better choice for multi-machine systems that form a pool. ASF allows you to start relatively small and easily scale the distribution of the architecture to even hundreds of machines. This said, you could even mix AAS and ASF and have the main application deployed as AAS and the back end at some point re-architected as ASF.

Table 15-2 provides a list of functions that only AAS or only ASF support. Functions not listed on the table work the same (or don't work at all) in both scenarios. From a pricing perspective, note that there is no charge for the Service Fabric itself. All you pay for are the actual computing resources you enable on it. In this regard, pricing follows the same rules as an Azure virtual machine.

TABLE 15-2 AAS and ASF capabilities

Azure App Service ONLY	Azure Service Fabric ONLY
Automatic operating system updates	Remote Desktop access to server machines
Switch the runtime environment from 32-bit to 64-bit	Freedom to install any custom MSI package
Deploy via Git, FTP, and WebDeploy	Define custom startup tasks
Integrated SaaS available: MySQL and monitoring	Support for Event Tracing for Windows (ETW)
Remote debugging	

Important To be deployed in an Azure Service Fabric, your entire application must be converted to a Service Fabric application. This entails installing the Service Fabric SDK and using ad hoc application project templates from within Visual Studio. More information on the SDK can be found at *https://docs.microsoft.com/en-us/azure/service-fabric/service-fabric-get-started*. Note also that Service Fabric is similar to Cloud Services, but Cloud Services is considered a legacy technology that has been fully replaced by Service Fabric.

Using an Azure Virtual Machine

Somewhat between AAS and ASF is an Azure Virtual Machine (AVM). If you need more than just a single monolithic application but, at the same time, the application requires substantial changes to be packaged up to be ASF compliant, then going for an AVM can be a savvy choice.

An AVM is what the name implies—a server machine virtually delivered to you empty and at your full disposal as far as configuration and setup are concerned. At its core, an AVM is a sample of Infrastructure-as-a-Service (IaaS) whereas both ASF and AAS are samples of a platform as a service. All Azure virtual machines come with free load balancing and auto-scaling capabilities. Once a virtual machine has been created on Azure, you can publish your application directly from Visual Studio.

Regarding costs, the most economical AVM starts a bit over $10/month while a reasonable one costs you at least ten times more. This amount should be added to the costs of the software you install, such as the license of your own SQL Server. All in all, though, an AVM represents the simplest and easiest way you must migrate to Azure from an existing on-premise configuration.

> **Note** More details about the various hosting options for Microsoft Azure can be found at *https://docs.microsoft.com/en-us/azure/app-service/choose-web-site-cloud-service-vm*.

Deploying from within Visual Studio Code

As discussed, automatic deploy to Azure is nearly instantaneous from Visual Studio. If you use Visual Studio Code, instead, you need some additional tooling to make it happen. In particular, you might want to consider the Azure Tools for Visual Studio Code as available from Visual Studio Marketplace. (See *https://marketplace.visualstudio.com/items?itemName=bradygaster.azuretoolsforvscode*.)

Deploying to Linux

The cross-platform nature of ASP.NET Core makes it possible to host the same application on a Linux machine, too. The common approach is to publish the application files to a local folder and then upload (via FTP, for example) the image to the server machine.

There are two main hosting scenarios for Linux: hosting on a machine equipped with Apache or Nginx. Another option is to use Amazon Web Services and the Elastic Beanstalk toolkit. (See *https://aws.amazon.com/blogs/developer/aws-and-net-core-2-0*.)

Deploying to Apache

Deploying an ASP.NET Core application to an instance of the Apache server means configuring the server environment to act as a reverse proxy server. We have already touched on this aspect in Chapter 14, "The ASP.NET Core Runtime Environment." Let's briefly recap.

To instruct Apache to act as a reverse proxy, you need to have a *.conf* file located under the */etc/httpd/conf.d/* directory. The sample content below tells Apache to listen on any IP addresses through port 80 and all requests received through the specified proxy machine. In the example, the proxy machine is 127.0.0.1 on port 5000. In this case, Apache and Kestrel are assumed to run on the same machine, but just changing the proxy pass IP address makes the trick of using distinct machines.

```
<VirtualHost *:80>
        ProxyPreserveHost On
        ProxyPass / http://127.0.0.1:5000/
        ProxyPassReverse / http://127.0.0.1:5000/
</VirtualHost>
```

You also need a service file to tell Apache what to do for requests aimed at the hosted ASP.NET Core application. Here's a sample service file.

```
[Unit]
    Description=Programming ASP.NET Core Demo

[Service]
    WorkingDirectory=/var/progcore/ch15/simpleplage
    ExecStart=/usr/local/bin/dotnet /var/progcore/ch15/simpleplage.dll
    Restart=always

    # Restart service after 10 seconds in case of errors
    RestartSec=10
    SyslogIdentifier=progcore-ch15-simplepage
    User=apache
    Environment=ASPNETCORE_ENVIRONMENT=Production

[Install]
    WantedBy=multi-user.target
```

The service must be enabled from the command line. If the above service file is named *progcore.service*, the command line is as below:

```
sudo nano /etc/systemd/system/progcore.service
```

For more details refer to *https://docs.microsoft.com/en-us/aspnet/core/publishing/apache-proxy*. In particular, you might want to look at the aforementioned documentation for aspects like adding SSL and firewall settings, rate limits, monitoring, and load balancing.

Deploying to Nginx

Nginx is an open-source HTTP server that is growing in popularity; it can easily serve as a reverse proxy as well as an IMAP/POP3 proxy server. Its primary characteristic is the use of an asynchronous architecture to process requests instead of a more traditional thread-based architecture like that of more canonical web servers such as Apache and older versions of IIS. For this reason, Nginx is often used in high-scalable scenarios and as a proxy as opposed to highly trafficked websites. (See *https://www.nginx.com*.)

Let's see how to configure Nginx to a server as a reverse proxy to host an ASP.NET Core application. All you do is edit the content of the file */etc/nginx/sites-available/default*, which is a JSON file with content similar to the lines below.

```
server {
    listen 80;
    location / {
        proxy_pass http://localhost:5000;
        proxy_http_version 1.1;
        proxy_set_header Upgrade $http_upgrade;
        proxy_set_header Connection keep-alive;
        proxy_set_header Host $host;
        proxy_cache_bypass $http_upgrade;
    }
}
```

By changing the value of the *proxy_pass* property, you indicate the location of the Kestrel server, if outside the server machine or listening on a port different from 5000.

Like we have seen for Apache, this is only the first step toward a full configuration of the environment. It's enough to forward requests to Kestrel but not to manage the lifetime of Kestrel and its .NET Core web host. You need a service file to start and monitor the underlying ASP.NET Core application. The way you do it is the same as we've seen for Apache. For more information, see *https://docs.microsoft.com/en-us/aspnet/core/publishing/linuxproduction*.

Docker Containers

Containers are a relatively new concept that attempts to replicate the role of containers in the shipping industry. A container is a unit of software that contains an application and its full stack of dependencies and configuration. A container can be deployed to a given host operating system and run without any further configuration.

For developers, containers represent the dream scenario in which any code is running locally—on the mythical "my machine" where everything works—and it also runs in production. The operating system is the only common ground to guarantee containers to work once deployed.

Containers vs. Virtual Machines

At first sight, a container has a lot in common with a virtual machine. However, a fundamental difference exists between the two.

A virtual machine runs on top of some virtualized hardware and runs its own copy of the operating system. Also, a virtual machine needs all binaries and applications required for the scenario for which it is built. Subsequently, a virtual machine can be several gigabytes large and usually takes minutes to start.

A container, instead, runs on top of a given physical machine and uses the operating system installed on the machine. In other words, a container is just expected to deliver the delta from the host operating system to the environment you need to have for the applications to run. As a result, a container is usually only a few megabytes large and therefore takes seconds to start.

In the end, both containers and virtual machines isolate an application and its dependencies from the surrounding environment, but multiple containers running on the same machine all share the host operating system (see Figure 15-13).

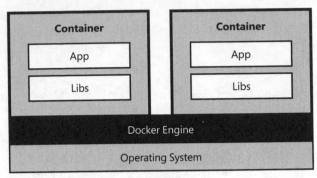

FIGURE 15-13 Containerized architecture

From Containers to Microservice Architecture

Just the fact that multiple applications can be packaged to run side by side on the same virtualized operating system has led to a new approach to software development known as *containerization*.

An application and its configuration are packaged in a special format—the container image—and deployed to a container-enabled server. In DevOps terms, this also means that the development environment can be "snapshotted" and turned into an independently deployable piece of code that just runs on a given operating system. More, it can be easily ported from server to server, and it keeps on working as long it is transported on a compatible container-enabled infrastructure, whether public or private cloud or even a physical on-premise server. The slogan of containerization is then "build once, run anywhere."

Containerization leads to breaking up monolithic applications into distinct pieces, each deployed to a distinct container. An SQL database can go to a container, a Web API can go to another, and a Redis cache can be yet another distinct container. Furthermore, distinct containers are independently deployable parts that can be scaled or painlessly updated/replaced in the future.

Docker and Visual Studio 2017

An ASP.NET Core can be easily made compatible to Docker by simply selecting **Enable Docker Support** while creating the project, as shown in Figure 15-14. The effect is that a few text files are automatically added to the project.

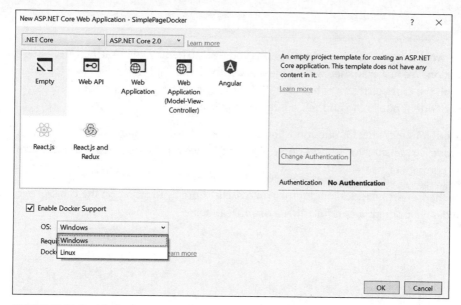

FIGURE 15-14 Enable Docker support for an ASP.NET Core application

The most important of those files is *dockerfile*. Here's sample content.

```
FROM microsoft/aspnetcore:2.0
ARG source
WORKDIR /app
EXPOSE 80
COPY ${source:-obj/Docker/publish} .
ENTRYPOINT ["dotnet", "Ch15.SimplePageDocker.dll"]
```

The project also contains a couple of other files in a new folder named *docker-compose*. When the folder is selected, the Build menu changes to show the Docker build option. Clicking it causes the image to be created and deployed to the registry of the underlying container-enabled server. To test it locally on a Windows machine, you need to install Docker for Windows.

Once the Docker image has been created, the sample application runs from an unusual IP address, typically 172.x.x.x. (See Figure 15-15.)

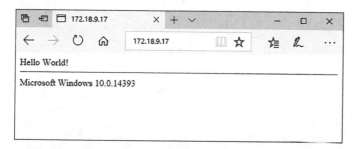

FIGURE 15-15 Running a Docker image

The actual files of the Docker image can be inspected in the *obj/docker* folder.

Summary

In this chapter, we went through the various options you have to deploy your ASP.NET Core application to production. We first examined what it means to publish the application files to a folder and how to deal with the cross-platform nature of ASP.NET Core. In doing so, we distinguished between framework-dependent publishing and self-contained applications.

Next, we went into more details about hosting on Azure and explored the various services, including Service Fabric, virtual machines, and App Services. Finally, we briefly touched on the whole theme of Docker and containers.

In the next chapter, we conclude our journey on ASP.NET Core by focusing on the topic of migration and brownfield development versus full rewrite of applications.

CHAPTER 16

Migration and Adoption Strategies

The most expensive part of a building is the mistakes.

—Ken Follett, "The Pillars of the Earth"

ASP.NET Core is not the newest version of ASP.NET 4.x. Despite its unfortunate (but deliberately chosen) name, it's a whole new framework, albeit deeply inspired by the current ASP.NET and in particular, by the ASP.NET MVC framework. Overall, we would not go too far from the truth by saying that ASP.NET Core is ASP.NET just as one would rewrite it today. It's more modular and with a smaller memory footprint than classic ASP.NET, and it can target multiple hardware/software platforms. For example, new ASP.NET Core applications also can now run natively on a variety of Linux and Mac OS platforms.

ASP.NET Core is not simply a new web-oriented framework. It is a web framework, but it still needs an underlying general-purpose framework. It's the underlying framework—the .NET Core framework—that ultimately provides the cross-platform capability. Regarding development impact, ASP.NET Core plus .NET Core is a combined platform of the same order of magnitude as ASP.NET and the .NET Framework released in 2002. Luckily enough, the gap between the new platform and the current is much smaller today than it was back in 2002.

At any rate, ASP.NET Core changes the way web applications are developed on the Microsoft stack. Refreshing some skills is inevitable for the entire team. Hence, writing for the ASP.NET Core platform is a cost to consider, beyond the budget for the application to build. How then do you approach ASP.NET Core if you're a decision maker within your company and how to sell it if you're a consultant willing to help?

In this chapter, we'll try to nail down the promises of the new framework to the real benefits.

In Search of Business Value

Let's be honest. No customer would pay to change an application that works for another application that just works. At the same time, no software is a dead thing that remains static and immutable once in production. Business changes and so applications should ideally change with it; sometimes, that means radical rewrites. A big rewrite is an option when radically new business opportunities appear on the horizon or when attractive new technologies make their debuts.

ASP.NET Core doesn't create new business opportunities, but it's quite an interesting technology to look at. Determining how interesting and beneficial it could be, is the question. ASP.NET Core has little to do with enhancing an existing application to cope with new business requirements. However, the moment new business requirements come along, upgrading to ASP.NET Core is an option to seriously consider.

Looking for Benefits

All in all, I believe there's a lot of unnecessary hype around ASP.NET Core. As I see it, the hype amounts to pure enthusiasm without clearly explaining the business benefits of the switch. When it comes to making this decision, though, finding good business reasons to drop a relatively new system for a brand new one that works the same as the old one gets tricky fast.

One heavily emphasized benefit is that ASP.NET Core enables your code to run on multiple platforms. This is true, but only if you rewrite all of your code to address the .NET Core framework. Most literature also emphasizes other benefits such as performance improvements, modularity of the code, and open source code. The really geeky points such as the brand-new middleware and the extensive use of dependency injection through the framework are also emphasized.

While I am far from saying these are not benefits at all, the real impact they might have on the business just depends on the business itself. Paying for a faster application when you are not experiencing slow response is pointless. Paying for the potential to scale up when you have an established business and no expectations to grow exponentially is pointless, too. What's the value in having Microsoft open-sourcing the code of ASP.NET for a company that outsources most of the development? And the list can go on. Let's try to view the most popularized benefits of ASP.NET Core with a more critical eye.

Multiple Platform Support

The .NET Core framework is a full rewrite of the .NET Framework specifically created to compile on a few different platforms in addition to Windows. Hence, an ASP.NET Core application that targets the .NET Core framework can also be hosted on a variety of Linux server platforms. To be precise, the .NET Core framework can also run on Mac OS, but for the purpose of hosting, it makes no difference at the moment because no hosting platform is based on Mac OS. At the same time, though, having the .NET Core framework also target Mac OS at least enables developers to compile their ASP.NET Core application on their Mac laptops natively.

As I see things, the cross-platform nature of ASP.NET Core applications is the most relevant business value it has. Some might argue that because it's still a web application, it can already be reached from whatever platforms and operating systems. The true point, though, is hosting more than reach. There are a lot of companies out there who just don't consider ASP.NET because of the license necessary to run Windows Server or are restricted to use open platforms like Linux. (This sometimes happens with some public government agencies because of the false perception that adopting open platforms is really "free as in beer.") Furthermore, Windows hosting is still more expensive than Linux hosting. It's not a huge difference, and the difference is likely shrinking, but Linux tends to be a bit cheaper, which makes ASP.NET worth considering. Finally, a cross-platform ASP.NET is beneficial for companies because it enables them to save some further money running applications on cheaper Linux machines at least for (integration) testing purposes. Also, the Linux hosting ecosystem is larger than on Windows (see Mesos, Marathon, and Aurora) and doesn't lock you down to a single vendor.

Improved Performance

It would really be surprising if a totally rewritten framework weren't significantly faster than one that is 15 years older. So, by all means, ASP.NET Core is faster than classic ASP.NET. Let's see why first and then have a look at some quick objective numbers.

First and foremost, the ASP.NET Core pipeline is async, and this guarantees that the minimum number of pooled threads are busy at any time. Also, the pipeline is redesigned and extremely modular. Finally, Kestrel is really amazingly fast in dispatching requests. Next, there's the whole point of the memory footprint per request which is about five times smaller in ASP.NET Core.

The memory footprint point deserves some further attention. As discussed in Chapter 14, the HTTP runtime pipeline has been completely restructured. Until ASP.NET Core, ASP.NET application requests were processed in the same runtime devised two decades ago for what has now become ASP.NET Web Forms. The beating heart of the old pipeline was the notorious *system.web* assembly. Many suggest the *system.web* assembly as the main culprit for the poor performance of classic ASP.NET applications, though I only partially subscribe to this view. The *system.web* assembly was tailor-made for ASP.NET Web Forms, and it was so beautifully done that it survived for two decades. When Microsoft introduced ASP.NET MVC, it opted for adding only the necessary runtime extensions to the same runtime. Because of this design decision, ASP.NET MVC never had the thin and tailor-made runtime it deserved. By design, it was given a larger runtime summing up the capabilities of two radically different application models—Web Forms and MVC.

Worse yet, a few years after introducing ASP.NET MVC, Microsoft also launched Web API. Web API was designed from the ground up and given its own runtime for processing requests, but it still relies on the ASP.NET runtime for hosting. As Figure 16-1 shows, any application that uses ASP.NET MVC and Web API has probably three times the memory footprint it really needs. And this is not caused by the notorious *system.web* assembly.

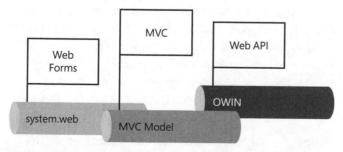

FIGURE 16-1 The notorious composition of ASP.NET frameworks

Another aspect of the improved performance of ASP.NET Core is its modularity. The entire framework ships in the form of NuGet packages, which allows you to cherry-pick just the features you really need. In classic ASP.NET, the runtime was only partly customizable because some HTTP modules could be disabled, but the entire request processing pipeline was, for the most part, hard-coded. In you run only ASP.NET, your code can have a chance to run sooner than in ASP.NET Core.

As far as numbers to support the improved capabilities are concerned, you might want to look at the benchmarks published at *https://github.com/aspnet/benchmarks*. The numbers there might not give an absolute measure of how fast your application can be. It's still a benchmark, so the numbers will realistically be much smaller for a realistic application. However, the ratio between of the benchmarks for ASP.NET and ASP.NET Core will likely be the same. And that ratio says ASP.NET Core is about five times faster in the number of requests it can serve in a unit of time. This said, though, keep in mind that every application is different in terms of the number of actual requests it handles.

Finally, a little-known point about performance is the actual power of application fine-tuning. By simply swapping *AddMvc* with *AddMvcCore*, you can almost double the speed of a request, at least for the initial part of the processing. One experiment demonstrated that the time to serve 1 million requests with ASP.NET Core dropped from more than two seconds to 1.2 seconds simply using the core configuration. For more details, see *http://bit.ly/2wuvhDl*.

Improved Deployment Experience

Classic ASP.NET supports a deployment experience that ASP.NET Core marketing defines as framework-dependent. In other words, the application ships only with its own binaries, which means the necessary framework is expected to be already installed on the server. Multiple applications can share the same framework though some applications might need different versions of the same framework. In this case, both frameworks must be installed, and subtle issues might arise. It's the notorious "DLL hell," or something very similar to it.

ASP.NET Core brings an additional deployment experience—self-contained deployment. In this case, the application ships with its own binaries as well as the entire framework. The application takes its own space and could run in total isolation no matter what it installed on the server. This solution guarantees unparalleled isolation at the cost of increasing the necessary disk space by an order of magnitude, typically growing from a few megabytes to a few dozens of megabytes.

As discussed in the previous chapter, you can host ASP.NET Core applications on a variety of web servers, most notably IIS and Apache on Linux. However, the deployment experience is not limited to the options we already covered in Chapter 15. Although not really common, you can still host an ASP.NET application in a completely custom minimal web server possibly forking an open-source web server project. At the very minimum, such a web server must implement *IHttpRequestFeature* and *IHttpResponseFeature* interfaces. A starting point can be found at *https://github.com/Bobris/Nowin*.

 Note If you are using Windows and if the ASP.NET Core application targets the full .NET Framework, you can even host it as a Windows service. An example is *https://docs.microsoft.com/en-us/aspnet/core/hosting/windows-service*.

Improved Development Experience

The ASP.NET Core programming experience is simply awesome. The redesigned framework is really good and well-architected. It's probably a little bit too over-engineered, but all current best ASP.NET programming practices have been incorporated. You will hardly find a better framework—for a few years at least.

Also, you are no longer limited to Visual Studio as the programming environment. You can now use Visual Studio Code to develop your application, which is free and lightweight in comparison to Visual Studio or even to JetBrains' Rider. Visual Studio Code, just like Rider, can be used on different platforms as well.

From a purely programming perspective, Microsoft unified the MVC and Web API controller model and added native dependency injection. Also, the modularity of the middleware is extreme, and you really have the unprecedented chance to write just the code you need and no additional line.

Open Source

The entire source code of ASP.NET Core can be found at *https://github.com/aspnet*. From there you can navigate in a number of repositories to find the various packages that form the framework as well as documentation and samples. All projects are frequently updated by hundreds of Microsoft contributors and members of the community.

The open-source movement is a strong statement about the Microsoft commitment to ASP.NET Core. And if you have doubts about the framework, consider that there hasn't been a new version of classic ASP.NET MVC since February 2015. Sure, classic ASP.NET MVC is pretty much done, and there's not really much to add, yet that is a sign that the entire development effort has been moved to ASP.NET Core. So, in the end, embracing ASP.NET core is a purely a matter of time. And in the short run, it's also a matter of finding some concrete business value in it.

Favoring the Microservice Architecture

The microservice architecture is quite popular these days because it combines well the core idea of a service-oriented architecture without the bureaucracy of the SOA tenets. Essentially, a microservice is an independently deployable software application that is autonomous and with a well-defined boundary. A microservice can be written in whatever language and using whatever technology because it's independently developed and deployed, and it communicates through standard channels, whether HTTP/TCP, message queues, or even shared databases or files.

ASP.NET Core lends itself to implementing microservices because of its lightweight nature, speed, and flexibility. Also, the support for Docker contributes to making ASP.NET Core even more interesting in a microservice perspective.

Brownfield Development

It should be clear by now that adopting ASP.NET Core is not a matter of upgrading to the next version of a framework or product already in use. As an example, upgrading to ASP.NET is not the same as upgrading from SQL Server 2014 to SQL Server 2016. When upgrading SQL, all your tables, views, and procedures will remain fully functional, and you have additional features (such as native JSON and versioned tables) to leverage at your earliest convenience. Upgrading to ASP.NET Core provides no such smooth transition. At the very minimum, you spend money to rewrite the same system as before, not to mention the costs of training developers—any developers—for that and the subsequent, though temporary, dip in productivity. You also need to possibly consider costs of adapting the continuous integration (CI) pipeline to .NET Core CLI tools if you use CI. You have the same system as before on a new framework at a price that depends on the skills and attitude to learn from the team members.

An easy consideration is that no customer would reasonably pay to replace a system that works with another system that works. This idea leads us straight to brownfield development.

In software, the term *brownfield development* denotes a scenario in which a new system is developed taking into careful account existing systems. In other words, brownfield development is about developing new software under the constraints of existing systems and technologies. You might want to be very cautious before adopting a disruptive framework like ASP.NET Core in a brownfield development scenario.

To add ASP.NET Core in a brownfield scenario, you have to first move toward a more distributed architecture in which the overall behavior of the system results from the composition of multiple independent components (microservices). In this context, you can seriously consider replacing one or more components with new components that just plug in and use a new, even disruptive, framework. In summary, in front of a disruptive framework change, you must decide what's legacy and what's not. And you need to consider replacing non-legacy components. On the topic of evolving a .NET architecture toward microservices, see the e-book at *https://aka.ms/microservicesebook*.

In the end, brownfield development with ASP.NET Core is realistic, but often quite expensive. The balance is all in the concrete business value it delivers. This can only be seen case by case and business by business. Finally, consider that if you use brownfield development, the sole fact that you are forced to select what's legacy and what's not is a step on the way to reduce the technical debt.

Note Just to remain in the ASP.NET space, note that component vendors still make most of their revenues out of ASP.NET Web Forms products because companies focus on their own businesses and use software really as a service. Companies would reasonably consider deep refactoring or rewriting only when the business scenario changes (for example, because of scalability issues or new opportunities to seize). Scalability is one of the most abused words, especially regarding ASP.NET Core. I don't think that every company out there has scalability issues. I would rather stress that good code scales reasonably well by default. So, when you realize you have scalability issues, often it's because your code is of poor quality.

Greenfield Development

Greenfield development is the opposite of brownfield development, and it occurs when a new software system is developed without constraints of any kind. As an architect, you are free to make best decisions without compromises. In this scenario, the point of determining whether to adopt ASP.NET Core becomes a purely technical matter.

Let's see a summary of the technical challenges that adopting ASP.NET Core poses to ASP.NET developers. Developers with no past ASP.NET experience might find this summary of the delta with previous versions of the framework to be of little interest. Before we get there, though, it's important to look at the .NET Standard story.

The .NET Standard Specification

The .NET Standard specification attempts to solve the problem of sharing .NET code across multiple versions of the same application—mobile, web, and desktop. The same class library might be shared by multiple applications with each targeting a specific version of the .NET Framework, and there's no guarantee that the class library only calls functions the framework supports.

The .NET Standard provides a nifty way to name and version a particular snapshot of the .NET Framework. So every version of the .NET Standard defines the API that any implementation of .NET must provide to be compliant. Put another way; once a class library complies with a version of the .NET Standard, it can be safely used by whatever application that targets a version of the .NET Framework compatible with the standard.

The latest incarnation of the .NET Standard is .NET Standard 2.0, and it goes hand in hand with .NET Core 2.0. That should be the minimum requirement for any new greenfield development involving ASP.NET Core. The .NET Standard 2.0 comprises a lot more classes than any of the previous versions (even ADO.NET classes are back). According to Microsoft, numbers more than 70 percent of the libraries on NuGet only use the API part of the .NET Standard 2.0.

Here's the framework signature in the CSPROJ file for an ASP.NET Core application that targets ASP.NET Core 2.0.

```
<PropertyGroup>
    <TargetFramework>netcoreapp2.0</TargetFramework>
</PropertyGroup>
```

And here's the signature of a .NET Standard class library.

```
<PropertyGroup>
  <TargetFramework>netstandard2.0</TargetFramework>
</PropertyGroup>
```

Note that to create a .NET Standard class library you have to choose a specific template in Visual Studio from a different node than regular .NET Core applications. (See Figure 16-2.)

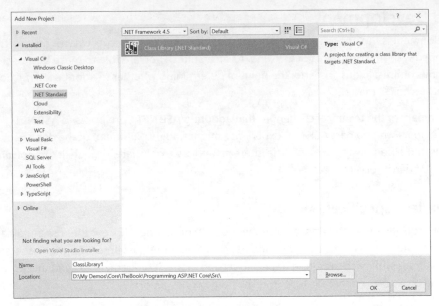

FIGURE 16-2 Creating a .NET Standard class library

What Is Different for ASP.NET Developers

In ASP.NET Core, a few programming chores require a different approach than in past versions of ASP.NET and familiarity with a new set of APIs. Table 16-1 lists the differences.

TABLE 16-1 Programming tasks different in ASP.NET Core

Task	Description
Starting up the application	The global.asax file is gone, and so it is the web.config file. The initial configuration of the application takes place in the startup file and also comprises tasks (setting up the web host) that were hidden in the folds of IIS and ASP.NET setup. The application is made of a collection of properly configured services. Furthermore, the framework introduces the notion of the hosting environment, namely an object that carries information about the current runtime environment.
Serving static files	An ASP.NET Core application serves static files directly without the intermediation of the web server. This behavior must be configured explicitly, but the configuration is so flexible that you can serve static files from whatever path and data source.
Passing dependencies around	Most classic ASP.NET applications use an IoC provider of choice to pass dependencies around. ASP.NET Core comes with its own DI subsystem that can't be deactivated, though it can be replaced with a compatible IoC that has been ported to .NET Core and also endowed with a special connector to the ASP.NET Core DI system.
Reading configuration data	ASP.Net Core no longer contains a web.config file to contain basic application settings. The configuration data is displayed as a hierarchical object model populated by a variety of data providers (JSON, text files, and database). Configuration data is passed around via DI.
Authentication	The authentication scheme is now based on claims and is no longer strictly based on a cookie. Concepts like identity and principal remain, but the API is different though conceptually compatible.
Authorization	The authorization API works as in classic ASP.NET, but ASP.NET Core provides a valuable extension in the form of authorization policies. You might want seriously consider policies.

As you can see, the vast majority of those changes apply before the control flow reaches the layer of controller classes. Controllers are substantially the same, and so it is for views. There are some extra features and improvements, but 99 percent of the code you have around controllers and views usually works unchanged in ASP.NET Core or with only minor fixes. And so it is for your programming skills.

Should I Go with ASP.NET Core?

Here's the key question: For greenfield development, is ASP.NET Core 2.x a viable option?

My current answer is simply yes. My forecast since the early beta days of the framework was that it would become a serious option to consider by the end of 2018. What was a lighthearted forecast in late 2015, now seems to be quite well addressed by facts and sentiment across the industry. And even a bit ahead of expectation. Fanboys and marketing people aside, the framework is really good, but this is not enough when it comes to real-world business and physical budgets.

In 2018, I expect the basic framework and, more importantly, a couple of satellite frameworks to reach an even higher level of maturity. In particular, I'm referring to Entity Framework Core and especially SignalR Core.

For data access, if you find the latest EF Core problematic, you have plenty of other options as we discussed in Chapter 9. A good alternative is to use micro O/RM frameworks. As for SignalR, it has been an official part of the ASP.NET Core family since version 2.1.

Is there anything missing? On the Microsoft front, I miss OData (there are no rumors about future support), and I would like to see an EF Core that supports system-versioned tables like SQL Server 2016 and newer. However, you will have to look at your own list of third-party dependencies to see which are not yet .NET Core–compliant that might jeopardize adoption.

Outlining a Yellowfield Strategy

Let's say that you want to take an existing application and rewrite it for ASP.NET Core. The scenario is a line-of-business application that needs a refresh and possibly a new architecture. In other words, the scenario is about rewriting the same line-of-business application to make it serve the same business needs plus something more.

I would not classify this as either plain greenfield development or brownfield development. It's a kind of middle way we could call "yellowfield" development. Essentially, it's a new application with no architectural constraints, but we are observing the nonfunctional requirement of preserving as much as possible of the code and expertise of the current production system.

Dealing with Missing Dependencies

When you embark on a big rewrite project, the architectural pillars might be different but to flesh it out with actual code you may wish to reuse the old code as much as possible to save development time and preserve some of the investments made. This is reasonable so long as it's worth the cost.

When it comes to this, you may face any of the following.

- You use some NuGet packages that have not been ported to .NET Core.

- You use custom DLLs you don't fully control that are not (yet?) available for .NET Core.

- You have layers of code depending on some obsolete Microsoft frameworks including ASP.NET Web Forms, Entity Framework 6, ASP.NET SignalR, OData, and Windows Foundation Services.

- You have portions of plain C# code that uses API calls no longer supported.

For any of those issues, you have two possible routes: reuse/adapt the source code or completely rewrite the source code underneath the same observable behavior. In the rest of this chapter, we'll develop a couple of optional strategies for reusing/adapting the existing code. A first good step, though, is to analyze what you have. Enter the .NET Portability Analyzer tool.

The .NET Portability Analyzer

The .NET Portability Analyzer is a Visual Studio extension you grab from the Visual Studio marketplace. (See *https://marketplace.visualstudio.com*.) The tool takes an assembly name in input (or even the entire current solution path) and produces a report in the form of an Excel file. (See Figure 16-3.)

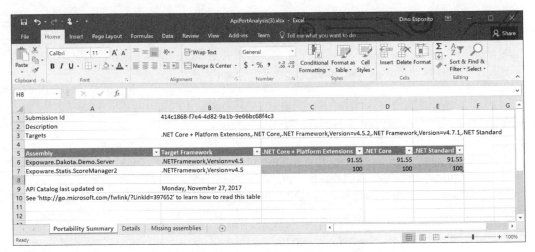

FIGURE 16-3 Results of a .NET Core portability analysis of a .NET 4.5 solution

The report gives you an idea of the effort required to make the code work successfully on .NET Core. To be precise, though, the tool is not just for .NET Core and can be configured for various targets, including multiple versions of the .NET Framework and .NET Standard specifications. (See Figure 16-4.)

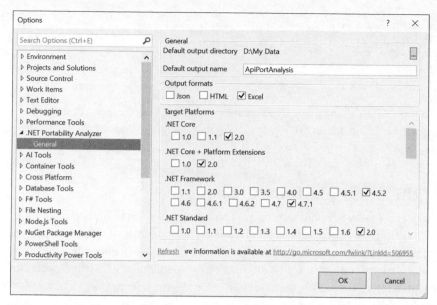

FIGURE 16-4 Settings supported by the .NET Portability Analyzer

Not only does the tool show a percentage of the code that works, but it also lists what's wrong and, in some cases, it even suggests changes to perform.

In general, the .NET Core team following two key guidelines. First, they only included classes really used by most developers. Second, for each necessary functionality, they only provided one implementation. In the full .NET Framework, for example, you have at least three different classes to place an HTTP call: *WebClient*, *HttpWebRequest*, and *HttpClient*. Only the last one is available in .NET Core. Hence, any assembly that uses, say, *WebClient* lowers the percentage reported by the analyzer, though fixing it is nearly straightforward. In general, a compatibility level reported by the .NET Analyzer that is superior to 70 percent is a very good response.

> **Note** The .NET Portability Analyzer is also available as a console application. You can get it at *https://github.com/Microsoft/dotnet-apiport*.

The Windows Compatibility Pack

The Windows Compatibility Pack (WCP) is a NuGet package which provides access to more than 20,000 API not included in .NET Core 2.0. At least half of these functions are Windows-only functions and touch on areas such as cryptography, I/O ports, registry, and some low-level diagnostics. To check if the code is currently running on the Windows platform and then see if the call is safe, you can do as below.

```
if (RuntimeInformation.IsOSPlatform(OSPlatform.Windows))
{
    // Call some Windows-only function added with the WCP
    ...
}
```

Also, you find in the WCP also some new APIs that are in not in .NET Core 2.0 and that enjoy a cross-platform implementation. In this list, you find *System.Drawing*, the CodeDom API, and the memory cache.

Postponing the Cross-platform Challenge

The portability analyzer is a tool you might want to run to measure the effort of porting or, at least, have a rough estimate of the effort it will entail. The effect of the analyzer, though, is significant only for the code components you directly control. If your existing application relies on external dependencies, there's not much you can do at the source code level. Common situations are dependencies on third-party NuGet packages or plain class library DLLs and dependencies on some Microsoft frameworks that for various reasons are not available as-is in .NET Core. Table 16-2 lists most common and popular .NET frameworks not currently available, at least in their original form, in .NET Core.

TABLE 16-2 Popular Microsoft frameworks not directly supported in .NET Core

Framework	State of the art
Entity Framework 6.x and older	Replaced by Entity Framework Core 2.0 and newer.
ASP.NET SignalR	Replaced by ASP.NET Signal Core
OData extensions for Web API	Not planned
Windows Communication Foundation	ASP.NET Core applications can consume existing WCF services through an additional dedicated client library (*https://github.com/dotnet/wcf*) but exposing WCF services is not supported. This extension is currently being considered.
Windows Workflow Foundation	Not planned

If maintaining the dependency on some of those frameworks or libraries is crucial for you then you only have two routes ahead. One is just keeping up the good work with the current non-.NET Core platform you're using. The other is moving the frontend to ASP.NET Core but postponing the cross-platform challenge. (See Figure 16-5.)

When it comes to creating an ASP.NET Core project, you can choose to target either the .NET Core framework or the full .NET Framework. By choosing the latter, you preserve the existing code in its entirety, at least the parts of it that deal with dependencies. In fact, you still have to rewrite the startup of the application dropping *global.asax*, *web.config*, and other classic ASP.NET practices.

ASP.NET Core unleashes its true power if the .NET Core framework is targeted. However, the general recommendation is to target the full .NET Framework only when necessary. But, at the same time, if targeting the full .NET Framework is necessary, you can probably move forward even without porting the code to ASP.NET Core.

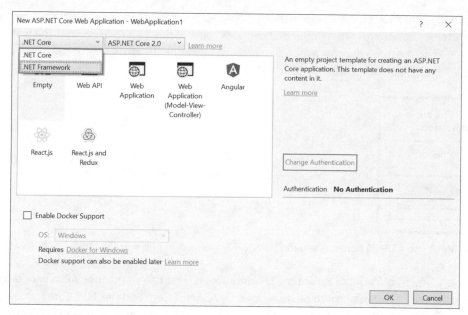

FIGURE 16-5 Choosing the target .NET Framework

Moving Towards a Microservice Architecture

Targeting the full .NET Framework for the sake of preserving existing critical code is an option, but it's an option that tends to maintain a monolithic structure in the resulting application. Let's delve a bit deeper into a quite concrete scenario: preserving the investment made on EF6 data access code.

EF6 and Bounded Contexts

Entity Framework Core and Entity Framework 6 look enticingly similar, yet they are quite different under the covers. The most relevant fact is that, in any case, you don't have to re-learn everything because the two frameworks share the same goals. Personally, because I always used a very limited set of functions from EF6 anytime I dropped EF6 code to an EF Core project, it always worked fine quite soon and only with minimal adjustments. I'm talking, however, of Code First code with no lazy loading, no grouping, no scaffolding and migrations, and no transactions—just plain queries and updates.

EF Core is steadily progressing, but it's a big rewrite and, as you might have already experienced in your career, any big rewrite takes a lot of time. As of EF Core 2.0, the team still doesn't recommend moving an EF6 application to EF Core unless you have a compelling reason to try the change. The recommended approach is to rewrite the data access layer with EF Core from the ground up, finding workarounds whenever you run into a feature that either doesn't exist or works differently. This approach to very basic CRUD code works acceptably well today. You can read the current roadmap of EF Core at *http://github.com/aspnet/EntityFrameworkCore/wiki/Roadmap*. I particularly recommend the section *Critical O/RM features* in the Backlog area.

Overall, what should you do with a significant EF6 data access layer when the application is being ported to ASP.NET Core? Here's where bounded contexts come handy. Figure 16-6 shows the first approach. You keep the application as a monolith and just postpone the cross-platform challenge and opt for the full .NET Framework as the target.

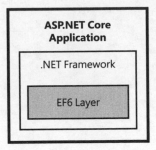

FIGURE 16-6 Moving to ASP.NET Core but targeting the .NET Framework to preserve EF6 code

Alternatively, you might want to isolate the EF6 data access layer to a standalone API and detach it from the main application, which could be developed for ASP.NET Core and the .NET Core framework. In doing so, you could also have EF Core and EF6 code partitioning the functionalities of the data access layer. (See Figure 16-7.)

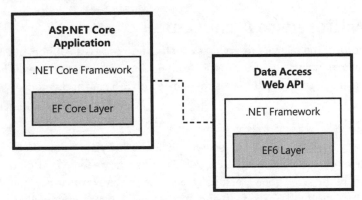

FIGURE 16-7 Separating the context of the main application and the context of EF6

This pattern, which ultimately leads to a microservice architecture, can be used as often as you wish, and it also finds a match in the *container* technology.

One More Word on Containers

When it comes to partitioning the application into smaller pieces, you start having a microservice architecture. Should the industry ever agree on a shared definition for the term *microservice*, then the definition wouldn't be too different from the following: A microservice is an independently deployable application that runs autonomously and uses its own technologies, languages, and infrastructure. Independently deployable, per se, simply means that the microservice can be deployed without affecting the rest of the application. The deployment can take place in many ways, including via containers.

Today, containers are often used within a microservice architecture. In general, you can containerize any web application or web API regardless of its architecture and technologies. All technologies are equal to the container's eyes, but inevitably, some are more equal than others. For example, you can containerize any .NET Framework application, but that would be only possible on Windows containers. Instead, a .NET Core application can be containerized in both Windows and Linux. Moreover, the size of .NET Core container image is much smaller than the same image for a non-.NET Core application. Finally, because a .NET Core application is cross-platform, the image can be dropped to a Linux container as well as a Windows container.

Summary

Nobody should adopt ASP.NET Core just because it is a new version of the old familiar ASP.NET framework. Instead, you should look to see if there is business value for you in ASP.Net Core. The primary value of ASP.NET Core is in its cross-platform nature, which concretely allows companies to save money by hosting applications—for production or testing—on cheaper Linux servers. Another factor to consider is the improved performance of the ASP.NET Core runtime and, at the same time, the extreme modularity of the framework that makes good fodder for highly scalable applications.

All this said, if you're not experiencing performance issues today and don't have significant extensions and architecture changes in sight, porting for the sake of porting is never a savvy choice.

Index

X - Y

Z